TIMES GONE BY

OXFORD

TIMES GONE BY

Memoirs of a Man of Action

VICENTE PÉREZ ROSALES

Translated from the Spanish by
JOHN H. R. POLT

INTRODUCTION AND CHRONOLOGY
BY BRIAN LOVEMAN

OXFORD
UNIVERSITY PRESS

2003

OXFORD
UNIVERSITY PRESS

Oxford New York

Auckland Bangkok Buenos Aires Cape Town Chennai
Dar es Salaam Delhi Hong Kong Istanbul Karachi Kolkata
Kuala Lumpur Madrid Melbourne Mexico City Mumbai Nairobi
São Paulo Shanghai Taipei Tokyo Toronto

Published by Oxford University Press, Inc.
198 Madison Avenue, New York, New York 10016

www.oup.com

Oxford is a registered trademark of Oxford University Press

Library of Congress Cataloging-in-Publication Data
Pérez Rosales, Vicente, 1807–1886.
[Recuerdos del pasado. English]
Times gone by : memoirs of a man of action /
by Vicente Pérez Rosales;
translated from the Spanish by John H.R. Polt;
with an introduction and chronology by Brian Loveman.
p. cm. — (Library of Latin America)
ISBN 0-19-511760-3 — ISBN 0-19-511761-1 (pbk.)
1. Chile—History—War of Independence, 1810–1824—Anecdotes.
2. Chile—History—1824–1920—Anecdotes.
3. Pârez Rosales, Vicente, 1807–1886.
I. Loveman, Brian.   II. Title.   III. Series.
F3094 .P4413   2002   983'.04—dc21   2002025115

Photograph of Rosales on p. xii, courtesy of the University of Chile
Photograph Archive, with special thanks to Jose Moreno Fabbri.

Photographs of drawings on pages 231, 233, 243, 250, courtesy of the
Chilean National Archives, with special thanks to Mario Monsalve.

1 3 5 7 9 8 6 4 2

Printed in the United States of America
on acid-free paper

Contents

Series Editors'
General Introduction

The Library of Latin America series makes available in translation major nineteenth-century authors whose work has been neglected in the English-speaking world. The titles for the translations from the Spanish and Portuguese were suggested by an editorial committee that included Jean Franco (general editor responsible for works in Spanish), Richard Graham (series editor responsible for works in Portuguese), Tulio Halperín Donghi (at the University of California, Berkeley), Iván Jaksić (at the University of Notre Dame), Naomi Lindstrom (at the University of Texas at Austin), Eduardo Lozano of the Library at the University of Pittsburgh, and Francine Masiello (at the University of California, Berkeley). The late Antonio Cornejo Polar of the University of California, Berkeley, was also one of the founding members of the committee. The translations have been funded thanks to the generosity of the Lampadia Foundation and the Andrew W. Mellon Foundation.

During the period of national formation between 1810 and into the early years of the twentieth century, the new nations of Latin America fashioned their identities, drew up constitutions, engaged in bitter struggles over territory, and debated questions of education, government, ethnicity, and culture. This was a unique period unlike the process of nation formation in Europe and one that should be more familiar than it is to students of comparative politics, history, and literature.

The image of the nation was envisioned by the lettered classes—a minority in countries in which indigenous, mestizo, black, or mulatto peasants and slaves predominated—although there were also alternative nationalisms at the grassroots level. The cultural elite were well educated in European thought and letters, but as statesmen, journalists, poets, and academics, they confronted the problem of the racial and linguistic heterogeneity of the continent and the difficulties of integrating the population into a modern nation-state. Some of the writers whose works will be translated in the Library of Latin America series played leading roles in politics. Fray Servando Teresa de Mier, a friar who translated Rousseau's *The Social Contract* and was one of the most colorful characters of the independence period, was faced with imprisonment and expulsion from Mexico for his heterodox beliefs; on his return, after independence, he was elected to the congress. Domingo Faustino Sarmiento, exiled from his native Argentina under the presidency of Rosas, wrote *Facundo: Civilización y barbarie,* a stinging denunciation of that government. He returned after Rosas' overthrow and was elected president in 1868. Andrés Bello was born in Venezuela, lived in London, where he published poetry during the independence period, settled in Chile, where he founded the University, wrote his grammar of the Spanish language, and drew up the country's legal code.

These post-independence intelligentsia were not simply dreaming castles in the air, but vitally contributed to the founding of nations and the shaping of culture. The advantage of hindsight may make us aware of problems they themselves did not foresee, but this should not affect our assessment of their truly astonishing energies and achievements. It is still surprising that the writing of Andrés Bello, who contributed fundamental works to so many different fields, has never been translated into English. Although there is a recent translation of Sarmiento's celebrated *Facundo,* there is no translation of his memoirs, *Recuerdos de provincia (Provincial Recollections).* The predominance of memoirs in the Library of Latin America series is no accident—many of these offer entertaining insights into a vast and complex continent.

Nor have we neglected the novel. The series includes new translations of the outstanding Brazilian writer Joaquim Maria Machado de Assis' work, including *Dom Casmurro* and *The Posthumous Memoirs of Brás Cubas.* There is no reason why other novels and writers who are not so well known outside Latin America—the Peruvian novelist Clorinda Matto de Turner's *Aves sin nido,* Nataniel Aguirre's *Juan de la Rosa,* José de Alencar's *Iracema,* Juana Manuela Gorriti's short stories—should not be read with as much interest as the political novels of Anthony Trollope.

A series on nineteenth-century Latin America cannot, however, be limited to literary genres such as the novel, the poem, and the short story. The literature of independent Latin America was eclectic and strongly influenced by the periodical press newly liberated from scrutiny by colonial authorities and the Inquisition. Newspapers were miscellanies of fiction, essays, poems, and translations from all manner of European writing. The novels written on the eve of Mexican Independence by José Joaquín Fernández de Lizardi included disquisitions on secular education and law, and denunciations of the evils of gaming and idleness. Other works, such as a well-known poem by Andrés Bello, "Ode to Tropical Agriculture," and novels such as *Amalia* by José Mármol and the Bolivian Nataniel Aguirre's *Juan de la Rosa*, were openly partisan. By the end of the century, sophisticated scholars were beginning to address the history of their countries, as did João Capistrano de Abreu in his *Capítulos de história colonial.*

It is often in memoirs such as those by Fray Servando Teresa de Mier or Sarmiento that we find the descriptions of everyday life that in Europe were incorporated into the realist novel. Latin American literature at this time was seen largely as a pedagogical tool, a "light" alternative to speeches, sermons, and philosophical tracts—though, in fact, especially in the early part of the century, even the readership for novels was quite small because of the high rate of illiteracy. Nevertheless, the vigorous orally transmitted culture of the gaucho and the urban underclasses became the linguistic repertoire of some of the most interesting nineteenth-century writers—most notably José Hernández, author of the "gauchesque" poem "Martín Fierro," which enjoyed an unparalleled popularity. But for many writers the task was not to appropriate popular language but to civilize, and their literary works were strongly influenced by the high style of political oratory.

The editorial committee has not attempted to limit its selection to the better-known writers such as Machado de Assis; it has also selected many works that have never appeared in translation or writers whose work has not been translated recently. The series now makes these works available to the English-speaking public.

Because of the preferences of funding organizations, the series initially focuses on writing from Brazil, the Southern Cone, the Andean region, and Mexico. Each of our editions will have an introduction that places the work in its appropriate context and includes explanatory notes.

We owe special thanks to Robert Glynn of the Lampadia Foundation, whose initiative gave the project a jump start, and to Richard Ekman of the Andrew W. Mellon Foundation, which also generously supported the project. We also thank the Rockefeller Foundation for funding the 1996 symposium "Culture and Nation in Iberoamerica," organized by the editorial board of the Library of Latin America. We received substantial institutional support and personal encouragement from the Institute of Latin American Studies of the University of Texas at Austin. The support of Edward Barry of Oxford University Press has been crucial, as has the advice and help of Ellen Chodosh of Oxford University Press. The first volumes of the series were published after the untimely death, on July 3, 1997, of Maria C. Bulle, who, as an associate of the Lampadia Foundation, supported the idea from its beginning.

—*Jean Franco*
—*Richard Graham*

Translator's Note

This translation is based on the 1910 edition of *Recuerdos del pasado* (*Biblioteca de escritores de Chile*, vol. 3, Santiago: Imprenta Barcelona). In addition I have consulted the following editions: Santiago: Imprenta Gutenberg, 1886; Buenos Aires: Ángel Estrada y Cía., S.A., 1944, 2 vols. (with preliminary study and notes by Eugenio Orrego Vicuña); Havana: Casa de las Américas, 1972. Unfortunately there are errors, either the author's or his publishers,' that reappear in all of these editions; where I have been able to detect them, I correct them with appropriate annotation. I do not know of any scholarly edition of this book, which richly merits one.

The authorship of the footnotes in this translation is indicated by initials: VPR for notes by Pérez Rosales; EOV for notes that I have adapted from those by Eugenio Orrego Vicuña; and JP for my own contributions. I have not attempted a full annotation of the text, which would require an expertise that I do not possess.

In translating the chapters dealing with the author's stay in California I benefited from being able to consult the version published by my late teachers, colleagues, and friends, Professors Edwin S. Morby and Arturo Torres-Rioseco: *California Adventure* (San Francisco: Book Club of California, 1947).

For their assistance, I am grateful to Professor Pilar Álvarez Rubio, Verónica López, and, as always, Beverley Anne Hastings Polt.

—John H. R. Polt

Vicente Pérez Rosales

Chronology of Vicente Pérez Rosales

1807   April 5. Vicente Pérez Rosales born in Santiago, Chile. Both parents members of the upper crust of Chile's colonial society, wealthy, highly educated, politically involved.

1810–1814   Patria Vieja. Initial movement toward independence in Chile; maternal grandfather member of first Junta de Gobierno in Santiago (September 18, 1810). Factional and personal struggles between supporters of Bernardo O'Higgins and Carrera family. Members of both sides visit Pérez household.

1814   Spanish defeat proponents of independence at Rancagua; José Miguel Carrera fails to reinforce O'Higgins' forces.

1814–1818   Spanish "reconquista." Spain reimposes colonial regime. Pérez Rosales' grandfather and aunt sent to exile on Juan Fernández Island; mother imprisoned by notorious commander of Talavera regiment, Vicente San Bruno.

1817   Battle of Chacabuco (February 12); Spanish defeated by San Martín's army. Carrera brothers, Luis and Juan José, arrested in Mendoza by San Martín's forces.

1818   Chile declares independence (February 12); Spanish army defeats Chileans at Cancha Rayada near Talca (March 19);

Battle of Maipú (April 18) seals the independence of the country. Pérez Rosales, at 11 years old, flees to Mendoza as political exile. Participates in youth militia; witnesses execution of Luis and Juan José Carrera April 8, 1818.

1818–1821   Studies in best Santiago private school, has private tutors in French and English.

1821   Leaves Chile on English ship *Owen Glendower*. Abandoned by captain in Rio de Janeiro. Witnesses Brazilian independence movement (1822).

1823   Sails back to Chile on the *Doris;* meets Maria Graham, wife of ship captain.

1825   Leaves on the *Moselle* with other young rich Chileans to study in Paris.

1825–1830   Studies in Paris at elite school for Latin American and Spanish youth. Meets San Martín, many prominent intellectuals. Enjoys Paris theater, cafes, and city life. Witnesses 1830 revolution in Paris.

1830   Returns to Chile.

183?–1845   Returns to Chile; experiments at farming, cattleman, herb medicine, shopkeeper, bootlegger, smuggler, journalism. Lives on a farm in Colchagua off and on almost 10 years.

1835   Tries journalism; fined for insulting a priest he calls a swindler.

1842   Publishes a satirical article ridiculing the private and public responses to a plague of grasshoppers (importing turkeys to eat them).

1845–1846   Chile's first immigration law; Pérez Rosales goes to Magallanes on scientific expedition.

1846   Partner in a newspaper, *El Mosaico,* published in Santiago for 12 issues; prominent authors include Andrés Bello, Manuel Silvela, Juan García del Río; goes to Copiapó and *norte chico* mining districts on the steamship (August 1846).

1848   Leaves for California from Valparaíso (December 1848). Tries mining, running a restaurant, and other jobs with Chilean companions. Restaurant destroyed in San Francisco fire.

1850   Returns to Chile; named colonization agent in southern provinces (October 11, 1850). Helps settle first German immigrants at Valdivia.

1852   Publishes *Memoria sobre la colonización de Valdivia.*

1853   Participates in founding of Puerto Montt (February 12, 1853; date chosen to honor Battle of Chacabuco).

1854   Publishes *Memoria sobre emigración.*

1855   Intendente of colonization territory of Llanquihue.

1855–56   Travels overland to Buenos Aires, then sails to England and Hamburg as Chilean colonization agent and consul general. Meets Argentine ex-dictator Juan Manuel Rosas in Southampton.

1857   Published *Ensayo sobre Chile* (in French) to describe Chilean geography, customs, and opportunities for immigrants.

1858   Publishes *Manual del ganadero chileno* (written in Denmark after visiting a livestock exposition).

1859   Returns to Chile on the *Nueva Granada.* Appointed Intendente of Concepción. Translation of *Ensayo sobre Chile* published in Santiago.

1861   Pérez Rosales' cousin, José Joaquín Pérez, takes office as president. Marries wealthy widow, Antonia Urrutia, in Concepción; Pérez Rosales elected deputy in *Cámara de Diputados* (Lower House of Congress). Experiences poor health.

1870   Publishes "La colonia de Llanquihue, su origen, estado actual y medios de impulsar su progreso."

1875–1882   Publishes in *La Revista Chilena* and *Los Lunes* (Supplement to *La Epoca*); articles later collected in *Diccionario de 'El Entrometido* (Dictionary of a Busybody) (1946).

1876-1881   Senator of the Republic for the Province of Llanquihue.

1880   Member of National Manufacturers Association (*Sociedad de Fomento Fabril* [SFF]).

1882   Publishes *Recuerdos del Pasado* (much of which had been written earlier).

1884   President of SFF.

1885   Pérez's wife, Antonia Urrutia, dies.

1886   Pérez Rosales dies September 6 in Santiago.

1949   On the hundredth anniversary of the gold rush, his "Diary of a Trip to California" (*Diario de un viaje a California*) published in Santiago.

Introduction

Vicente Pérez Rosales died September 6, 1886, at the age of seventy-nine. His life and careers spanned the dawning of Chile's independence, its early nationhood, two foreign wars, two civil wars, the arrival of steamships, railroads, telegraph, the southern and northern expansion of the country's territory, the arrival of European, North African, Latin American, and North American immigrants. Pérez Rosales' life—he was born in 1807—took him from the alternating dusty and muddy rusticity of early nineteenth-century Santiago, a town without a printing press before 1812, to Rio de Janeiro, Paris, and California for the 1849 gold rush, to his country's far south, its northern mines, and to Germany as a diplomatic emissary and colonization recruiting agent for his country in the 1850s. At the end of the 1850s he returned to Chile, first as a provincial intendant (*intendente*) in 1859, and then was elected to Congress and later to the Senate in the 1870s.

Pérez Rosales' family belonged to the "political class" of aristocrats and pseudo-aristocrats that ruled South America's most "stable" nation in the nineteenth century. But he also belonged to Europe's and the Western Hemisphere's age of exhilarating technological, commercial, and political transformation. He was part of a world responding to the American revolution of 1776, the French Revolution of 1789, the philosophical "age of reason," the political age of upheaval, the attack on monarchy and the ancien regime, the struggle to create republics—and an age in which millions of Europeans left their homelands to resettle in the Western Hemisphere. In retrospect, the modernization that characterized the nineteenth century meant profound social volatility, unprecedented global movement of peoples, information, and commodities, a big step toward the networked globalization of the late twentieth century.

Pérez Rosales witnessed and participated in these amazing changes in the life of humankind. Unlike most people, he also wrote about them. And the stories he tells are fascinating, inspiring, and often hilarious. They put the reader "on the ground," experiencing the repugnant slave corrals in Rio de Janeiro in 1822, a shipwreck near Cape Horn, the mining camps of California, and the spectacular growth of San Francisco during the 1849 gold rush.[1] His journal with notes on his adventures in California, which he illustrated with humorous drawings, later served as a source for part of *Recuerdos del Pasado* (*Times Gone By*).

In *Recuerdos del Pasado*, the reader follows Pérez Rosales in Chile from north to south, from countryside to mining camps, to the far southern forests—for half a century. *Times Gone By* is a gift for historians of western Europe, California, and Chile. And its folksy, matter-of-fact, humorous and satirical style makes it a joy to read. The book is a treasure.

Literary critics put *Times Gone By* into a category called "*costumbrista*," a genre dedicated to customs and folkways, a description of popular culture and ways of life. But it is much more, for it takes the reader from the best Parisian schools of the 1820s, the theater and salons of the elite in Europe and Santiago, to the rough-and-tumble gold fields of California. It describes the sea voyages of three and four months between Chile and Europe and also North America. It relates, frequently firsthand, the operations of the first railroads in England and the lives of cattle rustlers and smugglers in the high Andes passes between Chile and Argentina.

It is almost impossible to read this book and not wonder how Pérez Rosales survived to write it. In the introduction to the third edition (1886), the editor, Luis Montt, remarked that "there would have been profound shock, had an astrologer predicted the great ups and downs in fortune to be experienced by this child born in 1807, in a town whose residents usually only traveled as far as their nearby farms in the summer."

---

1. Guillermo Feliú Cruz tells us in the introduction to the 1946 edition of *Diccionario del Entrometido* that the original pages of notes of Pérez Rosales' trip to California "are illustrated by Pérez Rosales' pen, and these drawings are famous for their obscenities. Today they are in the Archivo Histórico Nacional." Facsimiles are reproduced on pages 231, 233, 243, and 250; by today's standards there is little if anything obscene in them. Nevertheless one of the drawings (p. 41 of the manuscript), originally of a nude, was defaced by an anonymous reader with blue stripes to approximately the figure's waist.

Times Gone By is Pérez Rosales' best known and most celebrated book. He wrote many of its chapters long before the collected "memories" were first published together in 1882. Some had been published in newspapers and magazines in the 1870s. Before agreeing to publish *Times Gone By*, four years before his death, he had published various sorts of writing in Chile and Europe. He tried his hand at journalism in the 1830s and 1840s, founding the literary and philosophical "magazine" *El Mosaico* in 1846. With compatriots who had shared his time in Paris, he used *El Mosaico* to ridicule the Argentine "know-it-all" Carlos Tejedor and his colleagues, such as Domingo Sarmiento. Between 1850 and 1870 he wrote more serious essays and short monographs, among them several works on German colonization in southern Chile, a manual for cattle ranchers *(Manual del ganadero chileno*, 1858), and a popular geography (in French) to describe the country for potential immigrants (translated into Spanish a year later as *Ensayo sobre Chile*, 1857). These latter writings, erudite and didactic, were part of his "official life," intended to be of practical use for government officials, immigrants, farmers, and livestock breeders.

After 1870, Pérez Rosales gave license to his jovial skepticism, his acerbic secularism, and his anti-Spanish and anticolonial sentiments. Most of all he gave free rein to his biting sense of humor. Scattered articles and essays, some published in newspapers and later collected as *El Diccionario del Entrometido* (*Dictionary of a Busybody*), provide "definitions" of everything from "mines" to "political revolution" that departed considerably from those found in the Real Academia Española's authoritative *Diccionario de la lengua española*. As he tells the reader in the introduction, "Usually, what is said is less surprising than the ways in which it is said; people share most ideas, they are within everyone's reach. The difference is in the way that they are expressed and in style. Style makes singular the most common things, it strengthens the weakest, it gives grandeur to the simplest." Pérez Rosales' style exemplifies this notion in his short essay-definitions of such terms as "the alphabet," "irrigation," and "weather forecasting": "What predicts weather in one country may not be able to predict weather in another; what accurately predicts weather in one part of a country may be erroneous in other parts." This commonsense assertion is followed by a "learned" and facetious discussion of the variables (moon, sun, wind, atmospheric currents, etc.) that the ancients (Pliny, Galileo, Copernicus, and Descartes) and moderns used to predict the weather in Greece, Rome, England, and Italy.

In another entry to his "dictionary," the definition of "Bottles (Factory of)" turns into a discussion of why no such factory exists in Chile, how such an industry could be encouraged, and a call for bringing an immigrant family of "bottlers" to teach Chilean artisans and pave the way to establishing a real glass factory. Instead of a definition of "Bottles (Factory of)," Pérez Rosales offers recommendations for tariff policy, encourages increased immigration, and provides an acid commentary on the lack of entrepreneurship in Chile. The next entry, "*castigos*" ("punishments"), offers a brief philosophical discourse on penology and humanity ("punishment delayed seems more vengeance than punishment . . . when the criminal faces the gallows one no longer sees the ferocious bandit . . . but just another unfortunate victim of legalized murder, monstrously and inhumanly executed." The entry on "hygiene" begins with a parenthetical definition ("synonym of Universal Panacea") followed by a discussion of a Parisian charlatan's marketing of bottled "Seine Water" in the 1820s as a miraculous cure-all. Pérez Rosales noticed the importance of the labels on the charlatan's bottles, the appeal of the advertising, and the disclaimers (the labels told consumers that the water worked its miracles only slowly, and only when accompanied by a healthy life, good air, moderate habits, etc). Later he would produce "imported" spirits on his farm in the Chilean central valley. When he had success, he decided that he would "confess" by changing the labels and promoting the high quality of Chilean liquor. In short order the market for his product disappeared. Wealthy Chileans were willing to pay high prices for "imported" liqueurs, but not for local alcohol with fancy labels.

Perhaps most revealing is "listening" to Pérez Rosales as he reveals his definition of "mines," a place and part of his life that had become a partial metaphor for human relations.[2]

---

2. There are many editions of *Recuerdos del Pasado* and much literary analysis of Pérez Rosales among experts on Chilean literature. His other work is less well known, but the *Ensayo sobre Chile* (Ediciones de la Universidad de Chile, 1986) and the *Diccionario de 'El Entrometido'/ "Sueños que parecen verdades y verdades que parecen sueños"* (Editorial Difusión, 1946) include enlightening biographical essays, the first by Rolando Mellafe Rojas and the second by Guillermo Feliú Cruz. The ex-Director of the National Library, Enrique Campos Menéndez, published a sampler of Pérez Rosales' work in Vicente Pérez Rosales, *Páginas escogidas* (Editorial Universitaria/Biblioteca Nacional, 1986). Jaime Quezada, a Chilean scholar who has written several articles on Pérez Rosales, also published a more recent synopsis of his life with brief excerpts from his work and examples of some his drawings (*Vicente Pérez Rosales, Andanzas de un chileno universal*, Zig Zag, 1994).

"Mines"

When natural, they are [like] iron boxes with stubborn locks, where
with sweat one may open them, perhaps encounter gold, and
almost always, especially without experience, misery; but not
when they are artificial; because if hammering rocks rarely
brings riches, it [hammering] often produces good results when
wielded against the weaknesses of the human heart. Who fails, during
the day, to exploit some of these?
The mines of the doctor and his partner,
the pharmacist, are human infirmities.
Of the lawyer, human discord.
Of the bad priest, human credulity.
Of the tyrant, human cowardice.
Of the Parisian fashion designer, foolish female pride.
Of the flatterer, the vainglorious powerful and stupid.
Of the soldier-adventurer, pay for murder. . . .

In another essay, "Something that here we call 'Centralization'"
("*Algo sobre lo que por acá llamamos centralización*"), published in the *Revista Chilena* in 1877, Pérez Rosales spoofs Chile's overly centralized political and administrative system. The essay recounts the difficulties of a southern town's government council in finding a legal way to fund an outhouse/latrine (*bacín*) for use by the town's prisoners. According to Pérez Rosales, the regulations of national law made things ever so difficult, but despite the legal norms, there was "an inevitable consequence of the prisoners being fed and their chewing and digesting the victuals," and also a horrible odor from the nearby plaza where the prisoners did their necessities. In English, only Mark Twain could have told this tale so facetiously, mocking so inspiredly a political and legal system that required permission from the capital to expend funds to dispose of local waste. Unfortunately, as Pérez Rosales recounts, the artisan who manufactured the *bacín* had already delivered it to the local authorities, it had been put to use, and he had not been paid—because the ceramic fixture had not figured in the annual budget despite the council's request for his services. Unsurprisingly, the artisan hesitated to reclaim an item that had already been "in use" during forty-eight hours, preferring that the councilmen invent a way to pay him. "Not possible," said the authorities, at least not without consulting the Intendente, the provincial representative of the president. The payment was eventually made, after much red tape, numerous administrative procedures, approvals, reversals of

approvals, appeals to higher authority, and a final decision by the Minister of Interior. They could pay for the *bacín*, so long as they sent along the proper documentation and receipt.

Many other Chilean writers, especially in the political press since the 1820s, had resorted to irony, caricature, and ridicule—one must remember the liberal who gave himself the name *"el diablo político"* (the "political devil") in the late 1830s, writing an editorial column called "infernal politics"—until the government ran him out of business using the law regarding "abuses of the press." Debates over literature and theater in the local periodicals also resorted to satire, personal attacks, ridicule, and burlesque. Pérez Rosales engaged in that sort of personal exchange in his early journalistic ventures also, in the 1830s and 1840s. Indeed he was fined in 1835 for characterizing a priest as a "swindler." But in *Recuerdos del Pasado* and in the *Diccionario del Entrometido* he did not attack any particular government; his sense of humor and of human foibles were more universal. Pérez Rosales' descriptions of "local customs" from Paris to California, from Copiapó to Hamburg, remind the reader of Mark Twain's apocryphal report by extraterrestrials on the Planet Earth, *Letters from Earth*, a sort of interplanetary (the nineteenth-century equivalent of a trip from Valdivia to Buenos Aires, and from there to London) cultural anthropology written up by a sardonic philosophical humorist. Twain's heirs prevented publication of this work for many years, perhaps due to its spoof of religion; Pérez Rosales published his work while he still lived, making fun of himself, the institutions around him, and human folly. Yet there was rarely a note of personal antagonism in Pérez Rosales' writing in the 1870s; he applauded practical measures that made life better, he endorsed modernity at the same time that he took it with more than a grain of salt.

Memoirs were not common in the 1880s in Chile; less so those published before death and referring to those still living in so irreverent a manner. Pérez Rosales spoofed the powerful and the pauper, and especially himself in his many adventures. He recounted his dealings with San Martín, his encounter with ex-Argentine dictator Manuel de Rosas, with European literati, with bandits and *caudillos* in Argentina, and royalty from Russia, Germany, and France. He did not "tell all"; indeed he told his readers that he wouldn't do so, nor did he intend to be a historian.

The first "edition" of *Recuerdos del Pasado* was published in serial form in the columns of the Santiago periodical, *La Epoca*, then a second edition as a *separata*. He informs the reader in the prologue to the second edition in 1882 that besides causing laughter at himself and others, the publication of his collected memories would allow "evaluating what we are and what we could have been, had we been less remiss in following examples worthy of emulation." For the third edition (1886), "hopefully purged of some of the most embarrassing errors," Pérez Rosales explained how he came to assign the rights to publish the book to Nathaniel Miers-Cox. Miers-Cox proposed gifting the books and profits to an order of nuns that managed the *Santa sección de la Caridad*, tending the needs of the impoverished and disabled. The nuns would ask for alms and give a copy of *Recuerdos del Pasado* to the generous donors. In the introduction to the third edition, Pérez Rosales also lamented the numerous errors in the first two editions, but did so with his typical humor: "It's understandable that a printer changes [by way of typographical errors] an author's words from *llanura* to *blancura*, from *torreones* to *terneros*, *túmulos* to *tumultos*, etc., etc., but one cannot tolerate [changes] that introduce contradictions, such as *tímido* instead of *temido*, *no se podía* instead of *podía*, *desconocidos* instead of *conocidos*, *desairado* instead of *airado*, etc. etc. But enough, reproducing each of these errors, not to mention corrections of words and dates, would mean reproducing the entire book!"[3]

From politics to morals, from the benefits of immigration to the evils of prostitution, from slavery to aristocracy, from human avarice to human kindness, Pérez Rosales' *Recuerdos* leap across time, oceans, and continents. They tell tales of "Times Gone By" but remain "modern" in their fine dissection of human motivation and behavior as we approach the third millennium. The same is true for the short essays in the *Diccionario del Entrometido*, edited and published by Luis Montt after Pérez Rosales' death. Indeed Pérez Rosales' pithy definition of "justice" in the *Diccionario del Entrometido* seemed unfortunately apt in Chile in the present: "Justice almost ceases to be such, when confronted with power."

Recuerdos del Pasado has a special place for Chilean historians and historians of Chile. It depicts social and economic conditions in the country's first century of independence firsthand, it relates the everyday lives of people from the very peak to the bottom of Chilean society. It reveals common

---

3. The typographical errors listed by Pérez Rosales change the meaning from "levelness" [like a prairie] to "whiteness," "towers" to "veal calf," "tombs," to "tumult." The typographical errors that introduced contradictions: "timid" instead of "feared," " it was not possible" instead of "it was possible," "unknown" instead of "known" and "slighted or unrewarded" instead of "angry or irritated."

Chilean prejudices, myths, customs, self-perceptions, and stereotypes of other nationalities and ethnicities and popular culture. From independence in 1818 until the early 1830s the new country experienced considerable internal strife and political instability. Conservative forces defeated liberals at the Battle of Lircay in 1830, a milestone in the foundation of an "autocratic republic." Under three consecutive ten-year presidencies (Joaquín Prieto, 1831–1841; Manuel Bulnes, 1841-1851; and Manuel Montt, 1851-1861, the first civilian president since 1830), Chile established a relatively stable political system and experienced economic growth based on exports of minerals and agricultural products to world markets. The government encouraged foreign investment and expansion of trade, especially with England and the United States, but also with other European countries and Australia. Brief civil wars in 1851 and 1859 reconfirmed the autocratic republic but also made necessary some political liberalization in the 1860s and 1870s. Pérez Rosales' memories of *Times Gone By* recall this period of nation-building until 1860, the push to establish "law and order" and also to import the technological, economic, and intellectual advances of Europe and North America so cherished by Chile's governing elite. They also detail the diverse sources of opposition to imported ideas and ways of life as the global webs of North Atlantic capitalism enveloped Chile and the rest of Latin America.

In addition to its great value for historians of Europe, California, and Chile, and the entertainment it is bound to provide for other readers, this book also has a special place in my own memories of becoming a historian, and of my own learning about Chile. When I first set out to write a history of Chile in the 1970s, Pérez Rosales became an unwitting collaborator, an inspiration, and a source of "inside" information. He made researching history and writing history a joy, a gift not always conceded from archival files or historians of the past. I owe to Pérez Rosales the gift of laughing out loud, despite the annoyed looks of other patrons in the library, of imagining the dreadful circumstances described so matter-of-factly and dryly by Pérez Rosales. I am certain that, with this translation into English, his wit, insightfulness, and sometimes outrageous exaggerations will now be enjoyed by literally millions more readers over the years.

Not all was humor for Pérez Rosales. Sometimes, he was deadly serious, even in *Times Gone By*. His description of conditions in the Copiapó mining region in the 1840s and the brutal treatment of prostitutes, waitresses, washerwomen, and wives alike makes the reader cringe with pain. The unselfconscious language of racism employed by the miners, merchants, and roustabouts as recounted in Pérez Rosales' matter-of-fact reporting of dialogue reminds us all that racism was "taken for granted." Pérez Rosales also wrote seriously regarding German colonization at Valdivia (*Memoria sobre la colonización de Valdivia,* 1852) and about the general problems of attracting immigrants—as a counterpoise to many Chileans who opposed bringing "foreigners" to settle (*Memoria sobre emigración,* 1854).

Pérez Rosales had his practical side, along with his dose of upper-crust Chilean understanding of the uses of extended family and "contacts." By the 1870s he proudly confessed his pragmatism. He had avoided death in the streets of Paris in 1830, lived in the Chilean countryside by hook and by crook, survived treks in winter in the Andean mountain passes, escaped the vengeance of Argentine border guards whose horses he stole, faced racism and just plain wickedness in California's gold country, worked as a waiter in San Francisco, cussed like a miner forty-niner, lived as a diplomat in Europe, and returned to Chile to risk his life in primitive canoes during pioneering expeditions to the fabulous lakes, rivers, and forests of the southern frontier. Serving as local government official and colonization agent, and faced with the dilemma of providing suitable farmland for arriving German immigrants, he paid a local Indian to burn huge tracts of native forest.

Who authorized such a decision? A bureaucrat by appointment, Pérez Rosales never adapted to bureaucracy nor, strictly speaking, acted like a bureaucrat. He was an adventurer, often impetuous, and, for better or worse, hardly ever willing to "wait to see what happened." The colonists needed cleared land to farm; there was lots of forest. Burn some of it! If the trees were hundreds or thousands of years old, so be it. The Germans had been promised land. He owed his job to personal and family connections, but his social background made him partially immune to compliant careerism. In any case, his own self-described "indiscipline" would hardly allow him to be content with a low-key role as a vacillating civil servant waiting for instructions. He parceled out land to the immigrants, gave them axes, and sought to defend them against public and private depredations by Chileans who wanted to "sell for 10 pesos what was worth 1."

Pérez Rosales often lived "on the edge." Some Chileans denounced his unorthodox methods of buying and clearing land for "his" immigrants. He defended himself and helped found Puerto Montt in 1853 (Manuel Montt was president; he had defeated the rebels in a bloody civil war in 1851—the opposition tarred him a tyrant and Pérez Rosales gladly founded a town named in his honor).

Two years later Pérez Rosales was in Hamburg as the government's colonization agent and consul general. He passed over the Argentine Pampa, sailed to Brazil, then England, and met with ousted Argentine dictator Juan Manuel de Rosas in Southampton. Pérez Rosales found him quite civilized, and figured that his enemies had exaggerated his barbarism and ferocity. On the other hand, he noted that his innkeeper remarked that if Rosas wasn't busy killing people in England as he had in Argentina, it was because he knew that in England "it's just a step from murder to the gallows." After his conversations with Rosas he also noted that the ex-dictator believed that Argentines could only live under an absolutist political system; that he (Rosas) was the indispensable person who could contain the passions of his "crazy" countrymen.

In September 1855 Pérez Rosales arrived in Hamburg. In *Times Gone By* he describes the political and economic institutions of this city-state of 200,000 souls and his difficulties in promoting European emigration to Chile. To that end he published his *Essay on Chile (Ensayo sobre Chile)*. At the time, there existed no comparable geography and description of Chilean fauna, flora, social and political systems, customs, and national character. He wrote the book, in part, to persuade emigrants to embark to Chile and overcome the ignorance regarding the country on the continent and the negative propaganda spread by other colonization agents seeking to channel immigrants to Brazil, Mexico, or elsewhere. Pérez Rosales describes with glee and feigned anger the stubborn stupidity of French, Russian, and German officials who confused Chile with Mexico, Peru, and Colombia. But he also acknowledges the exaggerated nationalism of Chileans, who "have a low tolerance for unfavorable comparisons regarding their country."

The *Ensayo sobre Chile* is informative, eclectic, selective, and entertaining. Pérez Rosales explains that Chilean women marry early, that many are grandmothers by age thirty-one, and that they keep procreating until age thirty-eight, or even forty in the countryside, taking care of their own children alongside their grandchildren. In another part of the *Ensayo*, he details the history and qualities of "the Chilean horse," a history of cattle-raising since 1548, and also an abbreviated history of the country's pigs, goats, and sheep (and the poor quality of Chilean wool). In case potential immigrants should be apprehensive, "Chilean snakes may be taken in the hand with no concern," and "there is great undiscovered wealth in the sea life of Chile's territorial seas." Moreover, "the crustaceans and mollusks that populate our coasts are a precious resource for their number and the delicacy of their flavor." (No one who has spent any time in Chile could disagree with those observations.) For good measure, Pérez Rosales added that the Chilean bees would soon produce honey "that will compete with the European product throughout the regions bordering the Pacific Ocean." And for those concerned about medical technology, we are assured that there are good quantities of leeches in Chile, such good quantities that after use it is not necessary to save them. The small size of Chilean leeches is compensated for by their numbers; indeed "exports of this annelid have recently begun from Valparaíso." Part hype, part geography, part inventory of botanical, marine, and zoological resources, part cultural history ("Chilean generosity is always apparent, except in business negotiations"), the *Ensayo sobre Chile* never achieved the acclaim of *Recuerdos del Pasado*, but it continues to provide a snapshot of the country and of Chilean self-perception at mid-nineteenth century.

What sort of person would boast of the quantity of Chilean leeches and their effectiveness in the 1850s? The same individual who would report the price of pork in Valparaíso and the central valley, the scarcity and limited variety of reptiles, and the trade in ostrich feathers (113 dozen to California in 1850).

Who was Vicente Pérez Rosales? What was his family background? What sort of life could bring him to write the *Ensayo sobre Chile* in 1857, then publish such an enduring account of *Times Gone By* in the 1880s?

Pérez Rosales was born into a wealthy family, related on maternal and paternal sides to the upper echelons of colonial Chilean society. On his paternal side, he descended from the Spanish historian and merchant, José Pérez García, and Rosario Salas y Ramírez de Salas, part of the powerful Larraín extended-family, the so-called "eight-hundred" who dominated much of Chile's early history. In the late colonial era, Pérez García authored the *Historia general, natural, militar y sagrada del reino de Chile*, a chronicle of conquest and settlement of the Chilean colony. According to Chile's great liberal historian, Diego Barros Arana, "few men have written worse in Chile, than this Pérez García. He lacked any imagination, his writing was bereft of any literary art and without color or luster. . . . His contribution is strictly erudite, documentary." No one who ever read his grandson's Vicente Pérez Rosales' entertaining, bawdy, and colorful writing would have similar comments.

Vicente's father, José Joaquín Pérez y Salas, married Mercedes Rosales Larraín, a brilliant, highly educated woman who read widely and spoke French and English—which she taught to her son Vicente. Vicente had access to books, erudition, and the best of everything that colonial society could offer. His father died, perhaps from tuberculosis, when Vicente was quite young. His mother remarried to Felipe Santiago de Solar, a wealthy banker, merchant, and, sub rosa, an important political figure in the dying days of the Spanish colonial regime. Vicente's maternal grandfather, Juan Enrique Rosales, served on the first Chilean Junta in 1810 that swore loyalty to Ferdinand VII but then became a symbol for the independence movement. For the Spaniards who returned to Santiago in 1814, Rosales had chosen the wrong side. With the Spanish reconquest (the *reconquista*) of 1814-1818, he ended up, infirm and elderly, exiled along with other "patriots" to Juan Fernández Island.

According to Pérez Rosales, his stepfather contracted private teachers to supplement his studies in "the best private school in Santiago." Pérez Rosales learned French and English, enjoyed reading, but, as he said of himself, "I was a little undisciplined and ungovernable (*díscolo*). As it turns out, he was so ungovernable that his mother and stepfather put him on an English ship headed to Europe at age fourteen to see if he might learn some discipline on board. The English sea captain, Lord Spencer, dumped him in Rio de Janeiro, where he was appalled by the slave trade and the backwardness of Rio de Janeiro. He witnessed the Brazilian independence movement in 1822, then made his way back to Chile on the *Doris*, where he was befriended by the wife of the ship's captain, Maria Graham. Graham later wrote descriptions of her adventures in South America that became valuable "primary sources" for generations of historians.

Home in time for the earthquake that shook Santiago in 1822, Pérez Rosales leaves us a description of the terror that overtook the town, then of the abdication of Bernardo O'Higgins in early 1823. He also recalls increased numbers of French merchant and warships arriving at Valparaíso in the early 1820s. After independence in Chile, the elite looked to France as the center of culture, the measure of fashion, whether of clothes or literary and philosophical trends. Vicente's stepfather hosted French navy officers and merchants, joining with them in commercial ventures. He had his own small fleet that made war on the remaining Spanish vessels in Chilean waters.

Pérez Rosales' stepfather was also well educated and trilingual (French, English, Spanish). He helped finance the Chilean-Argentine invasion of Peru led by José de San Martín that eventually made Peru independent. The Pérez extended family would figure in Chilean politics for most of the nineteenth century, including President José Joaquin Pérez (1861–1871). Pérez Rosales himself would maintain correspondence with key government personalities from the 1840s on, especially Antonio Varas during the administration of President Manuel Montt (1851–1861). Family and political connections thus served Pérez Rosales well, if not always, from birth to death.

Along the way, however, both circumstances and his own penchant for travel and adventure put him frequently at risk. At age eleven, in exile with the Rosales family that had fled Santiago when the Spaniards defeated the rebels at Cancha Rayada in 1817, he formed part of the "youth militia" and witnessed the execution in Mendoza of Luis and Juan José Carrera, brothers of Chile's first dictator (1811). The Carrera family, "patriots" and rebels, had rather strong differences with Bernardo O'Higgins, the eventual Chilean "father of his country" and victor over the Spaniards at the battle of Maipú that defined the war for independence in 1817. All of these now legendary figures were visitors to young Pérez Rosales' home in Santiago. His family sought to take a neutral line between the patriot factions, but the execution in Mendoza made a lasting impression. It would not, however, be the last execution or revolutionary bloodshed witnessed in Pérez Rosales' long life. Neither O'Higgins nor San Martín moved a finger to save the Carreras; some had it that they ordered the executions. In any case, after independence the O'Higgins and Carrera factions continued to war until the most famous Carrera, José Miguel, was killed and O'Higgins abdicated the country's "Supreme Directorship" and went into exile in Peru.

In 1825 Pérez Rosales, a number of half-brothers, cousins, and other young Chilean aristocrats (perhaps totaling thirty-five), including sons of two independence war heroes, Francisco de la Lastra and José Manuel Borgoño, sailed on the *Moselle,* around Cape Horn to Brazil, on their way to France. Perhaps prejudiced by his earlier misfortune in Rio de Janeiro, Pérez Rosales found little to like about the city in 1825, or for that matter when he revisited Rio in the 1840s, 1850s, and 1860s. He says that there wasn't a single building, including the imperial palace, that compared with any of the public or private buildings of "our present-day Santiago."

Unhappy with the *Moselle*'s captain, the Chilean party changed vessels in Rio de Janeiro for their voyage to France. Along with family members and friends his age, Pérez Rosales would receive schooling and lessons in life in Paris. At age eighteen, he would thus join other Chileans and Latin Americans in a small colony of upper-class youngsters who studied under Leandro Fernández Moratín and then Manuel Silvela at the Liceo Hispanoamericano in Paris. Until after the July 1830 revolution in France, Pérez Rosales lived the life of a well-off student in the best schools for émigré Latin Americans in Paris. He rubbed shoulders with distinguished visitors, political and literary, and shared with his cohorts the streets, libraries, theaters, and amusements of Europe's, if not the world's, intellectual capital.

On his return to Chile in 1830, after first impressing the locals with his fashionable ways, he spent the next decade doing a bit of everything, but never very successfully. Politics had taken a turn against his stepfather who was in exile with his fortune greatly diminished. Pérez Rosales lived much of the time outside Santiago, south in the central valley, and his biographers gloss over this period—as does Pérez Rosales, for the most part, in his *Recuerdos*. He tried his hand at farming, retail trade, cattle and tobacco smuggling from Argentina, designing theater sets, journalism, bootlegging, and quack medicine. From the mid-1840s until the 1860s, in contrast, his adventures in the country's northern mines, in California, in Chile's far south, and then in Europe are well known and amply covered in *Times Gone By*. What is clear in retrospect is that during his life the eleven-year-old boy who witnessed the execution of the two Carrera brothers in Mendoza went from marooned teenager in Rio de Janeiro to an education in Paris, from impoverished roustabout, cattleman (and cattle rustler), smuggler, fraudulent "doctor" and "pharmacist," bootlegger and distiller of local liquor with imported labels, miner, and "forty-niner" in California, explorer, founder of settlements in Chile's far south, Chilean Consul General in Hamburg, back to Chile, Senator of the Republic and founding member and president of the Council of the National Manufacturing Society (*Sociedad de Fomento Fabril*).

By the 1860s his world travels had more or less finished; as Chilean historian Rolando Mellafe put it in an introduction to a reprinted version of Pérez' *Ensayos sobre Chile*, a temporary bout of poor health convinced him that "his life as a globetrotter, who tested his luck and defied fate" had come to an end. He decided to begin another life, dedicated to politics and home. Perhaps partially for that reason, at the age of fifty-four, he decided to marry. And marry he did, a wealthy widow named Antonia Urrutia. At approximately the same time, Pérez agreed to be a candidate of the National Party (Montt-Varista) for the province of Chillán. Once elected he again fell ill; his substitute (*suplente*), José Gabriel Palma, replaced him in the Chamber of Deputies. In the 1870s he served in the Senate and continued writing humorous short essays. His pragmatism made him little tolerant of high-minded, principled, and dedicated "political oppositionists," as illustrated sarcastically in his

"Primer of the Trendy Opposition" ("*Cartilla del opositor a la moda*") published in 1876 in the *Revista Chilena*: "For diffusing your political doctrine, erase from your dictionary the words discussion, justice and truth; put in their place, argument, partiality and lies. . . . Never tire of repeating that [the government] has done things poorly, or at best half-asked; never suggest how they might have been well done or improved, otherwise you will enter the difficult road of practicality. . . . [All bad things] come from above, the rain that made roads impassable, destroys bridges. . . . Only the favoritism and lack of foresight of the government could cause such calamities. . . . if crops are lost and the price of bread goes up, it must be the government's fault for not prohibiting exports in time . . . and if there is litigation, and as usually happens one of the litigants loses, tell the aggrieved party that the government is to blame for appointing incompetent and corrupt judges . . . and if anyone in your town opposes government authority, don't bother finding out the reason for the government's action, just say that the [opposition] was defending civil liberties and rights brutally violated by the soldier . . . and if the soldier defends himself against knives drawn against him, call him an executioner, hired assassin or a cuckold."[4]

By the 1870s Pérez Rosales clearly had no use for feigned idealism and righteousness, but he never lost his own idealism regarding human volition and the prospect for a better future, if not for himself with the infirmities of old age, certainly for Chile and humanity. Pérez Rosales lived an extraordinary life in extraordinary times. Only the greatest of good luck allowed him to survive his adventures and live almost to the age of eighty. For the reader, his good luck is also ours. *Recuerdos del Pasado* is Pérez Rosales' irreverent history of his life, and that of Chile from 1814 to 1860, published only four years before his death.

In the preface to the second edition (1882) Pérez Rosales tells the reader that since it was written after the book, the preface should really be the postface (*postfacio*), that he'd written the book to tell his compatriots "what we were, to better evaluate what we are, and what we might be, if we had lived in ways more worthy of emulation." He also apologized for the uneven style, the lack of continuity, the omissions, because "between the serious and ridiculous, grief and happiness to which we humans are subjected, often there is no [real] transition." In this first English edition of *Recuerdos del Pasado—Times Gone By*, John Polt has

---

4. "Cartilla del opositor a la moda" in *Vicente Pérez Rosales, Páginas escogidas* (Santiago: Editorial Universitaria/Biblioteca Nacional, 1986: 261–263).

brilliantly translated Pérez Rosales' prose and added historical and literary notes for English-speakers; future Spanish editions will do well to
consult these notes to eliminate errors that have been reprinted since the
first edition published in Chile in 1882 as a serial in the periodical *La
Epoca*. Readers in English and Spanish will benefit from Polt's efforts to
make sense of some of the errors that Pérez Rosales himself complained
about when he wrote the preface to the third edition in Spanish shortly
before his death.

Time now to become immersed in *Times Gone By*. Revisit through
Pérez Rosales' eyes the Santiago of 1810, sail to Rio de Janeiro in 1821, go
to Paris in 1825, then back to Chile 1830, to the Andes blanketed in
snow, then to California for the forty-niners, and back to Europe in the
1850s and then return to Chile as it finished its third civil war of the
nineteenth century. But be prepared for surprises, to laugh, and to laugh
out loud along the way.

Brian Loveman
Solana Beach, California
November 2001

TIMES GONE BY

Contents

I

Why the Santiago of 1814 to 1822 can't hold a candle

to the Santiago of 1860.

W hat sort of place was Santiago in 1814? What, back then, was this city that has grown so big for its age and that along with its more or less justified claims to metropolitan status still harbors the petty ways of a village?

Apart from the wonderful Chilean sky and the impressive view of the Andes, the Santiago of 1814, the delight of its happy citizens, was, for the newly arrived foreigner, a remote and dismal town, whose low and crudely fashioned buildings, though neatly lined up along straight streets, lacked any architectural distinction. The value of this jewel of the so-called Kingdom of Chile was further reduced by the filth in which it was set, for though it rose on the fertile plain of the Mapocho River, it was bordered by the Mapocho dump on the north, the Cañada dump on the south, the Santa Lucía dump on the east, and the San Miguel-San Pablo dump on the west.

If the fringes of Santiago were garbage, what might one call the countryside beyond it, in view of the apathetic and self-satisfied character of its solid citizens? Only the eastern valley of the town was, thanks to the waters of our Chilean Manzanares[1] and of the sparkling brooks that flow from the foothills of the Andes, an authentic garden in comparison with the empty fields that stretched north, south, and west from our capital. The plain of Maipo, a veritable oven where the summer sun burned down unobstructed on the thirsty stonecutter, boasted only bleached-out rosemary bushes instead of trees, and puny ephimerous down instead of grass. To use the poetic expression of our Chilean peasants, not even the finch greets the day out there.

Back then, who could have looked at our smug and slow-paced way of life and imagined that in time those useless empty spaces first visited by the muddy Maipo in 1820, when it joined part of its abundant stream with the ever scanty and wrangled-over waters of the Mapocho, would be where the locomotive now roars and rushes through the cool groves that surround countless valuable farms, in each of which industriousness, art, and the comforts of life seem to have found their natural home! Who could have imagined that those foul shacks that extended the city beyond the old Cañada dump would be replaced by parks and sumptuous villas fit for a king, and, what is more, that the dump itself would become the Alameda de las Delicias,[2] an avenue that can well be the envy of polished Europe's finest city! Miracles, all of them, born of our immortal 12th of February 1818, when we broke through the wall that separated us from the rest of the civilized world and decided to manage our own affairs as we saw fit.

But let us not get ahead of ourselves.

Even twenty-four years after the time I am speaking of, Santiago had only 46,000 inhabitants. Seen from the Santa Lucía heights, its many trees made it look like a village of farmhouses lined up along streets whose narrow sidewalks were often invaded by the protruding buttresses of churches and convents or by the columns of the more or less pretentious houses of wealthy citizens—and this is no cause for surprise, because the invasive impulse of Church and Money is never idle.

Our capital had only one marketplace and one main square, where, along with the best shops, you would find the cathedral, a convent, the governor's residence, the city hall, and the forbidding jail, which, as occurred in every town founded by the Spaniards, flaunted its austere iron grate and the filthy hands of the prisoners who grasped it while granting audience to their daily visitors. Every morning you would see, just out-

---

1. *Manzanares,* the river that runs through Madrid. JP.
2. Now called Avenida Bernardo O'Higgins. EOV.

side the arches of this gloomy building, two or three bloody corpses laid there by the police so that their relatives might identify them.

From the doorway of the jail led a street that joined what we now call the Calle del Estado and that displayed a line of crude wooden huts and dilapidated stalls, called bargain shops, instead of the clean and attractive little stores that now crowd around the columns of the Fernández Concha Gate. Behind those repulsive establishments lay an expanse of baskets filled with not very fragrant slipperlike shoes and waiting for Saturday to come around, when for four *reales* they would once more provide footwear to the sons of the first families of the metropolis, for it seemed to be the norm that these shoes should not last the young gentlemen more than a week.

In the place of what is now the Fernández Concha Gate there was a low dark archway that held the most luxurious shops, veritable emporiums where the buyer could find, commingled in the most democratic fashion, sumptuous Chinese fabrics, brocades, gold lamé, laces, chintzes, crockery and glassware, rosaries, beads, children's toys, pictures of saints, Chinese skyrockets, sugar, chocolate, *mate,* hardware of various sorts, and everything else in God's creation, all of it illuminated at night with pure tallow candles set in candlesticks of no less pure copper, with their obligatory accompaniment of snuffers and tallow spills.

In the middle of that square, which served equally for processions and bullfights and for the parades of the troops, stood an enormous bronze fountain always surrounded by water sellers, who used gourds to fill the barrels carried by their animals and then supplied the town with drinking water; and on each side there frequently stood one or two gallows for condemned criminals, in spite of whose gloomy presence the aristocratic square was never for a moment bereft of that sinister instrument of mortification, the stake or *rollo.*

When he was laying out the regular design of the capital, Valdivia never dreamt of the height that its buildings would eventually attain, for its streets, wide enough for houses of a single story, are narrow for those of two; and one story more is all it would take to plunge them into perpetual shade.

The houses were provided with courtyards, corrals, and gardens; their entrances were guarded by enormous doors, whose stout leaves boasted rows of shining copper bosses to make them even more solid; and none of those belonging to the high and mighty lacked a proud triangular sort of gable that crowned the doorway and displayed in its center the carved coat of arms that testified to the owner's noble rank.

Foreign luxuries had not yet even dreamed of invading us, and so the halls of our great moguls displayed nothing but Chilean ones: whitewashing instead of wallpaper; instead of cut velveteen carpets, Indian mats or semi-carpeting that only covered the center of the room and left the space along the walls free for the chairs, placed in keeping with the rigid moral standards of that time, because those intended for the ladies were always placed on the side opposite to that where only the male sex was to sit. From this placement so little conducive to amorous skirmishes you can deduce the anguish suffered by lovers, though word has it that they made up for it later, either through the gratings of the windows that faced the street, or over the walls of the corrals. In addition, wooden tables inlaid with more wood, bearing solid silver candelabra, displayed religious images, decorated Peruvian knickknacks, peacocks made of silver filigree, and bowls, censers, and vessels for drinking *mate,* all likewise of silver. The wall decorations were limited to one or two mirrors framed with artistically arranged mirror fragments, some picture of the family's favorite saint, some frightful huge portrait of a titled ancestor painted in the style of good old Josephus Gil.[3] The entire panoply was lit with tallow candles; and in winter the parlor was warmed with hardwood coals, glowing in a mighty brazier of solid silver that rested on a handsome stand in the middle of the room.

Less well-to-do families displayed the same amenities in their parlors as did the wealthy, but on a lesser scale. Except for the piano, very scarce in those times, or the harpsichord, instruments that the poor replaced with a guitar leaning against the wall, and for full carpeting, in place of which the poor had a piece of straw mattress draped over a frame under which you could hear the little mice at play, once you had seen one parlor you could say you had seen them all.

External luxuries were another story. Their chief symbol was the two-wheeled calèche, for such a carriage was only used by the nobility. This frightening vehicle—its wheels at the rear, with six-inch spikes protruding from the board that joined them so that street urchins would not add their own to the great hulk's already overwhelming weight, with leather straps to suspend its chassis, with tires consisting of iron fragments attached to the wheels with enormous nails—was, for the well-to-do, a Noah's ark pulled along by a single mule, whose back, to top it off, had to bear the coachman, a fat mulatto with his poncho and his broad-brimmed hat.

The streets along which this vehicle so conducive to an active digestion bumped its way were not convex but concave; and down their middle, bordered by large stones, ran the waters of the Mapocho.

3. José Gil de Castro, a Peruvian mulatto who painted several of the liberators. EOV.

Then we had what were laughably called streetlights. These consisted of a lantern that the police obliged each householder in dear old Santiago to hang at his own expense over his front door, so that its single tallow candle might shed some modicum of light onto the solitary street during the early evening hours. But since the police specified neither the type of lantern nor the size of the candle, many a paper lantern and expiring puny stump of molten tallow shed their wretched light, or darkness, onto the none too clean sidewalk that lay before them; and I say "none too clean" because if, half a century later, those small sanitary establishments that our people baptized with the name *chaurrinas* were not accepted, I leave it to the reader to deduce what might have been the state of sanitation half a century earlier. In order, therefore, to avoid stumbling onto something repulsive, every lady who went out calling at night would always be preceded by a servant who, armed with a stick and bearing a lantern, would constantly halt, either to illuminate the passage over the streams running down the street along which they were walking, or to do the same for the sewers of those to be crossed, which, when they overflowed, would spread a disgusting flood over extensive segments of the road.

But let no one think that by our talk of sticks and lanterns we mean to show that back then the capital of the Kingdom of Chile lacked security police at night, because there was such a police, and it bore the curious name *serenía,* just as its troops were called *serenos,* though, to be sure, to this day no one has been able to determine whether this name is derived from the chilly dew *(sereno)* that fell on the officers on clear nights or from the serenity with which they bore the downpours on cloudy ones. Along with his primary obligation, the *sereno* was charged with frightening away the devil and being the ambulatory clock and barometer of the town. The stillness of the night would constantly be broken by the inharmonious bellowing of these men, who after a harsh but thundering *Ave Maria Purissima!* would shout out the time marked by the ancient clock of the Jesuit church, and then the state of the weather.

One day, after visiting all the houses in the neighborhood, there came into my parents' home, with copious accompaniment of boys and onlookers, a tray in whose center a folded napkin concealed a mysterious object. What might it be? Why were those pious women so quick to cross themselves as they approached the tray? Why indeed, but that there, present in body and soul, was the true and authentic shoe of the devil, with its worn nails, its drooping heel, and its sulfur smell! Contemporary reports had it that the night before, as the devil was crossing in front of the church of the Jesuits mounted on another devil who had entered the body of a mare, he had been so alarmed at hearing the enthusiastic *Ave Maria* blasted at him by a *sereno* singing out the time that in his fright he had lost his stirrups, and as he had dashed off cursing down the street, he had lost that shoe.

There was no scarcity of such clear demonstrations of the state of innocent credulity in which our people lived in colonial times, for I remember another equally itinerant and mysterious tray that, after the battle of Chacabuco, bore, instead of a dirty clodhopper, half a peck of pigs' tails, which were said to be appendages that in the heat of that clash our soldiers had cut off the Saracens, as the Spanish soldiers were then called.

Yet if it is true that Santiago did not enjoy the ease and conveniences that make for what the English call comfort, it is equally true that in the process of acquiring them we have been losing that plain and loyal brotherly feeling, that enviable openness with which every homeowner received the families, whether friends or strangers, who came from another neighborhood to settle in his own, for the welcoming message was always accompanied by offers of food and drink. This brotherly feeling was most intense with relatives and guests, especially at mealtimes. No sooner had the meal begun than the lady of the house would look for a tasty morsel on her own plate or in the olive dish, which was never absent from the table; and picking it up with her own fork, she offered it with an elegant gesture to her guest, who would quickly do the same with his fork and return the compliment to the lady with a courteous salute. When some special delicacy or notable culinary production was being served, the master of the house would instantly remember the friend or relative who was most fond of it; and a goodly portion of the succulent dish, in a covered vessel tucked under a clean napkin, would at once be on its way to the beneficiary's home. Still, this was nothing in comparison with the message that accompanied the gift, a message that was, is, and shall be as long as men inhabit this Earth, the quintessence of every courtliness past and future. It read as follows: "I am sending you this morsel, because I was enjoying it." This "I was enjoying it," which no one uses today because we find it so difficult to translate it into deeds, was used in Chile at that time; and I'd wager that were the worthy Victor Hugo to get hold of it, he, who dedicated whole pages to conveying the meaning of the foul words that the angry Cambronne uttered,[4] would devote three volumes to that "I was enjoying it."

4. Pierre-Jacques-Étienne Cambronne, one of the generals of Napoleon, appears in Victor Hugo's novel *Quatre-vingt-treize* (1874) and utters some suitably disguised expletives when the Battle of Waterloo is seen to be lost. JP.

In 1814 Santiago's fair sex, though not as artfully adorned as it is today, was worthy of the designation "fair" that has always suited it. Its headdress, in place of the European hat, consisted only of the Chilean woman's own incomparable hair, the graceful mantilla, and some flower newly plucked in the garden. Girls wore simple braids and only put them up into a bun when they married. As for rice powder, velvetine, brilliantine, and every other trick ending in -ine, they were nowhere to be found; but in their stead you could hear all day on the streets of Santiago the screeching voice of an old woman who went from door to door calling out: *"Obleas! Pajuelas! Solimán!"* The first of these were some ill-formed wafers from which the writer of a letter cut pieces to seal his correspondence; the second were cotton wicks treated with sulfur that served as matches do today; and the third, corrosive sublimate, was the indispensable precursor of every sort of feminine makeup.

Back then, paleness and circles around the eyes were only indications of sickness, dissipation, or sleepless nights, and never fancied themselves lures for lovers or marks of beauty, as happened later. Thanks to the simplicity and cleanliness of short dresses, never defiled by the soil and the filth of the streets, the elegant *santiagueña* everywhere showed one of her most innocent and powerful attractions, that well cared-for and well-shod foot that the Anglo-Saxons never fail to admire when they visit southern regions; and so not even in his wildest dreams could anyone then imagine that the imitative urge would bring the women of Chile to hide their feet under the dusty folds of a disgusting street-sweeper's broom, which is exactly what today's long and luxurious costume is. At that time a cross-eyed but elegant and wealthy young Spaniard took to hiding her defect by carefully arranging for a lock of her lovely hair to fall accidentally over her left eye, and just to follow the fashion the Chileans covered one of their orbs. A woman in the advanced stages of pregnancy wanted to give a more acceptable shape to her two opposing protuberances, and she put on a *guardainfante,* forerunner of the crinoline; and the Chilean maidens, without having any *infant* to *guard,* put on their *guardainfantes,* too. An old Frenchwoman, to hide the wrinkles on her forehead, decided to scatter a burst of false curls over that fallow field; and the women of Chile hid and continue to hide their smooth and lovely foreheads under those preposterous appendages that can suit only an old woman or a horse. But let us not despair, for all these little tricks do not affect the Chilean woman alone; they come to us from abroad.

Our schooling in those times was embryonic, to say the least. For women it was simply a matter of learning to read, write, and pray; for men who did not intend to enter the Church or the law, it consisted of reading in a sing-song, writing ungrammatically, and knowing bits and pieces of the multiplication tables, always excepting the nines. I forgot to mention that the alphabet had one letter more than it does today, a Maltese cross, which preceded the letter A and was called "Christus."[5]

Our boys' schools, which we attended from our tenderest years till the age of seventeen—all in short jackets and looking disreputable, not for lack of means but through excessive sloppiness, despite the whip and the broom handle quite skillfully wielded by our stern progenitors—consisted simply of a long room divided down its middle by a narrow table that separated the pupils into two bands so that they could the better vie for the laurels of learning. One side of the table was called Rome, and the other, Carthage; and a symbolic painting showing the head of a donkey, a whip and a paddle hanging from its muzzle, served, by its location, as the punishment of the defeated and the victor's prize.

The teacher or *dómine*, who, like all those of his ilk at that time, deserved to be called Don Tremendo, sat on a dais at one end of the room, the table before him holding, beside a few samples of penmanship and some scribbled primer, a stout paddle and the accompanying whip, true engines of instruction and human knowledge in a time when the brutal saying, *They'll never read if they don't bleed* was thought to be supremely witty and thoroughly true.

As for higher education, the less said, the better, because everything was taught in Latin, just to make it all clear to us. Why even mention studying the Spanish language? Who would waste his time studying a language we all knew from birth? Such, they say, was the opinion, for his sins, of our worthy Don Juan Egaña when he was asked whether the study of Spanish grammar should or should not be one of the subjects taught in our schools. And since by chance the subject of the Spanish Academy's grammar has cropped up, today's wise men might as well know that in 1814 there was no trace of any such contraption in Chile. In the conversations that I chanced to have with the distinguished patriot and learned jurist Don Gabriel Palma about the education received by the youth of Chile in those times, he assured me—and this fact was subsequently confirmed by the old Generals Lastra and Pinto—that in 1815, when he was the Latin teacher in the seminary, he surreptitiously, and as a merely supplementary frill, taught his students some rules of Spanish

---

5. *Christus,* "the cross that precedes the letters or alphabet in a primer and teaches us that all things should be begun in His Holy Name" (Real Academia Española, *Diccionario de autoridades*). It was the custom to place this cross at the top of a letter or other document. JP.

prose style, because no one would at that time have dared to teach such trifles in public. Nowhere would you have found a Spanish grammar or dictionary, because these two foundations of our language did not appear among us until early in the year 1817, and then infrequently.

No one can equitably deny Palma the glory of having been the first teacher of Spanish grammar in Chile, or deny General Don Francisco Antonio Pinto that of making our nation's government for the first time take a hand in this improvement of public schooling when in 1825, as Minister of the Interior, he ordered that the special study of Spanish grammar form an integral part of the high school curriculum. But I do not want to get ahead of myself and break with the order that the dates impose on me.

Cimarra, a Chilean term for playing hooky, derived from our word for wild, was surely invented for the boys of my time. We would come to school early; and if our teacher was the least bit late in opening the doors, we declared ourselves on strike and without further delay marched off to the river and challenged the plebeians there to see who would be the lords of the wooden bridge that day. On it and under it, because the river was almost always dry, we thrashed it out with stones and fists until it was time to return home, our bodies full of bruises, and our heads, of excuses to ward off the consequences of parental anger, though always in vain, for the handle of the feather duster never failed to clean our ribs of the little dust that the punches had left on them.

When I remember that as little men of fourteen or sixteen we sneaked out every afternoon after dinner, behind our parents' backs, to run over roofs and attics, using stones attached to long strings to capture the kites of others; when I remember what parental effort it took to get us to stay a few moments in the parlor after we had *greeted the company*, and then see how today's boys not only come to greet visitors without being called but do not even let us open our mouths in their eagerness to act the grown-up before their time; when I remember that we thought a Sunday wasted if we had not spent it riding, roping, looking for a fight, climbing trees, tearing our clothes, getting muddy, and even stretching a cord from one sidewalk to the other so as to lift up passing dogs, and now I see that on Thursdays and Sundays our chief promenade is swamped with self-satisfied little students, that each one of them is more elegantly got up on ordinary days than were we on holidays, that not a one is without his cane in lieu of his handkerchief, though his nose needs the latter more than his childish feet need the former, that wherever they may be they rush to occupy the most prominent sofas, with no thought for yielding them to the ladies, and that when they are alone their affected gravity makes it seem that with their mind on some Dulcinea they are hunting for rhymes for some amorous plaint; when I hear them, all puffed up, putting in their two cents' worth concerning the most perplexing points of law, the most intricate religious questions, the fickleness of women, and even the ennui produced in them by their disenchantment with life—at such times I feel humiliated by my past. The heights scaled by today's children can be compared only with the depth of the abyss in which those of my time were raised.

The public diversions of that Santiago that had only just banished the rustic underskirt also had a special flavor. The races at La Pampilla and the Llanito de Portales, in the open fields and without galleries of any kind, brought nobles and commoners to sit on piles of sheepskins and vie for the prize, whether for speed or for the powerful muscles of their horses' chests, an amusement that, stimulated by song and drink, would inevitably end in spills and a few uncivil stabbings. On the crude seats of the cockfighting ring, no less democratic than the races, the marquis and the poultry man sat shoulder to shoulder; for all their differences, neither of them, carried away by the noise of the bets and the fluttering of the cocks, paid the least attention to the imagined or real importance of his neighbor. Bullfights and equestrian games of skill alternated with religious festivities inside and outside the churches. On the birthdays of the rich, the diminutive band of the garrison marched eagerly through the streets and played in the courtyards of the wealthy birthday child. The swaying ceremonial gait, the frilled shirts, the knee britches and golden shoe buckles, which normally accompanied formal receptions, contrasted with the pealing of bells and the fireworks and frightening rockets that thundered in the air on the king's birthday or on the arrival of a new governor and captain general of the Kingdom of Chile. Visits to Nativity scenes, and *comisiones,* which were aerial battles among kites, some of them made of as many as a hundred sheets of paper and which, as they fell to earth with the consequent tangle of strings, had homeowners in an uproar, ripped tiles off the roofs, and led to squabbles in the streets and, often, to blows and knifings—all these amusements, as well as that of bringing prisoners out of jail to club dogs to death in the streets, provided excitement and topics for the most varied conversations in those happy times.

As for theater, there was little or nothing to be seen, because its place was almost entirely occupied by puppet shows, its true precursors; and so only rarely did one of the dreadful old chestnuts or farces that used to be performed in our convents as religious allegories replace the jokes of Josesito, now called Don Pascual.

Those religious plays, very popular back then, were never without their Saint Peter or their Saint Michael with his

I am the angel who comes
From Heaven's celestial blue,
Whom God Himself has sent
To wage fierce war on you,

and along with them, the Moorish King, the Devil, the clown, the sassy servant girl, and every other bit of nonsense that bad taste could turn into a character. The costumes clashed violently with the personage they were supposed to portray, and all that was lacking was for some ordinary fellow to step out to play Julius Caesar with his grenadier's boots and his brace of pistols at his waist.

You can imagine the degree to which the theater was in its infancy in 1814 if you know what it was even in 1820, in spite of having as its father and supporter a man as active, intelligent, and patriotic as was Don Domingo Arteaga, without whose zeal who knows how long we would have had to settle for simple theaters like that of Ña Borja's tavern. We have this most energetic entrepreneur to thank for the establishment of the first Chilean theater, founded in 1818 on the Calle de las Ramadas, moved in 1819 to the Calle de la Catedral, and finally settled in 1820 in the former Jesuit Square, which is now O'Higgins Square.

Since the morality of theatrical performances was questioned by the staunch partisans of the king, our patriots, turning the theater into a weapon, once they had written these two verses of Don Bernardo de Vera in big letters on the curtain:

Virtue and vice are here portrayed;
Behold yourself and speak your fate,

decreed that the performances were always to begin with the national anthem, with words by the same Vera and music by the violinist Don Manuel Robles, and that they were to be limited exclusively to dramas that, like *Rome Unfettered,* were most pertinent to the current political situation of the country.

At any rate, neither actors nor audience were aware of their proper role in the theater. During the battle scenes, the spectators cheered those on stage; when there was dancing, the spectators drummed out the rhythm; and when some character was in hiding and another seemed to be looking for him in vain, there was always someone who helpfully called out from the audience, "He's under the table."

I can remember two typical occasions.

One time the famous actress Lucía, the best we had, was booed; and she in turn, as brazen as you please, berated the audience, contemptuously tossing at it the foulest language that could ever come out of the mouth of an angry fishwife. True, they took her to jail; but it is also true that the next Sunday, thanks to some contrite flattery she concocted for the audience, they went back to applauding her.

Three soldiers were always stationed on police duty on the orchestra level, armed with rifle and bayonet: one on the left, one on the right, and a third at the main entrance. At that time it was becoming customary not to smoke in the theater; but an Englishman who had no patience with prohibitions, especially in America, forgetting that by his side stood a soldier and above his head was the box of Don Bernardo O'Higgins, the Supreme Director, took out a cigar and calmly set to smoking it. The soldier admonished him, the Gringo paid no attention; but no sooner did the soldier venture a new admonition, accompanied now by a threatening gesture, than the Gringo leapt at him like a rabid cat and grasped his rifle with the aim of taking it from him, and between the two of them there arose such a furious storm of blows and punches that Othello and Loredano on stage and the audience off stage forgot all about the smitten Edelmira to concentrate their attention on this new development. O'Higgins, who did not want to take a back seat in the matter, leaned out of his box and in a loud voice shouted to the soldier, "Look out, boy, hold on to that rifle!" At this point the soldier, gaining new courage, liberated the rifle from the British grasp, and a hearty blow with its butt stretched the Gringo flat on his back. And what happened next? Not a thing. The incident was considered closed, and Edelmira regained the attention due to her.

But not everything was fun and games in that Santiago of the olden days and of San Bruno, because in it one's personal security was hardly worthy of the name. Rumor, there being no newspapers, was constantly reporting some robbery or murder committed in one of the known haunts of crime, such as Pasos de Huechuraba, San Ignacio, Portezuelo de Colina, La Dormida, Cuesta de Prado, Cuesta de Zapata, Llanos de Peñuelas, and other places whose names I omit because, unlike these, they were not in very frequent contact with the capital.

Journeys were made on horseback; but no one traveled without his brace of pistols, his machete, and often his blunderbuss, the machine gun of former times, which you loaded by pouring a fistful of balls into its trumpetlike mouth.

On toward the end of September, roundup time, you would see a great commotion of carts, mules, and peasants on horseback at the doors and in the courtyards of the landowners who were getting ready to take their families to their country places. The carts, the only vehicle in which ladies, children, and their female servants traveled, were monstrously heavy antediluvian contraptions whose crude wheels had tires made of rough chunks of carob wood fastened with pegs of the same material and whose axles, thick wooden cudgels shaped as best could be with a hatchet, did not stop their creaking from the moment they got under way until they arrived at their destination. Only sixteen years later, that is, in the year 1830, was the iron tire first introduced into Chile to improve this important Noah's ark. In it, along with the mattresses that covered the central space to mitigate the force of the jolts produced by the uneven surface of the roads, and the silk curtain that adorned the entrance, you would always find, in the most free and friendly company, mistresses and servants, children, baskets of oranges, baskets of hard-boiled eggs and cold meats, little baskets of sweets prepared by the nuns, the solid silver chamber pot, bags of flour, jerky for the stew, the dreaded cannula for blood-letting, and the ever-consoling guitar. With these paraphernalia, and at the slow pace of the heavy oxen, by the end of a day under the burning sun you would reach something that imitated an inn and lacked everything except discomfort. It took four days to reach Valparaíso; it could take more or less time to reach the ranches where these springtime caravans were headed.

Santiago's merchants often sought their stock in Buenos Aires, from whose market, on muleback and over the dangerous Andean passes, they brought into Chile the goods they could not find in the village that was Valparaíso.

How much time, how many lives, were wasted then simply traveling!

We must not, therefore, look only at their political institutions to explain the backwardness in which some nations live. The forced isolation in which the children of one and the same country find themselves in their homes, the lack of constant and easy communication among them, contribute, along with defective institutions, to the lamentable backwardness of commerce, of industry, and of civilization itself. Roads and the elimination of distance make man more sociable, prolong his useful life; and with the experience thus acquired, his condition improves in every way.

Anyone who had seen Santiago in 1814 and seen it again in 1825 could rightly have said, "Either the great political and social events that have recently taken place in this town have not given it time even to put on a less tattered dress, or Santiago was born to remain the same forever." Physically, the Santiago of 1814 remained, ever so slightly retouched, exactly the same in 1825. Only to avoid annoying those *santiagueños* born in 1830 do I abstain from chronicling in detail how frightened we used to be on our fine Cañada promenade when some cow would escape from the filthy slaughterhouse of San Miguel and, with dogs and mounted cowboys in boisterous pursuit, would come crashing across the roadway in a fury, sweeping everything before it. True it is that in 1830 the president no longer had to wear a red sash and golden tassels, as it is that in 1830 we began to get rid of those heavy calèches and to adopt, fortunately but slowly, lighter wagons and coaches, though fairness obliges us not to forget that these vehicles would be washed in the middle of the street with ablutions of gutter water splashed on them with gourds or watermelon rinds.

Yet let us not mock our humble origins; those ragged villages, Santiago and Concepción, were the cradles of our fathers, and from among those rags rose the giants to whom we owe freedom and fatherland.

Now that I have given a summary description of the stage on which my earliest years were played, I shall go on to recount, in chronological order, the little that age has not yet managed to erase from my memory.

I I

Valparaíso. — My first lesson in international law. — Francisco de la Lastra. — José Miguel Carrera. — The defeat at Rancagua. — Osorio. — Juan Fernández. — Juan Enrique Rosales. — His daughter Rosario. — My mother is imprisoned. — Felipe Santiago del Solar.

In the summer, then as now, many of Santiago's families, in search of relaxation and better air, would trade the comforts of their aristocratic homes for the rustic and uncomfortable hole in the wall that was their country house or for the no less uncomfortable lodgings that they took in one of our seaports, where they went to bathe, to dodge the waves, and to look at the ships, and for the ladies to collect little seashells to take back to Santiago as presents for their friends.

And people were right to flee from so unsanitary a town in the summers.

Seeking to breathe purer air, my family was then breathing the air that at that time circulated in disheveled Valparaíso, an atmosphere that if it was foul back then at least deserves a prize for constancy, because it has managed to maintain, if not increase, its sterling qualities until the present time.

In 1814 our Valparaíso was barely beginning to emerge from the shell that enveloped its almost embryonic existence. The aristocracy, the merchant class, and the warehouses of the port were united in clustering around the main church; and the governor lived up in the closest castle, which was one of the three that defended the harbor against the depredations of pirates. What is now the elegant Almendral was a kind of long street made up of little shacks and an occasional tile-roofed hut, a miserable area on the outskirts of town through which screeching carts and a few mule trains passed on their way to the harbor, bearing local products for shipment and the meager consumption of the village. The whole beach, from that end of the bay to the other, was deserted but for the visits of the tides; drawn up on it, among the sargasso and near some stakes where the fishermen would hang their nets to dry, you could see some of those shapeless hollowed-out tree trunks that we still call canoes.

Nor was there an easy passage from the harbor to the Almendral, for when the sea at high tide crashed violently against the rocks of the cave called Cueva del Chivato, it cut the deserted beach in two. I remember that the police, in order to prevent the robberies that would take place in this narrow passage at night, placed a stake there from which they hung a little paper lantern with its fine tallow candle, the kind that sold at five for a *real*. When we recall that even shoes had to be ordered from the shoemakers in Santiago, we have all the proof we need that, next to San Francisco in California, which had similar resources, no town in the known world has surpassed Valparaíso in the rapidity of its growth or in its relative importance on the waters of the western seas.

An imposing sight among the handful of cockleshells that rode on the waters of that empty bay was the handsome *Essex,* an American frigate of forty guns commanded by the dashing Commodore David Porter. Her jolly sailors up in the hill quarter and her no less jovial officers in the flatlands gave the sleepy village a festive air that, since it was a good thing, could not last long.

Old mother England and her proud and recently emancipated North American daughter had once more had disastrous recourse to arms. Their ships sought each other out on every sea to destroy each other; and just when the inhabitants of Valparaíso were enjoying the presence of the *Essex,* they were terrified to see the *Phoebe* and the *Cherub,* two powerful British warships, appearing at the entrance to the harbor and racing under full sail to draw close enough to fire on her. A volley from our castles sought to show the attackers, with the plumes of water raised by our cannonballs, how far our maritime jurisdiction extended and that we proposed to keep it neutral; and the English seemed to understand this, since that day and the following they limited their actions to sailing close-hauled back and forth beyond the range of our guns.

I remember that on the afternoon of March 28, when some of the officers of the *Essex* who had come in search of fresh provisions were in the midst of emptying a few bottles in the home of the Rosales family, the sudden sound of her cannon made them all snatch up their caps and, without further goodbye than the cheerful and cocksure young blade's "Farewell forever!," dash into their boat shouting hurrahs. Many families went up on the hills to get a better view of what they figured was going to happen; we saw that the *Essex,* taking advantage of a fresh breeze and trusting in her greater speed, was getting ready to run the blockade, since she could not let herself be drawn into the unequal combat that lay before her. At this point the English ships, fearing that the coveted quarry would escape them, attacked her right in the harbor. The wind failed the *Essex* on her second tack, leaving her in so defenseless a position that we thought she had run aground; and right there, despite the shots fired from our fortresses to keep the English from continuing in their act of aggression within our very waters, the *Essex* was demolished and vanquished.

That was the first practical lesson in international law that civilized England impressed on my memory, for she never made even the slightest amends to the friend into whose home she had trespassed.

When we returned to Santiago we soon saw that the year 1814, a year of disturbances and follies, of glories and disasters, was not to come to an end without writing the epitaph of the first state of our emancipation on the blood-stained tombstone that watches over its glorious remains. But since it is not my aim, in dredging up these memories, to enter the domain of history, no one should be surprised if I leave this task to a pen better qualified and limit my notes to recalling the private events that I have myself witnessed and to depicting them just as they appeared to me, leaving aside all commentary and arbitrary judgments.

At that time Colonel Don Francisco de Lastra was governing in Santiago with the title of Supreme Director of the State. He was a fine upright gentleman, who, after having served in the royal Spanish navy, had unhesitatingly plunged into the revolutionary maelstrom in the service of his country's liberty. Unfortunately, the honorable character of a gentleman and pure disinterested patriotism were not then qualities sufficient in themselves to maintain anyone at the heights of power. That could only be achieved if those worthy qualities were accompanied by the bold and wary nature that is the inevitable companion of ambition, and Lastra was as little ambitious as he was excessively trusting.

Of the two political factions that were doggedly struggling to gain control of the reins of the state, that of the Carreras held the upper hand. Its leadership consisted, among other very distinguished learned and worthy men, of the brilliant Don José Miguel Carrera, the dainty Don Luis, and Don Juan José, the giant of the family. All three brothers were soldiers and equally fervent patriots. Don Luis and Don Juan José recognized Don José Miguel as the head of their family and of their party, both for his intelligence and knowledge of military matters and for the universal respect that he had managed to gain ever since he first returned to his country from Spain.

This young man, whose life fills pages as brilliant as they are sorrowful in the history of our early years as an independent nation, had come to Chile shortly after the inauguration of our first attempt at a congress, having already established an honorable record by giving up a secure and, for a man of his age, brilliant position in Spain as lieutenant colonel of hussars in the king's army in order to take on the uncertainties and dangers of a revolution whose outcome was in doubt but that might perhaps lead to the emancipation of his fatherland from Spanish rule.

His lucky star made him welcome in every salon, along with his well-proportioned figure, his stature rather tall than middling, his jovial and mischievous character, his clever conversation peppered with Andalusian jests sharpened by his natural wit, the easy manner of the gentleman soldier, his imaginative and always elegant dress, and his exquisite gallantry with the ladies. It combined with his republican ideas, his unrestrained boldness in expressing them, his utter lack of reticence when it came to facing the dangers that might arise from his frank and lively manner, and his knowledge of military affairs to gain him the esteem of thinking men; and, along with his unaffected bearing, his carefully displayed scorn for the privileged classes, and a generosity bordering on extravagance, it made him the idol of the troops and the common people.

Endowed as he was with these qualities, and when he found it so easy to be learned among the learned, a Lovelace[6] with the womenfolk, coarse and prankish among the lower orders, and soldierly when in barracks, it was plain to see how far our Chilean Alcibiades might have gone had his

6. *Lovelace,* the rake in Samuel Richardson's novel *Clarissa.* JP.

ambition to be first among all allowed him to await the fruition of the events he and others were preparing, rather than precipitate them.

The Carrera brothers, and most especially Don José Miguel, were close friends of the Rosales family. It therefore came as no surprise to us that when we returned from Valparaíso we found that madcap José Miguel, as my grandfather Don Juan Enrique Rosales affectionately used to call him, and his brother Luis hiding in our house, having just escaped from Chillán prison, where the political storms had carried them.

It is far more difficult and even dangerous than one might think to steer a middle course in politics. My family had no reason to be hostile to Lastra and every reason to think well of Carrera and of his gallant rival, O'Higgins; and all of these showed nothing but friendship and respect to my parents, who responded in kind.

The presence of the Carreras in our house and the nonchalance and even imprudence with which Don José Miguel came and went at night, received visitors shrouded in capes, and sent out his emissaries, all alarmed our family, which feared that the current of events might at any moment make it guilty of acts that it did not condone but that friendship forced it to tolerate. This situation could not and did not last long.

The night before the violent overthrow of the Supreme Director Don Francisco de la Lastra, Don José Miguel had a heated, though friendly argument in the vestibule of our house with my mother, Doña Mercedes Rosales. He was trying to calm her, countering her serious admonitions with merry jokes, until finally the lady shook her fan at him and said these words, whose full meaning I came to understand later: "How long are you going to carry on with this craziness, José Miguel? Believe me, it's going to come to no good end. At least wait for my father to get here." Don José Miguel, who at that moment seemed to be more concerned with what he was thinking than with what he was hearing, burst out in a booming laugh, looked at his watch, snatched up his hat, and in an affectionate way said, "Don't you worry, Merceditas. Just figure that the bird's already in the cage; and just in case, bolt the front door." And with that he headed down the corridor toward the coachhouse door, which is the one he generally used, and disappeared.

The next day Lastra was overthrown.

On the fresh morning of the first day of October of 1814, the sleepy Santiago of 1809, which in 1810 had become embroiled in the revolutionary whirlwind that inaugurated the period of political emancipation for what was known—though I don't know why—as the Kingdom of Chile, turned into a restless town alternately seized with feverish bouts of joy and fear, hope and despair, and for good cause, since at those very moments the country's future as an independent nation was being committed to the mutable fortunes of war in the heroic village of Rancagua.

With the nation's government still unstable because of the convulsions that had shaken it and that invariably and naturally occur in the course of a people's political regeneration, the leaders of the patriotic party had been taken by surprise in the midst of a fratricidal revolution by the Spanish forces that under the command of Don Mariano Osorio had come to reconquer the country and were marching on its capital. Belatedly they had repented of their folly but had been forced to take refuge in defenseless Rancagua, where at that moment they were making the most desperate efforts to defend themselves.

Those who had supported our political emancipation and were barely beginning to enjoy its enviable fruits could not accept the loss, at one blow, of what they had acquired at so great a sacrifice. Santiago, agitated by day, did not sleep at night. With horses dashing up and down the streets, seditious exclamations, cries of "Long live free Chile!" and "Down with free Chile!," rumors, and reports that were confidential but always terrifying and always spurious, the most cruel anxiety took hold of the minds of those who felt imperiled, while a frenetic joy arose in the partisans of the crown.

No one as yet knew what was happening as October 2 dawned, a dawn as doleful as it was glorious for our battered arms. Messengers came from the scene of the catastrophe driving their horses to the limit and shouting that all was lost; and since everyone remembered Osorio's haughty threat to "those exercising authority in Chile" that if they did not surrender to the royal troops he would wage total war and leave nothing standing, the expectation was, of course, that what was assumed to have happened in Rancagua would also happen in Santiago if the city should resist. Before sunset and throughout the sad night of that bitter day, ragged remnants of our army, men and women on foot, carrying some of their possessions on their backs and leading their little children by the hand, with terror marked on their faces, streamed into the southern quarters of town, while all that could be heard anywhere was the terrifying exclamation, "The enemy's coming!" But what truly struck terror into distressed Santiago was less the confirmation of our defeat than the conviction that our scattered troops would immediately and precipitately retreat into the Andes. Churches, public treasuries, military stores—the fleeing leaders of the battered patriots seized on everything to deprive the conquerors of supplies, and so whatever could not be carried off was sacked.

On his way to Aconcagua, Don José Miguel Carrera met in my parents' house with my grandfather Rosales to calm him and assure him that the disaster of Rancagua was not definitive, since in a few days, after regrouping in Aconcagua, he would once more drive the Spaniards from Santiago. O'Higgins, another close family friend, did not seem to share these hopes; as he took a hurried leave of us after learning that Elorreaga's troops were pursuing our scattered men in forced marches, he told my father with fury painted on his face, "All of this is no one's fault but Carrera's!"

When soldiers were fleeing, how could the ordinary citizen who had committed himself to the cause of freedom not flee? People of modest means, seeing that the rich fled, grew even more afraid and fled as well; and thus for many days after the catastrophe at Rancagua the dangerous slopes of the Andes were populated with demoralized soldiers, women, children, and old people, who saw their salvation only on the far side of those snow-covered peaks. The isolated houses of the primitive farms of the day sheltered those patriots whose age or ailments kept them from following the others to Mendoza, in Argentina; my frail old grandfather, accompanied by his children and grandchildren, and with his loving daughter Rosario Rosales as his tender support, went into hiding in the huts of Tunquen de las Tablas, near Valparaíso.

After these citizens had fled and left their fully stocked houses behind, robbery, pillage, and often death naturally held sway in the unhappy city; and this chaos and commotion only came to an end with the arrival of the first detachments of the conquerors, and especially with Osorio's ostentatious triumphal entry into the city, which took place on the ninth.

Not all the inhabitants of Santiago were supporters of independence; there were also a great many families loyal to the colonial regime, and the proof of it was the great enthusiasm with which the people, dressed in their Sunday best, celebrated in the arrival of the conqueror the happy event of the return of Chile, then a prodigal son, to the fold of the Crown of Castile. Triumphal arches, flags and silk hangings on the balconies, the tolling of bells, all proclaimed the general rejoicing; and on the pavement of the streets, an abundance of flowers marked the route taken by the procession that so proudly accompanied that auspicious redeemer who subsequently was to bring forth so many tears from the very ones who were then receiving him so joyfully.

Rancagua was, then, the tomb of our infant Chile, which, like Hercules, displayed its willpower and its strength even in its cradle. Born on September 18, 1810, Chile had plunged into the hurricanes that always arise in the course of a stormy political emancipation, with no compass to guide it but patriotism; and only after four years of struggle in which, along with a few understandable blunders, it had always displayed every civic virtue, every kind of heroism, and all the patriotic poetry that can embellish the human heart, did it succumb like the phoenix, leaving behind those glorious ashes that were to spring to renewed and perpetual life in Chacabuco under the name of the New Fatherland.[7]

After the curtain had fallen to separate the first act of the bloody drama of our emancipation from the second, Osorio, and after him Marcó, following an ill-conceived, arbitrary, and cruel policy, seemed intent only on losing no opportunity to provoke a reaction with their blunders. It may well be that, as some Spanish authors assure us, Osorio, on coming to Santiago, intended to follow a conciliatory policy that by winning the hearts of the stern republicans whom he had just beaten might achieve with gentleness and equity what could never be expected from an ill-conceived severity; but if there was any such intention, it was unfortunately only a momentary flash of common sense. That man's heart was not good; and if it was, then it must be admitted that the stimuli of fear and bad counsel can drive the soundest spirit to commit bestial deeds.

From the very day that he set up his office in the house of the Conde de la Conquista, where he was first lodged, this dreadful commander began so artfully to repudiate all the harsh statements that had been attributed to him and to make such a show of humanity and natural kindliness toward the conquered that these came even to believe in his sincerity. I can still remember seeing very respectable men in my parents' house raise their hands to heaven in gratitude for so unexpected a blessing. The reason for such gratitude was, however, quite short-lived, for the ink with which the promises had been signed was not yet dry when that wolf, whom history has tried in vain to exculpate, saw the trusting sheep within range of his claws and lunged at them.

As long as our country exists, Chileans will preserve the memory of the brutal and senseless tyranny that Osorio, twelve days after his entry into Santiago, inflicted on all the heads of families and men of distinction who honored their country with their talents and their virtues. On the afternoon of November 2, 1814, the appearance of Santiago's main square, filled with persons whose faces mirrored simple curiosity or grief

7. Chileans refer to the period from 1810 to the defeat at Rancagua in 1814, before the Spanish "reconquest" (1814–1817), as the *Patria Vieja* or First Fatherland. The *Patria Nueva* or New Fatherland begins with the victory at Chacabuco in 1817. JP.

or the satisfaction of revenge, was the logical consequence of the assault that in the pre-dawn hours Osorio had carried out against many of the unsuspecting leading citizens of the reconquered capital. In an area before the gate of the prison, kept clear by the line of soldiers who held back the crowd, there stood, for reasons unclear to most, some fifty wretched horses, some with saddles, others bearing simple sheepskins, and most of them with rope or leather halters instead of reins. What simple bystander could have imagined that this train of ill-treated animals, so miserably equipped, was the sole means of transportation that a senseless cruelty allotted to illustrious exiles to take them to Valparaíso, their first stop on the road of martyrdom that led to prison on the remote island of Juan Fernández!

And yet it was true. Before nightfall and amid the pained silence of the spectators, broken only by an occasional brutal imprecation from a sergeant of the Talavera regiment, a group of more than forty estimable patriots was seen walking slowly and feebly out through the prison gate; despite their merits, the respect due to their white hair, and the consideration that a virtuous heart always feels for the unfortunate, they were forced, and practically pushed, to mount and head off toward the port under heavy guard while their sorrowful and ridiculous appearance served to provoke brutal merriment.

Thus, bearing with them only the clothes on their backs and finding no relief on their arduous voyage but what they could purchase from their guards with what little gold they might have chanced to have on their persons when they were arrested, Rojas, Cienfuegos, Egaña, Eyzaguirre, and Solar went to meet their fate, along with many another prominent patriot so well known that I need not mention him, for it goes without saying that there was no distinguished name but it appeared on the list of the banished, no prominent family in Santiago but it mourned the fate that awaited its relatives or friends.

Bounteous Nature, which has ever endowed the women of Chile with both the delights of beauty and the charms of virtue, seems at that time to have taken special pleasure in joining youth, beauty, and an inexhaustible treasure of filial love in Rosario Rosales. When on the gloomy night of that odious act of repression this young girl was startled by the shrieks of the family of her aged father, Don Juan Enrique Rosales, as they saw a detachment of soldiers bursting into the house and dragging him from his sickbed to throw him into prison, she quickly wrapped herself in her shawl and, acting on her own, not realizing what she was doing, she followed, distraught, after those who had robbed her of her only treasure; but when she reached the prison and heard the clanking of the bars that shut him in, nature reasserted herself and caused her to fall in a faint onto the cold flagstones of that fearful place. Her brothers, who had followed that unhappy embodiment of filial love, took her home; and no sooner did she regain consciousness than, haunted by the thought that her father would be killed, she ran in terror to knock at every door where instinct told her she might find someone who, taking pity on her plight, might intercede for the preservation of so precious a life. Since all she found, however, was good will and disconsolate helplessness, this angel of filial love succeeded in overcoming every obstacle that the stern Osorio placed in the way of all who sought to speak to him at the critical moment of the deportation, and in vain she poured out her supplicant tears onto the foul boots of that tyrant. Don Juan Enrique Rosales had been a member of the first Patriotic Junta established, to the shame of Spain, on September 18, 1810,[7a] and so it was necessary that he, along with his companions Marín, Encalada, and Mackenna, should pay for so atrocious an offense against the Crown of Castile.

Rosario, accompanied by her brother Joaquín, followed her captive father's convoy until he and his companions in misfortune reached the village of Valparaíso after an arduous voyage of three days. In that hamlet, which I shall refrain from describing here because of the emotions that the sad memories of that time awaken in my old heart, there then lived, to the good fortune of the new arrivals, the kind and beneficent Spaniard Don Pablo Casanova, who as an act of charity—the only appropriate term for what he did—looked after the prisoners during the three days they remained on land while the bark *Sebastiana,* which was to transport them to Juan Fernández, was being made ready.

Meanwhile, Rosales's daughter, seeking to gain permission at least to join her aged parent in his exile, repeated in the house of the commander of Valparaíso the scene that in Santiago had yielded only a cruel rebuff from the commander Osorio. Thus the day after her arrival she went to lay her tears and her pleas at the feet of the governor of the port, who at that time was a Spanish naval officer named Ballesteros.

I shall reproduce here the words with which in more tranquil times my aunt told me this episode in her eventful life: "After an hour of anguished waiting, Ballesteros condescended to grant me an audience. He was sitting in his office, apparently conferring with some army officers. The cold 'What was it you wanted?' that the governor directed to me with unblinking curtness without even deigning to offer me a seat im-

---

7a. All editions read 1812, but Professor Brian Loveman informs me that the correct date of the first junta is September 18, 1810. JP.

mediately demolished the slim hope that I had entertained before coming into his presence. Impassively he listened to me stammer out my request; and when I saw that instead of answering me in the moments when my tears forced me to be still, he seemed to occupy himself by absentmindedly scribbling something on a sheet of paper and then for some reason crossing it out, it seemed useless for me to insist. Just then the governor harshly shot at me, 'That's enough crying, madam. Forbidden means forbidden!' and I don't know how I kept from dropping dead on the spot. I couldn't leave the room. The image of my sick father, dying alone in exile, with no friendly hand by his side to close his eyes, had left me as though petrified; and when the governor saw this, irritated, it seemed, by my continued presence, he took hold of me, half courteously and half brutally, and led me to the door of his office, through which he tossed a piece of paper and then cavalierly turned his back on me. God inspired me to pick up the paper from the floor. As soon as I read it, I saw that it contained these words that only the governor and I could understand: 'permit her to board ship, as though for a journey.' Later I found out," my aunt added, "from the *Sebastiana*'s purser that among other things that the governor had discussed with the ship's captain, he had told him, 'If that rascal Rosales's girl wants to go with her father, let her; she's no less a rebel for being a woman.'"

That saving piece of paper scornfully dropped on the floor, which my aunt kept as a relic till her dying day, is now in my possession; and I preserve it as incontestable evidence of the spirit governing that time, when Osorio's subordinates had to seem brutal even when granting a favor.

The life of the aged patriot Don Juan Enrique Rosales, that of his daughter Rosario, and that of each of the victims who for the same offense shared the anguish and privations of exile in Juan Fernández from the day of their imprisonment until March 25, 1817, when O'Higgins repatriated them, is a drama that I do not intend to recount here.

One of the inhabitants of Santiago who did not leave for Mendoza or for Juan Fernández or the vaults of the castles of Callao was my stepfather, Doctor Don Felipe Santiago del Solar, whom I called and to this day call my father. He was one of the wealthy staunch patriots whom Osorio's policy had either to win over or drive into bankruptcy. Having failed to achieve the first part of this terrible dilemma, Osorio plunged wholeheartedly into the second, burdening Solar with so many taxes and forced loans and contributions that but for the business connections his important firm maintained in Buenos Aires he would have been completely ruined. All this, however, seemed insufficient to the pitiless commander; he wanted to strike at a more sensitive spot to force the incorrigible insurgent into submission, and his exquisite cruelty suggested to him the idea of wounding the rebel's heart by imprisoning my mother.

The tenacity with which Osorio sought to destroy Solar's financial position suggests that this suspicious ruler had some inkling of the role that the ardent patriotism and wealth of his victim were to play in the process of the emancipation of America, for as soon as the year 1820 arrived suspicion turned out to be premonition, as can be seen from the historical document that I copy here, since not everyone is familiar with it:

Lima, October 4, 1833

The State acknowledges its obligation toward Don Felipe Santiago del Solar in the amount of sixty thousand pesos in partial satisfaction of the amount awarded to him by the Congress on December 3, 1832, as payment for the outstanding debts arising from his outfitting of the Army of Liberation that came to Peru in 1820 under the command of General San Martín, said amount to be paid in the manner and at the times that the current state of the treasury may permit.

To be duly noted in the General Accounting Office and the National Treasury. *Gamarra.*

To be noted in the General Accounting Office. Lima, October 8, 1833. *Arriz.*

To be noted in the National Treasury. Lima, October 8, 1833. *Burgos.*

Less than three weeks had passed since the departure of the *Sebastiana* when my family received the next blow. It was on the afternoon of November 17; and on the verandah that led into the garden my father was attempting in vain to check the tears drawn from his wife by the painful thought of her aged father's exile, when he was interrupted by the surprising word that a carriage under military guard had just stopped by our front door.

My brother Carlos and I ran to see what this meant; we soon saw an officer emerging from the carriage, short, corpulent, broad-shouldered, thick-necked, with a lively face and a great brown mustache. He was dressed with some affectation; and on his tall shako, which was hardly appropriate for his stature, he wore the crown and heraldic lions of Spain, shaped in brass. We were frightened to see this individual, who, after unceremoniously crossing the first courtyard, followed by two soldiers, reached the entry hall and called out, "Anybody here?" My father came out to meet him and, greeting him as Don Vicente San Bruno, asked him to what he owed his visit. San Bruno replied, "I'm not looking for you. One thing at a time; but don't you worry about that, because we'll meet again soon enough. I'm looking for Doña Mercedes Rosales, and it's a pity that rebel should be so good looking. . . . Come on, let's not waste any time!" When he told our beloved mother that she was under arrest and was about to seize her by the arm, Carlos and I shouted and lunged at San Bruno, who continued on his way while sending two poor boys sprawling on the courtyard stones with the back of his hand.

I I I

Marcó's tribulations. — Chacabuco. — A great soirée in honor
of the conquering army. — The coat of arms of Chile. —
The defeat at Cancha Rayada. — Second emigration to
Mendoza. — The death of Luis and Juan José Carrera.

B y this time Don Mariano Osorio was no longer in charge. He had
been succeeded by another proconsul, named Casimiro Marcó del
Pont, less competent than his predecessor, though no less cruel. The prisoners on Juan Fernández, from whom we received only infrequent news,
were still subject to the whims of their jailers on that New World Ceuta,[8]
lacking all hope, while in the hearts of their relatives and other patriots in
the so-called Kingdom of Chile, helplessly crushed by the abuses of arbitrary power, a store of affronts was building whose explosion, once it
came, was bound to sweep Spanish rule from our soil forever.

8. Ceuta, a Spanish city on the coast of North Africa, was long used as a place of banishment. JP.

As a matter of fact, on the far side of the Andes an expeditionary force that aimed at a liberating invasion had been formed in 1817 by the tireless zeal of the gallant colonel of mounted grenadiers Don José de San Martín, at the time governor of Mendoza, with the support of the heroic fugitives from Rancagua, whose ardent valor and patriotism were crying out for bloody vengeance. It is thus not surprising that Marcó, his mind troubled by the threatening news of these warlike preparations, should have been brought to exclaim in one of his bad moments that he would deprive the Chileans who were enemies of their king of everything, even of their tears. Fortune, however, had decreed otherwise; and it was written in the book of fate that an exiled Marcó would repay the exhausted tears of his Chilean victims with his own.

On one of the long hot days of January of that year, in the dark spacious parlor of an old and well-known Santiago mansion called the Carrera house, a handsome gentleman some thirty-five years old, tall, blue-eyed, with a prominent nose and black hair, was restlessly walking up and down. His preoccupied air, his constant glances toward the street through the half-opened window, as well as his agitated gestures of impatience, all showed that he was momentarily expecting news of some important event. At about 3 p.m., when at that time of the year all is quiet during the siesta, one of those ragged chicken peddlers who used to come from the countryside into the capital to sell their modest stock of merchandise crossed the courtyard with his chickens slung from his shoulder, stopped at the door of the entrance hall, and uttered the standard cry, "Nice fat chickens, get your chickens!" My father, for none other was the silent and restless character whom I now bring once more onto the scene, shuddered as though struck by a spark of electricity when he heard that voice, apparently not unknown to him; and signaling to my mother to keep me busy and out of the way, he rushed out of the parlor, ordered a servant to take the chickens, and, as soon as he thought he was alone, took the peddler by the arm and disappeared with him into the adjoining study.

Who might this unprepossessing individual have been? What was the meaning of his being so mysteriously shut in with my father? These were questions to which my mother, more concerned with maintaining the isolation of the study and its surroundings than with satisfying my childish curiosity, replied only by telling me to be still.

A moment later the peddler, looking like a downcast beggar, left the house and, stretching out his hand for alms to everyone he met, disappeared down the Calle de los Huérfanos.

Only four years after these events could I draw from my mother's mouth the explanation of the enigma of the chicken peddler. In her autograph album the lady preserved a small piece of paper that, if rolled up, could be taken for tobacco inside the leaf of a cigar. On this piece of paper you could easily read the following: "January 15. Brother S.: I send you 4,000 pesos for the ducks. Within a month Brother José will be joining you." The ostensible peddler was one of the many spies and messengers used by the governor of Mendoza, both to keep up the spirits of the patriots languishing on our side of the Andes and to keep Marcó guessing. The date indicated the day on which the army would set out; the pesos, the number of soldiers; and Brother José, the name of the illustrious liberator Don José de San Martín.

I never saw my father's face more radiantly happy than when he sent the supposed beggar on his way. Several visitors came by that evening, all speaking in whispers, all gesticulating more or less vehemently, and all showing signs of that joy produced by the imminence of some happy event.

From that day on I could not but notice an unusual degree of animation in the streets of Santiago. Couriers were constantly dashing from the palace as fast as their horses could bear them, sometimes heading for the north of the Kingdom, sometimes for the south. Troops were ordered up from the south, then commanded to stop en route and scattered in detachments among all the Andean passes, because San Martín managed to conceal the route taken by his troops so cleverly that there were times when the royalists thought they saw the threatening ghost of the army of liberation looming in each and every gap between the mountains.

The eleventh of February arrived, and with it so much beating of drums and blowing of bugles, so many horses racing about the city while at the same time the few troops still left in Santiago were seen hastily marching out by the Cañadilla, that the town had all the appearance of a military compound in the process of striking camp after a surprise alarm has sounded. There was not a single face that did not clearly show its anxiety. Fear and hope struggled within every heart. Some said that San Martín, at the head of more than ten thousand men, had already crossed the mountains and was pouring out onto the unhappy Kingdom of Chile a flood of heartless rebels who were devastating everything; others, that San Martín only had a handful of men, worn out from their march and so poorly armed that at the first sign of the royal troops nothing would be left of them.

Then came the night that I recall so vividly. After evening prayers, every outside door was either hermetically sealed or barely open and under careful watch to avoid the excesses of the mindless mob, for whom looting was a necessary element in any denouement. Silence alternated with noise. There were moments when you could have heard a fly pass overhead and moments that thundered with the imprecations of the mounted patrols in hot pursuit of those impatient insurgents who gave way to their pent-up frustrations with premature shouts of "Long live Chile!" One of these rash citizens flitted like a ghost down a hallway of our house just as six soldiers on horseback dashed into the courtyard and, with great clattering of sabers and horseshoes, penetrated halfway into the entry hall, where they encountered our family. When the commander of the squad haughtily ordered him immediately to hand over the insurgent who had just taken refuge in his home, Solar, unperturbed, picked up a candelabrum and, inviting the soldiers to follow him, made a tour of the whole house, as though intent on nothing but the surrender of the fugitive, of whose entry he declared he was quite unaware; and he played his part so well that after looking even under the mattresses of the cots, where he knew very well they would find nothing, he kept up the search until he had led them to a flat area adjacent to the roof. They thus saw themselves obliged to give up their useless pursuit, returned cursing to the parlor and to their horses, and, casting angry glances at everyone, left the house redolent of the sweat and droppings of their horses.

But the funeral bell had begun to sound its last knells for Spanish power, whose end began on February 12, 1817, on the glorious slopes of Chacabuco, to conclude with the forever memorable victory at Maipú. On the afternoon of that day a frightened Marcó received vague reports of the defeat of the royal forces under Maroto in Chacabuco; and without waiting for their confirmation, he fled in terror, accompanied by some of his subordinates, toward the coast at San Antonio, hoping to find some Spanish ship that would offer him shelter. But a courier had taken off after him at breakneck speed to report these happenings to Don Francisco Ramírez, the owner of the farm at Las Tablas where my family had hidden immediately after the surrender of Santiago and the arrival of Osorio; and so Marcó fell into the hands of my angry uncle, who with his farmhands took him to Santiago and turned him over to the conquerors and the custody of Aldao, captain of grenadiers in the army of the Andes, on the 24th.

No one should be surprised to see me passing so lightly over the political events that I have witnessed in the course of my life; it is not a political history that I am writing, and if now and then I seem to stray from my purpose, I do so in order to divulge some little-known facts or to give unity to my narrative by recalling the incidents that motivated these memoirs.

With San Martín's entry into Santiago, the house of Don Juan Enrique Rosales, who was still languishing in exile with no consolation and no guardian angel but his selfless daughter Rosario, traded its mourner's crepe for a ball gown; the gloomy silence left by the violent removal of its owner yielded to the most animated and cheerful eagerness to decorate everything. Wanting to give the heroes of Chacabuco a small token of their gratitude, Rosales's daughters and sons-in-law outdid themselves in organizing the most lavish soirée that the circumstances of the time allowed, sure that their exiled father, far from considering his house profaned by such rejoicings while he languished in exile, would bless his children's attentions toward the brave warriors to whom we owed freedom and fatherland.

O'Higgins had just been proclaimed Supreme Director of the State on the memorable 16th of February, and the joy of the Rosales family seemed all the more justified because it was known that the most urgent desire of this gallant leader was to repatriate the eminent Chileans confined on Juan Fernández.

To show the simplicity of customs that prevailed in those days, I shall give a rapid account of the ball I have mentioned, which, were we to see the likes of it today, we should consider ridiculous but for the sacred purpose that brought it into being.

My grandfather's house stood on the same ground occupied today by the palace of the hero of Yungay[9] and, like every good building in Santiago, had its two courtyards that provided light from both sides to the central portion of the house. Awnings made of sails brought from Valparaíso for this express purpose were stretched from the house out over these courtyards, and sails also served as carpeting on the rough pavement of these improvised rooms. Lighting was supplied by many martial chandeliers made of concentric circles of bayonets hanging point down, in whose sockets tallow candles were placed, with rings of paper at their base to keep them from dripping. A multitude of myrtle arches and mirrors of every size and shape adorned the walls; and some of the doorways and windows were covered with appropriate translucent paintings produced by the coarse brush of the painter Dueñas, whose best student, Mena, would begin to paint a tree by marking a mud-colored perpendicular line on the canvas with a ruler, and then take up a brush thoroughly soaked in green paint and smear it over an area about the size of a watermelon at the end of the straight line, which he called the trunk; if he did not write "This is a tree" below that stick and green club, it was because he did not know how. On each of the courtyards musicians sat

---

9. *The hero of Yungay,* General Manuel Bulnes, conqueror of the Bolivians at the battle of Yungay in 1839 and later president of Chile. JP.

behind a likewise painted screen, and a musical flying squadron was held in reserve to step in wherever it might be most needed. What most drew the attention of the capital, however, was the explosive notion of setting up, on the street outside the front door, a battery of mountain artillery, whose replies to the toasts and patriotic speeches being delivered within must have left no window unbroken throughout the whole neighborhood. The inner rooms were adorned as luxuriously as the times permitted, and a profusion of conjoined flags endowed the whole with the harmonious appearance that its ingenious ornamentation called for.

In the central space of that vast and ancient building a very long table had been set up, on whose lace-trimmed cloths stood treasured bowls and platters of solid silver brought out of storage for this special occasion, as well as the ancient and highly prized Chinese porcelain. The most exquisite dishes of the time were all represented on that bounteous board, along with turkeys with gilded heads, bearing flags in their beaks, stuffed piglets with daintily curled tails, holding bright oranges in their mouths, Chiloé hams, almond cookies prepared by nuns, others baked with flour and eggs, fudge, candied egg yolks, and a million other delicacies, not to mention many wedges of Chanco cheese, spiced olives, pickled onions, and other fiery tidbits whose flames were to be put out with local wines from Santiago and Concepción and not a few Spanish ones.

It was decided that the ladies would come crowned with flowers and that no man should fail to wear a red Phrygian cap with borders of blue and white ribbon.

I hardly need say what an impression this merry and, by that day's standards, most sumptuous soirée caused in Santiago. It began with the Argentine national hymn sung in unison by all those present and followed by a twenty-one gun salvo that jolted every house in the neighborhood. Then came the minuet, the contredanse, and the rigadoon, favorite dances of the time; and in them the fair sex of our country displayed its youth and elegance, as did the phalanx of brilliant Argentine and Chilean officers who with their heroic deeds had won for themselves the ever honorable title of Fathers of their Country.

The warrior's somber frown gave way to the amiable smile of gallantry as the youthful heroes who had risen to the call of patriotism strolled merrily from room to room, acknowledging at that moment no rank but what was conferred by true merit and no fatherland but the common soil of America. There the glorious son of Yapeyú[10] shook the dainty hand of the valorous Lieutenant Lavalle with the same cordiality

10. *Yapeyú,* the birthplace of San Martín. JP.

as he did the calloused hand of bold O'Higgins,[11] and no one asked the nationality of the Uruguayans Martínez and Arellano, the Argentineans Soler, Quintana, Beruti, Plaza, Frutos, Alvarado, Conde, Necochea, Zapiola, and Melián, the Chileans Zenteno, Calderón, and Freire, the Europeans Paroisin, Arcos, and Cramer, or of many another whose origin escapes my memory, such as Correa, Nozar, Molina, Guerrero, Medina, Soria, Pacheco, and all those whose military obligations allowed them to grace the joyful occasion with their presence. The cream of Santiago's patriotic youth was also there, along with the few old men whom Marcó's cruelty had failed to exile, the merry and quick-witted Vera, and that famous expert in military fireworks, Father Beltrán, who, when asked to fit our cannons with wings so that they might cross the Andes, had quickly turned himself into a Vulcan whose arsenal turned out bolts of lightning for the Jupiter of our independence.

The general gaiety reached its zenith at the table. The informality that is the firstborn daughter of the grape melted away the reserve of the guests; and the vicissitudes of the recent battle of Chacabuco, as recalled and recounted, glass in hand, by the same heroic youths who had just taken part in it, and accompanied by the thunderous noise of the artillery salvos, filled the house and the whole neighborhood with the merriest commotion of cannon fire, music, and hurrahs that Santiago had ever heard since the day of its founding. Toasts were the order of the day, and every toast shone for its terse forceful expressiveness. How flat those laconic but energetic outpourings of souls quivering with patriotism would seem to us today, when we normally measure the quality of a toast by how long it takes us to propose it! We used to toast with our hearts; now we do so with our heads.

Standing in the midst of his staff, San Martín, after a brief but stirring patriotic toast, held the glass in which he had just drunk as though to throw it onto the floor and turned to the master of the house to ask, "May I, Solar?" After my father had replied that the glass and whatever stood on the table were there to be broken, not a toast was proposed but a glass was thrown to the ground so that no one might later desecrate it with toasts of a contrary persuasion. Thus the floor took on the aspect of a battlefield covered with smashed glasses and bottles.

The Argentine national anthem was sung twice, the second time by San Martín himself. Everyone stood up, two black servants with trumpets were brought into the dining room, and all were electrified to hear, accompanied by the majestic virile sound of those instruments, the

11. Juan Lavalle was an Argentinean, while Bernardo O'Higgins was a Chilean. JP.

rough but true and steady bass voice of the hero who since his crossing of the Andes had not ceased for a single moment to be the object of universal veneration. The Chilean anthem could not contribute its thrilling sound to the celebration because that symbol of unity and glory had not yet been born; it was not adopted by the Senate till September 20, 1819, and first sung, with Chilean music, a week later.

This was also the case of the Chilean coat of arms, which in very embryonic form appeared next to that of Argentina on the screens and paintings that decorated the courtyards, for it was only three days after having adopted our national anthem that the Senate approved the original design of our national emblem. This consisted simply of a dark blue oval in whose center stood a white Doric column surmounted by the word *Libertad,* above which appeared three five-pointed stars representing Santiago, Coquimbo, and Concepción, which were the names of the three great political divisions that made up the country at that time. This design was bordered by laurel branches tied with tricolored ribbons, and the whole shield was flanked by trophies composed of weapons, flags, and broken chains.

We might at this point recall the origins of our national emblems. From the first political squabbles of 1810 until the time of Don José Miguel Carrera's propitious participation in our revolution, Chile had no flag but the flag of Spain, nor any coat of arms other than that of the kings of Castile, which makes us suspect either that our fathers were not thinking of an absolute separation from the mother country or that, if they were, they were afraid of letting it be known. To Don José Miguel's intrepid patriotism we owe the bold and timely end of indecision: in 1812 he displayed to the astonished eyes of the people of Chile our first tricolored flag, blue, white, and yellow, which was approved the following year by the Senate and which was to bear stalwart witness to so many glorious deeds and so many misfortunes. Stunned but not defunct after the dreadful catastrophe of Rancagua, it came to glorious life again in 1817, its original yellow dyed red, as Vera so poetically put it, by the blood of its defenders. Once the legendary lion banner of Spain had been driven forever from the soil of Chile, there rose in brilliance in the blue of our free skies that single fair star that has ever been, is, and will be the precursor of the boldest military triumphs.

Once our soirée had come to an end, everyone turned anew to the task of consolidating the great work so happily begun at Chacabuco; and the first thought of all was to bring home, as soon as possible, the patriots whom Spanish cruelty was holding prisoner on Juan Fernández. It was feared, and rightly, that once news of what was happening in Chile reached Abascal, then viceroy of Peru, those unfortunate patriarchs of our leading families would soon be transferred to the vaults of the castles of Callao; and so they would have been if the Spanish brig *Águila* had not fallen into the hands of the patriots as she entered the harbor of Valparaíso, mistakenly thinking it to be still under Spanish control. Now she set out immediately for the island; and since Don José Piquero, commander of the prison there, offered no resistance when asked to surrender his charges, these had the good fortune of being able to embark in freedom and return to the bosom of their disconsolate families on March 25, a month and a half after the memorable battle of Chacabuco.

These intervals of happiness between the storms of the past and the tempests that the future still held in store for us before the conclusion of the epic of our emancipation did not last long. Life then was a life of contrasts: you passed directly from laughter to tears, and from tears to laughter. How could Marcó have foreseen that his own edicts of pillage and torture, which only a day earlier had filled the royalists with vengeful rejoicing, were to serve, a day later, to plunder and torment those same royalists, on whom fell the inexorable law of retaliation, an eye for an eye and a tooth for a tooth! And how could those who indulged in ecstatic celebrations, trusting in what seemed to be a secure future, imagine the depth of the abyss into which the uncertain fortunes of war would plunge them at Cancha Rayada!

The ever memorable year 1818, a year of tears and glory, and the foundation stone of our independence, was just beginning when the defeat at Cancha Rayada turned the joy and hope of daily strengthening our liberty into the most cruel disillusionment. It is impossible to describe the effect that the news of this catastrophe, which took place on March 19, had on the citizens of the capital, who were all the more surprised for being so little prepared to receive it. At the time of the defeat at Rancagua in 1814, not all the inhabitants of Santiago who favored the cause of emancipation thought it necessary to cross the Andes to save themselves from the ire of the royalists, because, although their patriotism was sincere, their deeds had not yet been such as to mark them as incorrigible rebels; in 1818, however, Cancha Rayada found very few *santiagueños* still wearing the mask that had protected them, since they had most jauntily tossed it away after the glorious victory at Chacabuco. The wildest panic thus took hold of hapless Santiago; and with the instinct for self-preservation constantly spurred on by the muddled news brought by those fleeing from the battlefield, all thoughts were of seeking refuge on the far side of the Andes.

Moving a whole unprepared and distressed population struck no one as impossible. The spirit of "every man for himself" surmounts all obstacles in the way of flight, for even the most insuperable seem small to the eyes of fear.

It was frightful to see the mass of people on foot and on horseback who were sweeping everything before them on the well-known road past Chacabuco into the Andes; wherever you looked among the highest peaks, you would see scattered groups of men and women on foot, some leading their children by the hand, others seated to catch their breath, and most of them begging other refugees for food that would allow them to continue their flight.

To suggest how families less well off than mine must have suffered on this trek, let me say that for nine saddle mules supplied us as a special favor by Loyola, who ran carts to Valparaíso, my father paid fourteen thousand pesos. We could of course take nothing with us; everything was left behind in charge of a faithful old servant, as though we were to return the same day. I remember that while our mounts were being saddled and mattresses were being tied even on Solar's pampered horses, the rest of the family was busy hiding the jewelry and our remaining silverware beneath the floors of the interior rooms, while many sacks holding a thousand pesos each were being thrown, unseen by the servants, into the well in the rear courtyard. Then, at 3 P.M. on the 23d of March, we set out on our flight to Mendoza with little more than the clothes on our backs.

Thus we had not yet finished celebrating the return from Juan Fernández of my old grandfather Rosales and his inseparable daughter Rosario when we were forced to try again and more effectively to save that venerated trunk of our family tree; but all the sufferings on our way would have been bearable, had not a new and unforeseen misfortune caught us by surprise on the arduous slope of Las Vacas. The mule on which my mother was riding stumbled, throwing her from the saddle; she would have been smashed to pieces against a rock had not my aunt Rosario, that martyr to familial devotion, leapt from her mount to place herself between the rock and her sister's body, saving her life at the cost of breaking her own thigh with the impact. Until we reached Mendoza, an uncomfortable stretcher was the only conveyance that in our flight we were able to provide for that extraordinary young woman, who seemed to be destined to suffer for each and every member of her family.

Thus we arrived in the poor village of Mendoza, where, like everyone else, we sought winter quarters; and since Mendoza boasted a sort of school that, being the only one in town, seemed in some ways to resemble an educational institution, all the male children of the Chilean refugees wound up there.

Meanwhile the arrival of these refugees spread the most acute panic in Mendoza.

That region of the former Viceroyalty of La Plata, lacking both troops and the resources for raising them, now faced a possible avenging invasion by the victorious Spanish army as well as the disturbances produced everywhere by the slighted ambitions of the Carrera brothers, the declared enemies of O'Higgins since before the disaster at Rancagua. It seemed as though the first heroes of our emancipation, to whom our country's cause owed so much, could not collaborate with the heroes of the New Fatherland. The specter of rivalry arose in the patriotic breasts of those fathers of our liberty; and that principle, so noble when it strives for man's betterment, went astray in those times and sought only the extermination of the opposing faction. The Carreras had the misfortune of losing out in this fratricidal struggle, and the author of these lines had the painful experience of witnessing the final scene of that bloody drama.

Mendoza was at that time under the command of Don Toribio Luzuriaga, who, to lighten the burden of its sparse garrison, had ordered arms and military training to be given to every schoolboy over the age of ten. When, filled with pride and joy, I first loaded the gun that was put into my hands; when, with my companions, I marched along to the rhythmic beat of the drum; when with speed and martial bearing I obeyed the commands of the army captain who served as our instructor, how could I have imagined that soon thereafter, with the same weapon, to the same rhythm, and obeying the same orders, I would serve to mark off the somber space occupied by two benches where Don Luis and Don Juan José Carrera, close friends of my family, were to be shot!

Both brothers, one using the name Leandro Barra, the other that of Narciso Méndez, had fallen into the hands of their enemies and were held incommunicado and in chains in the Mendoza jail. On April 4, the day before the battle of Maipú, we were horrified to learn that the prosecutor Corbalán had called for the death penalty for both defendants; this sentence so deeply perturbed the public that the very men who seemed most intent on carrying it out were obliged to shore up its authority by submitting it to review by three jurists, Galigniana, Cruz Vargas, and Monteagudo.

Never was so serious a matter resolved in a more hasty fashion; and this happened because with San Martín's beaten army about to clash with the conquerors at Quecherehuas, it was feared that the least rumor of a new defeat would plunge Mendoza into a revolutionary turmoil of which the Carreras would soon emerge as leaders. Monteagudo and Cruz Vargas were of the opinion that, hard as it seemed, the sacrifice had to be made. On April 8, at three in the afternoon, the unhappy prisoners were notified that they were to die that day at five. At the same time, the student soldiers were called to arms; and at four o'clock sharp they were drawn up on the town square near a low wall next to the jail, against which stood two benches that were to be the final seats of two victims of human brutality.

Thinking that we should be obliged to fire on the victims, our parents protested; but after the governor had replied that there was no lack of veterans for the job, the deadly process went ahead.

The crowd grew steadily, until we could barely maintain the line that held it in check so that the executioners could do their work unhindered. At a quarter to six the great commotion that we noticed among those guarding the jail told us that the drama's terrible denouement was about to begin; in this we were not deceived, for the bells of the nearby church began the ancient death knell that besought the town to pray for the souls of the condemned.

A moment later, hand in hand in deathlike silence, the two illustrious victims, Luis and Juan José Carrera, appeared at the gate of the jail, men who had shown me so much kind affection in happier times, when, in the bosom of friendship and together with José Miguel, they confided to my mother their fears and hopes for the future of our country, or their frequent madcap escapades. Bareheaded, in leg irons, preceded by four soldiers, followed by a picket of riflemen, and flanked by two priests, they hobbled across the short distance between the jail and the benches. Their faces were pale; the demeanor of the dainty Luis, as calm as Juan José's was agitated; and it seemed that those unfortunates had much to say to each other before their death, because not for a moment did they stop talking to each other in a low voice, until, as they arrived at the end of that fatal journey, the priests had to tell them something that I did not hear but that, after an involuntary shudder, made them turn to their spiritual escorts, thank them, and passionately press a crucifix against their breasts and kiss it reverently.

Resigned and as though exhausted, they sat down; asking the executioner not to blindfold them, Luis put his handkerchief to his face and exclaimed, "This will do!" This last indulgence was denied them; but as the rifles aimed at them and the priests began to withdraw, raising their voices to deliver a final consolation, both brothers suddenly leapt up as though impelled by a single spring and, to the consternation of the startled spectators, tore off their blindfolds and rushed into each other's arms, there to remain in agitated silence for half a minute. It was their last farewell to brother, life, and fatherland!

I have never been able to forget the terrible impression made on my soul by this solemn, wordless, and unexpected protest against the atrocities—which continue to this day—committed by man, the so-called highest being in Creation.

After the executioner's hand had returned these unfortunates to their seats, their souls flew to heaven through the smoke of a single volley. Luis fell forward motionless; Juan José swayed for a moment on the bench, pronounced some words that my emotions kept me from hearing, and then collapsed.

I V

How Lord Spencer repaid the kindnesses done him in Chile. —
Brazil. — The first steamship to reach Rio de Janeiro. —
What people thought of steamships in those days. — Slavery. —
Brazil's achievement of independence. — The famous writer
Maria Graham. — The earthquake of 1822. — O'Higgins. —
National holidays. — Chile in 1824. — A remarkable
proclamation by General Luis Aury. — Camilo Henríquez's
views on immigration.

Though in 1810 Chile was called a kingdom, it really resembled a
farm rented to a bad tenant less concerned with the future of the
property than with his own profit; and only on the day it came once more
into the hands of its rightful owners could it begin to enjoy the benefits
that always flow from direct contact with the civilized world after a time

of misguided isolation. Once its gates were thrown wide open to commerce, foreigners came to its free shores from all over the world, and our ports ceased to be the exclusive preserve of Spanish vessels.

The finest of the foreign warships that in 1821 unfurled their flags in Valparaíso Bay, until recently quite empty, was the elegant British frigate *Owen Glendower*, whose commander, Lord Spencer, nobler in his name than in the deed I shall recount, enjoyed, like many another foreigner, the hospitality of the Solar mansion in Santiago.

One day, whose date I am loath to remember,[12] this good lord was sitting next to my mother on a sofa overlooking the garden and seemed absorbed and amused by the sight of the damage inflicted on some bottles of snuff (which my good grandfather, Don Juan Enrique Rosales, used to prepare and for lack of a better place hang against the garden wall to dry in the sun) by a tall, thin boy who, for all his sickly appearance, was quick to take advantage of the opportunities that the visit of this haughty Gringo offered for the full display of his destructive impulses. Every half bottle brought down with a well-aimed stone, leaving the rest hanging by its neck, seemed to meet with as much approbation from Spencer, in the form of that silent approval that the Yankees bestow on a "good shot," as it met with reproof from the lady, who, lacking more active means of reprimand and after several telegraphic signals of disapproval, could no longer tolerate what she was seeing and managed, for my sins, to exclaim, "Look here, Vicente, I'm sick and tired of this!"

The noble Englishman saw this expression, so inconsequential and so frequent on the lips of Chilean mothers, as an opportunity for him to requite my family's attentions by saving it from seeing the name of Rosales stained by the future conduct of a son who at so early an age had managed to exhaust the patience of his own mother. Buoyed by this happy thought, he proposed to the lady that he take the sickly boy to Valparaíso and lodge him on board his frigate, where in the company of midshipmen of his own age he might enjoy himself, get some exercise, and even learn some English. My mother said no, my father said yes. Four days later I was off to Valparaíso, on the fifth I slept on board, and on the sixth I awoke on the open ocean, seasick and on my way to Cape Horn!

Lord Spencer's visit had been a farewell call, but he had kept this to himself once he had hit on the idea of repaying my family's services in so strange a fashion. On his orders I was cast to live among the sailors in the bow of the ship; the officers were ordered to avoid all contact with

12. Cf. the opening sentence of Don *Quixote*: "In a certain village in La Mancha, whose name I am loath to remember . . ." JP.

the poor prisoner; my little trunk with clothes was thrown into the hold; and with nothing but what he had on, a seaman's hammock for a bed and no food but the coarse rations of the crew, sick, dirty, covered with tar from head to toe, and unable to understand what was happening to him, the poor helpless boy suffered for seven weeks, which is what it took the *Owen Glendower* to reach Rio de Janeiro.

Once the frigate had anchored in that beautiful harbor and rendered and received the customary military salutes, the downcast exile, with never a friendly hand stretched out toward him, was put into the crew's boat, which carried him to what they call the Praia Grande and abandoned him there in the most cruel fashion. Alone, bewildered, penniless, and in danger of perishing of hunger and want, two thousand leagues from home among people who did not even speak his language, that victim of a heartless madman would not now, bowed down by age, be calling up memories that still make him shudder, had not God, desiring not to give up on humanity, sent Mr. Macdonald, the frigate's first lieutenant, to his aid. This officer, moved by compassion for the boy, set off after the boat and became the guardian angel who saved him. He asked whether I had brought letters of recommendation! Then, shocked at what was going on but not daring to do more for fear of offending Spencer, the old seaman placed two gold coins in my hands, urged me to stay close to a shed that served as sleeping quarters for black slaves, recommended me to the care of their overseer, and left me.

Ah, youth! My belly full of bananas, guavas, and sugar cane that an old black woman taught me how to chew, I slept that night on the floor among my new companions as I might have slept in the softest bed.

Toward noon of the next day, three gentlemen jumped out of a boat and headed for the shed in search of me: the British consul, the Spaniard Don Juan Santiago Barros, and Don José Ignacio Izquierdo, a Chilean. To judge by the way they approached me, my filthy, tar-smeared appearance must not have caused a very favorable impression. Guided by what worthy Macdonald had told them, they were looking for the son of one of the leading families of Santiago; what they saw resembled, more than anything else, a scullion in dirty rags. All this, however, changed as soon as I told them my parents' names. Señor Izquierdo exclaimed in surprise and with enthusiasm, "Mercedes's son? Gentlemen, I'll take charge of this boy; I'm a close friend of his family's." Don Juan Santiago Barros said, "I'll take him; I'm Solar's agent here." At this point the consul intervened and said, "No one has a better claim on him than I, because it was I whom Macdonald first asked to get this young gentleman home and not either of you."

How often such things occur in the course of our lives! Hardly ever is there more than a single step between happiness and misfortune. My providential protectors had to reach a compromise, and it was decided that I would be lodged with Barros and would take turns eating with each one of those rivals in kindness.

I remained in Rio de Janeiro, capital of Brazil, for about two years before an opportunity to return to my parents' home arose. To avoid useless repetition of what so many have written about the bay and about the capital of this South American colossus, I shall say little or nothing. For my purposes it is enough to indicate that the bay, among the world's most sheltered, with a mouth barely two kilometers wide, measures thirty kilometers from north to south, and twenty-six in width; that the city, while somewhat haphazard in its layout, possessed in 1821 every kind of civil, military, and religious establishment and every convenience that could make life pleasant in those times; and that all of it was set, as it still is, in the most imposing and picturesque landscape.

As an example of the progress of steam power, King George IV of England had just presented the Regent Dom Pedro of Brazil with a small steamboat, powered by a high-pressure engine, for cruising on the bay. It was only natural that a phenomenon of this sort, able to move and cleave the water without aid of oar or wind, should cause the greatest astonishment, and so the day of its maiden voyage bells rang, the ships at anchor in the bay decked themselves in all their finery, and the *Santa Cruz* and the *Cobras* convulsed the air with their thunderous royal salvos. But what a letdown after so much ado! Once that heavy contraption got under way, the countless boats and skiffs that crowded the waters to escort it were forced (who would believe it nowadays?) to reduce speed in order not to leave the regent's sloth of a vessel behind; and when Don Santiago Barros, who was with me in one of the accompanying boats, saw this, he gave me this angry lesson in republican statecraft: "Do you see what all the fuss is about, my boy? Well, let me tell you, and don't you forget it, that it's the people who with the sweat of their brow have to pay for all these knickknacks, these useless toys for kings. This thing isn't worth a damn, and it never will be!" And small wonder that that worthy son of Old Spain should hold these opinions when the Inquisition of that time taught that the use of the steamboat is a sin, a kind of sorcery and a machine that could not function without the aid of the Devil or without an express pact with that invisible artificer. What wouldn't the old Spaniard say now, were he still alive!

Still, let no one think that vessels propelled by steam did not reach Latin America until 1821, because late in 1818 and with the name of "steam boat," in English, a small vessel of that type was successfully navigating on and near the island of Trinidad, and according to the *Correo del Orinoco* of the day, "it was a pleasure to see it push upstream." If that good Spaniard were alive today, what would he say to me! Nowadays, when we see the miracles of steam, of photography, and of electricity, we may perhaps suspend judgment on the limits to human power, but we can never deny it!

In spite of my youth, what most attracted my attention in Rio de Janeiro was slavery. Lack of muscular strength and great lassitude and drowsiness seem to be characteristic of the white race in the tropics, where the man of cold or temperate regions seems also to be exposed to diseases that sooner or later sap his natural vigor. These, I believe, are the factors that explain the need for the Negro in the economic development of the areas that lie directly beneath the sun.

The slave trade was not prohibited in 1821 as it is today. Vessels originating on the coast of Africa frequently reached the harbor laden with unfortunate new blacks who had been traded for liquor or torn from their primitive country by trickery, to be sold like work animals in the marketplaces of civilized peoples. The number of victims that this always heartless trade brought yearly from the coasts of Africa to those of Brazil was terrifying. According to official records, 20,610 blacks left Africa in the fifty-two ships that reached Rio de Janeiro alone with this dreadful merchandise in 1823, and only 19,173 arrived, after 1,437 corpses had been thrown overboard!

Many times did I witness these dealings, as inhumane as they are shameful. After completion of the customs formalities, the unfortunate merchandise entered a corral surrounded by arcades, where, distributed among the various agents and watched by robust overseers armed with whips, whose crack was often heard, it silently awaited a buyer. Before entering the corral, the Negro was thoroughly washed, which meant driving him into the sea with whips. He was next fitted with a loincloth; men, women, and children subsequently took up the position assigned to them in so repulsive a marketplace. The buyers then proceeded to a careful scrutiny of each personal quality of the unhappy black whom they wanted to buy. He was set up like a statue and examined from head to toe; he was made to bend over, to lift heavy weights or hold them up with his arms outstretched to give an idea of his strength; his chest and waist were squeezed to see whether he suffered some pain; then he was made to open his mouth so that the state of his teeth could be checked; in a word, these people were subjected to the sort of examination to which in Chile we subject horses before settling on a price. Once the animal had been sold he was turned over to trainers, sturdy and cruel mulattoes who, after teaching the blacks obedience above all, along with a little Portuguese, returned them to their owners, under whose yoke they were to live the dreadful life of the slave until they died. I have seen public whipping posts where domestic wrongdoings were punished with countless lashes; and I have also seen backs full of scars and scabs undergo new and frightful whippings, to which the passersby paid no more heed than do most of our people when they find a brutal driver vengefully beating his debilitated horse.

Before I turn the page on this matter, I must, much against my inclination, recount something that I witnessed while lunching one day in the home of Don Juan Santiago Barros. This gentleman wanted to give a present to a friend of his who had said that he needed a black girl as a servant for his wife; and so he had bought one, about sixteen years old and recently brought from Africa. To make sure that the present was worthy of its intended recipient, he had the girl come into the dining room, thoroughly washed and carefully combed, and naked but for a covering sheet. Once she was there, and in the company of all, he made her remove that cloth, with never a thought for the fact that I and a son of his were present! Once the unhappy creature, who seemed more like a mechanical ebony statue than like a living being, had been approved by those present, she was dressed and sent to her destination.

In mid-June of 1821 alarming rumors about the deterioration of relations between Brazil and her home country, Portugal, were circulating in the city, so much so that within a few days, as I saw that these rumors were increasingly taking on the tone of the most violent recriminations, I began to fear that I would witness the same melancholy scenes in Rio de Janeiro that I had witnessed in Chile in 1814 and 1818, since Brazil was also attempting to attain her independence. I was mistaken; Brazil's freedom cost neither tears nor blood, for it came simply as the natural and logical consequence of preceding events.

The demands of Napoleon I, determined to carry out his favorite scheme of a continental blockade against England, forced the house of Bragança, which then ruled Portugal, to take refuge in its American territories. Until that time, Portugal, like Spain, had in her colonies followed that inept policy of restrictions that provoked the emancipation of Spanish America; and since, once the royal family had come to Brazil, that fair part of the world had begun to enjoy all those freedoms and privileges that prior to that time only Portugal had enjoyed at her expense, she could not resign herself to return to colonial status when Dom João VI, her legitimate sovereign, returned to his European domain. At that time rights and privileges did not belong to the people but to the crowned heads who governed them. They came with the king, and they left with the king; and so no sooner did Dom João VI embark for Lisbon in March 1821, leaving his son Dom Pedro as regent of Brazil, than the painful effects of his absence made themselves felt. Brazil became once more a colony; Portugal, which, with her king abroad, had been almost a colony, once more acquired the despotic rank of mother country.

The Portuguese parliament, with little concern for the consequences of its acts, heedless of the causes of the recent emancipation of Spanish America and even more of Brazil's understandable reluctance at being demoted from mistress to servant merely by the departure of the king, determined imprudently to wipe away even the memory of her fleeting good fortune. To eliminate all traces of equality between the two states, it decreed that the prince should join his father in Portugal and sent a powerful fleet to Rio de Janeiro to escort him. The Brazilians, alarmed by what was going on and determined to have recourse to arms should that become necessary, hit upon the happy thought of first approaching the prince, offering him, through their representatives, the glory of turning the vast and wealthy state that he was governing into a sovereign empire, whose splendid scepter they would place in his hand if he did not abandon them. Dom Pedro accepted this great honor, and the city's mighty fortresses were notified of this fortunate development and ordered to force the Portuguese fleet, once it had arrived, to anchor beyond the reach of their batteries. The Portuguese troops that Dom João VI had left in Brazil to serve as a guard for his son were the only ones that sought to resist the new state of affairs by trying to establish defensive positions in their barracks; but the people, massed on the vast Campo de Santana[13] and, supported by native troops, surrounded and besieged them and soon forced them to yield and to surrender, with the sole condition that they would be sent home.

During those agitated days I had been offered the opportunity to return to my distant fatherland on the frigate *Doris* of the British navy. As she carried me off amidst the Portuguese vessels ready to weigh anchor and bear the unhappy news of Brazil's emancipation back to Portugal, I could see that they were taking aboard the remaining royal troops that had capitulated and were leaving those shores, never again to set foot on them.

13. *Campo de Santana,* a square in Rio de Janeiro, now called Praça da República. JP.

This great event, born of a tranquility and good sense that made it one of the most peaceful recorded in the annals of the emancipation of peoples, began in the early months of 1822 and was sanctioned by the happy sons of Brazil on September 7 of the same year with the exaltation of Dom Pedro I to the throne of the new Brazilian empire as Emperor and Perpetual Defender of Brazil.

I should be most remiss did I not here express the sincere gratitude that I owe the memory of the learned writer Maria Graham, widow of the ill-fated captain of the *Doris,* who fell victim to a fatal accident in the waters of the Cape. Her maternal attentions on the *Doris* more than made up for the unprovoked brutality that I received on the *Owen Glendower* at the hands of Spencer when he snatched me away from my parents.

Once I was home again in Chile, and although I was too young fully to appreciate my country's progress, because back then we were children till the age of seventeen and young lads beyond that of twenty, my mind was already beginning to be sufficiently independent to allow me to scorn received opinions or laugh at them. The history of earthquakes, which in 1822 added yet another page to its recital of disasters, offered me the chance to do both at the same time, for that earthquake, which, to be sure, was not one of the strongest to shake our land, brought forth additional proof—though, alas, none was needed—that superstition has not lost and will never lose its hold on the hearts of the ignorant, as long as mankind inhabits this sublunary world. There was every reason to be afraid and good cause for trepidation. Sidewalks and courtyards were covered with piles of shattered roof tiles. Amid the general consternation, the dashing to and fro and collisions with which the alarmed inhabitants tried to avoid the danger, and the shouts of "Lord have mercy!" raised to heaven, I could see a frightened priest struggling outside our front door to escape a woman who was grasping his cassock and dragging herself along on her knees while begging him at the top of her voice to absolve her of the sins she was confessing to him out loud. About ten-thirty on that fearful night it occurred to a venerable nun to declare that she had had a revelation that the quake was the forerunner of the end of the world and that eleven the next morning would be the hour of the Last Judgment. This terrifying news, which spread with lightning speed throughout Santiago, produced a general stampede into the squares and parks; without knowing what they were doing, educated men and ignorant, ladies and scrubwomen, everyone, great and small, had such quantities of beds and mattresses dragged to these places of safety that in no time they covered a part of the embankment, the public squares, and the newly constructed esplanade.

What would an enlightened man magically brought to Santiago have thought of us on seeing, among the mattresses, the glowing coals of the braziers that heated pots and kettles for the inevitable *mate,* and on noting the trembling with which the faithful sucked up their tea even as they implored pardon for their sins?

The dreaded hour finally came; and while some closed their eyes to escape their fear and others fainted away, the sudden and general clamor of the city's bells proclaimed to happy Santiago that thanks to the prayers of the nuns, a merciful God had pardoned the human race and granted it additional years of life.

But such fleeting incidents, which now and then cast a cloud on the intellectual progress of some of earth's peoples, can shed their discouraging, if not ridiculous light only on a small part of our civilization. Everything was progressing in Chile at that time, and progressing far more rapidly than one might have expected from the country's colonial past or from the quasi-independent life it had led since 1810.

We come now to the year 1824. The Supreme Director Don Bernardo O'Higgins had relinquished power, or rather had been forced to recognize that he could no longer manage public affairs without plunging his country into the horrid abyss of fratricidal struggle. On January 23, 1823, this Chilean hero had crowned his record of noble service with these solemn words: "Believing that under the present circumstances the tranquility of our country may be furthered by my ceasing to exercise the supreme authority of the State, I have decided to abdicate as Supreme Director and to assign my powers provisionally to a governing council composed of the citizens Don Agustín Eyzaguirre, Don José Miguel Infante, and Don Fernando Errázuriz."

He might have added what that hero of America, San Martín, had said four months earlier as he left Peru: "As for my public conduct, my countrymen's opinions will differ, but their children will render the true verdict."

The public life of O'Higgins, that great servant of his country whose virtues are far more evident than his defects, came to an end that once more proves the philosophic axiom that there is but a single step from the Capitol to the Tarpeian Rock.[14] The news of his resignation had not yet become known when, as he was about to exile himself forever from the Chile for which he had so often risked his life, he was arrested in Valparaíso by Ramón Freire as a preliminary to an investigation of his

---

14. *Tarpeian Rock,* a place on the Capitoline Hill from which, in ancient Rome, criminals were cast to their death. JP.

administration. Circumstances that others have recounted and that it is not the purpose of these memoirs to reproduce then led that pride of Chile, both civic and military, to the remote shores of Peru, whence his mortal remains could return to the bosom of his grateful fatherland only half a century later.

Every time that in Chile we celebrate our national holiday in September, I am automatically reminded of the ceremonies with which the patriots of 1824 celebrated the 12th of February, a date now almost forgotten but that more than any other has a claim on the fullest and most deserved homage of every Chilean. It was on February 12, 1541, that Pedro Valdivia founded our proud Santiago; it was on February 12, 1817, that the army of liberation, after having expertly and boldly solved the problem of crossing the Andes in the face of the enemy, gave us at Chacabuco our liberty, which the nation sanctioned the following February 12 with the solemn proclamation of our independence.

That was the day celebrated back then, and not the 18th of September; and only those who have witnessed those festivities, in which the wildest expressions of joy were mixed with those of the purest gratitude to glorify the fathers of our country, can rightly judge the effects that the gnawing tooth of time has even on the memory of those customs most deserving of immortality. On that day the flag beneath which we had proclaimed our independence was carried with great ceremony by the Supreme Director and placed on a throne in the city hall; and then, accompanied by all the civil, military, and religious authorities, it was taken to the cathedral, where, after the reading of the Gospel and in place of the customary sermon, our original declaration of independence, brought there for this purpose by the head of state himself, was read to the people in a loud and clear voice.

All we retain of those heartfelt commemorative festivities are the cannon salvos from Hidalgo Castle and the lights and other street decorations, which have been moved to the Alameda, because even what became the boulevard to our gay Pampilla (now the Parque Cousiño) has been quite stripped of its original democratic character and now serves only the carriages of the nobility, to the exclusion of the people's humble cart. How many of those who come to show off their carriages and their horses on our boulevards, how many of those who go to the theater, where the national anthem is still sung, more for the chance to show off the voices of the singers than for the meaning of its stanzas, a meaning that has even been changed to comply with foolish demands for the profanation of this historic monument—how many, I ask, remember, amid the rejoicing of the day, the men to whom they owe their country and their freedom and the ease and learning with which they are now blest?

During the first stages of our emancipation, the words "Fatherland" and "Chile" were not synonymous. "Fatherland" did not literally mean what we now call Chile, but the body of democratic principles that was fighting tooth and nail against the absolutists of the Spanish monarchy, and besides that, the very persons who were leading on the banners of independence. That is why back then we had a First and a New Fatherland. Only in 1824 did a decree give its proper meaning to the word "Fatherland" by commanding that "¡Viva Chile!" was to be shouted instead of "¡Viva la Patria!" on those great occasions that commemorated recent glorious events or those that gave us our liberty.

Those who say that old people live only on memories and obsessively find fault with everything that differs from what happened or was done in their youth, are telling the truth, but not the whole truth. At any rate, this rule does not apply to me, because as far as I am concerned what once is good does not become less so with age, nor, if something new is good, do I fail to recognize it quite as enthusiastically as I did when I was young. But since I am not alone in this, and since there are many who cannot easily remember the good things of the past, I think my readers will not take it amiss if, before going on to the year 1825, I give them a quick sketch of what Chile was like in 1824, which will let them deduce what she was in 1810 and allow us to render unto Caesar the things which are Caesar's.

Our national territory, which at that time stretched only from Atacama to the Chacao Channel, was divided into three large departments called Coquimbo, Santiago, and Concepción, and the districts of Valdivia, Talcahuano, and Valparaíso.

The department of Coquimbo bordered on the north on the province of Atacama of Upper Peru at the Sala Agua Buena River and the dunes of Atacama, and on the south on the department of Santiago at the Quebrada del Negro and the Tilama Pass. The southern border of the Department of Santiago was the River Maule, which separated it from the Department of Concepción, whose southern limits were the Vergara River, the hill of Santa Juana, and Point Rumen.

The jurisdiction of the so-called districts of Talcahuano and Valparaíso did not exceed the limits of these towns, while that of Valdivia reached as far as the Chacao Channel, which was the farthest outpost of our country's flag.

According to calculations whose correctness I have been unable to verify, in 1824 this country, a poor and remote corner of America known only for the blood and treasure that its fruitless conquest cost Spain, had 1,300,000 inhabitants between the two races, native and European, more or less pure or mixed.

From this one can easily deduce what, in 1810, must have been the degree of schooling, the inclinations, and the aspirations of this small and isolated segment of the human race, where the adage "God grant you money, son, for knowledge is of little use" set the tone for the nobility (almost always acquired by purchase), just as Scholastic hairsplitting did for our classrooms, as privileged treatment for Spaniards did for our commerce, as a surplus of food crops did for our ill-cultivated countryside, as "First God, then the King, and then the master" did for the common folk, as lance and plunder did for the Indian, while there were very few who felt the urge to learn by secretly devouring the few scientific, political, or technical books that smugglers or an always dangerous chance placed in their hands.

Who could believe that starting from so little, and in only thirteen years of independent life, thirteen years of feverish and stormy life in which triumphs and disasters, hopes and disappointments followed on each other while at every moment the life, liberty, and property of the heroes of the bloody drama of our independence were at risk, Chile could reach the year 1824 as successfully as she did!

In the history of the first years of our independence we find a fact worthy of the notice of philosophers and statesmen, namely, that those improvised heroes to whom we owe so much did not fail, even while wielding the sword in defense of their own lives, to plant for us institutions of progress, not even at those moments when our bleeding and penniless country seemed to be falling back, with them, into the slime of renewed colonial rule.[15] There are, in fact, very few among our present institutions that do not descend from identical or analogous ones established by those giants of selflessness and patriotism amid the horrors and anguish of war. In 1824 Chile already had, if not as perfected and flourishing institutions, at least as ideas to be developed in due time, a number of more or less matured plans to raise the republic to the rank of a civilized nation.

Several constitutions were adopted in the course of those thirteen years, and the judicial provisions of the one ratified in 1823 are still in force today, in 1874.

---

15. The government's resources were so paltry and its credit consequently so exhausted that in October 1818 the arsenal halted the production of cartridges because there was no money in the treasury with which to buy paper. VPR.

Today's administrative subdivisions in many ways reflect those of the past. What we now call an *intendencia* was then called a *delegación,* and many of today's *departments* were then called *districts.* True, the country was divided into three great sections, but who knows whether such a division, revived and improved, might not make it easier to scrutinize the activities of government and, through decentralization, stimulate the initiatives of the governed?

The Society of the Friends of Chile, established on August 5, 1818 to promote the country's progress in agriculture, commerce, mining, crafts, and trades, shows what a Ministry of Development, which Chile still lacks, could be.

Recognizing the pressing need to be as well informed as possible about the country they were creating, our leaders, on June 26, 1823, decreed the formation of a statistical commission charged with undertaking a scientific voyage over the entire territory of the country to examine its geology, its flora, and its mineral deposits, compiling all the data necessary for a complete statistical overview; and six months later, on December 20, a chorographical commission was established to produce a map of Chile, promote industry, and contribute to the national defense.

On May 21, 1823, a remarkable set of regulations on public order and morality was issued, from which, with the exception of some articles too closely reflecting those times, our current governors could learn a good deal.

The maintenance of order in the countryside, which only now has begun to be seriously discussed among us, was decreed on May 26 of the same year and entrusted to judges who, along with the functions of our present-day highway commissions, had the obligation to watch over the sanitary conditions of fields, men, and animals, the preservation of our forests, and the extension of cultivation.

A welfare commission was formed and charged with protecting and promoting all charitable institutions. The poorhouse was reestablished to wipe out mendicancy and take in the destitute of both sexes to give them work according to their abilities and take care of all their needs.

The demands of public sanitation were not neglected; the clearest proofs are the establishment of the appropriate commission and the prohibition of further burials inside the churches.

In 1820 the military hospital, titled State Hospital, was created.

Regulations were passed to promote and accelerate the process of civilizing the Indians, called brothers since 1813.

Public education and the administration of justice owe to our forefathers the creation of the Supreme Court, the Chilean Academy (established on

December 10, 1823, with three sections: moral and political sciences, physical and mathematical sciences, arts and literature), the Academy of Law and Forensics, the National Institute in the capital and in the departments, created in 1813, reestablished in 1819, and reorganized in 1823, convent schools for males and females, Lancasterian schools,[16] the National Museum, the National Library, and freedom of the press.

They enthroned the dignity of man with the abolition of slavery, flogging, caning in the army, titles of nobility, whether hereditary or purchased, and everything else that degrades mankind and makes it more ridiculous than it already is.

At the same time that the effects of cruelty and foolish pride were being abolished, everything possible was done to elevate the spirit and to rear men capable of bearing with justified pride the title of citizens of an enlightened republic. To this intent a Legion of Merit was founded in 1817 to recompense virtue and talent in every sphere of activity with what was described as "the nation's highest and most esteemed prize."

Rewards were also established for teachers and outstanding students. What so far we have not done and unfortunately seem not about to do anytime soon, the fathers of our country had already done in 1820. At that time six years of advanced study were preparation enough for a benefice in a cathedral or, in the case of laymen, for an analogous appointment in their field. In furtherance of the same purpose, the title of Distinguished Youth was bestowed on the student who most excelled in the uprightness of his behavior and the display of civic and moral virtues or in his scholarly or technical progress; and in addition to the special position that he was granted everywhere and the respect with which he was treated, he obtained the right to continue his studies free of charge.

Unlike what almost always happens now, public servants did not work without hope of reward; the proof is in the decree of June 3, 1820, which ordered that at the outset of every year the director of each treasury office submit to the appropriate ministry the service record of each employee so that those who had served at a lower level might be considered for new appointments.

All the expenses of the state had to be rigorously budgeted, and in those times one can even find evidence of the consolidation of our domestic debt.

To the men of that tumultuous and painful time, the art of war, that imperative need of the human race, owes the Military Academy, the

16. *Lancasterian schools* were those organized according to the system of the English educator Joseph Lancaster, under which advanced pupils were used as "monitors" to teach others. JP.

School of Navigation, the commission for drawing up a code of military justice, and the national arsenal for the production of weapons.

Our wounded veterans were not homeless beggars in those days because, in 1823, the hero fallen on hard times could already count on an asylum under the immediate supervision of the head of the armed forces, so that these unfortunates might lack nothing.

The decree of December 10, 1822, laid the first foundations for the National Guard in Santiago.

So as not to make this enumeration, however superficial, of what we owe to our fathers seem too long-winded, I shall conclude my survey by showing that they concerned themselves even with increasing the number of work days of the Chilean year, for while they pursued loafing and idleness even in their holiest redoubts, they managed to reduce the number of strictly observed feast days from forty to only twelve and to abolish completely the many half-holidays that almost always, especially in the smaller towns, turned into full ones.

Their solicitude watched over everything. For our fathers Spanish America was not a group of different nations, but a single state to be emancipated; and they did not consider this state's emancipation complete while any part of it remained under Spanish control. The contemporary history of Argentina and Chile had already recorded, from the time of the struggle to emancipate Peru, many deeds that testify to this truth; but as I have seen no mention of those others that reached to the farthest corners of Spanish dominion in America, my patriotic pride must be allowed to record here at least the first words of the remarkable proclamation that Don Luis Aury,[17] commanding general of the forces sent to attack New Granada, addressed to his compatriots on July 10, 1818, after having taken possession of the islands of Santa Catalina, Providencia la Vieja, and San Andrés, dependencies of that viceroyalty. This is what he said:

> Fellow countrymen! The powerful United States of Buenos Aires and Chile, desirous of cooperating insofar as possible in the emancipation of their oppressed brethren, have charged me with carrying out this noble enterprise in New Granada. I thank Heaven for inspiring them with sen-

17. All the editions consulted write *Luis de Mauri* in the chapter heading and *Luis Maury* in the body of the text; but the individual in question is Luis, or Louis Michel, Aury, a Frenchman by birth and a corsair in the service of Buenos Aires. See Carlos A. Ferro, *Vida de Luis Aury* (Buenos Aires: Editorial Cuarto Poder, 1976). As an epigraph and again on p. 87, Ferro's book reproduces exactly the proclamation that Pérez Rosales copies here. I thank Professor Iván Jaksić for his guidance in clearing up the confusion. JP.

timents so magnanimous. May their unity and wise conduct be our guide in our future operations.[18]

And what shall we say now of the then current ideas about the importance of immigration as a complement to the great work undertaken with so many sacrifices? In *Camila,* which the famous patriot Camilo Henríquez wrote for our theater to sow the seeds of legitimate progress in the minds of the public, one of the characters says, "If America does not forget Spanish prejudices and adopt more liberal principles, she will never be anything but an overseas Spain, as wretched and benighted as European Spain. To remedy her lamentable depopulation and her backwardness in agriculture and arts and crafts, she must attract foreigners by means of impartial, tolerant, and benevolent laws."

Thus nothing escaped the eyes of those extraordinary men, who shifted the warrior's sword to their left hand to leave the right free to wield the organizing pen, and with the same ease took the steel once more into their powerful right to defend their country's cause and their own lives.

In 1824 we had four diplomatic missions abroad: Don Joaquín Campino was minister plenipotentiary of Chile in Buenos Aires; Don José Antonio Irizarri, in Europe; Don Miguel Zañartu, in Peru; and Don Ignacio Cienfuegos, in Rome.

In Chile only the enemies of her liberty were considered foreigners, and talent was rewarded with the most sensitive public posts. Dauxion Lavaysse became director of the Statistical Commission; Alberto d'Albe and Carlos Lozier were put in charge of the Chorographical Commission; Zegers, or Zeggers, as they wrote back then, was chief of the bureau of foreign affairs; Bayarna was director of the Military Academy; Ocampo had a voice in what was then called the National Chamber. In a word, the Chile of those days was capable of making her own the illustrious names of San Martín, Cochrane, and Blanco; and the descendants of those bold officers who on land and sea generously brought us their precious and so badly needed contributions of blood and learning continue to bestow on us days of glory as though their ancestors had had no fatherland but our own.

18. *Correo del Orinoco* (Angostura), No. 17 (1819). VPR.

V

The Baron de Mackau and the corsair Quintanilla. — My voyage to France. — Rio de Janeiro. — Le Havre. — The Paris of yesteryear. — María Malibrán García. — A young son of Fernando VII. — The Duchesse de Berry. — Silvela's school. — The mathematician Vallejo. — Don Andrés A. de Gorbea. — Don Leandro Fernández Moratín. — Don Silvestre Pinheiro Ferreira, our civics teacher. — Romanticism. — Alexandre Dumas. — General San Martín in France. — General Morillo.

Among the European nations whose ships began to frequent our coast as soon as our war of independence permitted it, England and France were the most eager to gain the friendship of the new state that was just opening its coveted ports to the fruits of foreign industry.

This was one of the reasons that led the French Minister of the Navy to authorize the commanders of his Pacific fleet to offer free passage in their supply ships to the sons of Santiago's influential families who might want to continue their education in France. It fell to Admiral de Mackau, who later became Minister of State under Louis Philippe d'Orléans, to convey these generous sentiments toward Chile and even to have the pleasure of exaggerating them, as will be seen in the events that I shall recount and that, since they took place very much within my own family, are generally unknown.

In 1823 there were as yet no foreign commercial establishments in Chile, and the French had chosen the very prosperous firm of Don Felipe Santiago del Solar to receive their vessels and the merchandise that they were beginning to send from their country to our nascent republic.

The Baron de Mackau, commander of the French naval frigate *Clorinda,* which at that time was riding grandly at anchor amidst the British and North American ships in the bay of Valparaíso, had gone to Santiago with some of his officers and was lodged in my father's house, where, to make his stay more enjoyable, he was treated like a king.

Chilean territory was not yet entirely free of Spanish rule, for the dreaded Quintanilla still dominated the vast range of islands to the south of Chiloé. This did not, however, stop our corsairs from devastating Spanish commerce from the waters of Valdivia to those of Guayaquil, for our feluccas, the only vessels we then had, were cheerfully plundering every Spanish merchantman they could get their hands on. The firm of Solar alone boasted four corsairs, whose flagship, *El Chileno,* had inflicted such damage on Quintanilla, capturing every supply ship sent to him from Peru, that in exasperation he fitted out a famous vessel, *La Quintanilla,* which, under the command of one Martelí, quickly demolished Solar's entire flotilla and forced *El Chileno,* the only boat to escape its talons, to seek shelter beneath the batteries of Valparaíso. Our worthy Baron de Mackau learned of what was going on from Solar. I do not know what they said to each other; but I do know what happened then, for the fact is that the dreaded *La Quintanilla* was presently captured by the frigate *Clorinda* and the no less dreaded Martelí found himself a prisoner aboard the French transport *Moselle.*

These merry pranks and others like them, which there is no need to consign here; the constantly increasing contact with foreign lands brought about by commerce; the arrival on our little-frequented shores of talented men like Lozier and of many another who, without being any great shakes in his own country came to make it big, and to do so effortlessly, in ours; the favorable reception that for these reasons the spontaneous hospitality of our drawing rooms accorded to everything foreign, even if the foreigner were nothing but a simple peddler adorned with the free and easy manner of the *commis voyageur,* the art of tying his tie, and the no less attractive one of being able to dance the newly introduced quadrilles and teach others to do so—all of this led many a father to think that an education, if it was to be good, could only be acquired in civilized Europe, and many a mother, and even daughters who until then had scarcely ventured into the field of social pastimes, to believe that the source of gallant conversation and the true *comme il faut* that charms a salon could be found only in France or England.

Thus even before we Chileans learned of the benevolent disposition of the French government toward the youth of America, Carlos Pérez Rosales and Juan Enrique Ramírez had set out, for England and Scotland, respectively; and on January 16, 1825, the French naval transport *Moselle* sailed for France from Valparaíso with a cargo of young Chileans.

Where were they bound, these young men, their parents' pride and hope, and the envy of those whose impecuniousness condemned them to the schools of their homeland? They were on their way to France in search of an easily acquired knowledge, never suspecting for a moment that wisdom awaited them there in quite the same way that gold awaited many another who twenty-four years later thought he would scoop it up by the shovelful in California.

The *Moselle's* merry passengers were Santiago Rosales, Manuel Solar, the four Jara-Quemada brothers—Lorenzo, Ramón, Manuel, and Miguel—Antonio de la Lastra and his brother José, José Manuel Ramírez, my brother Ruperto Solar, and I.

Subsequent to this first expedition, but no longer transported by the French navy, others set out for the same destination: Calixto, Lorenzo, and Víctor Guerrero; Rafael, Santiago, and José María Larraín Moxó; Bernardo, Domingo, Alonso, and Nicasio Toro; José Manuel Izquierdo, Manuel Talavera, José Luis Borgoño, Ramón Undurraga, and Miguel Ramírez. Except for Manuel Talavera, Calixto Guerrero, Bernardo Toro, and Miguel and José Manuel Ramírez, all of these young men, including those who went on the first voyage, were placed in the famous school run by Don Manuel Silvela,[19] unique in its time both for the renown and intellectual qualifications of its celebrated teachers and for the great number and wise distribution of the various branches of human knowledge that were taught there.

19. Manuel Silvela was a Spanish émigré. JP.

What remains of all that gilded youth of Chile that in search of learning crossed the seas to envied Europe? Only memories of fruitless efforts and three witnesses to the overall failure: Don Rafael Larraín Moxó, Don Domingo José de Toro, and the feeble hand writing these lines.

Unless he has first given them a basic education, it will always be a mistake for a father to separate his sons from family and country and send them to Europe to study in twisted French or bad English what they can learn in good Spanish in Chile. A young man should go to Europe only when, after receiving an education and learning in Chilean schools all that can be learned there, he wants to perfect his professional training or acquire that other knowledge that marks the man of the world and that can only be acquired in the intercourse with all manner of people that comes with travel, in the thorough study of men's customs, and in direct contact with the children of the most civilized nations of the Old World.

And so those of us who went there came back having learned little more than the wretched ABCs, unable even to claim that in knowledge we could match those who, bemoaning their inability to follow us, had never left Chile. Yet in all fairness it must be confessed that to this day no one has managed to excel us in useless learning, in Frenchified language, or in opining ex cathedra on every subject.

I see, however, that I have strayed from my voyage aboard that famous *Moselle* that caused us so much suffering. We sailed on her accompanied by the prisoner Martelí; and after a voyage of thirty-six days, during which I again rounded Cape Horn, I could for a second time gaze upon Rio de Janeiro and that terrible Praia Grande upon which I had been cast four years earlier, abandoned by the refined cruelty of Lord Spencer.

Rio de Janeiro in 1825 was the same overgrown village as in 1821, just four years older, a town of slave traders, haphazardly laid out, with no thought for cleanliness and no provision for sanitation after midnight, for since there were no fixed sanitary depositories for those residues whose name so struck Victor Hugo when issuing from the mouth of an angry Cambronne, barrels whose only lid was the open air above them came down from every direction to infect the shores of the bay's placid waters. With a few exceptions, the more splendid the appearance of nature in that place, the greater the negligence and slovenliness of its sweaty inhabitants.

Then, as in 1830, 1845, and 1860, when I had occasion again to visit that imperial capital, I did not find a single building, including the imperial palace, that would bear comparison with any of the public or private buildings of present-day Santiago.

I was struck then by the church that was joined to the palace and served as their majesties' oratory or chapel, not so much for its architecture as for the kind of singers that made up its great choir. Who would have thought it! Those singers whose silvery childlike voices accompanied the holy sacrifice of the mass, all of them sons of the then dismembered Italy, were victims of that immoral mutilation that fits one as a harem guard in polygamous Turkey. The same effect that this act, sanctioned by human greed, produces in a calf, it also produces in a man. Those unfortunate choristers had the voice of a woman, the face of a child, and a bloated body and abdomen. Were they happier than other men? Who can say?

At that time, Brazil, whose good fortune had spared her having to pass through any of the storms that had almost unmasted our ship of state in our struggle against the Spanish mandarins, had already, on March 25, quietly ratified her constitution, which her children, for reasons unknown to me, call the third oldest in the world.

The favors that are bestowed as freely as those the French government bestowed on us usually come at a high price. We had to leave the *Moselle* in Rio de Janeiro because of the harsh and almost brutal treatment we had received at the hands of her good captain; and continuing our voyage on board a French boat commanded by Captain Blatin, we reached the entrance to the English Channel one hundred two days after leaving Chile and shortly thereafter found ourselves in the interesting French port called Le Havre de Grâce.

There seems to be a competition among the English Channel, the Bay of Biscay, and the Caribbean to see which should outdo the others in its equinoctial storms. The annual shipwrecks in those turbulent waters are counted not by tens but by the hundreds. Cherbourg, Le Havre de Grâce, whose name proclaims what it was before human skill and effort made it what it is today, and many other ports are clear proofs that any bad anchorage or even hint of an anchorage can be made into an excellent harbor. That is why it is shortsighted of us to neglect the roads leading to the dangerous ports between Valparaíso, itself a bad harbor, and Concepción Bay. If the French had found, where now the great harbor of Cherbourg stands, the natural advantages offered by the port of Topocalma and by the shallows and lagoons of Vichuquén and Boyeruca, and if, in order to make the Seine navigable from its mouth on, the French had counted, as we count in Talcahuano, with shallows that the flood waters of the Bío-Bío fill and that pass right by Concepción and flow out next to the harbor, how much more easily could they have built the harbor of Cherbourg,[20] and for how many years would the Bío-Bío by now be open to river and ocean traffic, bypassing the dangerous bar at its mouth!

What a job it was to build the port of Le Havre! Construction had barely commenced on the breakwaters that were to protect it from the inroads of the highest tides, which wind would turn into raging seas, when during the night of January 15, 1525, a third of the town's population drowned in a sudden rise of the waters that threw as many as twenty-eight vessels into the moat of Gravelle Castle. Similar accidents occurred there in 1718 and 1765, and on the former occasion the force of the wind was such that even today people speak in shock of how a thirty-six-pounder cannon was ripped from its emplacement along with its gun carriage. Well, thanks to human effort, that same place today boasts the safe and very busy artificial harbor where we had just landed.

No one thought of linking the Seine to the sea by battling against the bar and sand banks that its rough waters created at its mouth, as we have several times thought of doing with our Maule, believing that an artificial increase in its waters might push the bar out to sea, a notion whose absurdity is made plain by a study of the mouth of the mighty Amazon, whose violent waters, even while forming a bar, push out forty leagues into the sea without mixing with those of the ocean. The mouth of the Seine is used only to take advantage of the shallows that the low tides left on its eastern shore. These shallows, enclosed by walls and deepened by the dredge and the crowbar to the level of the lowest tides so as to turn them into spacious esplanades of calm water, are now the anchorage where, side by side in symmetrical rows and with no need of an anchor, the hundreds of ships that yearly visit that port lie, after an easy entrance protected by breakwaters, as secure as in a cup of milk.

In 1825 Le Havre had three basins of water linked by canals, and the three could easily hold up to two hundred deep-draft vessels. As a place to live in, there was nothing remarkable about it. On the contrary, the only impression made on my memory by that fortified town (of the third rank, to be sure), with its moats, arsenals, and shipyards, its four stern and unwieldy gates, its scanty population, which consisted of only 22,000 residents and 4,000 transients, and its purely military and mercantile character, was of what human skill and labor can achieve when struggling determinedly against the material obstacles that nature sometimes puts in the way of their aims.

• • •

20. It is, however, Le Havre and not Cherbourg that lies at the mouth of the Seine. JP.

I left Le Havre the way a migratory bird leaves the way stations on its route; on the fifth day after my arrival in envied Europe, and after a tiresome all-night ride in the tumultuous coaches of Lafitte & Caillard, I found myself in Paris, that celebrated city, center of all that is good and all that is evil, of the merry and the sad, the home of good taste and ridiculous excess, and the favorite spot for idle pastimes and dissipations, baptized by good old Victor Hugo with the pompous title of "the brain of mankind."

When it comes to regaining their youth, cities have the advantage over men. Few in this world have seen more years go by than the ancient Lutetia, a town that Julius Caesar himself called an *oppidum,* which shows that even back then it had pretensions to the rank of capital. Compared to the Paris of my third visit, that of 1859, the Paris that I first saw in 1825 was like the figure of a deformed man scratched onto a wall with chalk and charcoal, by the side of an artistic portrait displayed in a museum. That does not mean that its palaces, its churches, its academies, and the museums that hold so many treasures were not then in existence, because most of these marvels of the human spirit did already exist; but it seems truly incomprehensible how such precious jewels could be set in so crude a mounting, scattered as they were and as though hidden in a huge overgrown village that had been expanding as chance would have it with no plan of any kind, a town of twisting dead-end streets, some wide, others as narrow as could be, and most of them dark, humid, and fetid, their pavement in disrepair, wretchedly lit by whale oil whose feeble light was supplemented by earthenware jars filled with tallow and burning wicks that the police would place by the potholes to keep vehicles from overturning.

That Paris of 1825 was gone by 1859. Louis Philippe d'Orléans had already begun to transform it by extending its limits, surrounding it with powerful fortifications with the appropriate gun emplacements, and laying out elegant streets from one side to another, when his unexpected successor, Napoleon III, with the threefold aim of depriving the city's revolutionaries of their natural lair, giving work to the idle hands always ready to join any disturbance, and beautifying the city by means of costly demolitions that spared nothing, drove through the midst of that ancient and intricate labyrinth the splendid wide streets that now bear the pompous title of avenues.

There was nothing elysian about the Champs Élysées other than the cleaner air that you could breathe there as you left the center of town. The Bois de Boulogne was a small wood reserved for royal hunts and, because of its isolation, the place dedicated to the bloody requital of personal offenses.

The opposite side of town had, for the same use, the forest of Vincennes, differentiated only by the two blackened towers of the fortress that stood at its entrance and served as a Bastille, and in whose moats a doleful monument marked the spot where the Duc d'Enghien had been murdered on orders of Napoleon I. Apart from this, the constant movement and agitation, the idlers, the joys and storms, the fashions, the follies of the coquettes, the dissipations, the aristocratic balls and those others distinguished by the can-can, the caricatures and witticisms, the duels, the wealth and poverty, live and reign in that great city today just as they lived and reigned back then.

In Paris you can live on pennies or on millions and still, with pennies or with millions, be always poor and in debt up to your neck.

Foreigners are right to praise the perfection of the musical and dramatic performances that are the delight of that metropolis. The general belief is that no actor can make a go of it if he does not succeed in Paris.

The Paris of my youth had nine theaters of some importance in their time, in addition to many others of lesser or even least standing. If you wanted to soak in classicism and hear the French language spoken with academic perfection, you went, until 1827, to the Théâtre Français, where the celebrated Mars was still performing. If you wanted your fill of jokes, barbs, and puns, you had the Gaîté; for horrors like the terrible *Thirty Years, or The Life of a Gambler,* there was the Porte Saint-Martin, the Théâtre de l'Ambigu, and others; for merry light music, the Opéra Comique; for music serious and also merry, though of another school, there was the Théâtre Italien, filled with the lithe trills of the frigid Sontag,[21] whose throat seemed to hold a nest of nightingales, and the powerful, moving, supple voice of the incomparable María Malibrán García, the pride of Spain and the delight of France, Belgium, and England, where she performed in turn, an artist who, according to the newspapers of the time, was worthy of being served and adored by both Thalia and Melpomene; and for majestic music they had the Opera, famous then for the richness of its sumptuous decorations and for the voice of the one tenor whom the French recall with pride, Nourrit, who committed suicide when he learned that another man sang as well as he did.

For the gay exhibition of erotic fantasies, no soil is more fertile than the boards of a stage, and not because their devotees find there better

21. *Sontag.* All editions consulted read *Santag,* but the author evidently refers to Henriette Sontag (1806–1854), a celebrated German soprano, who made her Paris debut at the Théâtre Italien in 1826 and returned in 1828. She was admired for the excellence of her voice but considered unexpressive and cool in her acting. JP.

and cheaper charms than what they might find without, but because of every man's itch to possess whatever other men admire. On the stage of the theater, as on the stage of life, this seems to be a general rule, even though we all know that where fiction is everything, everything must be fiction.

Nonetheless, in the wandering guild of those who earn their living imitating the vices or virtues of others, hiding genuine tears beneath counterfeit laughter, or bestowing ardent kisses of tenderness on those whom they would gladly send to blazes, now and then you will find sincerity, which necessity obliges to be insincere. Such was the case of the artist I have just mentioned, the justly famous María Malibrán García, daughter of the celebrated tenor García and sister of the well-known Viardot whose voice charmed the Russians in the imperial theater of St. Petersburg. Malibrán was an actress only on stage. I still remember an incident I know to be true and whose details appeared, discreetly disguised, in *Le Constitutionnel* in 1828.

One morning it occurred to one of those idle men, be they enviable or worthy of pity, whose wealth sometimes exceeds the demands of dissipation, to send Malibrán a perfumed sheet of paper enfolding a bank note for a hundred thousand francs and inscribed with these brief lines: "Mademoiselle: A moment's private interview, its day and time to be decided by you, is the boon requested of you by your obedient humble servant, Heine." The letter and its enclosure were returned with this laconic reply: "I am not for sale; and if misfortune should oblige me to forget my duty, it would not be with you. M. M. G."

Heine conceived the generous whim of handing both messages to the editors of *Le Constitutionnel* with the request that against suitable remuneration they print some philosophical observations on them. The editors limited themselves to publishing both notes, along with the initials that authenticated them and with this single remark: "Now let them say that money will buy anything!"

And since my pen has somehow strayed onto the terrain of gallant deeds, I shall devote the ink it still holds to recount an instance of Spanish gallantry that managed to capture the attention of the news-hungry capital of France for two whole days, which is practically forever.

At that time, in 1828, one of the pupils in the school, enrolled there by the Spanish ambassador, was a pleasant young fellow whose face reflected, as might a good mirror, the features that Fernando VII himself must have displayed as a boy. I naturally do not know which of these two reasons, if not both, accounted for the respect with which this young man was treated; all I remember is that we were schoolmates, that his name was Fernando Solís, and that he called the ambassador his father. It was Fernandito who told me the banal little story I shall now recount, to which he was a witness in his so-called father's home.

The Spanish embassy had decided to put on a lavish party in honor of the brilliant Duchesse de Berry, who was at the time the least disliked person among those who made up the court of the devoted old huntsman Charles X of France; and this, as is always the case, sufficed to produce an admiring chorus of Fortune's spoiled favorites, to make tailors, dressmakers, and hairdressers work overtime, and even to cut the Gordian knots that closed many a purse that could not be otherwise opened. I had already seen the guest of honor from quite close up at the Théâtre du Gymnase, a name that at her request, and because he considered her the patroness of the arts, the good Charles X had changed to that of Théâtre de Madame. The truth is that I had failed to see, in her splendidly decked-out little figure, either the beauty or the admirable elegance that the flatterers of the court attributed to her.

Marie Caroline de Bourbon, widow of the murdered Duc de Berry, must then have been at least thirty-nine years old; but these years, which for a Chilean woman can sometimes even mean old age, had not yet ravaged the duchess's true charms, for she could still feel rightly proud of a matchless complexion, silky blond hair, well-rounded arms, and two tiny feet that, though ever so slightly pigeon-toed, were the delight of connoisseurs, a fact of which she was well aware. This merry and capricious Neapolitan was, furthermore, the mother of the Duc de Bordeaux, heir presumptive to the French crown, later Comte de Chambord and currently pretender to the royal name of Henri V; and this fact augmented the consequence she enjoyed in her own right.

It was then the custom at court balls to lay carpets out onto the sidewalk of the street leading to the palace gates and to station handsome young men at the threshold to receive the female guests as they arrived and accompany them into the building. One of the sudden downpours that frequently descend on Paris had just soaked the carpet placed on the sidewalk in front of the embassy, in addition to filling every pothole in the street's wretched pavement with water, when the duchess's carriage arrived with much clatter of horses and footmen in livery. That night the dazzling guest was wearing a pair of stockings reputed to be worth the fabulous sum of five thousand francs. Who could think of exposing such an artistic masterpiece and the accompanying splendid shoes to be defiled with smears of vulgar mud? The greeters at the door were in a quandary. A single long step would suffice to reach safe ground, but a step too long for a woman. What might be the solution? Laying down a board would be ridiculous; to go for another carpet would cause delay; lifting the lady in one's arms, as one young Frenchman proposed, was too disrespectful. Wild confusion reigned, until one gallant young Spaniard among those assigned to the embassy serenely placed his elegant three-cornered hat in the mud and held out his hand to the new arrival, saying, "This way, your highness." This graceful gesture of refined gallantry was admired and applauded by all; and his courteous sacrifice, accepted without hesitation by the duchess, gained the happy son of old Spain the honor of escorting the lady all that evening, as well as the praises of the prying reporters of the press. Official history is silent about what happened later; as for unofficial history . . .

Soon this sweet child of thirty-nine will reappear in my narrative, so little given to gossip, and then we shall see the difference between fame and fact. But let us not deprive freer and fancier pens of the right to paint or describe Paris, a very Dulcinea of a town that has the power to convert all who visit her into amorous Don Quixotes.

The return of Fernando VII to the throne of Spain had populated France with learned Spaniards whose liberal ideas obliged them to seek asylum beyond the Pyrenees; and I had the good fortune to become closely acquainted with several of these eminent men: the renowned mathematician Vallejo and the distinguished men of letters and of the law Moratín, Silvela, Ferrer, Salvá Saavedra, Mendíbil, and Maury.

A school for Spaniards had just been established at 9 rue de la Mi-Chaudière under the direction of Father Prado and Professor Vallejo, to whom I owe my inclination toward the natural sciences and what little I know of them.

Vallejo was a tall portly man with puffy small but intelligent eyes, a high forehead, and a formidable nose. When he walked alone he moved slowly, his progress almost always interrupted as though by suspension points. Fanatically devoted to the science that has made his name immortal, he would work through many a night so absorbed in his calculations that when the school bell rang reveille, he thought it was the signal for lights out and was greatly surprised when, leaving his study, he stepped into bright sunlight. These sleepless nights and constant cogitations gradually so weakened his head that he finally conceived the delusion of having found an infallible means of freeing mankind from the disastrous effects of earthquakes.

He had taken a special liking to me; and since in our recesses and even during our joint excursions into the environs of Paris for the purpose of training me in map-making he never spoke to me about anything other than his *Quakeblocker,* I soon became convinced that the learned professor would eventually go mad. This was all too true, for I had the painful experience of seeing him taken off to the hospital in Lyons, which at the time was famous for the treatment of madness, that saddest of human ailments.

Those whom political transgressions force into exile always form, in their places of asylum, groups in which they can vent the laments and grumblings that their common misfortune fosters. Among the many Spaniards who at that time were atoning in France for the sin of sensible patriotism, one who stood out for his frequent visits to the premises on the rue de la Mi-Chaudière was the distinguished mathematician Don Andrés Antonio de Gorbea; and to be sure, never in my contacts with that eminent educator did I dream that I was dealing with the future Chilean of whose learning and special training in the natural sciences his students in Chile would be justly proud.

The wretched state of Gorbea's finances in France can be gathered from the pleasure with which in 1825 he accepted the meager salary of five hundred pesos that Don Mariano Egaña, who was the Chilean minister plenipotentiary, offered him to go to Chile as a teacher of mathematics. Toward the end of that same year the poor exile came to our school leading his little son Luis de Gorbea Baltar by the hand to entrust him to the fatherly care of Vallejo, who in happier times had been his mathematics teacher. Luis de Gorbea Baltar was my fellow-student in Prado and Vallejo's school during all the time that I remained in that educational institution, until I transferred to that of the eminent jurist Don Manuel Silvela. Thus Luis did leave his country to obtain an education, and thanks to his devoted father's sacrifices he was placed in the reputable school that Prado directed in Paris. I have tarried over this insignificant event so as to restore to Señor Gorbea his reputation as a father devoted to the education of his son, a reputation that the latter seems to have attempted to deprive him of when he wrote to Don Salustio Fernández, Gorbea's biographer, that he had never gone abroad for his education.

In 1822 another victim banished from Spain lived in the shelter of a poor garret at 117 rue d'Orléans in the city of Bordeaux. To judge by the furniture in that miserable refuge, you would have thought that the tenant's poverty was extreme, though, to be sure, such a conclusion seemed to be contradicted by a collection of some three hundred books that, in the absence of shelves, were carefully lined up on the bare floor of the apartment. On the bindings of these books appeared the names of Lope de Vega, Solís, Moreto, Calderón, Cervantes, Rioja, Argensola, and other leading lights of the Spanish Parnassus. The master of so unenviable a den, a man of medium height, rather stout than thin, with large head, bulbous nose, lively little eyes, thick lips, and a fair though wrinkled and faded complexion, was then over sixty years of age, and his favorite occupation seemed to be leafing through his tomes, taking notes on them, jotting things down, and ordering his manuscripts.

On the afternoon of the first of November of the abovementioned year, this curious recluse had just written these words in small but clear letters beneath the title of one of Lope's comedies: "Ghosts, some fine verses, and lots of nonsense," when he heard someone knocking at his attic door. With rare exceptions, poetry and poverty have been and always will be inseparable companions, and so when the unfortunate old man heard the knock, no longer having anything to pawn to pay the rent due that day and chagrined by the cruel thought of having to sacrifice his books, the sole constant companions that brightened his exile, he dropped his pen, rose with an effort, and opened the door in deep distress.

The man who had been knocking was tall, thin, of a sallow olive complexion, with a large curved nose, cross-eyed, too, and standing so straight and stiff that he seemed to be Don Quixote in person coming to succor the damsels in distress of Parnassus. No sooner was the door open than mutual cries of joy and surprise were heard and the two fell into each other's arms, exclaiming "Manuel!" and "Leandro!"

The newcomer was Don Manuel Silvela, the learned jurist known in the Roman Academy of Arcadia by the name of Logisto Cario; and he had come to aid the leading dramatic poet of the Classical school of the nineteenth century, his friend Don Leandro Fernández Moratín, the celebrated Inarco Celenio of the same learned body.

Five years later the important Spanish and Spanish-American school known until 1832 by the name of its learned founder Silvela was flourishing on the rue de Monteuil in the Parisian Faubourg Saint-Antoine. Although the appearance of that remarkable man gave no sign of the talent hidden within, hearing Silvela speak once, with his easy cadences, his ever opportune and pertinent replies, his clear and erudite explanations, brimming with maxims and precepts that flowed effortlessly from his eloquent lips, was enough to gain him the respect and affection to which such enviable gifts entitled him.

In that huge and important educational institution, which from the day of its founding became the refuge of every penniless Spanish intellectual who ate the bitter bread of exile, Don Leandro Fernández Moratín taught Spanish literature, Silvela, Ferrer, and Mendíbil taught the classics, Dom Silvestre Pinheiro Ferreira, a former minister in Portugal, taught civics, and the mathematician Planche replaced Vallejo, who had just gone mad. Except for Planche, who was French, all those I have named and many others who contributed their stock of learning to the education imparted in that exemplary institution owed their involuntary residence in France to the restoration of the Bourbons in Spain.

Nonetheless, as I had occasion to discover later, what some French biographers declare about Moratín is not accurate. This author was not driven out of Spain by royal edicts but by his own excessive timidity. He thought he would be persecuted as were others; this, and none other, was the reason he faced death by starvation abroad.

This profound and witty writer was ever the victim of his modesty and timidity, which choked him into silence and even made him appear simpleminded whenever a stranger suddenly joined the company of friends whom Moratín was captivating with his delightful and always illuminating discourse.

Never have I known a man of letters more devoted to the purity of the language or more strictly observant of the laws of the Classical school. In these two capital respects he was uncompromising with everyone, and ultimately even with himself, for as his devotion turned into obsession he began to scribble emendations on everything he had written up to that time. He would have continued to do so if Silvela, annoyed by what he called sacrilege, had not one morning taken away his books and manuscripts. Yet it was in our school that Moratín gave the finishing touches to his work on the origins of the Spanish theater; and as I kept catching him in contradictions, his fondness for me made him confess that he was the author of that amusing pamphlet titled *La derrota de los pedantes (The Pedants Routed)*, a work that could have ruined him in Spain had it borne his name, for a literary affront that wounds men in their self-esteem is always unpardonable.

Moratín had his hands full with my New World pronunciation; when least I expected it he would leave me speechless with an inspired smile and his inexorable refrain: "Keep studying, my boy; you can't always hide nonsense under an exotic accent." On three occasions I took my first literary efforts to him to get his opinion. Each time he made me read them aloud and then, without a word, placed the sheets in an envelope, sealed it, and wrote on it: "I forbid you to rework this draft. Reread it in six months, and your own opinion then will be what mine is now."

If writers, new and old, did the same, how much drivel would be spared the light of day! They would be astounded by what they had considered masterpieces only six months earlier.

The ease with which Moratín composed verses was extraordinary; had he not been such a slave to perfection, he could no doubt have said of his comedies, as did Lope de Vega,

> More than a hundred times I sent a play
> From pen to stage within a single day.

I remember that a month before he died, as he was chatting with me about the raucous soirée that some blasted cats had held in the attic the night before, he peppered his speech, despite his ailments, with such displays of wit that I asked him, in my usual foolish way, "Why don't you write an epic poem, sir, that will demolish all those rascals?" "My, my," he replied, "an epic poem, eh? All right, my boy, get ready to write; everything you need is right here on the table." I obeyed at once; and had I not seen it with my own eyes, I would never have believed that that old man, racked with pain, his digestion in ruins, could still have in that extraordinary head of his, along with the inexhaustible stream of philosophical epigrams that flows only from age and experience, the fresh mischievous imagination of a child. In very little time and with very few pauses he dictated to me, in a canto and a half of octaves, the first part of the most original and amusing feline epic. Moratín was sitting by the stove as he dictated; and seemingly tiring of his effort, he asked me for the manuscript so as to give it the finishing touches. Unfortunately I obeyed him; and as soon as the paper left my hands it went from his into the flames, with the requiem, which dismayed me, "That's enough nonsense!"

Moratín was unmarried and had no desire to marry; he feared women, but he never treated them with the cruelty shown them by Quevedo.[22]

One month after this feline adventure, the Muses, dressed in mourning, attended the funeral of the man who had until then been the leading dramatist of the nineteenth century. Moratín died in my arms on June 21, 1828; and in 1853 you could still see a modest tomb, paid for by his students, in the Cemetery of Père Lachaise, between the grave of Molière and that of La Fontaine.

While he was alive, no one had given him a thought; had it not been for Silvela, he would have starved. After his death, however, every newspaper in Europe lamented the loss that Spanish letters and the Classical school in general had suffered. Fernando VII himself, the king of Spain,

22. Francisco de Quevedo (1580–1645) was the author of much satirical prose and verse. JP.

who was not always evil when he followed his own inclinations, wrote with his own hand to Silvela, asking for Moratín's printed and manuscript works so as to have them published under his royal patronage, and conferring on whoever might be his heir a life pension of four thousand *reales* to be paid from his private purse.

Spain was not the only country to banish her sons in those days; Portugal did the same. The former minister of João VI, Grand Master of the Order of Christ, and learned legal author Dom Silvestre Pinheiro Ferreira, driven from Portugal, came to Silvela's school, the refuge of several outcasts, thereby increasing both their number and the stock of learning disseminated by that outstanding educational establishment.

Our civics teacher was then some sixty-two years old. His body was small but well proportioned; his forehead, broad and imposing; his small eyes, lively and intelligent; his nose, large and curved; and his mouth, similar to that which we see in statues of the author of the *Esprit des moeurs*.[23] Pinheiro was a true polyglot and left works written in several languages. During the time that he spent at the school in the modest but honorable role of a simple teacher of civics, not once was he heard to mention the elevated position he had held in his country, nor did he fail to make use of every free moment to complete those works that were to bring immortality to his name.

Until 1826 the conflicting literary schools of Classicism and Romanticism waged an underhanded but extremely bitter war in France. The Classical school was the despot of the classrooms and could count on the legacy of learned antiquity and on the vitality that its restrictive rules drew from the inexorable non plus ultra of what was then called "good taste," based on the masterworks of the phalanx of brilliant minds that the age of Louis XIV had given France. Romanticism, struggling to break free, had until then been unable to bring down a tree held up by such mighty roots; and it would have remained under the yoke of the rules codified by Boileau in his *Art poétique* for who knows how much longer, had not the remarkable mind of Victor Hugo, a young man at that time, taken upon itself, fearlessly and resolutely, the task of liberating the prisoners of Classicism by bringing to the stage his famous *Hernani*, which, like a hurricane, swept away every Classical rule that stood in its way.

23. Pérez Rosales writes *Espíritu de las costumbres;* but since he habitually translates everything into Spanish, I take this to be a translation of a French title. I have found no work with this title in Spanish or in French and suspect that the author is citing from memory and referring to the *Essai sur les moeurs et l'esprit des nations,* by Voltaire, of whom there is a celebrated bust by Houdon. JP.

I attended the first performance of this drama, most reluctantly staged by the Théâtre Français, which until then had been the throne of the purest Classicism. On the first day, the impression made by the bold defiance embodied by this work was not as stormy as I expected; but from then on, the uproar, inside the theater and out, that its performances produced among the modern and old-school literati who attended them was so great that the performances of *Hernani* became more cacophonous than theatrical. The Classicists organized companies of derisory whistlers; the Romantics, companies of approbatory clamor and supporting fists. The simultaneous shouts of "Down with this play!" and "Away with bad taste!," accompanied by the shrillest whistling, were answered by the drumbeat of feet on the floor and thunderous replies of "Let 'em perform!" "Long live Victor Hugo!" and "Down with reaction!" The battle of shouts was followed by that of shoves, and shoves were followed by blows; at the sound of "À la porte!," so common and so feared in French theaters, you would see, coming out through the doors but still entangled and cursing (and in their chaotic exodus dragging along even the unfortunate policemen who were trying to separate them), knots of men of letters who in their blind fury were ready to spill their last drop of ink in support of their party.

A few days later splendid dramas, comedies, and farces began in effect to appear, in which the two parties made merciless fun of each other. To sully the Romantic system, the Classicists put on a frightful farce in which they had a child being born in the first act while one or two other characters are killed, and then in the third act this child dies of old age, in the midst of so many other deaths that even the prompter stuck his head out of his box to kill himself with the candle snuffers. The Romantics replied with *Avant, pendant et après*— before, during, and after the revolution—a most remarkable work, concerning which the ardent Classicist Silvela told me, "And the worst of it, my boy, is that that drama interests people, draws them in, and teaches them something." Moratín, less given to compromise than Silvela, only brought out, as though speaking to himself, "What a waste of talent!"

From that point on, the strength of the two schools that had been fighting for the presidency of the Republic of Letters in France was equally matched. Such equality could not, however, last long, because once the minds of the young writers were freed from the somber precepts of Classicism, the new school acquired masses of recruits; and so hardly had Hugo appeared on the stage when the celebrated Alexandre Davy Dumas, a poor young man just turned twenty-six, boldly entered the lists of innovation.

This remarkable author, product of his own studies and works, had begun his arduous literary career with some novels and projected plays that gained him nothing. Steeped in the precepts of the English and German schools and excited by the success just achieved by Hugo, he managed, through the influence of the Duc d'Orléans, in whose office he was working as a scribe, to get the austere Théâtre Français, the throne of Classicism, to allow his just-completed *Henri III* to be performed there. The opening night of this drama in 1829 was noisy in the extreme; and if at the opening of *Hernani* the shouts of the innovators restricted themselves to jeering the Classical precepts, at that of *Henri III* one could hear imprecations even of "Death to . . ." against poor Racine and the dreaded Boileau, according to whom there was no salvation for an author outside the rules of his art of poetry.

It was written that the triumph of Romanticism with its unbridled but attractive liberty was to be complete. The bell was tolling for the reign of the precepts of Aristotle, Horace, and Boileau, the Ten Commandments of good taste according to the strict Classicists—and small wonder, because the stubborn rules of an antiquated school, defended only by tradition and an occasional writer of the first rank, were under simultaneous attack from Goethe in Germany, Byron in England, Hugo in France, Manzoni in Italy, and Espronceda in Spain, where the memories of Calderón, Lope, Tirso, and Alarcón lay so near the surface, and from a reinforcing swarm of innovators like Dumas, Rivas, Tapia, Gil, and many others who seemed to be springing up everywhere.

I first saw Dumas in 1829, at the opening of his *Henri III*, and I met him twenty-seven years later. At the time of the earlier occasion, as he himself told me laughing, he had only twenty pesos a month on which to live in Paris; by the time I met him, he had already squandered fortunes and enjoyed an income of eight thousand pesos, all derived from his pen. Such is the power of letters in what many call frivolous France, which nonetheless houses true merit in palaces and reserves the wretched garret, the usual shelter of our poets, for idleness and incompetence.

Why should not I, too, portray this remarkable author who enjoyed such success in the literary world, even if I must make use of the brush with which in the old days Mena used to paint trees for the decorations of our theaters? Dumas was of normal height, rather stout than thin, with the complexion of a mulatto and black eyes as mischievous as they were lively. His mouth held an enviable set of teeth whose whiteness flashed in frank and frequent bursts of laughter, and his head was covered with a veritable fleece of curly wool. His talent exceeded his solid education, and it made him the king of the popular writers of his day; as he wrote, he had the knack of delighting his readers, tricking the press, and lying with the greatest of ease. In his lifetime he dictated more than anyone could copy, and he made short work of the sin of plagiarism by declaring that any idea that could be dredged up from any book was fair game. Poetry, finally, was his Dulcinea and a part of his life even among the pots and pans of his kitchen, where the father of *The Three Musketeers* frequently displayed his culinary talent.

Those who have nothing better to do than to peruse these lines have no doubt noticed that all my teachers had large noses; and since they were all known to be learned men, the question naturally arises: Might there be some more or less direct relationship between that facial appendage we call the nose and the intelligence of its bearer? In popular speech, having a long nose means being foresighted. Quevedo had a big nose; so did Cervantes, and I am sure that Moreto and Solís, Lope and Calderón, if their portraits are to be trusted, were not underendowed in this respect. Ovid was not called Naso because he was snub-nosed, and what worthy Cicero lacked in the way of a nose was made up for by the formidable *cicer* or chickpea that adorned such nose as he had. True enough, Socrates was snub-nosed; but that rather proves the excellence of large noses, because there is no rule but has its exception. I shall therefore entrust this problem to the physiognomists and go on spinning my reminiscences of those times—alas!—past.

The year 1829 had begun and nothing had disturbed the peace and quiet of Silvela's school, when an unexpected event suddenly sowed the seeds of raging discord in that temple of learning.

General San Martín, the hero of the Andes in 1817, the soldier who had refused a presidency in Chile and a crown in Peru, the selfless patriot who, according to poison tongues, had stowed away in the Bank of England funds derived from his position and from less than honest transactions during the brilliant period of our struggle for independence, was still living, poor, alone, and forgotten, in the European exile that with such remarkable willpower he had imposed on himself when he had no more enemies to defeat in America.

San Martín had just come from a school in Brussels where he had obtained a scholarship for his attractive only daughter Mercedes, whom he had brought with him from Buenos Aires. As soon as he had learned that in Paris there was a Spanish and Spanish-American school where many Argentineans, Chileans, and Peruvians were studying, he hastened to visit the sons of his former companions in hardships and triumphs.

San Martín's presence in the school overjoyed the Chileans and Argentineans but produced silence in the Peruvians and displeasure in the Spaniards. The general came to the school on foot, despite the distance that separated it from his modest dwelling. He wore a gray frock coat, fully buttoned, and suede gloves of the same color; and he carried a heavy walking stick. At first he did not recognize me; but when he saw me rushing to embrace him with delighted shouts of "General!," he embraced me most cordially, then held me at a distance while looking at me carefully and asking where I was from and of what family. My reply seemed to call forth a tear of tenderness in those proud and serene eyes that had so often faced and despised death on the fields of battle. That scene, during which he affectionately embraced in turn every student who came to greet him, was the perfect image of what happens in a family when a beloved father unexpectedly comes home. The memory of this remarkable man was a true marvel, for there was hardly a member of any of our families about whom he did not solicitously inquire.

Since these recollections have turned out not to be the posthumous work that I had intended, I have had to omit many a page whose historical import makes its publication as yet premature; but I now restore the following pages to their place, since on sober consideration they neither deviate from my personal yarn nor invade the territory of stern Clio.

I never failed to accompany my beloved general back to his lodgings whenever he came to visit us; and one day, as we sat enjoying the shade of the beautiful trees of the Tuileries, our conversation came to touch, among other matters, on the following.

The general, who seemed to enjoy loosening my tongue, said, "So even a schoolboy had to shoulder arms at Mendoza, eh? My, my, I'm really delighted to have such a charming comrade in arms at my side after all this time!"

"General," I replied, "it seems to me that the comrade you've just discovered is not one of those who are ornaments to the art of killing to the sound of music, because if I entered, or they entered me, into service as a mere auxiliary with his sword still virgin, that's exactly how I left it, and so it's never occurred to me to do what so many other soldiers of my ilk do, that is, to hide that virginity and play the hardened strumpet so as to claim the rewards of service."

The old soldier burst out laughing when he heard this, and, without letting me go on, asked, "What were they saying about the Argentineans in Chile when you came over here? Did they still remember the Army of the Andes?"

"Sir," I answered, "there are things that can never be forgotten, and the crossing of the Andes is one of them."

"That's fine," he replied, "but that's not exactly what I wanted to find out. Do I still have those few genuine friends that I had in Chile when I left there? Because friends in name, my dear friend," he went on, affectionately laying his hand on my shoulder, "are just as numerous around the man who's in a position to award jobs, as his genuine friends are scarce."

Moved by the expression that appeared on the general's face as he finished his sentence, I answered, "When Freire came to power, many of your close friends, since they were also friends of O'Higgins, fell silent, and others, like Solar, whose home you visited so often, have been torn from the bosom of their families in the middle of the night and made to pay in exile for the crime of having befriended the hero of Rancagua."

"And so for the same reasons," San Martín replied animatedly, "my reputation must not be all it might be over there."

"That's true," I said, "because . . . I don't dare . . . ."

"Do dare, my dear fellow," he said to encourage me, "just imagine you're talking to one of your schoolmates. 'Because,' you were saying . . . ."

"Because just as O'Higgins has his enemies there," I continued timidly, "so, too, you have yours, because very few among those who cherish the first period of our emancipation fail to blame you and Don Bernardo for the disastrous death of the Carreras, whose execution they call pointless and brutal murder; and gossip also accuses you of dirty dealings in the administration of the money that Chile entrusted to you for use in the liberation of Peru."

When he heard this, San Martín violently buried his face in his hands and remained in this tense position for so long a time that he might as well have been calling up painful memories as feeling the bitter resentment that human ingratitude always evokes in generous hearts. I was beginning to regret my excessive frankness in answering him when he straightened up and breathed hard, muttering, as though to himself, "Lousy Gringo, miserable little admiral, who thought he'd been robbed whenever there was something he couldn't pocket! Excuse me, dear fellow, I don't know what I was thinking of. So that's what they say over there? Well, I suppose they have their reasons. And now you tell me: What would you Chileans have done with three Argentineans who, because rightly or wrongly they'd been not only poorly received but even persecuted by the Chilean government, had, with the most patriotic intentions, turned to being, two of them, revolutionaries, and the third, a bloodthirsty outlaw? What would you have done, if these three Argentineans had fallen into your hands, when you saw law and order in danger and Chilean blood shed by the third of these foreigners at the very gates of Santiago? Would you have needed the advice of an O'Higgins or of a poor San Martín to have them shot? As for dirty dealings," he continued, smiling sorrowfully after casting a sarcastic glance at his clothes and minutely examining his thick chamois gloves, shiny with use, "you can see for yourself!"

Poor friend! I still regret having touched on so repulsive a topic during that conversation, for embezzlement was the last thing San Martín could be accused of. I knew how scrupulously he had administered the funds that had come into his hands, but I was ignorant of many of his acts of generosity toward the country for whose freedom he was fighting. I did not know that the ten thousand pesos—an enormous sum at that time—given to the hero by the city of Santiago to pay for his return to Buenos Aires had been donated by him for the construction of what is now our National Library; nor did I know, among other generous acts of that beautiful soul, that even the propagation of smallpox vaccination cost San Martín a third of the income from an estate he owned in Santiago, yet San Martín was a poor man!

When I returned to Chile toward the end of 1830, my close relationship with this old and revered friend, with whom it was as pleasurable to converse as it was instructive, came to an end. I lost sight of him at that point; and twenty-nine years later I had the painful experience of finding only clear but sad reminders of him in the home of his son-in-law Balcarce, which stood a few kilometers from Paris on the banks of the turbid Marne. There, under the care of the lovely granddaughters of that hero of our independence, his modest furniture was kept religiously in place in the small room he had occupied, and on the night table that stood beside his cot you could even see an ashtray among whose cold ashes lay the remains of his last cigar. On the walls of that room, which the whole family called "Father's room," hung some weapons, and among them that oilcloth hat and curved sword with a chain in place of a guard that had served as glorious emblems for the patriots of Chacabuco and Maipú and that are perfectly reproduced in the equestrian statue that adorns the entrance to our broad and well-known Calle del Dieciocho.

Sad indeed is the fate of the great benefactors of humanity when the history of their worthy deeds is entrusted to myopic pens that, like pedantic literary critics, dare in their smugness to judge what they are incapable of imagining, let alone writing. The heroic deeds of San Martín have been ill served by those who have made bold to comment on them; in what is the height of foolishness, I now see the spread of a mad insistence on linking Bolívar and San Martín, not to erect altars to these venerated fathers of our American fatherland, but to put them in the dock of the accused, to compare them, to draw sacrilegious conclusions from the comparison, and even to use it to flatter local pride, as though the fatherland of Bolívar were not also the fatherland of San Martín.

San Martín and Bolívar are nothing but the two sublime halves of the one sacred and indivisible whole that the hand of the nineteenth century shaped for the redemption of America. These two halves were placed in different hemispheres; and each, acting spontaneously in the field that fell to his lot, decisively and gloriously carried out the task that abnegation and patriotism imposed on him. Bolívar would not have done more in the southern part of the continent than the son of Yapeyú could have done in the north. What would have become of one without the other? Those two sublime halves, therefore, were born to complement each other, and it is always unjust to compare them.

But I see that my recollections make me stray from the narrative order imposed by dates, and so I return to the consequences of San Martín's visit to Silvela's school.

The Peruvians and the Spaniards, whose alliance against the Chileans and the Argentineans I have never been able to understand, began to isolate us and even to attack us surreptitiously; yet the troubles would have ended there but for another incident, as fortuitous as the presence of San Martín in our school, that occurred a few days later and made the situation worse, creating additional fuel whose explosion was to close the doors of that remarkable establishment forever.

General Morillo, that valiant and fierce soldier who had fought against Bolívar in Colombia, a hero to the Spaniards, a monster of cruelty and opprobrium for the Americans, also came to visit our school. The body of this rough and robust soldier, with his cold and piercing eyes, in whom the general's epaulets could not hide the coarse shell of his fierce instincts, was covered with scars. My classmate Torres, whom he had placed in the school, told me that during periods of changeable weather it was impossible to get to sleep when he was near, because as he slept his old wounds would then draw from him not groans but roars of pain. This soldier's presence in the school pleased the Spaniards and, for some reason, the Peruvians—who, though they did not come out to meet him, were glad of his visit—as much as it displeased the Chileans, Argentineans, and Colombians, among whom there was one who had to be held back from going to insult Morillo in the very reception hall.

The result of these two visits was inevitable; if the July Revolution of 1830 had not come to give a new direction to the antagonistic spirits of the school's one hundred eighty students, there is no doubt that the theretofore peaceful, orderly, and edifying activities of an institution still venerated by all who knew it would that year have ended in brawls and turmoil.

V I

Symptoms of the July Revolution of 1830. — The conquest of

Algeria. — The July Revolution. — More on the Duchesse

de Berry. — The ridiculous finale to the Parisian visit of

the Dey of Algiers.

C harles X of France, a king whose passion was the hunt, was punctilious in his religious devotions and strongly attached to the rights and privileges enjoyed by his predecessors before demagoguery and ungodliness had come, as he used to say, to shake the foundations of the peaceful and legitimate throne of his forefathers. He could not bear having occasionally to steal precious time from the pleasures of the chase and those of hearing his mass in the comfort of his royal chapel in order to attend to the affairs of state, and even less could he bear having to put up with the blasphemous authority exerted over him by parliament by virtue of an outlandish political institution called a constitution. He was old, none too bright, more good-hearted than ill-intentioned; and his reluctance to yield to the enlightened political demands of the age stemmed only from his desire resolutely to defend what he considered rightfully his, the heritage of his forefathers. Since the extent of this heritage had already been defined by these forefathers with the ringing phrase "La France, c'est moi!" it was hardly surprising that at the least sign of encouragement from his corrupt courtiers he set out wholeheartedly on the perilous road of restorations and on August 8, 1829, named the hated and energetic Prince de Polignac his prime minister to carry them out.

Parliament, which had just forced Villèle from office because of his reactionary tendencies, was alarmed but by no means intimidated by this new ministry and not only took up the challenge but in no uncertain terms expressed its disapproval of the sovereign's imprudent and dangerous policy in adopting such measures.

The reply to this unexpected defiance was a royal decree dissolving the parliament. Next came an appeal, as the saying goes in such cases, to the judgment of the nation; and the parties plunged frenetically into the electoral struggle. One side represented the sacred cause of sound principles; the other, that of ancient royal privileges supported by the brute strength of bayonets. Since neither side was prepared to yield and since it is an unquestionable fact that in a political battle the first to succumb are the leaders, it was clearly Charles X who was most exposed to this danger in case of defeat, and not his ministers, as his simple mind had led him to believe.

The imprudent sovereign, deaf to all advice and shut up in Versailles, where his mind was occupied only with the deer hunt in his royal forests, could not see what was happening outside, and the blare of the hunting horn kept him from hearing the roar of the political storm that his ministers were rashly provoking as they staked his crown on a single and most dangerous game of chance.

We all know what can happen to the best of laws when special interests are involved and particularly when the results of heated elections are exposed to fraudulent manipulation, just as we know how much rancorous energy the victims of injustice store up in their hearts and how enthusiastically they seize the chance for revenge. From what so often happens among us, then, you can deduce what must have happened there at that time, because when men of like ideas find themselves in like circumstances, they are alike also in their actions.

The government's newspapers set about disseminating the most outrageous doctrines. According to them, the reelection of deputies that had been members of the dissolved chamber was not only illegal but an act of rebellion; Polignac's personal organ, *Le Drapeau blanc,* had the audacity to roar, "Down with budgets, down with concessions, down with the Constitution! Plain bayonets are more than enough to bring the unruly mob to their senses!" To the further dismay of the defenders of the constitution, the rumor was spread everywhere that their efforts would be vain and even dangerous because the government, should it lose the vote, was prepared to have recourse to a coup d'état that would sweep away every concession that "the monarch's benevolence had bestowed on the country," and perhaps leave the bold innovators in a state worse than what had obtained before constitutions and demagogic novelties had begun to raise their impious heads.

Incredible as it may seem, in many parts of the kingdom fires were even set to provide pretexts for mutual recriminations and stir up the masses. The royalist papers, in reply to the charges of the constitutionalists, declared that all these ills were due to the Revolutionary Directorate, which designated the victims and chose and liberally remunerated their executioners.

In the midst of this disorder and these preparatory threats, everyone's eyes naturally turned to the army; and since the troops might become contaminated, an international insult that France had sustained three years before at the hands of the Algerian authorities provided Polignac with the opportunity to insulate a substantial force from the constitutional party, using it to add luster to his government while also holding it in reserve as a reliably royalist defense against the government's enemies. The logical result of this happy thought seemed to be to mount an overseas expedition, and one was soon mounted.

Those dens of obstinately incorrigible pirates, Numidia and what was formerly called Mauritania, whose depredations had been punished successively and in vain by each and every maritime power in Christendom, would perhaps, to the shame of civilized nations, have endured for many more years, had not an injustice on the part of France and the insulting act with which the sovereign of the Regency of Algiers responded to it sounded, in 1830, the last hour of independent existence for that African state.

Since the time of the Republic, France had owed large sums that Algerian merchants had advanced her for shipments of grain, and the debtor seemed to be in no hurry to reestablish her credit. Since the demands for repayment were, however, becoming more frequent and insistent, the French consul in Algiers, M. Deval, had been entrusted in 1827 with settling the matter, with a view more to getting rid of those demands than to satisfying them. According to what Abd-el-Kader himself told me years later, the consul's subterfuges so annoyed the Dey that, bursting into insults against France, he struck poor Deval in the face with his feather fan. As was to be expected, this rather intemperate act of Hussein Pasha's not only wiped out France's debts at a blow but transformed her creditor into a debtor. A French fleet soon came to blockade the Algerian ports, but only after three years of this blockade did the political need to remove troops from demagogic influences so as to have them ready for later use turn the blockade into an invasion.

On May 16, 1830, a powerful fleet commanded by Admiral Duperré set out for the coast of Africa from Toulon, convoying transports that held a landing force of 36,000 men under the command of the famous old Marshal Bourmont.

The expedition reached its destination on June 13; on the 14th it landed in the bay of Sidi Ferruch, just outside Algiers; on the 19th it won the memorable battle of Staouéli, defeating 40,000 Bedouins; and on July 4 Hussein Pasha, under vigorous attack from the French and after seeing the demolition of his own residence, the castle built in the capital by the mighty Emperor Charles V, surrendered, receiving permission to transfer his person, his treasures, and his favorite odalisques to the British fleet that was there as an observer.

The capture of Algiers was announced with carefully premeditated fanfare in the middle of a performance at the Opera at 11 P.M. on the 5th. The music stopped and the famous and esteemed tenor Nourrit dashed onto the stage proudly waving the lily banner and proclaiming the news of the happy event to the audience. All of us, Frenchmen and foreigners, left the building without waiting for the conclusion of the opera, and the cafés and streets of news-hungry Paris were soon filled with rejoicing masses. The enthusiasm of victory soon faded, however, before the political concerns that deeply worried most of the sons of that great city. For them, whatever was not the triumph of their ideas was simply trivial; and right they were, because their liberty was in peril and the electoral campaign, in which intrigue, promises, threats, and political fanaticism had openly played a part, left no room for other concerns.

No one was prepared to compromise, to split differences: it was all or nothing.

The Duc de Doudeauville, the Comte de la Ferronays, the confirmed royalist Martignac, the Comte de Chabrol, and many another partisan of absolutism had been stripped of their ministries for having tried to give conciliatory advice.

The expectation of an electoral defeat for the ministry then so provoked the royalists that they became imprudent enough to assume that the government was preparing a coup d'état that would once and for all smash those who disturbed what they called blissful public tranquility.

England, whose mind was ever active, was watching events beyond the Channel attentively though, it seemed, impassively; she realized that this possible coup would inevitably entail political upheaval. The *Times* of July 5 therefore asked what England should do in case France again followed the path of revolution; in order to prepare public sentiment, it was careful to reply that whatever domestic changes a revolution in France might bring about, England should maintain a policy of strict non-intervention, unless France should attempt to reach beyond her borders with the intention of disturbing the peace of Europe.

From August 3, the day of the opening of parliament, the dreaded coup was advanced to July 25; and on the 26th the *Moniteur* published the decrees that rode roughshod over constitution, oaths, and institutions, abolished parliament, muzzled free speech, and restored the privileges of yesteryear in their full force.

The first reaction of an offended nation was shock—not the shock born of fear, but that momentary paralysis during which a man seems to gather his strength before, in the next instant, falling in a frenzy on the offender. That afternoon at three o'clock I was coming back from my swimming lesson; and since I already knew all that was happening, I, unlike many others, was not surprised to learn that twice the usual number of sentries were on duty, to observe detachments of soldiers slowly patrolling squares and boulevards, and to see half the population of Paris out in the streets, forming silently menacing groups here and boisterously confrontational ones there, and tearing down the ominous posters with the immortal decrees that were to prove so costly to Charles X.

The court removed to Saint-Cloud, leaving the unfortunate city under the command of that Marshal Marmont, Duc de Ragusa, to whom so much misconduct is attributed. Villèle had abolished the National Guard, and so only some units of regular troops and the *gendarmerie* were left in Paris, a total of fifteen thousand men, who were considered sufficient to bring even the most stubborn revolutionaries to their senses.

On the morning of the 27th, police units, assigned to seizing all dissident newspapers before they could be distributed, visited printing establishments, destroyed their chief pieces of equipment, and imposed fines and other punishments on the editors for the least item published without previous permission from the authorities.

The diligent but imprudent Mangin, the prefect of police, then had the cafés and reading rooms shut down, in spite of which broadsheets rained down on the streets from invisible presses, and people calmly read these sheets before the very bayonets of the many patrols that were crisscrossing the city.

As threatening crowds gathered, incited by students from the Polytechnical School and the Faculties of Medicine and Law, factories and workshops closed down, as did the gates of the Tuileries, the royal palace of Orléans, and the elegant shops of the rue de Richelieu, the rue Saint-Denis, and the rue de Saint-Honoré. Troops occupied the squares, the boulevards, and every other corner of the city that might serve as a gathering place.

But all was in vain; it was written that blood should flow, and flow it did, since the troops had no other way to contain the angry populace, which, though unarmed, attempted to snatch away the prisoners that the gendarmes had been taking to maintain order. That first blood was the fuse that produced the immense general explosion that, to the terror of mankind and as a lesson to tyrants, drowned the most charming capital of civilized Europe in blood for three days in a row. During the night of that day, and during the next two days, the infuriated people broke open the doors of armories, set up barricades by overturning carriages in the streets and filling them with paving stones, turned houses into fortresses and every square and crossroads into a battlefield where boldness, bravery, and rashness seemed to be vying to see which could wreak the greatest carnage.

Black flags flying over many a building; bells sounding the alarm; the roar of the royalists' cannons; that of their rifles; the shouts and tumult of the combatants; the sidewalks made slippery by pools of blood; the dreadful piles of corpses that surrounded the burned-out or still burning guard posts; the crosses over the half-dug graves by the famous colonnade of the Tuileries, with terrifying inscriptions denouncing tyranny; the rafts loaded with human corpses, launched one after another on the waters of the Seine in the direction of Saint-Cloud, bearing placards proclaiming, "Make way for the people's justice!"—all of this announced the inevitable and disastrous fall of the elder branch of the House of Bourbon in France.

And what was Charles X doing while his good Parisians were being butchered on his orders? It is said he was hearing mass when the news came that the triumphant populace, seizing every carriage it could find on the outskirts of Paris, was coming after him, prepared to overwhelm the detachment of his guards.

Meanwhile the Duchesse de Berry, that sensitive and delicate creature whom we have seen in the Spanish ambassador's ball vying with her sex in the art of pleasing, showed herself to be more lively and alert than the sanctimonious Charles by fastening a brace of pistols over her riding habit and preparing to face the angry citizens of Paris and rekindle the feelings of loyalty that the monarch's ineptness had extinguished. Charles X, astonished when he saw the duchess's resolute demeanor and heard of her reckless intentions, stopped her and shouted, "What are you going to do?," to which she angrily replied, "Defend my son's inheritance, since you either can't or won't!" Then there was great commotion in the palace; and the duchess, arrested by order of the king as she was coming down the stairs leading into the courtyard, exclaimed in her desperation, "My God, now I understand my full misfortune in having been born a woman!" These words, like those that genteel historians attribute to General Cambronne at the Battle of Waterloo, are wholly apocryphal. At the time there was no mouth in Paris but what repeated the words that the pampered and refined little duchess, converted into a fury, had actually allowed to flow from hers to denounce the weakness and effeminacy of the whole royal family, which stood around her crossing themselves, because that kind of language could only be heard among fishwives. Poor duchess! The subsequent story of her life was an outlandish odyssey in which, till the day she died, the terrible and the absurd vied for the leading role.

Meanwhile the shrewd Louis Philippe d'Orléans, who seemed to take no part in the enormous upheaval he was witnessing, continued nonetheless to be its most powerful animator and the secret leader of those thoughtful men who considered a constitutional monarchy the only government suitable for France.

What an admirable people the French are, and how easily they pass, in the words of a favorite popular song, from love to battle, from seriousness to wit, from ardor to calm! For three days this people fought with a seemingly uncontainable fury, yet those three days were filled with examples of the noblest generosity. Riding roughshod over every obstacle, the citizenry forced its way into the palace of its kings, and ragged beggars sprawled on their throne; yet not one case of theft, not one work of art vandalized (with the exception of busts of Charles X) gave evidence of the passage of those rustic republicans through the royal halls of the dethroned monarch!

On the 30th, when the dreadful roar of battle had fully subsided, and while the rubble of what had been the archiepiscopal palace, the barracks, and the guard posts were still smoldering and the blood that had soaked the pavements and the barricades was still fresh, I ventured out of the Faubourg Saint-Antoine, eager to learn the fate of the Chileans who were then in Paris. With a good deal of effort, since I had repeatedly to climb over barricades, and filled with a fear more easily understood than described, after an hour and a half I reached the rue d'Artois, where Don Javier Rosales and other compatriots of mine were living. My chest was covered with tricolored rosettes, which a multitude of women dressed in all their finery were charmingly distributing to passersby, themselves placing them with elegant gestures and patriotic words on every lapel they encountered on the streets.

Don José Joaquín Pérez, who at that time was the secretary of the Chilean legation in France, excited by my accounts of what I had seen on the huge battlefield I had just traversed, went out with me to discover the meaning of a disturbance that was then under way on the rue Lafitte. We reached a barricade that almost completely blocked the door to the house of old Lafayette, whom the shouts of the crowd had forced to come out to be taken to the palace of the Duc d'Orléans, and who was struggling to break free of those who were trying to take him there in a sedan chair. We approached, and hardly had we heard that venerable son of revolutions say, "Let me be, my friends; I'll go on foot! *Je suis jeune aujourd'hui,*" when a mass of people rushing in from one end of the street, and another of regular troops unexpectedly coming from the other end, caught us in a most risky and dangerous trap. Although, as Fate would have it, the opposing forces, instead of attacking each other, ended up by fraternizing, the fright we experienced then has yet to be equaled.

The 31st was, in Paris, the day for enthusiastic demonstrations. That day Louis Philippe, abandoning all pretense, went on horseback to the Hôtel de Ville, where Lafayette was waiting for him. Hand in hand, the two stepped out onto the balcony overlooking the square; and there, amid the most clamorous enthusiasm of thousands of spectators, I saw them embrace each other. Louis Philippe was from that moment on captain general of the kingdom, and eight days later he was proclaimed king of the French.

Charles X and his son had already abdicated and chosen the coast of Scotland as their future place of residence. Both were received there with the same silent indifference that bade them farewell as they left the coast of France.

Le Figaro, a small but very witty French newspaper of that time, charged with writing the obituary of the ex-king of France, limited itself to these words: "The July Revolution was a disaster for the rabbits of Scotland."

But let us not concern ourselves only with misfortunes and political upheavals. Let us for a moment follow our worthy Hussein Pasha, whom, after the loss of his African domains, we last saw taking refuge, with his treasures and his odalisques, on board the flagship of the British fleet that was observing events in the Bay of Algiers. What does the reader suppose was the exiled monarch's first thought after settling into his new quarters? Perhaps to turn to the Sublime Porte? To beg England for her valuable assistance in the recovery of his lands? To offer an indemnity to

France? None of that, not on your life! The first thing that occurred to him to help him forget the mischance that in an evil hour was brought on his head by his hand's readiness to apply his fan to the face of a crooked consul, was to go live it up right in Paris.

That is exactly what he did; and the unfailing gallantry of the French, not satisfied with putting him up in the palace of the Tuileries, decided to dazzle the defeated guest with a magnificent performance of *Mahomet* in the royal theater of the Opera. That night so many curiosity-seekers swarmed to the theater that we barely managed to find orchestra seats at twenty-five francs apiece. The two boxes facing the stage, converted into one and adorned with Oriental splendor, drew the attention of the public, since they were to lodge the African visitors. As the performance was about to begin, a universal agitation, accompanied by lively whisperings, announced the entrance of the procession all were waiting for, whose members slowly and solemnly went about taking their places. The Pasha, whose bulk quite packed his chair and who must have been about sixty, though he looked younger, was a man rather tall than short, flushed of face, of florid complexion and Hellenic profile. His eyes were lively, his brows thick, and his beard carefully spread over his chest. He wore a long cloak of finest cashmere and, on his head, a shiny tall kind of headgear lavishly adorned with precious stones; at his waist shone the diamond-studded golden hilt of a damascene dagger. Behind this exotic personage, who called to mind the figure of the Great Lama, two powerful blacks took up their stations like two statues of ebony, harem guards in Berber caps, embroidered vests, and baggy trousers, displaying the gilded handles of their fierce daggers. Flanking this silent centerpiece—for this trinity impassively watched everything—were, so to speak, two wings composed of nine lovely Algerian ladies, in whose faces nature seemed to have delighted in massing the fuses that might cause all the powder in French hearts to explode. Like schoolgirls, they were all dressed alike, their costumes closely resembling those worn by wealthy Greek women, but with such an abundance of pearls and jewels that one could well say that each of them carried a whole treasure on her person. Despite the exquisite thin veil glittering with bits of silver that with studied negligence was draped over the faces of those angels worthy of an altarpiece, we could make out that eight were brunettes with wide black eyes and one a blue-eyed blonde, and that the oldest among them could not have been over twenty-two.

The performance began with the usual solemnity; but the public, instead of watching the stage, aimed every opera glass at the enchanted box where the ardent imagination of the French expected at any moment to see the fantastic tales of the *Thousand and One Nights* come to life. In vain did the silver voice of Nourrit, the matchless one of Damoreau Cinti, the graceful leaps of Paul,[24] the charms of Taglioni, and the marvelously agitated little legs of tiny Montécu attempt to attract the customary attention of the public; none of these amounted to a hill of beans in comparison with the exotic visitors' box.

It was only natural that the Dey's wives should experience something similar with respect to the young men who were gazing at them, especially when they could so easily compare the apathetic dull lethargy of the stern and bearded patriarch with the courteous glances of so many handsome and gallant youths who seemed to desire nothing more than to find favor in their eyes.

Between the marvels of the electric telegraph and the marvels of the visual telegraph, I'll put my money on the latter. The former speaks only the language of the country in which it operates, while the latter speaks every language there is or ever will be. Mastering the former takes study and concentration; expertise in the latter requires only having reached the age of puberty. I engage in these reflections because how much the French must have said in Arabic that night, and the Bedouin ladies in French, became plain when two days after the performance all his timid spouses somehow flew from the trusting Pasha, just as a band of captive pigeons scatters when its keeper forgets to close the cage door.

Hussein, angered by what one must call an abduction, fell upon the eunuch then in charge and without further ado ordered the other one to cut off his head and hang it on the balcony as a lesson for negligent servants. The cries of the menaced black, blending with the Arabic curses of the Dey, brought the palace servants and guards running. They freed the poor prisoner from the furious hands that threatened him and warned his master of the danger he faced in France should he commit even the slightest homicide. . . . Change of scene! The helpless monarch sadly and silently ordered his bags to be packed, mounted a post coach with a single servant and his few remaining riches, and, as he wished the asinine country where a man cannot do as he jolly well pleases with his own property to the devil, I last saw him on the road that leads to the border of the Germanic Confederation.

Two weeks later I had occasion to see the abovementioned odalisques again, no longer bejeweled, but dressed in French style, walking about with new masters or in search of others, for those they had first found, content with plucking their finery, had abandoned them.

24. *Paul.* Mademoiselle Paul was a celebrated dancer and mime. JP.

VII

How wrong we are when we think the whole world knows us.
— Beginnings of the railroad in Europe. — Bordeaux. —
Wines and chicanery. — How to make use of sandy terrain. —
A lucky escape. — Tenerife. — Tropical seas. — South winds.
— Effects of a lack of drinking water at sea. — Doubling
and redoubling Cape Horn. — The Falkland Islands.

E very nation, no matter how insignificant, suffers from the inborn
weakness of thinking that all other nations are very much aware of
it, or at least that they are often concerned with it. Anyone who tries to
convince its citizens of the contrary therefore risks being considered a
fraud or having to suffer the displeasure of them all.

Chile was as little known in the Europe of 1830 as are the mountains
of the moon among the Chileans of today. This is a plain and simple
fact. For the overwhelming majority of Europeans, there are only two
nations in Spanish America, Peru and Mexico; in the dictionary of these

learned men, Peru and Mexico are synonymous with gold and revolutions, although it is very true that the foreign ministries of the great maritime powers do Peru, Mexico, and the other remote corners and peoples who are satellites of these stars, the honor of considering them capable of paying unjustified indemnities.

In Chile we all know each other; in the world at large, the nations that inhabit and reign over its surface know each other very little. It would, then, be as ridiculous for the Chinese to laugh at our ignorance because very few of us know that Nanking is not a fabric but a city, as it would be for us to grow angry because in China they have not even a suspicion that we exist over here.

I have allowed myself this digression so as better to find an excuse for the Parisian official who was to issue me a passport to Chile and who did not do so because I refused to sign a declaration that Chile and Mexico are one and the same thing.

"What country are you from, sir?" this official asked me.

"The Republic of Chile."

"What did you say?"

"Chile, sir."

"What's that? Chile—what a name!"

"Yes, sir," I replied with some annoyance, "Chile, one of the American republics. What's so odd about that name?"

"Aha, aha, *de l'Amérique*, eh? . . . *Chili* . . . Chile, wait a minute . . . Chile. Why don't you just tell me what town you're from, sir, because I've never heard of any Chili."

"I'm from the city of Santiago, sir."

"The devil!" the learned official exclaimed at this point. "Why didn't you come right out with that in the first place?" And turning to his clerk he dictated these words: "V. Pérez Rosales, a native of Santiago in Mexico."

When I heard this outrageous rubbish I fired off an expletive and exclaimed, "Chile, not Mexico!"

"Well, get out of here," the Gallic geographer said at this juncture, rising from his chair, "and don't you come back till you know what country you're from!"

A month and a half later I returned to the same office, from whose direction the recent July Revolution had expelled the learned expert in geography for whom you had to say "Mexico" if you meant "Spanish America"; and with some difficulty, though not as much as before, I solved my problem.

It was no easy matter to travel in the Europe of 1830; it was all done in carriages similar to those operated by the enterprising Carpentier on the southern roads of our Chile before the railroad came to liberate voyagers from such tortures. At that time the railroad was barely beginning to show signs of life in bustling Europe, and one can well say that the need to reduce the cost of transporting the products of the coal mines is chiefly responsible for the existence of this instrument of wealth and human industry.

The first rails were nothing but hardened and leveled dirt. They were followed by wooden beams on which the wheels of the cars ran smoothly. When this invention gave surprisingly good results it was modified by the addition of narrow strips of iron to protect the wood from wear; finally, rails were made of iron alone, each one a meter long, with its ends resting on large stones sunk into the soil and serving the same purpose as wooden ties do now. These railways, much used in the coal mines to amplify the strength of the horse that pulled the cars, soon extended beyond the mines to serve commerce in general. In 1829 I had occasion to travel between Portsmouth and London, through the county of Surrey, on a railroad of this kind, where a single horse trotted along pulling three cars with more than ten tons of cargo.

Steam traction was also beginning to be tested at that time; and thanks to the invention of the famous Oliver Evans, a small three-horsepower engine that I saw operating in Newcastle began, with its automatic movements and surprising strength, to astonish all who observed this marvel of physics and mechanics, which, placed in the midst of twenty cars, would push ten even as it pulled the other ten, just as a powerful horse might do with the most insignificant weight. It was, however, only experimental and could not be used on a large scale, not only because of the defects of the machine, but also because it had not yet been shown that friction against the rails, aided by the weight of the locomotive, provides sufficient traction for pulling the cars of a whole train. Consequently the locomotive ran on cogwheels, and the rails on which it ran were also cogged. Who, looking at these modest beginnings, could have seen in them the results that today lie before us!

Battered and sleepless thanks to the heavy carriages of the great firm Lafitte & Caillard, toward the end of 1830 I arrived in Bordeaux in search of a ship that would carry me back to Chile.

Bordeaux is located on the northern bank of the deep and placid Garonne, a river that rises in Spain and after a navigable course of more than a hundred leagues enters the Bay of Biscay with the name Gironde. The city lies twenty-five leagues from the mouth of this valuable waterway; at the time I am speaking of, it had a population of a hundred thousand souls and was considered one of the richest and commercially most important in France. Within its irregularly laid out confines there was no lack of beautiful squares, broad streets, gardens, and public promenades; and among them stood the historic remains of a Roman amphitheater and the ruins of the Palais Gallien. Furthermore, Bordeaux had the best and most beautiful theater in France and the famous bridge with its seventeen spans, three-quarters of a mile long, built over the navigable waters of the Garonne. In addition, this port, which could hold more than a thousand ships and boasted docks, huge warehouses, shipyards, and every facility required by navigation and commerce, was made an even more pleasant place by its fine climate and by every establishment that philanthropy, religion, sciences, and arts require in a center of civilization.

Since wine is one of the chief treasures of the south of France, and since Bordeaux is the center of that industry, the first thing a traveler thinks of is a visit to the vineyards, the chief wineries, and above all the cellars where the wine is stored and undergoes special treatments, which are always hidden from the eyes of indiscreet curiosity. After spending a month most attentively visiting the wine-growing regions whose products are exported from Bordeaux and taking note of all the statistics I could get hold of, I confess that I was unable to understand how so strictly limited a production, which, though large, could not possibly satisfy the needs even of purely domestic consumption, managed inexhaustibly to pour out cases, barrels, and whole shiploads to the most remote corners of the earth.

Who but one initiated in the mysteries of the *conditura vinorum* of the ancient Romans could solve the problem of explaining why, when the good labels of Médoc are so limited, there is no corner of the earth, no matter how obscure and unknown, where the table of the rich man with contacts in Europe does not proudly bear bottles of Lafitte, Margaux, or Latour, wines so scarce that they never moisten the lips of countless European drinkers eager and able to buy them at any cost?

Chateau Lafitte is not even a French firm, because it belongs to Mr. Samuel Scott, who ships every barrel of wine produced by its 180 acres to England. Chateau Margaux belongs to the wealthy banker Aguado, to whom the Europeans pay court so that he will leave them some part of the wine produced by its 200 acres of not yet fully planted vineyards; and Chateau Latour, in a good year, only produces about 110 barrels of wine.

As luck would have it, in Bordeaux I ran across an old schoolmate who at the time was working for a major wine exporting house, which, like all of them, boasted of being the only one to export the genuine article. "Bear in mind," my artless schoolmate told me, "that here the only surplus wine that is or can be available for export has to be either very bad wine, produced from the very worst harvests, or counterfeit wine that has about as much of the grape about it as I have of a Frisian horse. All the good wine produced in the south of France isn't enough for the gullets of the big shots of France and England, but don't you worry about that, because we're here to make up this deficit and supply our foreign customers. There's nothing," he added, "that has a more or less sugary juice that can't be used to make wine, and just as in their dairies the English have the pump of their well that they call 'the black cow' and that lets them send more and more milk to market, so here we have sugar cane, honey, pears, apples, sugar beets, and from time to time, believe it or not, even bunches of grapes, to make and multiply our wines. Aroma, taste, color—these are nothing to worry about as long as we've got essence of muscatel, elder and grapevine flowers, strawberries, campeche wood for dyes, sunflowers, red lac, and other such trifles."

All of this does not mean that artificial wine is always more harmful than natural wine. In fact, it is far less harmful than natural wine when the latter is of such poor quality that it requires mineral additives to mask its acidity. These and other reasons help us understand the justification for the ingenious tricks of Monsieur de Jacourt and the no less admirable, though older, ones of the famous Baccius in his *Naturali vinorum historia,* published in Rome back in 1596.

But counterfeits do not surprise me, because both in the physical realm and in the psychological, bad merchandise that does not seem good will not sell. What surprises me, what drives me wild, is watching the magisterial and self-satisfied air, the matchless solemnity with which many of the supposedly best connoisseurs of wines sip and savor their glasses of the artificial stuff, extolling it before their guests as *grave pur sang* and showing them, just to clinch it, the brand name, the seal, and even the catalogue of the reputable exporting house.

Falsified wine, or rather, the art of falsifying wine, was born the same day as the grapevine. The Greeks suffused their famous Chios, so appreciated by the Romans, with seawater; according to Pliny, even good old Cato, for all his sterling reputation, falsified wine so perfectly that he managed to fool the best bibber of his time. The prudent reader can calculate how much more he might have done had his name been merely Lafitte, Margaux, etc., etc.

During my excursions through the wine districts I frequently had occasion to cross part of the great sand flats that there they call *landes,* which somewhat resemble those that in Chile form near the mouths of the rivers, as in Talcahuano, Boyeruca, and some areas along the banks of the Bío-Bío. Such dunes, whose moving sands are not only unsuitable for cultivation but, driven by the wind, invade whatever cultivated lands lie near them and make them sterile, and which not many years ago were considered entirely useless in France, are now a genuine source of wealth there. Agriculture has succeeded in conquering the instability of the sands and has, furthermore, found useful trees to plant there.

I have no doubt that what is done in the *landes* of France we could as profitably do with our own dunes. The procedure for stabilizing and utilizing the moving sands is exceedingly simple. The French peasant begins by building a fence that will block all traffic over the sandy area that he wants to utilize; then he levels it with a rake and at the appropriate time spreads chaff, mixed with cheap grass seeds, over the ground at the rate of about nine bushels per acre, using a short-toothed rake to cover the mixture. The seeds soon sprout and achieve a respectable development, as grass always does, even if set on a bit of damp cotton; and soon the interwoven roots form a true carpet, whose fabric, as long as the hooves of animals do not disturb it, completely checks the instability of the sands, so that trees planted in them can begin to grow. The peasants, who to avoid sinking into the sand walk on enormous stilts, immediately plant the terrain with that kind of coastal pine called pinaster, which is characterized by its long and thin bunched needles. This planting occurs as soon as the sowing is completed; and the sapling, about a meter high, raised beforehand in seedbeds, develops admirably in the sandy soil. The local people thus achieve the triple benefit of giving solidity and fertility to dunes long considered useless, of obtaining an abundance of fuel and lumber, which they previously lacked, and, finally, of channeling into commerce the great quantities of resin that the pines produce upon the simple removal of strips of bark from their trunk and the placement below of vessels to receive the resinous sap that flows from these wounds.

Although I have often glimpsed the protective action of the guardian angel who seems to watch over the preservation of my life, never have I seen the hand of Providence more clearly than when I started my return voyage to my country in the last months of 1830.

There were three ships in Bordeaux completing their lading before setting out for Chile: the *Petite Louise,* the *Newcastle,* and the *Carlos Adolfo.* The captain of the first, without the least plausible reason, refused most obstinately to allow me to occupy a good cabin on board his ship. When I went to inspect the vessel's accommodations he was so rude to me that much to my regret I was forced to go on to the *Newcastle.* Her captain, who seemed to be cast from the same mold that gave human form to his ill-mannered colleague on the *Petite Louise,* refused me the cabin that, though it was not his best, I sought to occupy; the reasons he alleged were so nonsensical that they amounted to chasing me off his ship. Irritated by being thus unjustly excluded, since I had never haggled about the cost of the passage, I went to the *Carlos Adolfo,* where Captain Ticaut, a model of civility, not only assigned me the cabin that I had chosen, but even offered me his own in case I should fall ill in the course of the voyage.

The three ships left Bordeaux at the same time and arrived in the Canaries almost at the same time, and from that moment on until the present day not a word has been heard of the first two vessels and their inhospitable captains!

We set off from Bordeaux in early September. After gliding down the deep and still waters of the Gironde, whose banks form a varied panorama, sometimes cultivated, sometimes covered by dense forests of pines and cork oaks, sometimes consisting of arid shifting dunes, we soon lost sight of the impressive tower or lighthouse of Cordovan, which illumines the entrance to that mighty stream; and shortly thereafter we found ourselves sailing on the famous Bay of Biscay, so feared for its storms. It seems that the three ships I have mentioned had the same aim of completing their cargo outside France, since they sailed as though in a convoy only two days apart and all anchored at Santa Cruz, on Tenerife, one of the main islands of the well-known Canaries in the European waters of the Atlantic.

These islands, which in the fabled times of old led Plato into his celebrated ramblings about Atlantis, and which only became known after stout Hercules got around to breaking open a way for the Mediterranean through the Strait of Gibraltar, were later baptized with the name Hesperides, and then, and for a long time after, with that of the Fortunate Isles; and their benign climate and the abundant products of their agriculture make them one of the many jewels that adorn the Spanish crown. This volcanic group consists of many small islands, one of which boasts the famous peak of Tenerife, which until 1765 was believed to be the world's highest mountain and the sole cause of the terrible earthquake that shook the surrounding islands from December 24, 1704 until January 5 of the following year. Another island, Fierro, has enjoyed and for many geographers continues to enjoy the privilege of being considered indispensable as the starting point for the prime meridian. There is no tropical fruit you will not find in these islands, and anyone wishing to taste malmsey wine would be ill advised to buy it anywhere else.

Six days after leaving the Fortunate Isles and saying our last goodbye to the *Petite Louise* and the *Newcastle,* which had refused me lodging and passage in Bordeaux, we found ourselves struggling against the forced immobility that the calms of the tropical zone impose on sailing ships. Frying under the hot rays of the sun, there we stayed day after day with no hope of even the slightest breeze that might carry us out of waters that, thanks to their stillness, their surface covered with abundant aquatic plants, and even their oily and metallic sheen, resemble stagnant ponds more than genuine seas.

Nonetheless, for the traveler who does not consider a voyage as a blank in his existence and therefore wants those days to be counted as part of his life, the seas of the tropics, despite their vexatious calms, also have their pleasing attractions. There is nothing more grand and imposing than the sight of the sky after the sun has sunk below those burning horizons. The sunset, which lasts at least half an hour every evening, is an immense and fantastic curtain of the brightest colors, which rises slowly over the illuminated base of the ocean and displays to the observer's astonished eyes such fanciful forms, so many shades of soft and bold coloring, so many golden and purple streamers that spring up, spread, shrink, and reappear when least expected, that only the imagination, but not the palette of the most celebrated painter, could ever reproduce them.

Nor is the sea, though asleep and covered with sargasso, devoid of charms. Schools of bream often illuminate the sides of a vessel with the sunlight reflected from their golden scales. The precious fish known as bonito, chasing after the flying fishes with the speed of lightning, peoples the air with flocks of these poor fugitives, which fall dazed and flapping on the decks, where amid the jubilation of the crew they find the very death they were seeking to escape, fleeing from the voracity of the pursuing fish or from the beak of the sea birds that catch them in flight. Now and then some frightful shark appears at the stern of the ship and follows its wake, to the horror of some and the amusement of others, until it almost always ends its visit on deck, pierced by a harpoon. The sargasso itself, drawn from the sea and spread on the deck for better observation, is a treasure for the naturalist, with the multitude of curious little fish, crabs, and mollusks that live in it. Since everything is extreme in those tropical regions, where even flies are usually poisonous, the roots that like strands of pink silk hang from the jellyfish we call Portuguese man-o'-war sting the skin so intensely that those whom curiosity tempts to handle the sargasso often end by screaming or cursing at having their fingers caught in those devilish threads.

Little by little, and by dint of patiently taking advantage of the slightest breeze, we managed to escape the calm and enter a region more frequented by winds, until we reached the latitude of Montevideo, where their intensity begins so to increase that one can well say that from one extreme of calm and heat we leapt with billowing sails to the other extreme of agitation and unpleasant cold.

Not only the lowlands of barren Libya breed furious hurricanes; from the broad plains of the Patagonian pampas, and for similar physical reasons, winds also frequently rush onto the seas that bathe their eastern coasts, winds so terrible that the mere name *pampero* makes the seaman tremble. Overtaken by one of these horrid gales we ran under bare poles before a wild storm for nine consecutive days; and at the worst of it the captain crowned our distress by announcing that our water supply was very low and that we should therefore have to ration ourselves most strictly. He authorized us to drink all the wine we wanted, as long as we did not touch water; and although this announcement at first rather caused rejoicing than chagrin, it soon increased the desperation caused by thirst, because one has to feel it and be unable to quench it in order to realize what a sacrifice such a calamity entails. During the brief moments when the ship's creaking and rocking allowed us to sleep we dreamt of rivers and lakes of fresh water, just as when you suffer the effects of poverty you dream of mountains of gold. To increase our desperation, we could see the horizon covered with squalls, while not a drop fell on our deck. On the seventh day of this torment fate took pity on us and discharged the most welcome and abundant of all floods onto the *Carlos Adolfo* and her thirsty passengers. Awnings were soon spread out, cannon balls were placed so as to shape them into funnels, hoses were attached to capture the enormous streams that flowed from them, and in less than three hours all of us, from the captain to the lowest page, entirely naked, because we needed to drink in water even through the pores of our skin, filled sixty barrels with that elixir of life, never before so jubilantly received. It was truly comic to see us fill even the intimate vessels of our cabins with water, for fear of finding ourselves in another drought.

With seawater, no matter how rough it may be, you can observe a curious phenomenon when a heavy squall falls on it: the rain forms a watery curtain that contains the wind, the waves cease to collide and break, and the sea is left without foam, even though its imposing billows continue to rise and fall.

Since we drank so much water, and the water contained so much tar after first running down the tarred rigging and then over the tarred sails, we were still as naked as Adam before his fall when our general delight was followed by a scene of the most ridiculous distress. The effects of this tar-laced water were certainly unpleasant, but very beneficial to the health of the downcast travelers.

With less stormy weather we continued on our way toward the waters of the Cape, until we had the misfortune of running into the most violent opposing northwester at the southern end of the Strait of Lemaire. During long hours, plagued by a steady drizzle and impenetrable fog, we withstood the dreaded attacks of those mountains of water that take the place of waves when the southern seas are whipped up by a hurricane-force wind. Nonetheless, after four days of resolute struggle we rounded the Cape; but since it was written that we were not yet to rest, we were already losing sight of the islands of Diego Ramírez to our east, broken remnants of the Andean range in that stormy region, when a sudden blast of wind broke the spar of our mainmast and threw it on the deck with such violence that the alarmed helmsman almost brought about our final ruin. So startled was he that we took on a wave over our bow that passed over the deck like a torrent and, besides dragging off two unfortunate sailors, our kitchen, and a launch stored near it, caused so much damage that we lost not only our recent hope of reaching our destination but also all hope of saving our lives.

Nevertheless, on such occasions man finds strength in his very weakness; and although nightfall was heightening the horror of our situation, we worked with stubborn determination, intent only on keeping afloat our ship, which the next day, driven by the wind and the currents of the Pacific, found herself once more so far to the east of Cape Horn that we could think of nothing but to seek some cove where we might repair the damage.

Two days after this distressing situation, the solid though unrigged *Carlos Adolfo* dropped her anchor in the shelter of Port Egmont on the deserted Falkland Islands.

How dearly we paid in those days for a voyage to Europe, a voyage that today is a mere pleasure jaunt!

Thus we found asylum in one of the world's most spacious and commodious harbors, and there, thanks to the steady calm of its waters, and freed from our buffetings, we were able to rest, sleep peacefully, and repair the damage to our ship.

The Falklands, also known as the Malvinas, are not three or four useless rocks fit only to be held as a strategic location at the mouth of so important a strait as that of Magellan. They are a whole archipelago, consisting of at least two hundred islands that form two sections, known as the Eastern Group and the Western Group. The islands of the former generally have low shorelines, while those of the second are girded by large rocks and bluffs that rise more than a hundred meters. There is no trace of trees or bushes on the archipelago; but its rich and abundant natural grasses lend themselves, in that relatively mild climate, to the raising of cattle, as was shown, at our landing, by the many cows and wild horses that the passengers of the until recently distressed *Carlos Adolfo* hunted with rifles.

The presence of domestic animals in such out-of-the-way islands stems from the many attempts made by some nations to seize possession of them, alleging rights that none of them seems to hold with any degree of clarity and perfection.

There are those who believe that the islands were discovered by Vespucius. Davis sighted them in 1592. Hawkins sailed along their empty coasts in 1594. Strong did better, for in 1600 he anchored in the strait that separates the two largest islands of the archipelago. The mania that the navigators of the age of Cook had for bestowing new names on whatever islands they found on their daring voyages, without giving a thought to whether these places were already known by some other name, is the reason why few islands have more appellations than these. The voyager Cowley called them Pepys; Richard Hawkins, Virginia, to commemorate the virginity of Queen Elizabeth of England; the French sailors of St. Malo, Malouines; and others called them Falkland. Whatever the case may be, Bougainville was the first navigator to take possession of them in the name of France and also the first to try to establish colonies in those cold and deserted places, founding the colony of Port Louis in 1763.

When she saw the islands thus occupied, England, which rightly or wrongly considered them hers, proceeded at once to seize them, establishing herself in Port Egmont and demanding that the French surrender the disputed sovereignty to Captain Mackride. When Spain, who looked askance at such cavalier confiscation of what legitimately belonged to her as an integral part of her American possessions, noticed what had happened, she assumed so threatening an attitude that not only did the English step aside, but the French, settling for repayment of what they had spent at Port Louis, ordered Bougainville himself to go with the frigate *Boudeuse* to surrender the islands, with the usual ceremonies and salvos, to Don Felipe Ruiz de la Puente, who, commanding the frigates *Esmeralda* and *Liebre,* took possession of them in the name of Spain on April 1, 1767.

But since the Spaniards had so many and such valuable American possessions to exploit that they were not about to waste men and money just for the foolish pleasure of holding on to something that at the time was worth nothing, they soon evacuated the colony, whose ruins we saw during our excursions on the islands. We all know of Argentina's claims to the Falklands after her war for independence, just as we know how much attention the English paid to those claims when, despite the protests of that republic, they took definitive possession of the disputed islands in 1833.

After a relaxed and cheerful stay of nine days at Egmont we once again, with a fresh breeze and clear sky, undertook our interrupted task of rounding, as they say, the Cape. We accomplished it so successfully that fourteen days later we dropped anchor in Valparaíso, one hundred seven days after leaving Bordeaux.

V I I I

My arrival in Chile.— The newcomer.—
The apprentice rancher.— The distiller.— Why our factories
fail.— The shopkeeper.— The physician.— My debut
as a journalist.— Consequences of sudden wealth.—
Tobacco and cattle smuggling in the Andes.—
Cast your bread upon the waters.

If in our day our proud Valparaíso seems so depressing and even repulsive to the new arrival from Europe who has not yet come to
know it, imagine the impression it made in 1830, with its unkempt gullies, its hovels defying the waves on the paltry bit of terra firma that lay
between the sea and the hills, a few ships riding at anchor in the bay,
and that endless street or country road lined by a motley collection of
huts and shacks and leading from what they called the port to the foot
of the famous old Polanco grade!

A foreigner, for whom America meant primeval forests, palm groves,
flocks of screeching cockatoos, and gold for the taking, would cross hill after

hill boxed up in those vehicles of Loyola's, known for their digestive effects and rightly called "goats" because of the way they bounced around. Eventually, his head full of bumps and his lungs full of dust, he would enter Santiago by the endless, dirty, and unkempt Calle de San Pablo, which began amid huts, *chicha* stands, and fields for playing *bolas*,[25] and reached almost as far as the main square of what we now consider our splendid capital.

Still, there is an unfailing change from adverse to favorable in the newcomer's impressions if he stays a while in our Santiago. The houses seem to grow taller, and their roofs, which at first seem so close to the sidewalks that they imperil one's hat, mysteriously rise to a more suitable height.

Then as now, Santiago at first shocked and subsequently pleased every traveler who closed his eyes as he left Europe and only opened them on reaching Chile.

Seeing myself, then, once more in my longed-for fatherland, and puffed up with that foolish self-satisfaction that invariably comes from having been overseas and leads us to pontificate about everything, I initially looked down on the modest and studious young Chileans who tried, with hard work, study, and concentration, to make up for what in the popular estimation was their greatest fault, not having bathed themselves in European culture. And this feeling of superiority was not unmotivated, because, in addition to the fatuous pride felt even now by those returning from magical Paris, at that time we enjoyed the prestige of the fashionable cut of our clothes, the astonishment of those who heard us native sons chattering in French, and an inexhaustible supply of amazing descriptions, amusing Gallicisms, varied and ever elegant knots for our neckties, and new steps to contribute to the dancing of the quadrille. In a word, for many a mother and not a few fools we had all the charms of newly unwrapped fashionable clothes.

But since fashion always changes, no matter how much something may be the rage for a time, it came to pass that once the fop was out of fashion and the answer to the terrible question, "How much is he worth?" became known, he was yesterday's news, and after two years of the most delightful *far niente,* the poor dandy saw himself obliged to look for something more solid to do with his life. This decision, normally considered meritorious, did not meet with the approval of Fate, which rarely smiles on good intentions; and at this point begins a whole rosary of mishaps and cruel blunders whose beads, not of gold but of rough wood, I shall touch only gingerly, since I do not aim to recount the dull life of an ordinary fool, but those things that in connection with it might yield some worthwhile practical result.

25. *Bolas,* a game in which wooden balls were made to pass through a revolving hoop. JP.

My inclination toward a free and independent life was as great as my aversion to anything that smacked of tamely accepting the yoke of public service; I thought, as does many a poor young man in love today, that simply renting a farm, with no resources but a short-term loan and a willingness to work, was all it took to bring home wife, wealth, and happiness.

I began by paying the obligatory tribute to rustic life that is paid by every newly hatched farmer who puts on a poncho for the first time: I acquired good horses, dazzling saddles, brutal spurs, a machete, a lasso, a leather strap, hobbles, drinking cups, another large horn cup, and saddlebags trimmed in silver; I forgot the language of Cervantes and took up country jargon; I competed in horsemanship and the use of the lasso with the best riders; I was up before the morning star; I worked like a mule; I got drenched by the rain and burned by the sun; I slept on the ground; and at the end of two years all that this pseudo-Frenchman, cursing himself, had to show for his effort was the clothes on his back and being two years older.

Battered but unbowed, he then sought to compensate for his agricultural disaster by perfecting what was then an infant industry in Chile, and he established a European-style distillery in the Department of San Fernando. The result of this new enterprise, however, if not quite the same as that of the first, was very similar, because being a thoroughbred Chilean, he had to yield to our national obsession of starting things not at the beginning but where they ought to end. Not only do progress and perfection not advance by leaps, but they presuppose the existence of first steps. A child crawls before he walks; a patent leather boot presupposes, as I have said a thousand times, tanneries and shoemakers' shops, and these, in turn, presuppose lasts, pegs, and, furthermore, hands that began by making slippers, then shoes, and finally boots. In my distillery I had to attend to the boiler, the still, the pipes, and the barrels, all at the same time. Back then, an inch-and-a-half valve was a treasure; consequently, when it broke, not even a treasure could buy a replacement in time.

The ceramic industry failed in Chile because we had the bright idea of beginning with fine porcelain when we had not yet mastered the plain jug and the simple rustic plate.

The glass industry failed because instead of beginning with ordinary glass bottles we had the nerve to begin with fine vessels and glass panes.

The beet sugar industry failed because the industrialist had to be a farmer, too, and the product, being Chilean, had to be of the finest quality.

Our textile industry is languishing because we would not start out with ponchos, blankets, and mattress covers; no, indeed, we had to start with cashmeres. And my distillery failed because instead of settling for a slight improvement in the condensing tube, I had to go all out; because instead of using domestic kettles, I had to have a delicate French still; and because instead of making better rotgut I was engrossed in making brandy, anisette, and other fancy liquors.

All this leads to the following sad but true axiom: Whenever you introduce an advanced industry into a country that lacks the basic ones, you guarantee the ruin of the entrepreneur.

Say what you will about not judging a book by its cover, the results of my enterprise will prove the contrary. To dress up my bottles I had sent to Europe for a lovely collection of labels on which gilded arabesques surrounded the words *Old Champagne Cognac;* and to make the illusion more complete, on the façade of my establishment a sign proclaimed in large letters, *Importer.* By the way, I hope none of the many importers of the present day will become upset and think I am alluding to them, because that kind of swindle only occurred in my time, and nowadays everything comes straight from Paris, or at least from Bordeaux.

Under the charmed cloak of this pretense sales grew so much during the first months that my patriotic pride rebelled. Seeing that I was myself attributing to foreigners a fame that properly belonged to Chile, I threw my European labels into the fire and wrote *Pure Chilean Products* on the façade of my building and *Coñac* on the labels of my bottles. From that point on, the business went to hell in a handbasket. Little had I suspected that when I threw off the cover of my merchandise I was throwing out its quality; it turned from good to bad, and no one gave another thought either to my liquor or to the champion of Chile's prowess in industry.

I then became a shopkeeper; and there was not a customer on whom with flattery and lies I did not shrewdly try to unload every sort of trash, assuring her that I was doing it only because she was who she was, and on condition that she not divulge the secret of prices as exceptional as they were ruinous for me. Wholesale dealings were "strictly on the up and up." My true invoice was locked away in my safe; the invoice especially prepared for customs purposes had already been sent off; and the buyer saw only an inflated invoice on the basis of which, and as a particular favor, "sacrifice" sales were made at cost.

Although there is a good bit of difference between a shopkeeper and a physician, my devotion to the natural sciences so reduced the distance between these two professions that, just as I officiously employed every flattery to sell my mercantile odds and ends, I went about gravely selling my scientific potions, pleased with my knowledge and, like so many others, little concerned with whether they might turn out to be passports to the next world. If the patient departed this life, the survivors and the doctor exclaimed, "Life is short! Who can argue with the will of God?" If the patient triumphed in his struggle against the physician and his ally the pharmacist and recovered, which happens even where there are doctors and boards of medicine, then no one thought of the will of God but only of the expertise of the skilled healer in whose hands the lucky patient had placed himself. I did not collect money for my visits, because there was no board to approve my arbitrary rates; but I did collect ingratitude, which licensed physicians do not, for the simple reason that if you sell your goods and swindle your customers you will make enemies but not ingrates. Ingratitude, as the word itself clearly shows, can arise only from gratuitous services; and how many gratuitous services do most of our physicians dispense to suffering humanity that would entitle them pompously to claim, as they often do, the title of humanitarians par excellence?

But I should not want the legitimate sons of Hippocrates up in arms because of what I have said. Science has always been sacred to me, and my words allude only to those who wrap themselves in her mantle and claim to serve the cause of virtue when all they are serving is their selfish ends.

In general, the physician who seeks renown does so more for his pecuniary benefit than for the mere sake of hollow insubstantial glory; if he frequently takes cover behind what we call humanitarian charity, he does so less with his unpaid charitable works than with his faithful obedience to the precept that "charity begins at home." I criticize not what these doctors do—they are within their rights—but the moral value they place on their acts and their failure to justify such value. Can a physician prosper without disease? Are not the diseases that afflict mankind the doctor's treasure, gold mine, and carriage, and the daily bread and education of his children? How, then, can anyone be so gullible as to think that a doctor, who is a man like any other, would try to wipe out or diminish the ailments that are his treasure, gold mine, and carriage, and the daily bread and education of his children?

But I have digressed more than enough.

The free time that I enjoyed behind the counter led me to leafing through my books; my books half revived my old love of letters; and since there can be no love of letters without scribbling, nor scribbles of this sort that do not find their way to the printing press and eventually serve to wrap a druggist's pills, so it came to pass that my guardian devil suggested to me that the low state of my fortunes was due to a mistaken choice of career and that I might foolishly undertake to replenish my scrawny purse by following the rosy path of letters. And so without further delay I set about to become a journalist.

In order to make a splash with my first attempts, I pretended, as do the members of the medical profession, to be concerned more with the good of others than with my own; and I sent off to a Santiago paper, well known at the time, a truculent article that made it crystal clear that a certain country priest whose name I do not care to remember, instead of serving his flock as an example of purity and honesty, was forging his bishop's signature in order to collect fees in excess of what parish regulations allowed.

There I was behind my tiresome counter, complacently waiting to be named a reporter or at least receive the sort of approbation that would qualify me for that rank, when I learned that my article had been denounced as libelous and, a few days later, that I had been convicted and fined an amount that exceeded my meager means. In vain did I go to Santiago, bearing, as belated evidence in support of what I had written against the priest, a piece of plaster from the church wall on which the ill-fated forgery had been pasted. All that the modest and honorable prelate, my good uncle Don Manuel Vicuña, whose memory I cherish in spite of all this, did when he heard my rueful account was to put aside in horror the strange document I was presenting to him and to send me off with the words, "My boy, I'm less chagrined by my own sins than by their having sent you off to be educated in France!" There was nothing more to be said. I shut my mouth, paid my fine, and took to my heels.

What was I to do now? After my initial shock, my foiled but irrepressible imagination soon suggested the path of mining, and so I became a miner. I staked claims, bearing false witness against myself and calling myself a professional miner, as do so many others who have never in their life seen a mine; and off I headed over hill and dale, resplendent in cap and *culero*,[26] looking for trouble. I was already weary of not knowing whether to dig down or dig horizontally, when my contrary fortune, ever ready to pamper me and then suddenly to turn its back on me, would have me find, in the dark recesses of an old shaft of the Willows Mine in the coastal hills of old Colchagua, the kind of deposit that veteran miners say jumps right out at you. Now I could rejoice and feel legitimate satisfaction at the chagrin that my unexpected success was sure to cause in all those who had looked down on my poverty! Wherever you go, gold is youth, is talent, is beauty, and so I had reason to be pleased with myself.

At the bottom of the dark and damp shaft, as I concluded the drilling that made that treasure my own simply because I had laid it bare, again

26. *Culero,* a leather garment that covers the belly and buttocks, used by miners to protect their trousers when sitting or sliding in the mine. JP.

and again I ran my smoking miner's lamp over the quartz face studded with golden veins and nuggets that seemed to guarantee my good fortune. That was a delightful moment, a dream—and nothing but a dream. My wealth consisted only of what was plainly to be seen, and it barely covered my expenses.

During the first moments after that deceitful discovery, my pick man had told the bearers that the boss was down in a well of gold to be had for the taking; the bearers told the other laborers, who told the passersby, who inflated the news as they took it to Curicó, whence, reaching colossal proportions, it leapt to Santiago. Presents from people who had paid no attention to me and letters even from those who had most despised me soon began their work of flattery, so that, as I sat at the mouth of the mine, depressed and shaken by new disappointment, I had the pleasure of receiving messages that concluded with these very words: "I trust that your great and well-deserved good fortune will not make you forget your many good friends, among whom one of the foremost has always been your most devoted faithful servant . . . ."

I have kept these letters in a book bound in black and titled *Bitter Lessons.*

As for the pastries and larded turkeys sent to me by persons who formerly had not so much as asked me to take a seat, I had them thrown into the mine as they arrived and told their bearers only that the mine thanked the generous sender.

As my instant fortune came to an end like the cones with which Cervantes compares human lineages, wide on top and coming to a sharp point below,[27] I sank from the regions of brilliance to my former station of contemptible fool. I was, furthermore, too poor to undertake any line of business compatible with the freedom of action that I have always tried to maintain, and I lacked any resources other than my good health and my remarkable ability to bear physical hardships; and so I struck an agreement with some men who were in the business of fattening cattle and set off for Argentina, where, buying cattle and serving as an intermediary between the dealers on either side of the border, I roamed about for eleven straight years without any respite but a sudden voyage to France and an occasional visit to my forsaken home, Santiago.

I am familiar with twenty-three passes over the Andes, and I cannot remember how often I traversed the ones I used most often, where you

---

27. In Part I, Chapter xxi of *Don Quixote,* the hero speaks to Sancho Panza of two kinds of lineages: those that descend from a great man and finally become a small point, like a reversed pyramid (not a cone), and those that from small beginnings come to be great. JP.

might say I lived during the summers. For my dealings in Salta, Catamarca, La Rioja, and San Juan, these were the passes of Antofagasta, San Guillermo, Doña Ana, No te duermas, and Agua Negra; and for my business in San Luis, Mendoza, San Carlos, San Rafael, and the outposts of Payen in the Patagonian wastelands, they were the passes of Portillo, Leñas Amarillas, Planchón, Maule, Longaví, Canteras, and Chillán.

On the basis of my Andean expeditions I have said over and over again how useless or at least how ineffective are the customs agents whom our treasury officials insist on posting at those passes, because there is not an agent whose vigilance cannot be easily foiled. When large-scale smuggling cannot be avoided, as is the case with tobacco in Chile, economic good sense prescribes only two means of putting an end to such immorality: either to reduce customs duties to the point where the risks of smuggling outweigh the profit, or to abolish them altogether. The former approach does away with a senseless burden on the honest merchant and deprives the dishonest one of an unintended reward. The latter approach would protect an industry that should long ago have become an important source of wealth for Chile.

Before I continue I want to record an event from my personal experience that can now be freely told, an event that redounds to the credit of one of Chile's richest, most hard-working, and most generous sons, and that provides yet another proof of the axiomatic inconstancy of Fortune, so that I can well advise anyone who has fallen on hard times, "Never give up!"

Back then, when the distinguished miner Don Zacarías Nikson was working the famous Millahue gold mine in Colchagua, there lived, on a modest property not very far from the ore-grinding machines of the wealthy Gringo, an honorable and quiet gentleman who, like me, was the target of the brutal blows of adverse fortune. Hounded by his creditors in Santiago and forced to sell for a song what little he had left in order to make good on his signature, this unfortunate gentleman knocked in vain on the doors of the Argomedos, Calvos, and Rencorets—the Rothschilds who monopolized the cattle trade in the bustling village of Nancagua—to get a fair price for his animals, because at that time a reluctant seller could set the terms of every deal, but not an eager one, and as far as I know this rule is as alive and well as ever. Our distressed seller, caught between going to prison for debt and going out on the highway to rob, was at a loss for what to do when chance, which sometimes is the mother of unexpected solutions, came to show him, if not a door, at least a window through which he might escape.

In those days one of the residents of Nancagua was that well-known, hard working, and delightful lady Doña Carmen Gálvez, whose matchless pastries were the delight of the abbots of our monasteries and the well-to-do sons of genteel Santiago. This lady, who was poor and therefore charitable, took pity on the travails of the afflicted cattle dealer and sent him off with a courteous letter of recommendation to Boldomávida, a neighboring farm where, she said, there lived a young man who, albeit Frenchified, had a better heart than he did head.

One morning, after riding around my fields—for there are no fields more ridden around than those of Chile—I was enjoying the shade on the porch at Boldomávida, a property I was farming at the time, when I saw, coming through the courtyard door astride wretched mounts, a rustic exhibiting some traces of the gentleman and a little boy who seemed to be his servant. The master was a young fellow of rather average height, black hair, pale complexion, and seemingly robust constitution. His clothes, though neat, did not conceal the poverty that was loudly proclaimed by his nag, his saddle, and the absence of the celebrated drinking cups that, along with the enormous rowels of silver spurs, were then the indispensable trappings of a prosperous countryman. The newcomer's greeting was rather timid than confident; but since there could be no standing on ceremony with a man recommended by Doña Carmen, we were soon sharing a bench and starting to chat like old acquaintances. He told me what was happening to him; he also told me that some dealers, when they saw that he was forced to sell, were offering him six pesos for a cow—seven if she was giving milk—and nine for an ox. He said that he had not come to ask me for more than that for his cattle, because, compelled as he was to sacrifice, he wanted only that his sacrifice should benefit a plain working man rather than heartless rich folk.

I was both moved and flattered; and after a short pause I told him, "What would you say to seven, eight and a half, and twelve pesos?"

"That, sir," he answered, "is even more than I could wish for."

"All right, then," I said, "the cattle are mine"; and as he was getting ready to go for them, I begged him first to do me the honor of lunching with me. He accepted; and when I noticed that as we were heading for the dining room he turned kindly toward his servant and told him, "Just sit over there in the shade; we'll be going soon," I ordered my foreman to take care of his horses and take the boy to the kitchen for lunch.

I shall be brief: when I received the cattle the next day I had the pleasure of making the unusual dealer a gift of a pair of suede trousers that, though not new, could pass for acceptable in comparison with the worn woollen ones he was wearing. My congenial guest received this insignificant present with a show of the purest gratitude; and as he gave me a farewell embrace, it seemed to me the beating of his heart betrayed his emotion. After this I lost track of him. Years and more years went by, and not the slightest trace of that cattle dealer remained in my memory, when, as I was signing some routine documents in the intendancy of Concepción in the year 1860, I suddenly noticed a great noise of shifting of chairs and courteous bowing and scraping coming from the neighboring room, occupied by my subordinates. When I asked with some annoyance what was the meaning of so much to-do, my secretary appeared and, with great marks of respect, ushered the wealthy Don Matías Cousiño into my office. Long before my last return from Europe I had heard talk of what an important role Don Matías played in Chile; and I was rising from my seat to receive him as he deserved when he, affectionately exclaiming, "Permit me to embrace you, Don Vicente!," warmly threw his arms around me.

I must confess that so unexpected a gesture left me speechless. "Do I know this charming gentleman and have I given him occasion to treat me so affectionately? What have I ever done for him, and where, and how? Might there not be some unfortunate mistake in all this?"

My very uncertainty refreshed my memory. That warm embrace whose cause I could not make out was not the first such embrace that I had received in my life; years before I had received another just like it from a poor rustic whom I had given a pair of used suede trousers at what was for him a difficult time.

"I have a complaint against you," were the first words addressed to me by that man, a Chilean Croesus in his wealth, though much superior to the Roman Croesus in his virtues. When with understandable concern I asked "Why is that?," he answered me with affectionate seriousness, "Because you've been back in Chile for almost four months, and since you don't want to collect what I owe you, you continue to be the slave of your public office, even against your will."

"Good Heavens, Don Matías," I replied, "what *you* owe *me?*"

"What a poor memory you have!" he answered. "I'll see whether I can refresh it." And taking me cordially by the hand, he managed by his words to make me admit, though shamefacedly, that it was I who had given a gift of suede trousers and he who had received it.

I shall not recount all that that noble and grateful heart did, after that meeting, for a former distributor of used clothing; let me only say that I have thought it essential to recall this brief episode in my life so that it may help to portray the superior character of that tireless servant of Chilean industry and commerce, Don Matías Cousiño, for whom the presence of someone who knew him when he was poor was an occasion not of shame but of proud satisfaction, which is never the case with a base heart.

I X

Revolutions.— Santa Cruz's War.— An execution in Curicó.
— The price of traveling without a passport. — The risks of
lying, even if opportunely.— I dodge San Carlos and flee to La
Rioja.— Natural riches between San Carlos and Famatina. —
Mummies. — Fossils.— Chilecito de Famatina. — Trade with
Chile.— Cattle prices. — Tobacco and tobacco smuggling. —
Erroneous view of the Andes as a single chain of mountains. —
The geographer Napp's mistakes concerning the base and eleva-
tion of the Andes. — The rewards of painting saints. —
My disastrous return to Chile.

The peoples of America would have been untrue to the ideals that led them to face the vicissitudes of the bloody struggle leading to their political emancipation if they had remained static after smashing the Spanish yoke. That great event, to which reason, justice, and the soundest principles of natural law impelled them, necessarily consisted of two stages: triumph in the struggle, and the building of an independent existence, phases that ought to have complemented each other and formed a single whole.

The Spanish-American republics had already entered fully on the second phase, although, by an easily understandable misfortune, they still offered the lamentable spectacle of disastrous civil wars, which pitted the more or less exaggerated patriotism of the builders against the irresistible demands of the patriotism of the soldiers. The nature and general tendencies of the human heart made this inevitable. These countries had only recently begun their life as independent nations, and their only qualification for worthily occupying so exalted a place was their triumph over the armies of Spain; and so it was only natural that the victorious warriors who had been proclaimed fathers of their country should seek to be the organizers and even supreme heads of the states that owed their nascent existence to their efforts. There were, however, many distinguished military leaders, and it was impossible to create a separate state for each of them, and even more impossible to tolerate any further delay in the full enjoyment of the indispensable political guarantees that protect the individual's life, liberty, and property; and so, without denying these warriors' merits, the peoples of America sought from the lawyer's gown and pen what they could not obtain from the soldier's simple sword, no matter how hardened in battle and how glorious. That is the origin of the fratricidal struggles that continue to this day in some republican states, and of the disorder that still leads many deluded Europeans to think that the word "republic" is nothing but a synonym of "revolution."

The military rebellion against President Orbegoso led by Salaverry in Callao in 1835 had, a year later, brought down on Peru the bloody intervention of Don Andrés Santa Cruz, president of Bolivia. This shrewd and ambitious leader had long been planning to endow his landlocked country with an outlet to the sea that would link it more directly with world commerce and thus facilitate the sale of the varied and abundant products of its rich soil. He now found himself with an opportunity to achieve his desires; but, misled by his own ambition, he foolishly chose, among the many means always available to the victor, precisely the one that might alarm his Chilean neighbors, who now saw, suddenly looming on their border, a very powerful state that under the name of Peruvian-Bolivian Confederation resurrected the Peru of old with all the power that its size and wealth gave it over the other states of the Pacific coast.

For this and other reasons, which I omit since very able pens have already dealt with them, the Chilean government declared war on Santa

Cruz on December 26, 1836, to which the proud Bolivian replied a month later with the solemn public proclamation of the new state whose creation Chilean policy sought to prevent. To consolidate it while also allaying the storm that threatened from the south, the shrewd Santa Cruz counted on his long-standing contacts in Chile, on the discontent among the defeated remnants of our *pipiolo* or liberal party, and above all on the resentment among our military, to whose ambitions the organizing talents of the distinguished statesman Don Diego Portales had recently dealt a mortal blow. As Chile, facing such political turmoil at home and the danger of a war abroad, sought to secure its imperiled future while maintaining domestic tranquility at any cost, it was not surprising that the year 1837 should begin its course to the sad accompaniment of foreign war, proclamations of a state of siege, and constant courts-martial.

Portales, the father of our country's reorganization, was misunderstood and therefore as detested at that time as his memory was later venerated even by his bitterest enemies. He imposed firm, unusually strict measures that crushed the revolutionary Hydra wherever it dared to raise its unpatriotic head. That genius, who paid for the well-deserved fame he enjoys today with his treasure and his life, had, in a moment of selfless exaltation, exclaimed, "If my father turned revolutionary, I'd have my own father shot." Portales never promised to do anything he did not intend to carry out.

We were thus under a reign of terror when, leaving my hired hands to drive the cattle I was taking from San Luis over the mountains to Chile, I rode ahead to reach Curicó, the capital of the former province of Colchagua,[28] whose governor at the time was the eminent and well-known author Don Antonio José de Irisarri.

As I entered the town's main square, which was so untidy as to look rather like a corral, and on which, as in every other village in Chile, stood only a humble parish church, a dirty jail, and a few unimpressive looking buildings, all surrounding an area overgrown with weeds and adorned only by narrow walkways of small stones that crossed it and offered some escape from the mud of winter and the dust of summer, I came upon so many people gathered there that my curiosity was aroused and I had to stop to find out the reason for such an unusual crowd. Would that I had simply continued on my way! For it had never oc-

---

28. In 1833 and 1865, the provinces of Talca and Curicó were carved out of the territory of that of Colchagua. Hence the author's references, here and later, to "the former province of Colchagua" or "what used to be the province of Colchagua." JP.

curred to me that the first thing to attract my attention on my return to Chile would be . . . the executioner's scaffold! Horrified, I observed that people were gathering in silent gloom in front of three stools, guarded by some grenadiers, that were about to be the dreadful final seats for three distinguished gentlemen whom a brutal and implacable court martial had, the day before, condemned to be shot. Their revolutionary plotting, which might perhaps have been checked by imprisonment or exile, was to bring to the scaffold, driven there by the iron hand of what we call human justice, the well-known citizens Don Manuel Barros, Don Faustino Valenzuela, and Don Manuel José Arriagada.

As the church bell rang ten, the bugle of the detachment of grenadiers, the personal guards of the provincial governor, announced with its usual discordant notes that the supreme moment had come; seconds later, in chains and with the customary fearful pageantry, the victims whose death would drown so many innocent families in tears and cover them with the black cloak of mourning appeared in the jailhouse doorway.

Terrified, my heart overflowing with sadness, I convulsively dug my spurs into my horse's flanks, turned it around, and galloped off toward Labarca's house; but before I could reach it the sound of a discharge announced to the distressed town that this frightful drama had reached its denouement.

The scenes of the tragicomedy of human life that we so eagerly act out are varied and disjointed. There I was, cheerfully on my way to conclude a simple business deal; and to reach my destination I had to pass through the horror and tears evoked by the funereal display of a political execution. Five days later that frightful backdrop and its dismal details had disappeared behind another curtain that displayed the most imposing unspoiled nature. The immense plateau of the Andes, that elevated frozen white sheet that stretches, broad and gleaming, to the north of the high peak of Planchón, replaced the cramped and gloomy square of stunned Curicó. The wild gallops of the horsemen crashing into each other in the course of the roundup had supplanted the steady march of the somber firing squad, and the mournful voice of the priest preaching contrition had yielded to the deafening shouts of the skilled cowboy on his horse, racing like a swift cloud across the open highland meadows in pursuit of the wild cattle. Such is life! One scene follows another and is followed by yet another, until actor and spectator alike are carried off by what sooner or later carries off everything in Creation.

At the time I am speaking of, the free importation of Argentine cattle through the southern mountain passes was not yet allowed, and those that were nonetheless brought in, which were many, because prohibitions that can be circumvented without risk are always useless, were brought behind the backs of the local authorities. The seller was responsible only for delivering the animals to a stockyard; the Chilean buyer took care of everything else.

When on April 20 I had completed my sales of cattle in the great corrals formed by the lava flows of Peteroa, I left my people to help the buyers and, accompanied by a single servant, headed for the pass of Las Yaretas, hastening to cross it before the solid dark clouds looming over those barren heights blocked my passage with the first snowstorm of the season. I was already treading happily on the first scattered and scrawny vegetation on the eastern slopes of the Andes when my cheerful commercial musings were rudely interrupted by the sight of five red blankets, that is, Argentine border patrols. These "red blankets," so called because the federal troops in San Juan and Mendoza wore symbolically blood-colored woollen uniforms, were as a rule thoroughgoing scoundrels whose arbitrary authority made them fearsome in proportion to their distance from populated areas. They came toward me holding their lances; when I told them that I was from Chile, they asked for my passport. Unfortunately the impression made on me by the executions in Curicó, the short time I had been in Chile, and, above all, my urgent need to sell my cattle before being overtaken by the snow had not allowed me even to think of asking the Chilean authorities for this stupid piece of paper. This bureaucratic lapse not only put an end to all my dreams but was on the verge of making me lose my very life.

Politically motivated terror did not exist only in Chile; suspicion and murder, insecurity and the gallows, were the plagues that the inflamed spirits of the battling Unitarian and Federalist parties[29] had set loose to devastate Argentina. In Chile executions were cloaked in legal niceties, but on the other side of the border the executioner's brutal axe rarely wore this sad disguise. The horrors of fratricidal war had compelled many distinguished Argentineans to seek refuge abroad, where, understandably struggling to return to their country, they took every opportunity to combat their political persecutors with their writings, with their intrigues, and with whatever other means they could find in their helpless condition. It was therefore necessary to proceed with great caution in those parts, because it was but a single step from suspicion to a rigged trial, and from there to the gallows or the confiscation of all of one's goods.

29. These parties supported, respectively, a unitary state and a federal one. They have nothing to do with Unitarianism in the religious sense. JP.

After the violent death of Quiroga, whose atrocities had earned him the title of Tiger of the Pampas, the power of Rosas was unchallenged; and he had distributed the provinces or states subject to his dictatorial authority among the most ferocious blind instruments of his absolute will. In Mendoza, and with the fraudulent title of general in command of the southern frontier at San Carlos, the governor was Aldao, the terrible and obese Franciscan friar whose bloody boldness had shocked everyone when, while serving as assistant chaplain of the Army of the Andes under the command of General San Martín, he had presented himself to Colonel Las Heras bathed in blood shed by his own hand in the fight at Guardia Vieja, on the way to Uspallata. In his youth he had been a bold and brutal womanizer, then a ferocious and bloodthirsty grenadier; but—who could have thought it!—true love had tamed this beast, and, unlawfully married, he would have remained quietly in Chile had not the Church authorities, according to what I heard from his own lips, launched him once more on the sea of adventures on which he had spent the first two thirds of his stormy life. When he assumed command of the southern frontier, age had already worn down his energy and, by 1837, changed the valor of the veteran grenadier, which in earlier times had frightened everyone into the timidity of the most unjustifiable cowardice. He feared assassination, distrusted everyone, and rare was the stranger in whom he did not think he saw a Unitarian.

My knowledge of the terrain where I found myself will explain the flood of worries in which my lack of a passport engulfed me; but my composure and growing familiarity with the human heart were to save me from this danger, as well as from many another in which I found myself in the course of my life. I told my Federalists that I was a Chilean businessman; that my passport was in the trunk that was following me with my baggage because I had thought I should not need it before reaching San Carlos, where I planned to stop; that if they had any doubts—because I could see that they were somewhat suspicious—I would give them my keys so that as soon as my baggage arrived they could assure themselves that I had no reason to deceive them; and that in the meantime I should go on to San Carlos, provided they would be so kind as not to detain my mule.

The chance to lay their hands on someone else's property without the owner's knowledge or consent was too good to be wasted; at least so I gathered from certain knowing winks exchanged by those honest troopers. These Argentineans, however, are smarter than they usually seem; and so they placed me under arrest, two of them to be in charge of me until my baggage arrived, while the other three, without bothering to return my keys, continued on the path I had just left, to pick up, according to them, some additional trails.

I confess that at first I thought I was lost. I had no baggage or anything like it. My saddle was my bed; and apart from that, what my servant and I had were saddlebags and small suitcases. What would be the outcome of my lack of foresight, of my improvised fabrication? It was obvious that those hoodlums would soon be back, and in no kind mood, and that there would then be no escape for me. Seeing myself in this predicament and with time running out, all I could do was to search my faithful Manuel's eyes for some relief that in my disturbed state I could not even remotely glimpse. Manuel understood me, and a bottle of excellent anise that he drew from a saddlebag the better to pass the time soon produced a free and cordial conversation among the four interlocutors whom an evil chance had brought together in that wasteland.

Manuel Campos, my devoted servant, was no ordinary man. He had been born in the mining country of Apalta and had been a highwayman among the hills of Teno; and Urriola, the intendant of Colchagua, had had his hands full trying to rid his province of this frightful bandit, this savage. In addition, he was a clever smuggler and the most skillful guide between the famous town of Chilecito in La Rioja and the outposts of San Rafael, in the pampas of Patagonia. Without recognizing who he was, I had saved his life when he was in a tight spot; this favor, for which even a beast is grateful, had so transformed the inclinations of his depraved heart that, though he continued to be fierce and bold with all other men, he was gentle, affectionate, and even timid with me.

Once the cheerful drinkers had reached the stage of bragging about their mighty deeds, a meaningful look from Manuel made me take hold of the pistol I always carried in my pocket; and while Manuel fell like lightning on the unsuspecting chatterer next to him, pushed him to the ground, and snatched away his dagger, I, with a determined expression, told his surprised companion to choose, in exchange for their two saddle horses, between a gold *onza*[30] and a bullet in his head. I shall not dwell on the fear that seized these two unfortunate agents of authority when faced with an attack as violent as it was unexpected. They settled for the gold coin. A moment later, for there was not an instant to be lost, we tied together my two packhorses and the two saddle animals that had brought us into this trap, mounted the two *pilones*[31] that we had just

30. *Onza,* a gold coin worth about sixteen nineteenth-century dollars. JP.
31. In Argentina *pilonar* means to cut off an ear; and in Mendoza they used to cut an ear off the best army horses, considering the consequent ugliness of the mutilated animals or *pilones* the most effective way to prevent their theft, so frequent at that time. VPR.

bought, and set off on the most frantic flight consistent with our need to spare our relief mounts.

This incident showed once more what consequences even the slightest lack of foresight can have under certain circumstances. My simple disregard for the formalities of the passport forced me to lie, the lie led to my arrest, the arrest almost led me into crime, and the action that made my flight possible could have brought me to the scaffold.

My fate was now in the hands of the astute Manuel; I confined myself to obeying his instructions, which for the moment consisted only in not sparing the spur and whip to get away from where the sellers of the horses had been left cursing. We realized that the trail left by the hoofprints of our animals would be vigorously followed, and we also knew we were in a country where the art of the tracker, comparable only to the instinct of the hunting dog, had reached sublime levels, for they say, ridiculous as it may seem, that a good tracker can tell from the track even whether his quarry is young or old. But as the saying goes, for every seven vices there are seven virtues. My good Manuel, who was not being followed for the first time, made use of all his virtues whenever a suitable occasion arose.

After four hours of a furious gallop over the wretched paths and hills and dales that lie between the town or fort of San Carlos and the second range of foothills, our *pilones* grew tired; we then continued at a walk until we reached the main creek that descends from the mountains to join its waters to those of the Tunuyán. With horses and riders standing in midstream, we changed to our original mounts, after which we hid the bridles that the tired horses of the soldiers were biting, drove these animals a short distance downstream until we reached a meadow, and there left them to their fate. We then retraced our steps and continued upstream, always in the middle of the creek, until, reaching a dry rocky place where no tracks would show, we set off across it and continued our way, always on guard but in less of a hurry.

Accompanied only by the old devil who had become my guardian angel, and with no spare horses but the two I had brought from Chile, I rode all that day and part of the night. We stopped to let our horses rest only when we thought it very unlikely we could be overtaken, and only on the third day did we light a campfire. On the fourth we entered the province of San Juan; on the fifth we found lodging in Calingasta, an Indian village in that poor corner of the world; and although we were sure that Benavides, who was then governor of San Juan, was far less suspicious and cruel than the friar Aldao, we did not consider our risky voyage at an end until we were in the home of the Chilean Díaz, an honorable small-scale miner in Chilecito, a town in La Rioja.

Except for a total lack of bread or anything like it, for we had already consumed our small remaining supply of toasted meal, we had fortunately not lacked for food, especially once we were able to light a fire, because I know of no region more bountiful in freely offering the traveler the means of satisfying his hunger. To this happy circumstance, however, the denizens of these almost empty lands owe their aversion to farm work, the untidiness of their dwellings, and the independent character typical of the hunter, whose shoe is a simple horsehide wrapping, whose bed is the ground, and whose blanket is the *chiripá* [32] that he wears over his trousers.

Curiosity leads the guanaco into the hunter's hands; the viscacha and the partridge are taken with a stick; to catch the tasty and defenseless armadillos that inhabit the country requires no effort on the traveler's part beyond picking them up, nor do they require a pot to be cooked in other than that formed by the small scales that cover their bodies. There is no dwelling, no matter how poor it may seem, where you will not frequently see fat quarters of beef or of guanaco hanging by the door at the disposal of neighbors and travelers. The man who tries to pay for the meat so generously offered is considered rude, or a Chilean.

And so we arrived in Chilecito and took shelter with compatriots, who, even if they are selfish in their own country, always make common cause when abroad; and for the time being I had nothing to do but rest from my exhausting voyage and wait for an answer to the letters I wrote to Mendoza to obtain the funds I had there. But evidently nothing was to work for me that year, because I received neither letters nor funds. Debtors cancel their accounts with the dead when these leave no papers, and with the living when they are hunted by the authorities.

Forced to change my plans, I decided to return to Chile as soon as the Andean snows would permit; but since I was unwilling to waste my time while waiting for the mountain passes to be clear, I busied myself with exploring and studying how an enterprising Chilean might profit from trade with Catamarca and La Rioja and with organizing the notes and recollections of my just-completed dash to La Rioja from the border at San Carlos.

I know few regions more interesting and less explored than these, through which unhappy chance made me travel from 24° to 30° south latitude.[33] Between these two parallels the mineral riches contained in

---

32. *Chiripá*, a cloth tied like a diaper over the trousers of the gaucho. JP.

33. Pérez writes (or his publishers print) "from 20° to 24° south latitude," but the area he speaks of lies between the latter parallel, which runs through the northern part of the Argentine province of Catamarca, and 30°, which runs just south of Chilecito. Furthermore, his text is contradicted by the subsequent reference to additional "excursions north of the 24th parallel," which would obviously involve the country between 20° and 24°. JP.

the broad eastern slope of the Andes, from the lower edge of the perpetual snows to the base of the second line of foothills, are such that if only peace prevailed they would suffice to astonish the world of mining with the treasures that lavish nature has hoarded there. Subsequent excursions north of the 24th parallel have shown me that this wealth, far from ending there, seems to grow more plentiful and extend without interruption into Bolivian territory.

The total absence of the vegetation that adorns and enriches the western slope of the Andes; the metallic appearance of the hills, cloaked in the most varied and frequently brilliant colors, dominant among which are red, brown, blackish, blue, pink, and ash gray; the geological formations revealed by impressive rock slides and by the deep canyons cut by rushing streams in the small level areas at the base of the mountains; the sight of stones fallen from veins of ore and lying on the roads as though on purpose to display themselves the better: everything proclaims that in time the virgin agricultural soil of that region will not be the only source of its inexhaustible riches.

Nonetheless, until now the horse of the skillful highland hunter races like a fleeting cloud over this silent but rich country in pursuit of the ostrich[34] or the guanaco, without the rider's having the least inkling of what treasures he treads on and leaves behind.

During my flight along the slope of the Andes that faces Mendoza and San Juan I had occasion to cross veins and loose rocks that when I examined them at my leisure on subsequent trips turned out to be, some of the purest galena, others of argentiferous galena, of arsenical silver with particles of ruby silver and filaments of pure silver, with chlorides such as those near La Huerta, and still others of very fine copper that, as they crumble, dye the hillsides blue and green.

At Gualilán there is gold in limestone deposits. Nickel appears in various places, and aluminum sulfate in many others; and I remember that as I was saddling my horse one morning I recognized from the bit's resistance to being lifted from the ground that the smooth black surface on which we had camped was nothing but an enormous mass of magnetic iron.

As one passes from the province of San Juan into that of La Rioja, the metals are generally pure, which is why the famous district of Famatina is considered one of the richest in the world. There gold is found in deposits of slaty texture, or loose in the sands of the rivers. The richest mines of chlorides, silver sulfates, and ruby silver are found on the Cerro Negro, near Chilecito, and those of pure copper, copper pyrites, and red

34. *Ostrich,* the South American rhea. JP.

nickel, at Tagué. I found coal only as I crossed the principal gorge that passes through the Pie de Palo Mountains in the province of San Juan. At Huaco, in the same province, there are hot springs called Hediondez[35] and springs of salt water.

Although mines of metals abound in those unexplored places, the same is not true of that more lasting mine, forests. North of Mendoza, no trees are to be found on the high or low plateaus of the eastern slope of the Andes. All one sees there, and not in clusters but very scattered, are the *algarrobillo,* the spiny *chañar,* spiny *farilla,* and genista, bushes whose wood is useless for construction. Along the slopes there are abundant grasses of the kind we call *cepilla* and *coironcillo,* excellent pasture for every kind of cattle, and in the valleys and along the streams, reeds, pampas grass, and *chilca.* Although this vegetation means little to the businessman, the case is very different with the botanist, in whose eyes even moss has its charms. The cacti alone could form an enviable collection. I have seen enormous bushy *melocacti* next to colossal branching columns at least a foot and a half in diameter and armed with spines as hard as steel. There are also various species of prickly pears, though with leaves smaller than those of ours, which are beginning to be put to commercial use in the breeding of the insects sold as cochineal red. There are cacti so small we might call them microscopic, and others that are so thin and dainty that they seem like bits of string tied together.

I have already mentioned the abundance of game. Would that there were not an equal abundance of the annoying swarms of *vinchucas* or assassin bugs that look like cherries when bloated with blood, and of poisonous snakes, the terror of inexperienced travelers forced to camp outdoors.

Notable among the birds of the region are a tiny and charming dove, which is to be found even in the patios of village houses, and the little green clouds of parakeets, which sometimes form fields of lively verdure in the midst of the most arid terrain, or make one think that trees that have lost all their leaves in winter are, thanks to the vivid greenery that temporarily adorns them, bursting with spring foliage.

In the course of one of my expeditions I took shelter in an interesting cave that faced the Cerro del Azufre. Abounding in remarkable crystallizations and stalactites, it served as a rustic tomb for five mummies of Indians that lay where the hand of some reverent kinsman had apparently placed them long before. These skeletons, perfectly preserved and squatting on a grass mat almost destroyed by the passage of time, seem to owe their preservation to some fluid in the atmosphere that inhibits

35. *Hediondez,* "Stench." JP.

putrefaction, since this phenomenon cannot be attributed simply to the temperature, which is often very high in those mountains. This conjecture is confirmed by the many dried horses that travelers, for amusement, leave standing upright in the mountains so that they will seem to be alive.

Another phenomenon that drew my attention were the fossils, which the delicacy of the petrified objects and the limited area where they were found showed to have been petrified instantaneously. I have collected some very interesting twigs of carob trees petrified to their most delicate tips, some cockroaches in the process of crawling, and a fat caterpillar in the hollow of a stick equally turned into flint.

Chilecito de Famatina, that hospitable hamlet of La Rioja that was the hub of my constant excursions, owes its existence not only to the very bountiful mining district in which it is situated but also to the constant activity of the wandering and hard-working Chileans, who never ask what country they are heading for as long as there is profit to be made there, and who baptize every corner of the world where they settle with the name Chilecito.

Although the plateau on which this mining and farming town is located lies at least three thousand meters above sea level, its climate is pleasant and healthful. The mineral deposits of Famatina are found in the great mountain range of the same name, which is one of the mighty ranges that spread out in those latitudes, breaking the apparent unity of the Andean system. Near the midpoint of this range rises the imposing snow-covered peak of Famatina, on whose eastern slopes and at amazing elevations are found its famous mines; but not one of these is being worked systematically or shows any sign of having been so worked, except for those left by the great international mining company founded in 1824 with so great an investment of money and effort, and which the fierce Quiroga gained the nefarious distinction of destroying when he murdered Professor von der Hoelten, who was in charge of the operations. What copious wealth lies abandoned there in that single peak whose rivers are thought to abound in golden sands like the Pactolus that enriched Croesus, and whose core is full of the richest ores of gold, silver, and copper, from its base to the mouths of the mines of Santo Tomás del Espino, which lie at the level of the eternal snows!

But why wonder at the neglect that mining suffered at a time when agriculture was reduced to scratching the soil with wooden rakes or antediluvian plows, to gathering the harvest with knives, and to piling the sheaves on hides and dragging them to the place where, as was our custom, they were to be threshed by the trampling of mares' hooves! It can fairly be said that in 1837 industry in the Andean provinces consisted of gathering natural products and immediately selling them, and of nothing else. The abundant means of supplying the basic necessities of life to a rustic population that evinced few desires, the extensive plains rich in pasture, and a climate that favored the natural propagation of cattle combined to give the impression of a pastoral society, which this in effect was. Because transportation by cart to Buenos Aires was so expensive, the landlocked provinces—Mendoza, San Luis, San Juan, La Rioja, and Catamarca—had at that time no seaport through which to ship and sell their products other than Valparaíso, Coquimbo, and Copiapó; and so it is not surprising that they should limit themselves to garnering the products of their herds, both because these yielded the greatest profit in their trade with Chile, and because the soap of Mendoza, the goatskins of San Luis, and the dried fruit of San Juan played only a very minor role in commerce.

This was not the case with what some called Corrientes, and others La Rioja, tobacco, although there was no large-scale cultivation in the latter province. From San Juan and La Rioja, veritable storehouses and points of transshipment for this commodity, cargoes of tobacco used to set out every year to bypass the useless guards stationed at our mountain passes, cargoes that ever since then cry out to our government, as do the plantings of tobacco in Chile, "Till when will you maintain the tobacco monopoly, that foul blot on our fiscal system and shameful curse on an agricultural and manufacturing activity that could flourish on our soil and that eventually, despite inept and timid ministers, will be one of our chief sources of wealth?"

At that time the price of Argentine livestock varied according to the point of purchase. In the corrals that border the pampas, south of San Rafael, a cow cost three pesos, an ox, five, and a horse, one and a half. In Mendoza, and above all in San Luis, a cow, with or without calf, four pesos, an ox, seven, a horse, twenty *reales,* and a select pack or saddle mule, five pesos.

My excursions and plans for future business did nothing to improve my financial condition. I had already been stranded in my exile for three long months, during which I had to supplement my funds by drawing on my scanty general knowledge of agriculture, mining, and above all medicine; but when I lost all hope of receiving something from Mendoza through my honest correspondent there, I decided to stop sitting around penniless and, in spite of the warnings and opposition of my good Campos, to make a bold attempt to cross the Andes at Pulido, a narrow pass where the perpetual snows lie at more than a thousand meters above those of Planchón.

I spent what little funds I had left on preparations; heeding no counsel but that of my pride or confidence in my own strength, I set off for the pass through the Sierra de Famatina, which I managed to cross despite the snow. Once those frozen white peaks lay behind me, peaks that I ignorantly thought formed the border between us and Argentina, I could not help casting something like a conqueror's glance at my silent servant, who limited himself to declaring mournfully, "Well, boss, I guess you know what you're doing. As for me, you know that I'll die wherever you do, because we're just at the start of this trip."

In effect, when we had crossed the high plateau that lies to the west of the Sierra de Famatina, the more or less orderly succession of high peaks that rise there showed me that this was another chain approximately parallel to the first. As I continued my march I soon saw, to my consternation, yet another long and imposing chain of mountains, called Guandacol, which to the west parallels the one we had just left and with it encloses the deep valley through which flow the waters of the Bermejo.

After five days of tenacious struggle in this excruciating voyage, blocked by snow, buffeted by howling winds that raise snowy plumes from those dazzling heights and often cast horse and rider into deep crevasses, lacking food that would allow me to hold out there for any length of time and a horse capable of further climbing, I was forced, much against my will, to turn back, follow the course of the Bermejo until it left the canyon, and seek shelter in the Indian village of Calingasta, where my calamitous retreat came to an end.

Writers on the geography of America are very much mistaken when, guided by the more or less capricious depictions found on comprehensive maps, they assume that the great range of the Andes is one uninterrupted chain from the northern limits of Chile to the waters of the Strait of Magellan. There is no such chain, no such continuity, except in the middle, and this does not include even a quarter of the total extension of the Chilean mountains.

From San Juan northward one observes a gradual broadening of the eastern base of the Andes, as well as the first appearance of ranges that, though they buttress the central mass, seem to follow a path parallel to it. These first elevations, which subsequently become individual ranges with snow-covered peaks, are separated by plateaus so high and of such a nature that the traveler who reaches the area of Atacama and Antofagasta cannot tell whether he is in the mountains or on the plains, in spite of being at an elevation that exceeds that of many of the highest mountains of southern Chile.

In the province of La Rioja, a man halfway accustomed to making geographical observations in his travels can easily identify three principal chains of mountains, separated by high valleys and each with mighty snow-covered peaks: the Sierra de Famatina, above which rises the impressive giant bearing the same name, with an elevation, according to the late Von der Hoelten, of more than six thousand meters above sea level; the mountains of Guandacol; and those that mark the watershed between the two republics. Yet the base of the Andes does not end with the eastern slopes of Famatina, because even farther east I have had occasion to cross the Sierra de Velasco, which almost parallels Famatina, with an average elevation of some two thousand meters.

On my voyage I had occasion to note the remarkable phenomenon that the slopes of all these lateral ranges are steeper toward the west than toward the east.

As I review the notes I made and compare them with subsequent trips, I can attest to the wholly capricious nature of Napp's affirmation, on page 67 of his *La República Argentina*,[36] that "south of the 32d parallel the Andean plateau narrows until it becomes a ridge that at gradually diminishing elevation extends to the southern tip of the continent." When the worthy Napp presented such an inaccuracy as fact, he either did so in keeping with the then prevalent aim of narrowing the territory of Chile at that latitude, or he took the opportunity to bolster in writing the correctness of the many lapses that appear on his map of the Argentine Republic with respect to its border with the Chilean Republic. The elevation does not begin to diminish at the 32d parallel, as he affirms, because Juncal, which is almost at the 34th parallel, is higher than the estimated elevation of Famatina and almost equal to that ascribed to Llullaillaco, which is much farther north, between 24° and 25°. Furthermore, the giant of the Andes, Aconcagua, rises almost exactly at the 33d parallel. The true progressive loss of elevation from the main body of the Andes that lies between the 24th and 34th parallels begins at the latter and continues, very unevenly, until it comes to an end at the waters of Cape Horn. Furthermore, though the plateau's elevation above sea level does, in fact, decrease, it is also true that its width, instead of turning

36. *La República Argentina: obra escrita en alemán por Ricardo Napp con la ayuda de varios colaboradores y por encargo del Comité Central Argentino para la Exposición en Filadelfia (The Argentine Republic: A Work Written in German by Richard Napp with Several Collaborators and Commissioned by the Argentine Central Committee for the Philadelphia Exposition).* Buenos Aires, 1876. JP.

into the "ridge" of the German-Argentine author, so spreads out at its base as to seem far more extensive than it is to the north, as is shown by the elevation of the hills on our southern islands, which are true foothills of the Andes, and by the explorations carried out by our mariners in the rivers Huemules and Aisen, between 45° and 46° south latitude.

Returning now to the interrupted account of my voyage, Calingasta at that time resembled what our Santa Cruz used to be, and its simple and peaceful inhabitants were small farmers who worked both in their fields and in the gold mines of the aforementioned Gualilán. In my day Calingasta was one of the obligatory storage points for the cargoes of tobacco that then leapt, as if by magic, over the mountains into Chile; and so, when the passes were open in the month of October and the Chileans came into town, you could find the same animation in this village as reigned in Valparaíso with the arrival or departure of a steamship.

I sought and found hospitality in the home of one Gómez, a simple and modest old Chilean who had long lived there and had acquired, in addition to a wife, an Argentine accent so strong that there was no word in the dictionary on which he did not impress the characteristic rhythm of our neighbors. I installed my bedding of skins beneath the thick bower of carob branches that my hospitable countryman assigned me as a bedroom; after eating my fill of cold *hapi*, a kind of jelly made of half-crushed and thoroughly boiled corn, I slept as in a princely bed, despite the swarm of fierce *vinchucas* that infested my new home.

On the following day I traded my seven battered horses for two robust sorrels and an excellent mule; and to bolster my host's confidence I made a present to his wife of a silver spoon, the last remnant of my glories to be found in my suitcase.

On the eighth day of my tedious stay in Calingasta—for my only occupation was trying to find out when the snows would allow me to escape my exile—Gómez and his charming wife were so kind as to leave me in full possession of the house while they went to Albardón. As I sat downcast on a bench, my feet in the sun, my mind in Chile, and my imagination roaming widely, my eyes fell on a religious image printed on a dirty old sheet of paper and tacked with a carob thorn to the head of the nuptial cot of the happy pair who were my hosts. Just to pass the time it occurred to me to apply a bit of color to Our Lady of Mount Carmel, which was the image displayed on that scrap of paper; and since on all my ultramontane excursions I have always had the company of a box of watercolors, which helped me to enrich my collection of vistas and of hard-to-preserve natural curiosities, I brought it out, and a moment later my work was done and that dreadful work of art had returned to its place, looking, with its new paint and from a distance, more like the king of diamonds than like anything else.

I was chatting with my faithful Campos in my quarters when, shortly after the owners had returned from Albardón, we saw them dash out the door, one shouting, "A miracle!" and the other, "Come see!" On hearing these shouts we, too, came running; and since I had by then forgotten the touch of makeup I had applied to the image, and since nothing in my appearance led my hosts to suspect that beneath it lay a genuine painter, it is hardly surprising that their shouts startled me at first and that then I had my hands full trying to persuade them that I was the cause of so unexpected a transformation.

As my simple hosts spread the story, the house was soon filled with curious neighbors and my humble bower turned into a studio for the coloring of prints and even the restoration of old oil paintings. The prints brought on sheets of paper torn from old missals or religious books offered no difficulty; but such was not the case of the oil paintings, for which the watercolors, the only and none too abundant paints I had, were of no use. Nonetheless, as my growing reputation obliged me to find a path out of every predicament, even if not always the straight and narrow path, I tried liberal applications of cooking oil on the back of the canvas to renew the colors and of egg white on the front to serve as varnish; and I got such good results that after twenty days of besmearing old canvas and filthy paper I had more than enough equipment for my voyage, in addition to a few coins that piously came to fortify my purse.

Such good fortune could not last long, and fate took care to prove it by a most unexpected occurrence that drove me from my safe and peaceful studio into the toils and dangers of the half-melted snows that awaited me in the Andes.

The modest artist's fame had attracted the eyes of the local authorities. This could be no ordinary man; the skills he displayed were out of keeping with his plain dress. Who might he be? Could he perhaps be a spy? Such were the questions they asked themselves, and not implausibly, because just at that time not only Chile was at loggerheads with the Peruvian-Bolivian Confederation, but the Argentine dictator Rosas had also cut off all peaceful relations with that state. I learned that on the night of the twenty-eighth day since my arrival in Calingasta a corporal of the "red blankets," my perpetual nightmare, had spoken with one of the neighbors, who had immediately approached my host and told him I was no Chilean but a Bolivian, and one of some importance, sent to La Rioja and San Juan by General Santa Cruz for who knows what purpose. He had concluded his fable by stressing the great risk Gómez would run if I was caught in his house, where they were planning to arrest me.

This news immediately brought to my mind the forgotten passport, my detention and consequent prank in San Carlos, my headlong flight, and every other cause for fear that might justifiably disturb the tranquility of a foreigner in that place and in my difficult situation; and since my poor host's eagerness to have me leave his house as soon as possible showed me there was not a moment to be lost, I made my preparations for the voyage to Chile with unheard-of speed and, only hours after that fearful warning and under cover of darkness, my intrepid Campos and I, with only four horses and a laden mule, left the hospitable home of the terrified Gómez and, much against our will, followed the difficult trail that leads from Calingasta to the well-known pass through the Agua Negra Mountains.

The October heat was already beginning to melt the snows that winter deposits on the high Andean passes, which in the north open earlier than in the south, yet are no less dangerous for the traveler who first braves them.

The snowfall that descends on our imposing white peaks in winter is a good deal more impressive when seen from close up than it appears from a distance. Hail is infrequent in the mountains, and only twice have I seen snowfall accompanied by wind. The snowflakes always float down like light feathers that sway, fall, rise, and whirl in the still air; they do so in such quantity that if you stretch out your arm you will be unable to see your hand. The winter snow of the Andes is dry, and the traveler caught in it can go on for hours if he has expert knowledge of the terrain. If he does not, he loses his way and dies, with the light feathers, still intact, gleaming white on his hat, his shoulders, and every other point to which they could cling. The snow covers all things, levels all things. It smoothes out every unevenness on the plateaus, and the outlines of the first streams that descend from the heights are so blurred that the landscape takes on a new appearance and only an experienced scout can tell—and then not always—where lies the firm ground and where the trap of soft snow that masks a dreadful abyss.

With the end of winter and the beginning of a milder season, new dangers arise for the first voyagers. The heat of the day melts the upper layer of snow; this water rushes downhill with a roar, forming dangerous torrents among the rocks and precipices. The cold of the night stops the melting, freezing sets in, and the next morning the traveler is faced, in place of the soft snow he trod the day before, with a crust of slippery hard ice that may support the weight of his horse without cracking but will cause it to skid and fall, or may be too fragile for the animal, which then at every step sinks into the snow up to its chest.

All these difficulties, however, would be child's play for the traveler did he not have to traverse precipitous slopes plunging into deep gorges. The very name that many of these passes bear tells us what they are; our rustics call them "Impossibles." A Spanish engineer was therefore as right as he was witty when he said of them, "Only the devil could have passed through here—and in his youth, too, because I swear he couldn't do it now!"

Nonetheless, by dint of strain and steady effort we reached the top, losing two of our horses in the process, which did not, however, discourage us, because if we did not overtax our two remaining ones they could bring us to the first Chilean settlement on the mountain road to Elqui. Struggling against the snows piled at the bottom of a deep ravine, at the top of which a crest of black rocks broke through the white sheet covering it, we followed the downhill trail toward La Laguna until, beset by cold, hunger, and exhaustion, we came upon one of the many snow-free caves that merciful nature provides for the Andean traveler. In one corner of that gloomy refuge, at whose entrance a crude stone wall kept out the wind, we found, much to our delight, the only treasure that could then save us, a small pile of horse dung, the precious fuel that the traveler in the Andes always gathers and uses sparingly so that it might serve whoever follows him on the same path. There I had some of what my good Campos called coffee, which is nothing but a cup of hot water into which a handful of earth has been dropped and which is drunk as soon as the earth settles. This drink, which foreigners may call what they wish, is not to be despised in the high mountains, especially by those suffering from asthma. I do not know whether our lungs need to breathe an air less pure than that of the highest peaks, or whether the boiling water's action on the earth infuses the air we breathe as we drink it with those earthen fluids lacking in the rarefied atmosphere; the fact is that my labored breathing returned to normal, and that thanks to such coffee and a half-heated piece of jerky I slept like a log that night.

The next day the "poor man's blanket," as my servant called the sun, had already been spread for some time over the dazzling surface of the Siberia where we found ourselves when, after I had finished the last sip of my morning cup of coffee, we set off in search of the canyon of the Turbio River, which rises on the far side of La Laguna. For a while, taking care not to overtax our hungry animals, we advanced cautiously between the massive Doña Rosa Range, which we left behind us, and the sheer range of Doña Ana, which seemed to be blocking our way on the north. Since the elevated body of water called simply La Laguna,[37] which is one of the chief sources of the Elqui River, lies between these two mighty massifs, we had to venture onto one of the steep and dangerous slopes that border it in order to reach the deep canyon that was to lead us to a place of human habitation.

Between the frozen lake, whose maximum diameter seemed to me not to exceed one kilometer, and the sloping heights through which we had to pass there lay one of those Impossibles, short but truly and extremely impossible. The thought that the slightest accident could plunge us from that height to the bottom of the terrifying abyss instantly made me shudder. It was impossible to retrace our steps; proceeding seemed equally impossible; but since between the certainty of starving to death and being frozen solid and the risk of falling to our destruction the choice was clear, we placed our fate in God's hands and spurred our horses on.

Holding our breaths, as one always does on such occasions, and with our eyes fixed on where the unsteady hooves of our constantly skidding mounts were treading, we had almost surmounted that peril when our pack mule, tottering from a violent fall and heedless of the shouts with which we tried to encourage it, slipped down the bank, while my horse, upset by an impulsive tug on the reins occasioned by that deplorable scene, also fell on its side, threw its rider some distance away, and inevitably followed the route that had led its unfortunate companion down the precipice! A moment later two unforgettable crashes told us we should never again see those brave and gentle beasts that had accompanied us so far. Stunned by my fall, seized by an indescribable vertigo, my spirits shattered, I owed my deliverance to the cool head of Campos. This faithful companion, at great risk, because the dangerous passes of the Andes are traversed far more safely on horseback than on foot, tenderly raised me from the ground and calmed me; a moment later, by sheer force, and plunging our daggers into the slippery ground as handholds, we managed to pass through the Impossible.

Now our equipment was reduced to the clothes on our backs and Campos's horse and saddle, and our food to a quarter of a guanaco that I had shot two days before and that fortunately had escaped the fate of our other belongings. According to my good companion's calculations, we still had some ten leagues' journey before reaching Tilo, which was the closest inhabited farm in those mountains. But I have no wish to tire

37. *La Laguna,* "The Lake." JP.

myself or the reader with the usual tales of travelers' ordeals. I am all for the laconic way in which *La Monja Alférez*[38] told the valiant story of her valiant life in four lines. I walked, I slept among rocks, I climbed mountains, I descended slopes, I suffered cold, I bore exhaustion, I lived for three days on only one cup of warm blood from the poor horse we had left. Had it not been for the strength of Campos, who left me and went ahead in search of help, and for the good heart of Señor Ságüez, who came to my rescue, there can be no doubt that between the Turbio, which a weakened man could not ford, and the rocks that border it south of the rapids of Los Piuquenes, someone would eventually have found, along with a human skeleton, a red briefcase that I still possess and that holds, written in pencil, my premature epitaph.

38. *La Monja Alférez* (The Warrior Nun) is the name popularly given to Catalina de Erauso, a native of Spain's Basque provinces, who in the early seventeenth century escaped from the convent where she was a novice and spent years living as a man. She served in the Spanish army in America and for her merits was promoted to the rank of *alférez,* corresponding to ensign or second lieutenant. She left an account of her military service but was also the heroine of a fictionalized pseudo-autobiography published in 1829. JP.

X

Juan Antonio Rodríguez, military commander of San Rafael.
— Threshing time.— Rodríguez is challenged. — He flees.—
Planchón Pass.— Customs guards in the Andes.— Chilecitos.—
Aldao.— The adventures of Rodríguez, continued.— His death.
— Rodríguez's itinerary and his papers.— The eastern slope of
the southern Andes. — A note by Rodríguez.

The twenty-sixth day of October of the year 1842 found me on the small but very fruitful farm Boldomávida, which I had just rented and which lies next to the one called Los Culenes in what used to be the province of Colchagua. There, to my surprise and that of others, I was resting from my travels between Mendoza and Buenos Aires, my expeditions to Salta, my comings and goings among La Rioja, San Luis, San Juan, and Mendoza, and my constant crossings of the Andean passes, which I had come to know so well that I had earned the enviable title of *baqueano* or scout.

How many political events had taken place in our country since the day of my flight from San Carlos!

The unexpected Treaty of Paucarpata; the unspeakably infamous rebellion at Quillota, headed by Vidaurre and leading to the unfortunate death of the great Portales; the bloody battle of El Barón on the hills of Valparaíso; the ever memorable victory of Yungay, in which the Chilean forces under the command of the brave and intelligent General Bulnes had destroyed the Peruvian-Bolivian Confederation that threatened us; the merchant flag of Spain flying peacefully by the side of Chile's; Bulnes rising to be chief of state, a well-deserved reward for his service; and above all, the law of amnesty, which allowed our exiled politicians to return to their homeland!

"First war, now work," I was saying to myself; and with my mind at ease about what the future held for my fortunate country, my imagination was once more powerfully drawn to thoughts of new expeditions.

As I sat by myself on the modest porch of my house contemplating my fields and drinking an Argentine *mate,* my imagination was busy roaming, if not over the scrublands of the icy mountains that I had crossed so often, then over the wide spaces of the pampas, whose mysteries were still unknown to me beyond the southern borders of Mendoza. At that time I had not yet undertaken my always disastrous adventures in that mysterious Patagonia where, I was assured, my endeavors could produce splendid results. It was only the disillusionment born of my earlier journeys that held me back and forced me, against my inveterate custom, to await a more favorable occasion before plunging into the unknown.

A favorable occasion, however, even if less than spectacular, soon arose and once more swept away my resolve to live quietly.

I discerned, heading up the road to the farm buildings, a drove of several horses and four oxen of remarkable size. My amazement increased when I saw that the drove entered my courtyard and that a cowhand, dressed in the Argentine fashion and riding a fine horse, dismounted and with a cheerful and respectful bow handed me a letter wrapped in a kerchief. At first I did not recognize him; but when I heard him address me by my name and call me "boss," I saw that the stranger was none other than my faithful old Campos, whom I had lost sight of four years earlier and who had sung the praises of what he considered my superlative qualities to his new employer until the latter had sent him from the fort of San Rafael, on the other side of the Andes, with a present for me.

The unexpected letter was signed by the celebrated Chilean Don Juan Antonio Rodríguez, a native of Loló, who for many years was the right arm of Aldao and the terror of the Unitarians, and who now, while serving as commander of the fort of San Rafael on the border between Mendoza and Patagonia, had taken it into his head to seek my friendship. The history of the dreadful Aldao's reign of terror in the province of Mendoza cannot be written without making very special mention of this terrible soldier of fortune whom the Argentineans still call a fierce bandit.

The arrival of my faithful Campos and his enthusiastic descriptions of the great beauty of those unexplored places; the abundance and cheapness of their countless cattle; what I knew about Aldao, whose friendship I stood to gain through that offered me by Rodríguez; and above all, the chance not to be hunted as I had been in San Carlos not long before, all propelled me once more onto the path of transandean adventures.

But a word of explanation is in order before I continue. Since pages torn from these notes have appeared in print, giving a mutilated account of some of my journeys, it seems to me that in order to preserve the proper order of the events I have witnessed, I should restore those pages to their context.

And so, turning once more to what was happening right then, I copy, without altering a jot or a tittle, the letter that a merry Campos had just handed to me wrapped in a kerchief:

LONG LIVE REASON AND THE CHRISTIAN RELIGION[39]

San Rafael, March 11, 1843[40]

Don Vicente Pérez Rosales

My dear sir:

Your good reputation has reached this place, which is why my trifling merit makes me bashful about seeking your friendship, which I hope you will not begrudge one who sincerely asks you for it.

I'm sending four little calves for you and your friends, and also, for your saddle, six broken colts that are not all bad even though I'm sure you have better ones there in Colchagua.

39. At that time the motto used on all official communications of the Argentine Confederation was "Long live the Argentine Confederation! Death to the Unitarian savages!," but the personage I am here recalling never employed it. VPR.
40. This date would seem to conflict with that given at the outset of the chapter, October 26, 1842. JP.

There is no point in mentioning our great scarcity of good gunpowder and small arms around here. Well, Señor Don Vicente, we pray God to give you health, and that's all from your friend who is eager to oblige you,

Juan Antonio Rodríguez

Along with this letter I received four fine oxen, the biggest I have ever seen, and three pairs of beautiful horses.

Who might this man be who sent me gifts without knowing me and asked me for favors without mentioning them? Let us follow his trail for a moment.

In 1833 not even in Europe did anyone suspect that mechanical threshers would one day be perfected to the point of replacing the flail over there and the hooves of mares in Chile at harvest time. And while we are speaking of machines, we could ask why humanity erects statues to honor those skilled in making and using machines for shortening life, and not those who strive to make machines to lengthen it. To Pitt and Ramsons[41] Chilean agriculture owes speedy and secure harvests, as it gathers in one or two months, depending on the extent of the fields, what used to require four, and then always under the threat of early rains. At harvest time half a million hands used to consume without producing, leaning on their rakes and waiting for months on end for the wind before processing the wheat. Is not the man who restored them to us more deserving than many another of statues that offer him to the veneration of grateful posterity?

Let my good intentions excuse this preamble, and let us continue.

On the northern flank of the Quiahue grade, in the maritime zone of what used to be Colchagua, there vegetated in 1830, like so many other ill-planted seeds of towns, a hamlet that bore the name Loló. The time of year to which these recollections refer was the threshing season, a time of very hard work that these good people made bearable by cheerful *intermezzi* of harp and guitar music and plenty of *chicha* to wash away the dust that stuck in their throats.

In the country, threshing and roundups were festivities to which no invitation was needed and where every well-behaved person with a good

41. William Pitt, an English inventor, developed a reaping machine in 1786. "Ramsons," of whom neither I nor my expert adviser, Professor Ken Alder, have found any trace, might be Robert Ransome, another English inventor of agricultural machinery in the early nineteenth century. JP.

144

horse could find hospitality. Under the commodious bower that was always set up near the workplace for the comfort and enjoyment of the helping hands there was never a lack of drink, good singing, or opportunities to show off one's horse and high spirits; and so it is safe to assume that at these performances, where everyone was simultaneously actor and spectator, the enviable peace and concord that ought to reign among Christian princes did not always prevail. This was all the more true if some foppish gallant came to join the crowd.

This genuine Chilean type, with his poncho and cowboy boots, is today almost forgotten; but back then he was the living reincarnation of the medieval knight errant, both in his way of life and in his tastes and inclinations. Like the knight errant, he went in search of adventures; like him, he sought tough men to conquer, wrongs to set right, rights to set wrong, and damsels to please, sometimes courteously and sometimes not, because some of these men were rude, and bullies, too. Just as the knight errant would not miss a tournament where he might display his valor and the invincible power of his lance, so the sun might fail to rise before one of our gallants would fail to show up at threshing time, at roundups, at horse races, and or anyplace else where there might be girls with whom to flirt, *chicha* to drink, songs to hear, verses with which to allude to those present, generosity and high spirits to be displayed, and shoving and slashing to give and receive, even if only for a refusal to drink from the same glass.

The threshing at Loló had been going on for four days, and nothing had disturbed either the work or the intervals of relaxation; but the fifth day came, and since it was to be the last, custom required an all-night celebration to bid farewell to the participants, with a bonfire to make up for the absence of the sun. Soon all beneath the bower were in the grip of a gaiety reportedly at fever pitch. The master of the house had made every effort to send his guests off in style, and nothing was lacking for the party: harp, rebec, and guitar, a spiked punch, wine, rolled roasts, and veal with plenty of chili.

A striking *huaso*[42] some forty years old, with deeply tanned face, powerful muscles, and a resolute mien, was enjoying all these delights, his arm around a singer and a glass of punch in his hand. This was Francisco Araya, a former laborer from Alhué, now well known as a loafer, who had put the crowning touch to his fame for brutal and unshakable valor in a dreadful duel fought with knives while the combatants were tied together by their left legs. On that occasion, Araya had forced his rival to save his

---

42. *Huaso,* a Chilean farmer or peasant. JP.

life by confessing that he was less of a man than he. Since he took pride in looking for a fight, it was to be expected, now that he was passing through Loló, that he would put in an appearance beneath the bower.

Facing him, but outside the bower, now hidden in the shadows, now visible by the light of the bonfire, a horseman seemed to be enjoying the spectacle of the carousal. This new personage, whose elegant dress and manner revealed him to belong to the aristocracy of the town, and who was tall, well proportioned, with bright cheeks on a fair face, blue eyes, aquiline nose, blond hair, and a red mustache, showed his participation in the festivities only by means of an occasional song that, while looking up at the sky, he sang under his breath at every loud boast—and there were many—that the bully Araya was constantly spewing forth.

During one of the intervals in the singing, a simple local fellow, tired of hearing nothing but Araya's voice, said to him in a roguish tone, "Don't talk so much, boss, because what's sauce for the goose is sauce for the gander, and there's no lack of those in Quiahue, and you never know what kind of bird you might stir up."

When he saw the sort of man who was interrupting him, Araya burst out laughing and exclaimed, "A bird, and in Loló? I hope I stir up two, because after one I'd still be hungry. And look here, you: you know what else? The man that can stand up to Pancho Araya hasn't been born yet, and just to show you, there won't be any singing of verses tonight unless I damn well feel like it, and if there's any objection, I'd like to hear it!"

He had not yet finished issuing this bold challenge when the stranger with the red mustache jumped down from his horse, shouldered the ruffian aside, and with one swipe of his dagger cut all the strings of his harp.

The blood of those who witnessed this unexpected turn of events froze in their veins, and deadly silence fell over all. Only the angry glares of the two remarkable antagonists spoke, as they exchanged glances that were death sentences and that, had they been forged of steel, would have filled the space between them with sparks. Few words are needed between men of this mettle. They understood each other, and with threatening gestures they immediately rushed out in search of their horses. Others in turn did the same; and a moment later, in the terrifying silence, a circle of mounted men had formed an arena in whose center, in blind fury and machete in hand, those two expert horsemen charged at each other in a frightful battle that ended only when with a hoarse dying scream a wounded body fell before the victor's mount.

Don Juan Antonio Rodríguez, in fair and open combat, had split Araya's skull with a powerful blow of his machete.

· · ·

As you leave the arid hills of Teno and cross the river of that name heading east up its canyon, you enter the picturesque and well-traveled road that leads to Planchón Pass.

Anyone who has explored the Andes only between Santiago and Atacama has no idea of the rich potential that the mysterious valleys of the south hold for agriculture and manufacturing. They display lovely evergreen vegetation, mighty waterfalls that offer cheap power near raw materials waiting to be exploited, and a climate that in many valleys surrounded by snow-covered peaks is milder than that of the central valley, for in them the vine, the orange tree, and delicate flowers are less exposed to unforeseen destructive frost. In places the natural moisture, without being excessive, makes irrigation unnecessary, and alfalfa need only be sown once to develop and reproduce.

Once it leaves Teno and enters the foothills of the Andes, the road to Planchón Pass is a delightful and extensive park endowed with every rare and remarkable attraction that only nature can create; and as one reaches the higher elevations, it presents a stern and imposing panorama of all a learned man needs in order to survey the mysteries of the second period of the Earth's formation. As one continues to climb, the vegetation seems to languish in the thinner air, for it diminishes in both size and vigor, so that once the traveler has passed the frontier post at Los Quenes, he begins to see dwarfed versions of what a few leagues below were massive trees reaching astonishing heights. This phenomenon becomes even more noticeable as one enters the zone of perpetual snows, for the cypresses that still grow almost on the very brow of the snowbanks are old by the time they reach a height of three inches. Before reaching these arid places the voyager begins to climb the slope of the volcano Peteroa, whose rocky dome, with its immense crater, forms the watershed between Chile and the Argentine province of Mendoza.

Within the very crater of this volcano, which is always active, though not violently so, there are some enclosures formed by lava and solid ice, along with scattered fissures that blast sulfurous vapors into the air. One of those enclosures is called the Main Square; and a traveler must lodge there if, riding at a steady walk for a day on hungry horses, he is safely to reach the pass of Las Yaretas, which lies opposite and where he can consider himself delivered from the terrifying snowstorms that frequently fall on the intervening white strip of Andean plateau.

On the rugged surface of that frozen snowbank stand scattered apparitions of pure ice called "penitents," whose whiteness, resembling that of ground glass, contrasts with the bare black ridges of the steep rocks that channel the blasts of wind and border the deep chasms hidden from the traveler's sight by piles of soft snow.

On the cool morning of February 18, 1830, four troopers and a corporal could be seen through the steam rising from the fissures on the Main Square of Peteroa. They seemed to be a cross between soldiers and country bumpkins and were struggling to saddle their horses as fast as possible to continue a hasty voyage eastward. They were Chileans and, being armed soldiers, could not cross the frontier, which seemed to suggest that they were not simply traveling but pursuing one of the many criminals who in those days, just as they do now, used to seek impunity for their misdeeds beyond the mountains. Their quarry, if they were pursuing someone, must have passed by the same place the night before; but he had not slept there. Recent traces of blood that showed on the ice and led toward Las Yaretas indicated that only one horse had passed through and that it had been very tired and wounded in the hooves; and so it was clear that if they hurried they could catch the fugitive before he reached sanctuary.

After several hours of following the track on trails and over passes until then unknown to their leader and finding nothing to encourage them in their arduous task, the corporal's determination was beginning to flag when the attention of one of the soldiers was sharply drawn to a dark object that seemed to be trying to hide behind a distant ridge of snow. They now accelerated their pace with renewed energy, but when they reached the icy "penitent" they found, to their great surprise and dismay, not the person they were seeking but a partly saddled dead horse.

The fugitive had therefore spent the night in the shelter of the block of ice, but where might he be now? The bloody track ended there; the one made by human footsteps hardly showed on the ice. Ashamed at being frustrated in their endeavor, because they were in fact pursuing someone, they determined to proceed at full speed to occupy the only pass visible, which lay not far off between two enormous black rocks; but they arrived too late, because they realized that they had caught up with the fugitive only when they heard the sound made by the collapse of an enormous eave of snow that projected over an abyss, onto whose bottom, cushioned by soft snow, desperation had cast their mysterious prey!

The astonished pursuers shouted with fright on witnessing this burst of desperate valor; and they had not yet withdrawn from the edge of the precipice that had dashed their hopes when they saw, alive and struggling in the soft white blanket that covered the bottom of the ravine, a man who, after climbing out the other side covered with snow, calmly shook out the blanket and hide he was carrying.

Don Juan Antonio Rodríguez had escaped from the pursuit that the death of Araya had brought upon him!

Don Juan Antonio Rodríguez did not leave his country as does a hardened criminal. He left because of one of those calamities that even prudence is sometimes powerless to avoid and that the law will not pardon.

He had been born in Chile, in a coastal district formerly belonging to the province of Colchagua, into an honorable family esteemed for its wealth in the former province of San Fernando. He had received quite a good education for such a remote part of Chile in 1790. The years of his childhood had been spent learning to read badly, write worse, and barely manage to count, as well as imbibing the trite moral maxims that, inculcated by ignorance, lead rather to fanaticism than to truly religious sentiments. Once he reached the age of puberty, his iron constitution, his extraordinary daring on horseback, a bravery that became proverbial, his talent for acerbic as well as amusing remarks, and his boundless generosity earned him a gallant reputation throughout the province that as late as 1850 still survived in the memories of the people of Quiahue.

In hiding, but steadfastly pursued after his clash with Araya, he disguised himself to go to the town of Curicó, where he learned from his friends that a certain jealousy on the part of the prosecuting magistrate and a not very uncertain thrashing received at Rodríguez's hands in the presence of the disputed damsel, had raised his unfortunate encounter at the harvest festivities in Loló to the level of premeditated murder. There was nothing for it, then, but to absent himself for a time from his country and to range, as a poor and helpless fugitive, over those mountains and those pampas where he had so often appeared as a shrewd, affluent, and renowned smuggler.

He consequently left without delay on what he was riding, as our peasants say, fleeing prison and the scaffold. When he reached the estate called La Huerta, he learned that the border guard had been instructed to detain him. But such guards had always been the least of Rodríguez's worries, even when, as was now the case, he had long-standing and serious accounts to settle with them. Without sparing his noble mount, therefore, that same night he skirted the guard by a route that he knew would allow him to pass without being heard.

No money is more wasted than that spent on these famous customs posts in the Andes, both because of the countless opportunities that the mountains offer for the evasion of their vigilance and because of the guards' lukewarm attitude toward the execution of their duties. Since the zeal displayed by the pursuers of Rodríguez seems, however, to contradict these facts, I consider it appropriate to explain the causes of so unusual a phenomenon.

Two years before the pursuit I have just recounted, Rodríguez was coming from the other side of the mountains with a fine load of tobacco. The best way to escape the vigilance of the guards is to make a detour; but since a detour requires time and therefore interferes with sales, Don Juan Antonio, who, without knowing any English, knew that "time is money," thought up the prank, as he put it, of leaving his cargo behind, sending his men ahead, having them lodge in the guardpost pretending to be cattle dealers, tying the guards up during the night, making them cross the mountains, and depositing them for twelve days in the Indian village of the Pehuenche chief Faipanque, who owned some ranches south of the Salado River.

The gift of a good horse that on Rodríguez's orders was made to each of the prisoners upon their release had not sufficed to crush the seeds of wrath and revenge that the heavy-handed maneuver had planted in the hearts of the protectors of the public purse, and one effect of their shame and desire for vengeance was that not even the governor of Curicó heard a word of what had happened. Their pursuit, then, was so vigorous that one could say they set down their feet where the fugitive had just lifted his.

As we have seen, Rodríguez did not spend the night in the Main Square of the crater of Peteroa but pushed on, without sparing his flagging horse, through the midst of that desert of hard ice until the noble beast, weakened by exhaustion and hunger, the skin at the base of its hooves torn by the sharp edges of the ice through which it was sinking, curled up next to a tall "penitent" and forsook both its life and the master it was bearing.

Forced to spend the night there, freezing to death and, for fear of being discovered, unable to light a fire, not even with the horse dung he was carrying, as does everyone who undertakes to cross Planchón, that man of iron waited for dawn wrapped in his saddle skins, sheltered by the still warm belly of the faithful companion that had brought him this far and that even in death made a present to him of its last remaining warmth.

The first glimmer of dawn found Rodríguez far from the public road, walking along one of the solitary paths that he knew and that had often saved him. The pelt that had covered his saddle was wrapped around his chest; his provisions were reduced to the last piece of jerky that he was devouring; his weapons, to the machete that had caused his misfortune; and his equipment, to his flint and tinderbox. But what could a man on foot on those white expanses do to escape the eyes of his well-mounted pursuers? And so they found him just as he was starting on the narrow and dangerous path that traverses the southern flank of the inaccessible rock that rises from an abyss and, with the snows of its level areas, feeds the first sources of the Salado.

What a dreadful situation for that unfortunate! If he continued to flee on that path, which if followed an hour earlier would have put many leagues between him and his pursuers, he was now sure to fall into their hands; to leave it was to plunge into an abyss whose depth was hidden by the fresh snow. At that dark moment he saw before him the prospect of a miserable and inevitable death, with only the choice of the means left to him; but for a soul of his mettle there could be no vacillation between dying on the ignominious scaffold of the criminal and dying smashed to pieces but free. When his pursuers called on him to halt, he therefore answered only with that frightful leap that, dragging along the icicles on the edge of the precipice, landed him on the bottom of the abyss, where he sank into the snow. His unique boldness doubly saved Rodríguez's life: because he did not land on hardened snow, and because his position at the bottom of the ravine cut many leagues from a route that, weakened as he was, he could not have covered without freezing to death.

Following a rushing stream, whose always perilous falls he negotiated by brute strength and by sliding and slipping, he came to the first yellowish meadows where the snows end. There, exhausted by his exertions, by hunger, and by fierce emotions, he found refuge in a cave, where the warmth of a fire restored him to life and where he spent the night, with no bed but the soil loosened by his machete, no blanket but the pelt he still carried with him, no pillow but his powerful but weakened arm.

Later, when fortune had placed him in more enviable circumstances, he told me that the next morning he had awoken more drained than rested, since when not dreaming that he was running, he had dreamt of being captured and seated on the executioner's bench, or of plunging into the abyss.

With the return of day and the certainty that he was free, this remarkable man quickly regained all the vigor of which the emotions of the night and the storm through which he had passed had deprived him; and continuing his way down, sometimes along the river bank, other times traversing ridges, he had the good fortune to be found and cared for by some guanaco hunters who were ranging through that area and who took him along until they left him safe and sound in Chilecito de Mendoza.

But, my readers might ask, what is this Chilecito that I keep mentioning? I shall explain.

The Chilean is by nature a wanderer; distances mean nothing to him if they offer a glimpse either of great profits or of great marvels. If he is not to be found everywhere, this is less for lack of desire than for lack of the means for satisfying his innate inclination. The burning sands of the Bolivian coast[43] are full of Chileans; thousands of them can be found in Peru; and in neither country does anyone deny that the Chilean laborer excels in energy, boldness, and hard work, unlike what occurs in his own country, where, having no one to whom he can display these virtues, he is not only lazy but comes to be meek and docile, though he is always haughty and proud abroad.

The first settlers who in pursuit of the Golden Fleece trod the enchanted shores of California were Chileans, and that change of scene sufficed to transform the effeminacy and apparent idleness of the scions of Santiago's first families into an enviable boldness and hard work. I have seen these men smile as they traded the soft touch of their kid gloves for the hard feel of the laborer's crowbar, and their linen shirts, stylish vests, and elegant coats of fine cloth for a plain and common rough woollen shirt. I have seen them sleep on the ground with no cover but a serape and no pillow but their hat, and, strong in their self-esteem, fearlessly challenge sun, rain, drudgery, and exhaustion. In California the sentimental dandy of Santiago and the farmhand of our countryside were masters and servants, valued boatmen, tireless stevedores, carpenters, adobe makers, gold panners, builders, and merchants. I have seen them change effortlessly from being strict and demanding masters in Chile to being humble servants of some mulatto who had struck it rich.

I have seen Chilean seamen calmly abandon a ship trapped amid the snows and terrible ice floes of the Baltic near Kronstadt, walk ashore over the frozen sea, and then travel from one jail to another until they reached Hamburg, whence I was able to send them home. I have seen them dashing and strutting about on a Bordeaux dock where they had just landed and did not know a soul, as bold and self-possessed as if they were still on the San Carlos wharf at Ancud. I have seen wealthy Chileans squander their money in every capital of Europe, with never a thought for the future; poor Chileans, trusting in their talents, seek the prestige and honor that in those centers of civilization flow from contributing to the advance of science and the arts; and Chileans, ordinary sailors and deserters to boot, cheerfully walk across France from Bordeaux to Le Havre in search of another ship on which to serve. The daring seaman who followed Cochrane to Greece was a Chilean; Chileans

43. Bolivia lost its seacoast to Chile in 1883. JP.

are the countless travelers who, their bag slung over their shoulder and a stick in their hand, are to be met everywhere in the Andean passes as they make use of the summer to march off in search of a pair of yet-to-be-broken oxen or of a saddle horse; and Chileans, too, are the founders and inhabitants of all the Chilecitos that stand at the eastern base of our Andes, because wherever Chileans gather in a foreign land, a Little Chile or Chilecito must needs spring up.

These Chilecitos, which, being nothing but a jumble of huts, farms, and fields, do not even deserve the name of hamlets, always offer the first prospect of hospitality to the Chilean who crosses the Andes. Natural colonies that grow up from chance and necessity, they are simply collections of Chileans both resident and itinerant, almost always composed in equal parts of honest men and dishonest. And that is not to be wondered at, because the eastern slope of the Andes is for the Chilean both the refuge of the wicked and the home and reward of the industrious, and so both the criminal and the good citizen seek sanctuary there.

Chilecito de Mendoza was, then, the place where the compassionate guanaco hunters left the poor fugitive. The miserable kitchen of a certain Cubillos, who not long afterward became the friend and subordinate of that terrible Rodríguez whose daring deeds as a warrior of the pampa kept the trumpet of Fame so busy, was the first step on the ladder that raised the helpless outcast to absolute power. That filthy place was a palace for him then.

Poor and alone, with no capital but the strength of his arms, no future but the path of crime, which lay broad and inviting before him in a place where personal bravery counted for so much and might made right, Rodríguez, who had not been born for crime, was able to control himself and resignedly offered his services as a farmhand to Cubillos, in whose house he spent the first months of his exile.

Cubillos soon found out who his strong and docile peon was, felt ashamed, and proceeded to get him work selling alcoholic beverages. From then on, as he pursued his small business, the Chilean Rodríguez was constantly to be seen in San Vicente, San Carlos, Luján, Chilecito de Mendoza, and any other place that might offer good prospects for the sale of the delicious *pichanga*[44] that he alone knew how to clarify. As he traveled about he gradually came to be known and esteemed by all, and with this esteem he laid the foundation for the affection and respect that those simple folk ever had for him. Rodríguez was loved not only as

44. *Pichanga* is what they call new wine in Mendoza. VPR.

a friend but also as an inexorable and impartial judge, and more than once people came to him as though he really were a judge. His decisions were never appealed, and there were times when this judge knocked one of the parties to the ground if he suspected him of offending his dignity.

The fame of the Chilean soon reached the palace of the ferocious and cruel friar whom hell seemed to have vomited up onto the unfortunate province of Mendoza. Rodríguez, tired of selling wines and excited by the tales of his friends' brilliant feats of arms in Argentina's civil war, wanted to join the army; and as soon as he heard that the friar-general wanted to meet him, he presented himself and asked to be accepted in the rank of private. The recruit's athletic appearance, his open and determined countenance, and the modesty of his request were enough to show that shrewd chieftain that, as he put it later, "a man like Rodríguez was what he'd long been looking for." A brief conversation with Rodríguez had in fact allowed him to discover in him the loyalty of a dog, a virtue unknown to him in men, the strength and vigilance of a warrior, so necessary at that time, and, along with an impetuous character, the innocent simplicity of a child. At that very moment he determined to become absolute master of the Chilean's will, and certainly no enterprise was ever undertaken more successfully. Rodríguez was Rodríguez only when his actions and thoughts had no relation to the actions and thoughts of his protector and father, as he called him; otherwise, that brave and generous *huaso* ceased to be who he was and became a physical and psychological extension of Aldao, placed at greater or lesser distance from the center.

Instead of being received as a private, Rodríguez was immediately enrolled among the general's personal guard and favored with attentions and preferences that came to offend his comrades. These, alarmed by the newcomer's sudden rise to favor, tried to make his service unbearable for him; but Rodríguez knew that game and made things so hard for them that their gatherings were more than once on the point of bloodshed and would have reached it had not the memory of his Chilean disaster contained the irate arm of the ex-salesman of wines.

Sure of the friendship of Aldao, whom thereafter he called his father, just as Aldao called him son, he sought, with the loyalty of blind and enthusiastic gratitude, a chance to "let himself be torn to pieces" for his benefactor. So drastic an opportunity did not arise; but there was no lack of chances to place himself at risk for the general, because the man that seeks danger finds it, and because it may be one of the few things that a man can be sure of enjoying in this life.

News came that some tribes of Chilean Moluches were infesting the pampas and that in collaboration with the scouts of the chieftain Baigorría they were devastating the province and threatening San Carlos from the uninhabited and dangerous frontier of San Rafael, which borders Patagonia. Rodríguez offered to confront them, bolster the defenses of the neglected frontier, and hold it, if necessary, against all comers. And so he did, which gained him the title of captain of the fort of San Rafael. From that moment on our soldier of fortune became a public figure and a frequent participant in the bloody encounters of the civil war whose dreadful sway so long devastated the Argentine Republic. But since my intention is not to trace his role in this war but to recount in a simple and straightforward manner those outstanding aspects of the private life of the exile of Quiahue that are most closely related to my own, it will suffice to say, before continuing, that in that deadly fratricidal war there was no man who hazarded his life more in the cruel clashes to which duty and devotion to his leader called him. There was hardly a spot on Rodríguez's body that did not bear the mark of a lance or a bullet.

Anyone who believes that while General Aldao was alive Rodríguez did anything except on orders of his commander or had a single idea not suggested by him has badly mistaken the character of this extraordinary man. Rodríguez was simply what a brave soldier has always been: his duty was to obey, and he obeyed without question. In addition, Aldao was for him, "after God," perfection itself and even a clairvoyant; and so, as far as Rodríguez was concerned, Aldao did not and could not command anything but what was just and necessary. Hence that mixture of delicacy and inexorable firmness with which he carried out even the slightest wish of his guardian spirit: delicacy, because Rodríguez's heart was never cruel; inexorable firmness, because that quality was demanded by his duty of obedience. His, however, was not the cruel inflexibility that delights in tormenting a fellow-creature, but one born of the profound conviction and inmost knowledge that what must be done is necessary and just.

I was talking to him one day at his new quarters at San Rafael, and in his plain soldier's way he had just handed me half of a beautiful watermelon that he had split for my enjoyment, when two soldiers came into the room leading a prisoner with his hands tied and of strikingly repulsive appearance. He was of medium height, powerfully built but deformed, with a sallow complexion and a treacherous look in his eyes. A deep scar, apparently produced by a cut that removed part of his nose and stopped only at his jaw, made the total impression produced by that unfortunate man indescribably repellent. Rodríguez, who seemed to recognize him, stood up and said, "Aha! So it's you, eh, Godoy? You ugly scoundrel, I knew I'd get you sooner or later!" And turning to the soldiers, he added, "All right, take him a good way off, so our friend Don

Vicente and I won't hear anything, and then into the river with him, because he's not even human."

This unexpected incident so terrified me that I could not keep the melon in my hands and, dispirited, set it down on the table. When Rodríguez saw this he dashed out of the room and shouted for the prisoner to be brought back, adding as he rejoined me, "You have no idea, Don Vicente, what rogues these deserters are; but since I've heard you say so often that it's very virtuous to forgive, why shouldn't we be virtuous here, too?"

When the prisoner appeared, he said, "Untie him. Kneel down at this gentleman's feet, you scum, and forget you ever knew me."

But though this chief, whom the Unitarians call a vicious bandit, so easily pardoned capital crimes when the decision depended only on his heart, in other circumstances the matter stood very differently. A short time after this incident, he received a firm, though ill-considered command to have one of his best soldiers shot; he gave the order, weeping and at the same time extending his protection to the unfortunate man's widow and children.

Captain Rodríguez was, then, less cruel than people said; and that is why he never headed his letters with the frightful motto, "Long live the Argentine Confederation! Death to the Unitarian savages!" but with this other one that he undoubtedly devised himself, "Long live Reason and the Christian Religion!"

The bitter hostility that prevailed between the Unitarian and Federalist parties had, before the death of Quiroga, reached such a pitch that even the saving word "mercy" had lost all meaning. Many of the Unitarians of San Luis and Mendoza, implacably persecuted, had sought refuge among the Ranquenche Indians whose frequent incursions, under the orders of one Baigorría, infested not only the area adjacent to their lairs, but also more distant regions, sowing fear and desolation everywhere.

Nonetheless, in the midst of so many atrocities, an act of individual virtue would now and then bolster one's faith in humanity. To the south and a little to the west of the city of San Luis lies the lake called the Bebedero, or Watering Hole. On the almost uninhabited terrain between the lake and the town there stood, at great intervals, occasional huts or bowers of untrimmed carob branches, serving rather as signs that someone owned those fields, which were used to raise cattle, than as permanent habitations for their proprietors. On a dark night of the month of March, 1844, by the light of two fine fires, the outline of one of these rustic bowers was reflected in the clear waters that lap the northern shore of the Bebedero. The light of the left-hand fire revealed some soldiers who had recently dismounted and were apparently preparing to bivouac there, and whose dress and diverse weapons gave them the aspect rather of bandits than of soldiers. Some wounded men were also to be seen among them; but this did not interfere with the merry chatter, laughing, and cursing of the others while they were preparing for rest.

Inside the hut, the firelight that seeped through the crude wall of branches fell on a man who sat on the ground, bound hand and foot, bowed as though with age, white of face, and with a red mustache. He seemed to be wounded, for his neck was bound with a blood-soaked kerchief. Near him sat a soldier armed with shotgun and dagger.

The leader of the troop and his deputy were talking privately near the second fire; and the appearance of the former was as handsome and pleasing as that of the latter was repulsive, for besides being short and deformed, he bore on his yellowish face the scar of an old knife wound that made it even more repugnant than it already was.

"Did you give the orders, Godoy?" asked the leader.

"Yes, sir: a rest for the horses, and about four hours of rest for the men, as long as we're in the saddle by daybreak, and that's all."

"A lucky shot, eh?"

"I'll say!"

"Do you suppose any of them got away? I wouldn't want these fellows . . ."

"No, no! How could they get away? Just as soon as you hit the Chilean, all those who were dashing off whipping their horses for all they're worth rushed us, like a dog who's after juicy meat scraps, to carry away the body; but there's no arguing with lances and sabers, and we left 'em all lying there."

"Now I'm glad that meddling Chilean didn't die. The friar's attack dog is finished now; Baigorría will have a mouthful with him! And is he tied up tight?"

"Why are you asking, sir? You tied him up with your own hands."

"Keep an eye on him. I'm going to catch a few winks."

"Everybody's snoring away, so it's only right for you to get some rest, sir."

A moment later, all movement had ceased, the fires were slowly dying down, and the universal stillness was interrupted only by the cries of the waterfowl on the lake, by the occasional violent snorts of the horses tied up around the camp, and by the slow footsteps of the sentinel who was guarding the prisoner.

At second cock's crow the appearance of three armed men at the entrance to the hut told the unfortunate captive that his time had run out;

but he was mistaken: it was the changing of the guard. Prisoners like him had to die in the presence of Baigorría. To make doubly sure, the trooper in charge entered the hut in order to check his fetters in person. The bound man, little imagining what was about to happen, felt a thrill when he sensed a gentle touch on his shoulder and realized that someone was cutting the leather straps that tied his almost numb hands behind his back and placing a dagger in them.

Moved by what had just happened to him and unable to account for the source of such unexpected assistance, Rodríguez—for the mysterious wounded man was no other than he—drew his feet under the poncho, cut their fetters with trembling hand, allowed some time for the circulation to return, and then, in an instant, pounced on the unsuspecting sentinel, knocked him to the ground with a powerful blow to the forehead, jumped over him, and dashed away to the lake. The sentinel's shouts waken everyone; and in a jumbled pack they follow Corporal Godoy, who purposely leads them astray, and rush off in full and noisy pursuit, leaving their coveted prey safe and sound behind them. At this point Rodríguez quickly rises from the mud that covers him, leaps bareback onto the best of the horses tied up there, pushes past two soldiers who try to stop his flight, and disappears like a fleeting cloud in the darkness and the dense mist that rises from the warm surface of the lake!

Two years later, on the occasion of my third voyage to San Rafael, Rodríguez told me of this adventure, adding, "No good deed is ever wasted!"

The bullet had entered near his throat and had somehow lodged by the nape of his neck without killing him. At San Rafael there was nothing resembling a surgeon, and so, had this remarkable man not displayed yet another instance of his valor, it is not likely that he could have lived to tell me the tale. When the fever and pain that his unwelcome guest caused him reached the point of trying our *huaso*'s patience, he took his dagger and, by touch, made a dangerous cut in his neck and then vigorously ran his hand over it from front to back and said, "There goes that millstone!" as he watched a bloody bullet fall to the ground, weighing a full ounce and carrying some fat with it.

The death of Aldao, which Rodríguez considered the worst calamity that could befall the province of Mendoza, completely changed the character and inclinations of his protégé. From that point on San Rafael became the seat of a new government only nominally subject to the authorities in Mendoza. Rodríguez built up his forces by enlisting every Chilean who came to his fort, whether brought there by poverty or past crimes; he acquired a stock of horses, arms, and ammunition, and with his resolute temperament he awaited the future with confidence. The towns of San Vicente, Luján, San Carlos, and Chilecito were drawn by his generosity to place themselves tacitly under his protection; although in theory they were subject to their local authorities, the only authority and leader they recognized was "the Chilean Rodríguez, the father of every honest Argentinean."

This adventurer was, in fact, the supreme tribunal to which those displeased with the sentences handed down by the provincial courts would appeal. No matter how complicated the case might seem, Rodríguez decided it instantly; he would hear the first litigant to appear before him and, on the sole basis of his account, pronounce his irrevocable decision. So convinced was he that "those crooks," as he called public servants, were bound to get everything backwards, that as long as his decision was diametrically opposed to theirs, he considered it right and fair.

The situation of the provincial authorities was as yet too precarious to allow them safely to challenge the armed disobedience of the Chilean rebel. Realizing the threat posed by his well-known boldness, they set about at once surreptitiously to undermine his power; and they succeeded in doing so, because Rodríguez lived entirely by his heart and not a whit by his head.

I had been suspecting their maneuvers for some time; and for some time, too, without seeming to take an active part in what I saw around me, I had been trying to counter that soldier's determination to avenge the affronts that he was firmly convinced were being offered to the memory of Aldao. Finally he opened his whole heart to me.

Without being a fanatic, Rodríguez was superstitious. He believed naively in witchcraft and ghosts, and the heart that never flinched in the face of enemy lances trembled like a child's before anything that smelled of the supernatural. He told me that as he was walking alone one night on the banks of the Diamante, where he had gone to weep unseen for the death of Aldao, his idol and his father, he had seen a friar dressed in white robes rise from the placid waters of the river and signal to him to draw near. "I felt, sir," he told me deeply moved, "that something was pushing me toward that phantom as if it were sucking me in. Without knowing how, I passed over the fence surrounding a garden that lies on the shore and approached ever closer to that ghost whose right arm pointed to the pampa to the east while his left arm pointed at my feet. I was about to fall into the river when I felt something holding me down and scratching my leg. I don't know how I kept from dropping dead with fright in that place! When I came to, everything had disappeared, and I found myself caught in some rosebushes into which I'd fallen.

What might this mean, Don Vicente? You've read so much and traveled so much: couldn't this be some warning from heaven? Because you ought to know that shortly before he died my father called me to him, squeezed my hand, and said, 'My son, if I die sell everything and go back to your own country; or if you don't do that, go right away with your troops and put yourself under the direct authority of the Dictator. If you stay here, never trust a Mendozan. They'll kill you!'"

The last words of that cruel friar were unfortunately prophetic for the adventurer, for they soon came true.

Upon concluding his story, Rodríguez leapt from his seat as though propelled by a spring and, in a firm voice and with his imposing head held high, pronounced these words that sent a shudder of fear through me: "I haven't obeyed him, and I don't intend to as long as a single man who speaks ill of Aldao is left alive! I'll show those boors that run things in Mendoza that, old as he is, Rodríguez can still break their back."

The dejection that follows exaltation soon overwhelmed that heart filled with gratitude, and he sat down in silence, his unblinking gaze fixed on the horizon.

Poor friend! Was he at that moment coming to the realization that he lacked the mental power to reach his goal? With Aldao dead, that restless spirit wandered aimlessly from one project to another, anxiously seeking some friendly mind that would direct his great capacity for action and make it bear fruit.

Then he took me by the hand and led me to our horses that were waiting outside, saddled, and without a word we rode out onto the pampa. After a short while he stopped, pointed to the south, and said, "Can you make out that high mountain down there, sir? That's the Gigante. Now turn your horse in the other direction and look around you as far as you can see. Did you see San Rafael, too? Now look at my hands," and he showed me a pair of hands as hard as iron. "Is all of this worth anything? All right now, everything you've seen is yours. Stay with me, don't go back to Chile!" I confess that I was so startled by this extravagant display of generosity, whose purpose was by now quite clear to me, that I could not immediately reply. Rodríguez, misinterpreting my hesitation, then added, "I know that all this doesn't amount to much for a man used to fine presents, like you; but let me make it plain, this is all just a stirrup I'm holding out to you so you can use it to mount to the position that my general used to occupy!" The situation was clear, but all I could understand was that once I was in possession of such a secret I could in no way remain in that place.

After exhausting every means of persuasion to discourage him from so mad a project, I made him concede the importance of my traveling to

Chile; and promising to do nothing until I returned, he escorted me as far as the snow line with a hundred lancers. There I explained to him the extent to which he was surrounded by traps and traitors, urging him not to confide his secrets even to his own pillow and to maintain his obedience like a loyal soldier, and above all to take no subversive step unless I was by his side. After I had made him promise all this, and with the despondency of one losing all hope, I gave my poor friend the last embrace he was to receive from me in this world.

The year 1848 had barely begun when in Chile we received the news of a powerful military movement organized in San Rafael and threatening to overthrow the established authorities of the province of Mendoza by marching menacingly on the capital. A few days later we heard that the leader of this movement, betrayed and defeated near Luján, had fled and been captured near Las Yaretas and given over to the executioner. The moldering bones of Araya, avenged now by the hand of fate, must have shuddered in their tomb!

Thus died, at the age of seventy-four and after a storm-filled life, the valiant *huaso* of Quiahue, the keenest sword of the merciless friar Aldao, Rodríguez, whose memory will ever be dear to the people living south of San Carlos, whose deeds will be remembered as long as men remember the fields of battle where shone the sword of that famous commander of the Patagonian frontier of San Rafael, whom his enemies called a vicious bandit and his friends, the loving father of all honest folk.

The death of Rodríguez, in whose company I had made several military-mercantile expeditions even beyond the Colorado River, which pours its waters into the Atlantic, also put an end to my interest in the cattle trade on the pampas, which consisted by turns of capturing wild cattle that, shouting and galloping at them, we managed to drive into places from which they could not escape, of forcibly seizing the animals that Chilean Indians had stolen in the province of Buenos Aires, and of assaulting the native villages of the pampas that were ruled by Baigorría.

How much natural wealth awaits the miner, and above all the cattleman, on that wild and almost unknown eastern slope of the Andes, between the famous pass of Planchón and 37° south latitude, and between the perpetual snows and the base of those bulwarks that, either descending step by step parallel to the icy summits, or striking out at a right angle to that line, gradually lose elevation until they become mere hills and blend into the vast plains of the pampas!

I still possess the original itinerary of this region that guided Rodríguez on his expeditions and that I owe to his trusting kindness toward me. When I first visited this remarkable man he had given up his own bedroom for my use. After retiring for the night I was disturbed by some bulges beneath the mattress. I reached under it; and, startled by the discovery that the bulges were made by numerous packets of papers, I withdrew my hand, supposing that these might be documents of such a nature that they could only be stored as close to their owner's hand as was the brace of cocked pistols he always wore at his waist.

As I was talking with him the next day about the names of some of the places we could see from where we were sitting, and how far off they were, he led me into his room, thrust his hand between my mattress and the boards of his cot, and from among several bundles of papers that, he said, contained sensitive documents and letters from Rosas and Aldao, selected the itinerary that I mentioned and that he kept in so unusual a repository.

This is not the appropriate occasion for publishing this important document, full of notes and corrections made by Rodríguez himself during all the time that he exercised his extraordinary power on the frontier; but since I shall say something about the suitability of those places for the easy development of the livestock industry, I prefer that my readers should hear from the mouth of its author what he wrote about the least opulent of them, those that lie along the course of the Atuel River from the spot called Juntas up to its source in the mountains facing Rancagua. Rodríguez's text is as follows:

From Juntas heading northeast until you reach Butalo, 8 leagues. Good grazing land, carob woods, swamps, extensive pampas with some hills toward the west. General Aldao camped here with the central division in 1833 because the land offers abundant resources and there are several freshwater lakes.

From here to that of the Puntano Passes called Puntano Milagüe, 8 leagues. Good grazing land with dunes and carob woods. In the shelter of a dune there were huts of the Guitrao Indians and their chief Barbón, all of whom died in 1833 when the vanguard of the central division came after them.

From here to Loncoboca, 3 leagues. Tall carob woods, *chañares*, dunes, water holes, and abundant forage along the river banks.

From here to Chilquita or Bain, 2 leagues. The same kind of country; a valley with good pasture flanking the western mountains; many wild cattle come to drink at a lake that lies in the middle of a nearby arid area.

From here to Soitué, 3 leagues. The same kind of good grazing land with great pampas toward the west. Wild pigs, many wild cattle; the mountains continue to the west. We cross the river toward the east at the

Paso del Loro because there is no road on the west bank, which we have been following for 6 leagues from Soitué. At the ford there is a gigantic carob and a former encampment of Indians that no longer exist.

From here to the Pampa de la Víbora (Tilulelfún), 1 league. This pampa is a good place to hunt ostriches with the bolas, because they are very abundant here. Good grazing land, pools of excellent water where the Indians camp when they come to invade San Rafael.

From here to Currulaca, 5 leagues. Good grazing, and carob and *chañar* woods. Immense numbers of wild fowl. Water is easy to find everywhere. Many pigs and wild pigs, as well as wild cattle and horses, that come to drink at this point along the river.

From here to La Varita, 5 leagues, the same kind of country with some signs of volcanic activity.

From La Varita to Los Marcos the distance is 14 leagues. In this stretch the river flows sharply toward the west; many tigers,[45] wild pigs, ostriches, and carob and *chañar* woods here.

From here to Bajada del Tigre, 1 league, narrow road, lakes, carob and *chañar* woods.

From here to Corral de Vicente, 3 leagues along a narrow curving path. A large shade-giving *chañar,* many carobs.

From here to Yuncalito, 2 leagues of broom, carobs, and *chañares.* Good grazing land and pools of rain water.

From here to Corral de Novillos, 5 leagues. Deep gullies near the river that could serve as corrals for a roundup; the country, as before.

From here to Real del Mundo, 4 leagues. Alfalfa fields along the river, because someone once camped or lived here; hilly toward the east.

From here to Real del Padre, 5 leagues; alfalfa and carobs.

From here to Las Juntas, 5 leagues. In the center of this place there is a round fort protected by steep slopes, with sparse *chañares* for shade. The road to San Rafael goes through this fort, and to the north there is a large wooded hill where Indian spies hide to catch our people when they go out into the fields.

I shall not further trouble the reader with a detailed copy of the itinerary that traces the course of the Atuel up to its sources in the Andes, a course that from the starting point called Las Juntas winds over flat and hilly terrain for one hundred forty-four leagues, according to Rodríguez. Suffice it to say that forage and sheltering trees for cattle stretch almost to the tops of the mountains; that in the place called Boca del Río,

45. *Tigers,* jaguars. JP.

twenty leagues from the last place mentioned by the itinerary, there are deposits of fine marble; that at Loncoboca, still farther up, there are excellent salt deposits; that at twenty-seven leagues from Loncoboca, at what they call Acequia del Atuel, after crossing over stones to avoid leeches, you come to some thermal baths called Aguas Calientes, which flow from "fields of pampas grass where the water bubbles up and where unless a man watches his step he will sink down as though into a deep well"; that whole forests of *molle* bushes are found in the grassy valleys that lie at the very foot of the high Sosneado; and that in the canyon that descends from its northern flank lie the bountiful salt mines of the Indian chief Maturano.

I have dwelt in detail on the natural advantages of the Atuel basin, which is considered less suitable for the raising of livestock than the other lands that stretch southward as far as the Río Colorado, so that no one may be surprised at the number of animals that graze there in complete liberty or at their extraordinarily low price.

The extreme abundance of year-round pasture to be found in the canyons, hills, and valleys of the eastern slope of the Andes, increasing from near Rancagua to the vicinity of the volcano Antuco, an area where I have traveled frequently, explains why Chilean cattle are constantly being sent to these places, in spite of the abundance and richness of our pastures and of the danger from the Indians once they cross the border. Between the Leñas Amarillas passes on the north and that of the volcano Antuco on the south, not only the domestic and wild cattle of the region but also thousands of Chilean animals are raised and fed, as Chilean ranchers from Quechereguas south entrust their herds to the Indian chiefs who own those empty lands.

Just as the pasture is more lush and more abundant as one moves southward, so also one notes a gradual change in the variety, thickness, and height of the trees, which in the north are limited to *chañares* and scrub carobs, with an occasional thorn bush, but toward the south not only become taller and more solid, but are reinforced by Chilean wild apple trees, terebinth, oaks, *guaigones,* and even cypresses, of which I saw many in the valley of Lagunas Acollaradas or Epulanquen near the source of the River Curileufu.

The abundance and richness of mineral deposits seem to be peculiar to the regions close to the Equator, because the farther a miner moves away from it, the fewer opportunities does he find for his exertions.

Except for the great open vein of silver that has been mined in Uspallata, whose last traces can sometimes be found in the southern mountains,

I have found no other mine of this metal, or of gold, in this region. Copper mines abound, especially in the Valle de los Ciegos near Planchón, and near the Río Tordillo, where I have seen vast landslides of very pure ore that no one was exploiting because of the difficulties caused by the absence of roads or the dangerous nature of such as exist. There are many large deposits of pure sulfur and aluminum sulfate; and on the high road from Planchón to San Rafael the traveler's attention is drawn most especially to a solitary and imposing lake of pitch that flows from a volcanic fissure and fills the air with sulfurous vapors. The arid shore of this sticky black deposit of bituminous substances contrasts with the whiteness of hundreds of skeletons of animals that were attracted to this place, perhaps by curiosity, and who died when their legs were trapped in it. Mines or deposits of excellent salt are found everywhere, especially along the road called Barsas de las Barrancas, which leads to Curileufu.

The trade that all these places carry on with southern Chile is limited to the rental of grazing lands and the export of animals, ostrich feathers, pitch for waterproofing jars, and salt.

Since time immemorial our purchases of animals from the Indians who live beyond the Bío-Bío have been, and continue to be, the principal cause of the thefts and offenses against Argentine property carried out daily by the natives from both sides of the Andes. Before concluding this part of my recollections, and as evidence for what I say, I shall therefore copy the exact words of a note that Rodríguez, in his interesting itinerary, dedicated to the commerce between the pampas and Chile. It reads as follows:

> A note on certain events and circumstances that must be considered with respect to the lands belonging to the Ñorquino Indians, who in their ignorance allow the Chileans to pass through. By means of threats, Zúñiga and Salvo, who know their language, get the Ñorquinos to let their spies go as far as Banquilmaco to trade, that is, to rob and raid along with the Indians to the east. These Christians[46] blend in with the thieving Indians, dress like them, and when undressed are indistinguishable from them; then they go on to join Baigorría's people and, after working hard at their robberies, come back, take their leave, return home dressed as they were before, and hand their plunder over to Zúñiga or Salvo, who sell it.

46. *Christians,* civilized men. JP.

X I

The Teno Hills. — Flogging.— Bands of thieves. —

Pay dirt.— Locusts and the Agricultural Society.— The new

decor painter for Santiago's theater.— Sarmiento, Tejedor,

and Argentine literature.

Back in 1847 I was renting Comalle, a ranch belonging to that distinguished writer and stern public official who, when he governed Curicó,
where it was located, used to write his friend Luis Labarca whenever a
rebellion threatened, "I'll soon go and make those rascals tremble at the
sound of my carriage wheels."[47]

At that time Comalle and the dense forests of Chimbarongo, as they
call them nowadays, were the lair of some famous bandits who skinned
their victims[48] and whose awful raids made the Teno Hills a fearful place;

47. The author refers to Antonio José de Irisarri, a Guatemalan in the service of Chile.
EOV. (Cf. Chapter IX.)
48. These bandits, called *pelacaras* or face-skinners, would skin the faces of their victims so
that they could not be identified. JP.

and since all measures adopted by the authorities to rid the area of this scourge had been in vain, I requested and obtained the position of sub-delegate for that dreaded section of the Department of Curicó, for the sole purpose of demonstrating that the lash does not always deserve the condemnation of humanitarians. The wealthiest landowners of the area were my diligent inspectors; under their leadership, the tenants took up arms and pursued the bandits everywhere, never substituting confinement for physical pain. Once the scoundrels had no place to hide and were not punished by receiving good shelter and food in what are called prisons but are in fact schools of heinous crime, they were forced to leave their theater of operations and seek beyond the Andes the impunity they could not find in Chile. It was not long before one could travel through the Teno Hills without carrying so much as a penknife.

At some point we must break the spell of ill-conceived humanitarianism. Insofar as man is an animal, he bears in his heart the seeds of the most abominable acts; and although it is true that instruction generally inhibits the growth and development of these terrible seeds, it is also true that instruction often brings them to perfection. Furthermore, instruction can have a moral effect only on the unspoiled heart of a child, who, holding as yet no firm notions of virtue or vice, has no reason to reject the path of honesty that a good teacher can show him; it is far from having the same effect on the heart of a grown man once he has come to know crime. Once a plant that at its birth can be uprooted with only a slight pressure of the fingers has been allowed to grow to its full development, it can be removed only by the spade or the axe. Hence the Spanish proverb, no less true for being trite, that "an old Moor can't be a good Christian."

It is precisely in the old Moor that the animal part of our nature dominates the intellectual, and the only way to speak to that animal part is with the lure of food or the fear of physical pain. How many brutal men have we not seen walking to the gallows with the most shocking calm! How many have we not seen, as they depart from prison, take leave of their companions with a cynical smile and a repulsive, "See you soon!" Are there any who approach the whipping post in the same fashion? Not one! It is physical pain that makes the tiger accept his trainer's head in his mouth without biting it.

Simple imprisonment teaches a hardened criminal no lesson but merely annoys him by not allowing him to indulge the countless vices in which he has been wallowing; and it is indisputable that when a man is caught in the act of tampering with fences, public safety would gain more from half a dozen lashes vigorously applied than from a year's reclusion under a better roof than he had before and with free meals better than those he had to work for while at large.

This does not mean that the imprisonment of a thief does not temporarily prevent him from continuing to steal as he did while free. But is it enough to deprive him of his freedom? Does the thief restore to his victim what he took from him by violence or cunning, except when chance brings his booty into the hands of the police? Does he reimburse the community for the expense of his temporary reclusion? If we decide to imprison the thief instead of giving him a good thrashing and sending him packing, so be it; but let us make him repay, by means of forced hard labor, the subsistence he owes society and the loss suffered by his victim.

The Pehuenche Indians also took part in the robberies and murders of the Teno Hills, a fact not generally known but which I was sure of before I became the satrap of that region. Bands of Pehuenches would come to the Department of Curicó every year supplied with ostrich feathers and pitch for sale, and no one suspected that this merchandise masked the robber's claw and the murderer's knife.

Under different disguises, birds of prey infested everything and were so well organized that I was at a loss for how to rid my jurisdiction of this plague. These gangs had branches in Concepción and Coquimbo. The animals stolen in either of these places were taken to the Teno Hills or the forests of Chimbarongo, where they were traded for those stolen in the other; and then new herders drove the Coquimbo animals to market in Concepción and the Concepción animals to Coquimbo. Since these transferals did not, however, always suit the gangs' joint interests, great herds of Chilean horses, which brought a high price in Cuyo, were handed over to the Pehuenches in exchange for cattle to be delivered the following spring. The Pehuenches were always very liberal in these delayed payments, financing their liberality by means of the thefts they carried out on the ranches of Argentina.

I was visiting Don Mateo Moraga, who had rented a farm in Teno and was one of my most active inspectors, when shortly after nightfall a blood-covered Pehuenche came to tell me that the chief of his village, Taipangue—who, as I subsequently learned, was nothing but a bandit of Spanish descent who was equally at ease in the role of petty chieftain as in that of simple honest peasant selling calves to be fatted—had just killed his brother by smashing his head with a stone. This complaint greatly perturbed me; and despite Moraga's efforts to make me wait for him, I was about to mount my horse and dash off with my accompaniment of *huasos* to this Taipangue's camp or village, when a Pehuenche woman appeared, also blood-covered and moaning and shouting that we shouldn't go unless we had plenty of men, because the chief had found out that her brother-in-law had come to denounce him and had had his people mount their horses and get everything ready to repel force with force. I immediately sent word to the inspectors Don Luis Labarca, the owner of Rauco, and Don Jorge Smith, Irisarri's son-in-law, to join me with their men; and an hour later, accompanied by Don Pedro Möller, a physician in Talca, we reached the camp. Although I had few men, because the others had not yet reached me, I thought that that would be the end of the matter, until the haughty replies, the sight of a bloody and apparently lifeless body, and an attempt to take a prisoner from me by force obliged me to attack without delay or compunction. Blood was spilled, to be sure; but it is also sure that the principle of authority was upheld. If I had delayed the attack; if, in keeping with the teachings of some compassionate criminologists who say that defense must exceed offense only insofar as strictly necessary to check it, I had set to measuring the length and depth of the wounds, I might not now be recounting this episode, which always comes to my mind when I see a poor constable attack a bandit with his wretched sword while the latter fires at him with his pistol, and the constable refrains from killing the criminal so that he will not be accused and tried for having been overzealous in his attack.

Be that as it may, the arrest of a wounded Taipangue and of some of his principal men, and the fear that the latter's confessions might shed light on the machinations of the other feather and pitch merchants, drove our hard-riding hillfolk to cross the border heading for the outposts south of San Rafael in the province of Mendoza.

The inhabitants of Santiago, who are always the directors and prompters in the tragicomic drama of our public life, were beginning to doze off when a Frenchman living on the ground floor of the Solar home (now the Hotel Inglés), poor in cash but very rich in schemes, having no trinkets or cosmetics with which to levy an indirect tax on husbands, came up with the original idea of exploiting both the married and the single by selling great expectations of wealth for very little money.

On my visits to Santiago from the ranch I used a room directly above that of this worthy entrepreneur; and I noticed that he never stirred when he was alone, but that as soon as someone was with him there arose such a noise of clanking buckets and such rattling as though of a coffee grinder that I heartily cursed having such a neighbor, until I saw the Frenchman run out onto the patio hatless and in his shirtsleeves, shouting like a madman, "Help! Help! Chile is a gold mine, and I know how to get at it!"

At the magic sound of "gold" the hubbub soon spread; people stopped at the front door to look, some came in, and the curious crowded the Frenchman's room. Open-mouthed they heard the hallelujahs with which the learned chemist announced to them that the soil of Chile was to a prodigious extent composed of gold, so much so that he had found this element even in the bricks of his room; with their own eyes they all saw, artistically arranged on a table, small mounds of different soils, each with a card indicating its origin, the quantity of gold it produced per cartload, and the fineness of the precious metal, represented by pellets displayed in a small jar by the side of each mound. The improvised laboratory also contained a small burner, some crucibles, flasks of mercury, some bottles of acid or other mysterious liquids, and, resting on a rather solid platform, something that looked like a machine, carefully covered with a rug.

The learned scientist, bombarded with questions and tired of speaking, made a present of two small packages of soil and two pellets not needed for his collection to those who seemed to him most likely to spread the news, after which he insistently begged his visitors to leave, since he had vitally important business to attend to. He then carefully shut his door with a combination lock, pretended to give some secret instructions to a companion who played the role of his servant, and disappeared, leaving his curious admirers, who seemed to envy the good fortune of the future dispenser of wealth, momentarily frozen in place.

Word of this astounding discovery had barely begun to circulate in Santiago when, as always happens in such cases, some ostensible alchemists appeared to support the claims of the discoverer by exploiting the simple credulity of rich and poor with the results of the false experiments they peddled. Serious and prudent men visited these offices of shameless larceny; I saw none leave them without carrying away some soil in his pocket, his face gleaming with satisfaction and his skull teeming with absurd hopes.

As a result of these assays, whose results the assayer made more or less encouraging depending on the greater or lesser fleeceability of the victim who had come to consult him, soon there was not a single old gold washing or stretch of yellow earth in the country that escaped notice; but since these properties were worthless without the secret for exploiting them, a secret that could be utilized only by the company that joined its capital to the knowledge of the inventor, a million schemes to find it out were soon under way. Each schemer thought he had some clue that would unravel the mystery; inventions sprang up everywhere and were carefully hidden from the envious glances of those who were left without such treasures. In a word, gold fever reached such a pitch that even many of those who started out deceiving ended up deceived, so true are the poet's words when he says that the thirst for gold always makes mincemeat of human reason.[49]

But the minds of ever-curious Santiago were not occupied only in trying to solve mineralogical problems, because in addition to the hullabaloo with the gold-bearing soil, another, brought on by an unexpected invasion of locusts around Maipo, came to be one of the favorite topics of discussion.

This proved to be the unfortunate occasion for our newborn Agricultural Society to demonstrate how good intentions outrun solid knowledge when such organizations take their first steps unguided by the hand of learning and experience.

Locusts, which devastate whole tracts of land in Argentina, do not move from one province to another here; when they do appear, they are less destructive than elsewhere. These voracious insects, which have even, and rightly, been called a plague, live and reign in some dry lands in our country, especially amid the eastern *pichi* brush of the province of Curicó, from which irrigation and the plow are beginning to drive them forever.

From time to time some section of our land is invaded by certain animals that disappear as rapidly as they appear, without anyone's having so far been able to explain this phenomenon. There are bird years, mouse years, ant years, moth years, flea years, etc., etc.

In 1855 the government was obliged to grant assistance to the farmers of Llanquihue, whose fields had been beset first by astonishing numbers of birds that destroyed their plantings, and then by hordes of mice that sprang up as if by magic south of the town of Osorno and spread farther southward like an oil slick, destroying everything until they reached the bay of Reloncaví, when they completely and inexplicably disappeared. The year before, it should be noted, birds were very rare in that area, and no one had even heard of the mouse that was soon to invade the land.

The farmers of Maipo and Santiago, who, like those of other provinces, are little concerned with determining the causes of these phenomena except when the calamity has already fallen on them, cried out to the government, which, then as now, was expected to do everything. The government always knows less about matters agricultural than do the

49. Pérez probably alludes to Virgil, *Aeneid* III, 56-57: "Quid non mortalia pectora cogis, auri sacra fames?" ("Oh cursed lust for gold, to what do you not drive the hearts of men?"). JP.

farmers; in response to their pleas it consulted the Agricultural Society, which ought to have known more than all the others put together about what measures should be adopted to wipe out that plague of Egypt.

The learned body thus consulted, fearing for its reputation if it admitted that it knew as much about locusts as the government did about agriculture, decided, after serious consideration, to propose a means of deliverance: the release into the infested fields of large flocks of turkeys and, to avoid thefts, the creation of a turkey police that would protect these useful workers from kidnappers and turkeycides.

This decision, which I am at a loss whether to call a plagiarism or imitation of the Portuguese remedy against fleas, along with the mad schemes for finding gold everywhere that had everyone in such a dither, made me once again take up my pen. At the risk of meeting with the same fate as on my first venture as an author, I ridiculed the incurable mania of thinking that gold could be had cheap and easy thanks to the inventive genius of a boldfaced charlatan, as well as the fear that intelligence is debased precisely when it most excels, by modestly confessing that it does not know what in fact it is ignorant of.

Fortunately, since in Chile what is written slowly is always read in haste, no one paid any attention to me; and to avoid new temptations, I hurried back from good old Santiago to my rustic Teno.

The monotony of rural toil soon exhausted my none too abundant stock of patience; and like a rudderless and ballastless ship driven by the Quixotic wind of adventure, I again crossed the Andes, weathered several storms under bare poles, and, badly damaged after struggling in vain against my contrary fate, dropped anchor in the cove called Teatro de la Universidad within the great bay Santiago.

The famous painter Giorgi had not yet come to Chile to show us what real theater decorations are. In our theater, called "de la Universidad" because of its location, there flourished the distinguished artist Mena, an expert in switching one thing for another for whom any decor would do as long as it contained what he called masonry.

"Please, we need a tree over here."

"A tree? Fine; we'll put in some masonry."

"Come on, no more masonry; what we need now is a mirror."

"A mirror? Well, sir, wouldn't a bit of masonry do just as well? What does the audience know about mirrors?"

Against the white background of the wings, Mena's trees looked like green dunce caps stuck on a cudgel. Next to masonry, the pine tree was his workhorse for theatrical forests; as for the backdrops, I shall let the reader deduce their nature and appearance from the above.

In rivalry with Mena and collaboration with my brother Ruperto I painted a complete garden set for the theater, which, though I say so myself, was the first halfway decent one in Chile. The public lavished praise on me, and I received it with all the modest compunction and nervous bristling of hair that mark the novice dramatist when the audience applauds the first of his dreadful farces.

At that time there lived among us the eminent and highly respected French painter Monvoisin,[50] who had come to Chile to lose, by dint of painting portraits the way Lope de Vega wrote his improvised comedies, the reputation that he had acquired in Europe. A master of his art and a friend, he was kind enough to visit my studio, where I had just painted a colossal tree for *Norma.* What sort of foliage might it have had when instead of greeting me he exclaimed in horror, "This is no tree, it's a salad!"

A few days later I had occasion to paint a small map on a screen; the next day the learned Argentine writer Tejedor said, in an editorial in *El Progreso,* that the theater's painters were so inept that instead of painting South America they had painted a ham!

I did not dare to stand up for myself, or rather for my brush, since I had not yet forgotten the earlier accusation; and so, with due prudence and moderation, I contented myself with painting over my unfortunate South America and replacing it with a portrait of the author of *Estudios teatrales,* ringed by a garland of "cruel damsels." Tejedor, unable to deny his resemblance to a billy goat when it was plain to the audience, saw this and tacitly made eternal peace with me, because he never again sought culinary resemblances to the innocent fruits of my brush.

And since Tejedor's name has come up, why not tell what he had a hand in, along with the work done by others who, driven and battered like him by the revolutionary storms that raged beyond the Andes, had been cast up among us in those extraordinary times?

As an ever-available *refugium peccatorum*[51] for Peruvians and Argentineans, Chile has served both of them as the wooden barrier in the bullring serves the hard-pressed bullfighter who with sword or lance has provoked the wrath of the pursuing bull. The number of fugitives who crossed the Andes and landed among us demonstrates both the intensity

50. Raymond Monvoisin. EOV.
51. *Refugium peccatorum,* "refuge of sinners," a term applied to Mary in the Litany of the Blessed Virgin. JP.

of their fear and the intensity with which they were hunted, though events have subsequently shown how powerfully panic can affect a man's mind if his conscience is even the least bit uneasy. Rosas himself, talking with me in England fifteen years later, told me that he had pressed the persecution rather to let Chileans learn directly what sort of men his enemies were than because of any fear that such blabbermouths might inspire in him. This does not mean that all, by any means, of the émigrés were men of little account in terms of talents, learning, and sincere patriotism, because to state that would be to state a falsehood, just as it would be to deny that in general the Argentineans failed to gain the respect of the country that gave them refuge. There are of course exceptions; but it is a fact that we were inundated with rogues, and boorish ones, too. The Argentineans forgot that the self-satisfied petulance that is normally tolerated in daily life is inadmissible in the Republic of Letters; once they were heard to say—because they frequented our printing shops—that the progress of journalism in Chile was due solely to them, the compassion that they often aroused turned to contempt.

Back then we Chileans were nothing like what we are now. Before, people did much and talked little; now they do little and talk much. A Chilean journalist never sought gain or literary glory, but the triumph of truth over the prejudices of the colonial era, and of republican principles over the capricious excesses of the authorities. The fathers of our country were intent only on educating the youth that was to succeed them, which was, in turn, more concerned with gaining and perfecting knowledge than with publicly displaying it in the press with cocky pedantry. This was the true reason why the Argentineans controlled our principal newspapers. The immigrants had asked the press for a chance to earn their bread, and the press had given it to them.

If, to determine the average level of the intellectual and literary talents that the Argentine immigrants brought us, we now apply the climatological system of noting the high and low temperatures of a region in order to deduce from them its average temperature, the observer's eye is instantly struck by the lively intelligence of Sarmiento and the foolish dullness of Tejedor. I mention these two in the same breath, not because I think that two minds so different can march in unison, but because of the rude and shameless arrogance with which both of them, in a corrupt Spanish, printed whatever bit of nonsense tickled their pens.

When Sarmiento first came to Chile he had more talent than learning or discretion. His fiery imagination, his impulsiveness, his inconsistencies, and his radically polemical spirit made him forget both the prudent respect he owed the intellectual progress, no matter how minute, of the country that was offering him refuge, and the dictates of his own conscience, since at the same time that he was praising the "purity of language," the "elegance of expression," and the "artistic perfection" of the splendid elegy that the dreadful catastrophe that fell on the Jesuit church on May 13, 1841, drew from the learned pen of Don Andrés Bello,[52] he boldly and foolishly wrote in the same pages of the *Mercurio,* of which he was then editor, that it was folly to study the Spanish language, because Spanish was a language dead to civilization, along with other literary heresies of the same stripe, mixed with rude insults to our poor Chilean literature. He considered us dim-witted; he told us that while the Muses happily caressed the Varelas and Echeverrías of Buenos Aires, in Chile they did nothing but sleep like a log; and not content with all this, he even christened us idiots because we were more concerned with expressing our ideas accurately than with increasing our stock of them.

To our shame, samples of Sarmiento's orthography are still to be found in the official gazettes of that eccentric literary era, an orthography that without the support of the government would never have passed from the imagination of dreamers to the world of realities. Nonetheless, if we are to be fair, we must admit that all the writings of that rough-hewn mind showed sparks of the most enviable creative imagination, and that even his reformed orthography, though not entirely his own idea, was more the product of his studies than of pretentious ignorance. In literary matters, Sarmiento was rather a madman than a pedant.

It is truly painful to move from the bold creative mind of the son of San Juan to the opposite extreme of sense and learning so brilliantly represented by the worthy Tejedor, who at that time was the editor of Santiago's *El Progreso.* If Sarmiento always displayed his natural talent in all his literary ravings, Tejedor only managed, in his, to show a lack of good sense and an abundance of gall in displaying that lack. Since he had to write about everything in order to fill the columns of *El Progreso,* the devil tempted him to proclaim himself the public censor of our theater. He found sin in everything, and his suspiciousness gave him such a talent for stripping the most innocent expressions and presenting them stark naked to the eyes of prudish mothers that he almost succeeded in bringing back the religious allegories that dominated our stage in the good old days. Next he tried his hand at poetry. Commending himself with all his heart to the peerless "cruel Julia," supreme lady of his most sugary sentiments, he "trembled" at Cape Horn "with the icy fever." To

---

52. *El incendio de la Compañía (The Fire in the Jesuit Church),* a poem of nearly 300 verses published in July 1841. JP.

make up for this and regain a normal temperature he decided to light into music and, with his dissertations, augment the stock of learning contained in his *Estudios teatrales.* He asked himself, "What is music?" and before another might rob him of the glory of answering, he answered himself, "Music is a manifold crystallization of the various stormy phases of matter, be they floating in the air or encrusted in the human heart."

When this bomb exploded, an explosion of which *El Mosaico,* a clever and witty paper that dared to challenge him, made good use, Tejedor, in a fit of pique and amid a chorus of laughs and derisive whistles, went off to Copiapó, where, however, not even the protection of *El Copiapino,* another paper edited by another Argentinean in that mining town, could shield him against the fierce stings of *El Mosaico,* which continued to pursue him until it saw him depart from Chile, to sin no more.

No more impure seed, none more loaded with dreadful Gallicisms, could have been found for the development of this kind of literature than that which the Argentine émigrés brought us, and so, far from our owing them the supposed splendor that according to them graced the Chilean press in those days, we owe them only the ocean of Gallicisms with which they flooded the modest but pure world of our letters. To this day we have not managed to rid ourselves of all the alien and affected expressions that we owe them and that would fill volumes.

XII

Passenger steamers.— Chief stewards.— Coquimbo.— Huasco.
— The port of Copiapó. — The city of Copiapó. —
The prospector. — The bamboozler. — The river and valley of
Copiapó. — Chañarcillo. — Juan Godoy. — The bootlegger. —
A voyage into the interior. — Admirable utilization of water.
— Chañarcillo again. — Bandurrias.— Pajonales. —
A husband is responsible for his wife's sins.

I lost hope of continuing my wild adventure-packed career as a cattle-man on the pampas when the revolutionary schemes that filled the mind of my friend Rodríguez forced me to break off my relationship with that redoubtable chieftain. Poor as always, but desirous of avoiding temptations as dangerous as they were flattering, I decided to sail to far-off Copiapó in search of a kinder fortune than I had hitherto found in the southern part of our country.

On August 28, 1846, I boarded the steamer *Perú*, headed for Copiapó. My arrival there was to increase, ever so slightly, the number of those unfortunate but intrepid beings who, spurred on by need and hope, risk their time and money on the lottery of the mines.

We were not yet out of sight of Valparaíso when a rowboat trying desperately to catch up with the steamer capsized; but our captain, a veritable machine, would not order even a momentary halt in the machine that was propelling us in order to save the drowning wretches, probably because his sailing instructions did not foresee such a maneuver. Some fishing boats brought there by chance gave that British machine a thousand-horsepower lesson in humanity that I am sure proved useless.

To avoid seeing that scowling face I went below to the passenger section; but any attempt to organize a protest was foiled by people coming and going, bumping into me, desperately calling for an attendant, and by the sacks and bundles that, along with the passengers, were milling about in the vicinity of the cabins until some steward packed them in, willy-nilly, just as they do with fish in a sardine factory before sealing them into their impenetrable prisons.

A steward on an English steamer in the Pacific is an absolute tyrant from whose decisions there is no appeal. It is also de rigueur that he know no Spanish, so as to leave you stranded between two pieces of baggage with a vacuous "No entiende" if you make a plain request. If, however, you adorn your request with a glimpse of a gold coin, the tyrant will yield scepter and crown to you and become the most abject lackey.

On a steamer there is absolute freedom of thought, as there is absolute tolerance in matters of dress. High-waisted tail coats rubbed elbows with low-slung loose-flowing jackets. Tall hats were perfectly at home next to short hats. No one paid any attention to his neighbor; everyone seemed to be absorbed by a single thought, business. Not wanting to be outdone, I tried to shake off the melancholy that I felt on once more leaving, and who knows for how long, the family that I so love and whose company I have so little enjoyed in the course of my harried life; and so I reclined on a sofa, where I was soon distracted by the gleam of two fair eyes that seemed to be intently fixed on me. It was the captain's wife, who struck me, whether because of the exotic figures surrounding me or as a natural effect of the seasickness that was progressing rapidly within me, as enchanting. I hesitated and meditated for a few moments and then, telling myself, "Here goes!" shot off two such arrows toward her as would have slain her without fail had not a harsh hissing voice intervened by saying, "Very well, I owe three hundred *onzas*." "I'll be darned!" I said, standing up with a start; and I saw that without my having noticed it, a gaming table had been set up near me and was being run by Don N., who was playing a cutthroat game of cards with several other men. The loser of the three hundred, a fellow of rather disreputable appearance, then stepped out with an affected mien to take the air on deck. I soon followed him, though for another purpose, since by now I was seasick.

Anyone who says that love conquers all things is talking utter nonsense; if he does not believe it, let him fall in love on board ship and he'll soon see his thoughts and actions ship out in another direction. That is what happened to me; my eyes met no further eyes, nor did my ears again hear the silvery tinkle of moneybags.

On the morning of the 29th I awoke in Coquimbo, a sad and gloomy-looking little harbor, even though its bay is one of the best in Chile; and despite the animation brought about by the arrival of the steamer, I chose not to disembark, fearing I should be left there if our machine of a captain should take it into his head to weigh anchor when least expected, as happened during almost every voyage. Coquimbo had not yet become what Valparaíso had been in 1822.

On the 30th, thanks to a very thick fog, we steamed past Huasco and had to spend some ten hours going back to find it. This is no port, no inlet, no cove, no nothing. On some low arid hills, little groups of miserable huts serve as both warehouses and habitations. The whole town would fit three times within the limits of the port of San Antonio de las Bodegas in 1838.

At seven the next morning we cast our anchor in the harbor of Copiapó, which as a port also does not amount to much, though it is superior in every way to Huasco.

Two lighters belonging to the customs service took us to the dock, and about two hours later I was in a carriage on my way to the capital of the province. The little harbor is surrounded by rocks that on the seaward side delimit the level stretch of sand, salt, and pebbles across which, always within sight of the sea, the road to the city runs for several leagues. Low round hills, bare and thirsty, are scattered across those plains, with the sun burning down on them with such force that people here believe that steel tools left exposed to it will lose their edge. Not one house is to be seen there, not one drop of water, not one little bush. After three hours' journey across this desert, you reach the river valley.

The Copiapó River is not only a river; it can also claim the honors of a fjord, because it sometimes mixes its waters with those of the ocean, though they are so scanty that this stream, like others in those parched northern regions, seems to be nothing but a relic attesting to past rainfall. As to why it should rain less now than before, no one has been able to say for sure. Some attribute it to the destruction of the forests; others, to a change in the direction of the earth's axis, because they deny that forests can attract water, citing as examples the torrential downpours that fall on the Argentine pampas, where not a tree is to be found. For the time being, far be it from me to enter into this dispute.

The *chilca*, the *péril*, and an occasional patch of grass struggle up through that loose and salt-encrusted soil, where vehicle traffic is difficult and most unpleasant because of the cloud of fine burning dust that pursues the traveler's carriage. The road to the city of Copiapó runs through the middle of this valley, and we reached the city's outskirts after eight hours of travel and after crossing numerous lagoons of fetid water that make up the river to the west of town.

Finally we reached the proverbial city of dreams, through which gallop the wild and varied ideas that are the charm and torment of the businessman; that place where the beggar gets bigger, the sandal magically turns into a boot, the old man into a boy, the greasy *culero* into an ample frock coat of fine cloth; a place where every man thinks he is a fount of mineralogical knowledge and laughs pityingly at the knowledge of his neighbor; a fertile field for the highly developed and profitable science of bamboozling,[53] which puts a deep dent in the pocket of the newcomer, who in turn bamboozles his successor, who afterwards does the same with the last to arrive; a place of fears and hopes; a place, finally, of miners who have made it and miners who have had it. This city, which we might compare to a large chicken coop where the chicken that today roosts on the top rung lets its droppings fall on the one below, only to suffer the same misfortune tomorrow, is located in a small well-cultivated valley between two rows of bare dry hills whose somber appearance sets off its lovely greenness and that of the countless small but productive farms that lie on both banks of the insignificant rivulet that is the Copiapó River.

Who could imagine now, as he travels through that country up the course of that tiny stream to the Paipote and Pulido Mountains, that it could ever have supported so abundant and splendid a vegetation as to merit the designation of pleasant fertile valley that our first historians bestowed on it! Just as the waters have left their parched channel as evidence of their former abundance, so the hills and valleys, with their vegetal names, immortalize the memory of the plants they once sustained.

---

53. The Chilean term *poruñear* means, in addition to cheating in general, the more specific form of cheating that consists of showing its victim a sample of valuable minerals falsely said to proceed from a mine that the swindler wants to sell. JP.

The town of Copiapó had already come of age by the time I am speaking of, because, although it was only formally incorporated in 1744 with the name San Francisco de la Selva, it acquired its renown as a fountain of wealth during the first years of the Conquest and has maintained it ever since. It is, thus, surprising that in 1713 its population only amounted to nine hundred persons, and that in 1846 it should still have been a million miles from what its natural resources would lead one to expect.

The layout of the town makes it irregular in shape, for it consists of only two main streets and a few others that have the appearance rather of country roads than of streets. Back then it had its square, its parish church and two monasteries, one Mercenarian and the other Franciscan, and, crossing the broad river bed, a ludicrous bridge made of rough-hewn beams laid by twos, some on crossed shaky posts, others on stubs of the broken branches of some willows that still survived in the mud.

The general appearance of this small village was very similar to that of the cities of San Juan and Mendoza. Among its buildings there were a few very fine ones; but almost all of them were made of adobe bricks, often badly packed, and their walls were not always quite perpendicular. The roofs, occasionally wooden but more commonly mud with a parapet facing the street, would leak at every hint of a shower. Nonetheless, for a man living in the mountains, coming into town was like coming into the valley of delights, despite the dismal nature of the place, its humid low morning fogs, its excessive midday heat, the wind, the unbearable dust in the streets rutted by the passage of carts and animals, and the swarms of annoying mosquitoes that at nightfall invade the part of town bordering on the meadows.

Anyone thinking that because he has been in Copiapó during that time he has been in Chile would be in error, just as he would lead his readers into error if, spurred on by the yen to write travel impressions, he should commit the folly of taking the ways of Copiapó to be indicative of those of the whole country. All that Copiapó had in common with Chile was the constitution, not always observed, and the laws, not infrequently broken. In this case, the sample did not reveal the whole, because the sample Copiapó was to the whole of Chile as an egg is to a chestnut.

It was difficult, if not impossible, to find more than four Chileans in any casual gathering of twenty-five gentlemen. Of gentlemen, I say, because the opposite was true in the case of the fair sex.

Just as a rustic clodhopper might owe the title of *Don* to his suddenly acquired riches, this village at first owed its premature title of city only to its mineral wealth; but it has managed to justify it with customs and practices that have less of the village about them than do many of those that live and reign in Santiago itself. There is no need there, as there is in other towns of its size, to hold one's tongue. Elsewhere, pity the man who cannot dissemble, and even more the one who does not praise what cannot be praised with a straight face. Our Chilean small towns, and even the mid-sized ones, unquestionably take on, in relation to Santiago, the character of a woman rivaling with another woman. Santiago bears the title of city: I want it, too; Santiago has a boulevard and a park with a fountain: I'll have my boulevard and park with a fountain, even if the schools, hospitals, and roads have to go naked.

Copiapó was a cosmopolitan town, largely inhabited by Argentineans from La Rioja, but with English, French, Chileans, Germans, and Italians, in addition to those who came from almost all of our sister republics. The only subject of conversation there was, and had to be, mines; and just as Valparaíso is one vast business office, so Copiapó was an immense pithead. Woe to him who might go there to live off his investments or by any kind of activity not directly connected with the mineralogical spirit of the inhabitants; he had either to take up mining or to get out.

After the customary greeting, the first question asked concerned the condition of the mine; the second, that of the wife; and let it be understood that if the greeting preceded the question, this did not occur out of courtesy, but because from a mile off the greeting revealed the present condition of the Copiapino miner's mine. Disarray in his dress, a worried air, an unsteady walk, holding his cane at its midpoint, were signs of ill omen; if he barely spoke above a whisper, if he made way for you on the sidewalk, if he bowed deeply, he was finished. But if a moment later, as often happened, he held his head high, walked firmly and steadily, tapped the ground with his cane, and spoke familiarly and smugly to persons whom not long before he had hardly dared to glance at, look out! He'd struck it rich or found a sucker. Even the fair sex—who would have believed it?—abandoned the names of its pastimes and its favorite adornments for such exotic words as leaders, shafts, bores, adits, and a thousand others in the same vein.

At social gatherings, dancing was more common than in Santiago. At the sound of "Polka!" the smoking room, which was always graced with a tempting lake of punch, would be vacated, and in no time everyone would be drawn up in parade order. In this army there were no wounded veterans; as good miners with plenty of experience, they all knew very well how to amalgamate the lump of old hard ore with the lively quicksilver of youth. The older and more creaky the bachelor, the younger and more tender the woman he chose for his partner. It was, thus, a pitiable, yet sometimes laughable sight to see those ill-caulked old corsairs, leaking port and starboard, trying to imitate the rapid and graceful movements of the newly launched little sloops, which sometimes caught them unawares from behind, sometimes from in front, while they were struggling to tack about. Fortunately the punch was, ultimately, the only harbor where they wound up dropping their anchors.

The young ladies did not have much to say, but they did all have a great desire to get married. The men talked of veins paying off or running out; the girls, also in the spirit of mining, yearned only to strike it rich in a canonically wedded husband.

Not all, however, was merriment in Copiapó, for in few places have I seen more anguish than there when the inexorable departure of the steamers was upon it. Days before this monthly calamity, the whole town was set in motion, running, bumping into people, asking questions, avoiding people, turning back, looking for silver, garnering silver, sending silver, waiting for silver, despairing of silver, and promising and swearing never again to contract obligations for silver. Once the steamer disappeared, however, so did the panting that came with relaxation; and just as a woman who has gone through a difficult childbirth, after promising not to fall into new temptations, falls into them anew, so the merchant went back to his habits, to new trials and new promises never to sin again, until he either grew rich or was ruined for good.

Among the inhabitants of Copiapó, as among all other children of this world, there also were, and still are, some striking human types that, though not exclusively Copiapeño, certainly seemed to be: the *Prospector* and the *Bamboozler*.

Both are skilled diplomats, and pagans, too. The god they worship is the one also worshipped by many governments, secrecy; and the devil they fear, exposure. Neither of these entrepreneurs needs to read the newspaper or so much as look over the passenger list of an arriving steamer, because even if they do not see someone coming from out of town, they smell him. Once this important information has been acquired, the prospector gets to work.

The first thing is to discover where the future victim is staying; next comes finding a way to meet him and talk to him in private. The first step is easy, but the second less so, because, after all, how do you just burst in on someone you don't know? How do you make an unexpected visit seem welcome, when there is no one to introduce the visitor and when the visitee may have come forewarned? Nonsense and child's play! Such obstacles were made to order for the prospector, and the prospector for overcoming them. He lies in wait until he sees the victim enter the building by himself; he follows him in and asks him whether Mr. So-and-So is staying there. When the reply comes as a question, "What can I do for you?" he immediately answers by thanking God for the good fortune of finding Mr. So-and-So all alone after so much effort, because, having heard that he is a perfect gentleman, he has come to seek his protection for a mine that he cannot operate because he fears that wealthy interests will wrest it from him, which would not happen if they saw "that you are a joint proprietor of El Tapado."

Who could hear this story, see the simple good-hearted face of the storyteller, and not grant the petitioner at least ten minutes in private? Once inside, he bemoans the lack of justice for the poor in Copiapó, because only yesterday a friend of his lost control of a rich mine, merely because he was poor and there was no one to speak on his behalf. He will explain how he made his discovery, point out the hill where the mine is located, and lament the persecution he has suffered for refusing to divulge the source of the ore samples he had been carrying. Then he says he thinks he has a little one on him . . . where might it be? Finally he finds it and hands you a lump of high-grade ore, saying that he's been allowed to keep it because it's so inferior, and that "you mustn't judge the quality of the mine by this one sample."

If you are an expert, he will notice it at once and ask you with the most innocent air, "Might this stone contain a little silver?" If he sees that you like the sample, he has you, ready to be milked for as long as you put off going to inspect the vein yourself or as long as you keep looking for some mysterious path mysteriously mentioned to the prospector by a mysterious woodcutter who died mysteriously at some mysterious spot. And the innocent babe will go on milking you until you decide to send all veins and mines and paths to the devil. To be sure, there are cases when the hoax does not work; but since no rock is too hard for the prospector, he keeps on drilling until it breaks. Or is broke.

A traveler therefore had to acclimatize himself in Copiapó to be immune from the endemic illnesses that used to attack, and still do attack, the pockets of the innocent newcomer to those mines of hopes and dreams.

The prospector is a wholesale dealer; the bamboozler retails the merchandise and even delivers. Rare is the tenderfoot who can escape him. Walking down the street and pretending not to walk in step with you, the bamboozler, with studied negligence, lets you catch a glimpse of what looks like a parcel of silver bars beneath his poncho. If you take the bait, he will immediately offer you a few nuggets of the same metal for your collection, but only on condition of the strictest secrecy, since they come from a little mine whose location he does not want to reveal so that no one will challenge his claim. If, being no expert but fond of mysteries, you accept the deal, you're sunk. Within moments the bamboozler will show up at your lodgings with half a bushel of arsenic in the form of bars copiously rubbed with a silver coin so as to give an appearance of legitimacy to his merchandise. Pure arsenic very easily accepts a silver coating, so that faced with that silvery repast, offered for sale by a seemingly simple fellow unaware of what he is selling (these are qualities sine qua non for the bamboozler), few greenhorns can resist temptation. After the required bargaining and the coughing up of a few gold coins, the buyer will be convinced that he has paid two for something worth twenty, and that after all there must be some profit in the deal.

Few arts are more highly developed and more lucrative than those we all know to be practiced by confidence men; and none of them is more common through all the stages of human life, from the point at which man first has use of reason to that of his death, than the art of bamboozling elevated to the level of a science.

Not everyone has it within him to achieve the title of refined bamboozler. To be a bamboozler, to make a bad penny pass for good, plain stone for silver ore, arsenic for bars of silver, vices for virtues, requires cheek, histrionic talents, shamelessness, knowledge of the human heart, the astuteness of the fox, and the relaxed and inoffensive appearance of the sloth.

The bamboozler does not live and reign only in the mines; the bamboozler flourishes in commerce, in industry, in the arts, in liberal, political, and religious studies, and in every corner of the world inhabited by man. He is partial to no one, at peace with no one, engaged in open warfare with the pocketbooks and the welfare of the human race; and the practitioners of his art, always lying in wait, are so numerous that we can say there is no hour, no moment, no instant or circumstance whatsoever in our lives when we are fully safe from some unexpected bamboozlement.

The tireless compiler who, after spending his days and nights with tattered tomes, inundates us with the publication of what he has copied and crudely stitched together and now peddles as the product of his own mind, bamboozles those who are new to literary studies.

The platforms and declarations of political parties and their candidates bamboozle the voters.

The prospectus of a newborn daily that offers impartiality and independence in politics bamboozles the subscribers.

The minister who wants a good job for a relative and gets a colleague to make the appointment so as to keep his hands clean bamboozles the country and the treasury.

The hypocrite, who with a contrite and anguished air kisses the floor in church so passionately that he lifts a brick with each kiss, is either on the lookout for a job as treasurer of a convent or wants to bamboozle some overpious woman.

When a newfound friend who knows that you just arrived declares himself your mentor and offers you his infallible protection, assay him at once and you will see whether he's bamboozling you.

The man who founds schools, claiming to foster learning but secretly seeking only to advance a particular set of views, bamboozles parents.

The old man with parchment hide who dyes his beard and mustache wants to bamboozle the girls.

The old woman who smoothes out her wrinkled skin with lard and cosmetics and, not satisfied with that, covers her face with a mesh veil with black flecks to disguise her yellow freckles bamboozles the boys.

The girl who paints rings under her eyes and pretends to be delicate, sensitive, and sickly bamboozles herself.

The fashionable young thing known for her spendthrift ways who suddenly reforms for no visible reason is trying to bamboozle some booby by making him swallow her frugality.

The woman of doubtful virtue is bamboozling when she tries to pass a trollop off as a lady.

Real prospectors, in partnership with the prospectors of pocketbooks, bamboozle everyone tempted by all that glitters.

The physician who does not come when called because, according to him, he has so many professional obligations, and who carries a notebook to keep track of his office hours, bamboozles the public trying to sell fame and good reputation wrapped in a package that contains quite the opposite.

The pharmacist bamboozles with panaceas that he sells as guarantees of enviable health; the manufacturers of medicines, with their usual warning against "cheap imitations," and the persistent homeopaths, with their little wonder pills.

The suitor bamboozles his beloved; she, her beau; the courtesan, her gallant; the husband, his wife, and the wife, her husband; and the true lover's eternal love is as much a bamboozlement as are ministerial promises at election time. In a word, bamboozlement, let people say what they will, is the endemic malady of mankind.

The constant talk of mines, the steady arrival of pack animals whose drovers, when there was no rich ore in the sacks, brought the very best, though in small samples, in their pockets on orders from the foremen and managers of the mines to whet the appetite of the owners, and especially my not having anything better to do, all impelled me to set off inland with the twofold aim of seeing what was to be seen and trying to find something I had never lost. Copiapó is a place where people think little and do much, and so no sooner had this thought fluttered through my mind than I was sitting on a mule, merrily riding along the well-known old road to Chañarcillo.

To reach the mines one had to cross the whole stretched-out city of Copiapó, on whose outskirts lay a no less stretched-out district called San Fernando. This place, which the Indians had owned in common, just as the Indians of Santiago owned Talagante, had been subdivided into plots about a quarter of a mile square, which the town had sold very successfully, for there was hardly one that was not expertly farmed and that did not bring its owners an income that would astonish our southern landowners. This stretch of the road is varied and pleasant, since it always runs down the middle of the irrigated plain that is the best agricultural land in the area.

My mule stepped lively and was so eager to rush on that it reminded me more than once of Iriarte's rented mule.[54] I rode through the Indian town, so to speak, arousing cheerful shouts of "That's the way to go!" from all who saw the easy amble of my enviable mount. In no time I was at Punta Negra, delighted to see those hills so saturated with mineral deposits that it seemed as though at every step I should stumble on an exposed vein of pure silver.

If anyone rides out from Copiapó for the first time with his mind filled, as is only natural, with thoughts of mines and discoveries, he will of course think, when he sees other travelers streak through the dust raised by the many pack animals that carry out supplies and bring back ore, that they must be on the way to stake a claim or bringing news of some rich strike. Often, however, the cause is neither of these, for everything here is in a rush: messengers, due dates, and even idlers just out for a ride, for the simple reason that almost all of them are riding rented horses or mules. I was suddenly startled out of my mineralogical musings by my mule's resolute turn toward the gate of a nearby corral. I headed it back toward the road, but to no avail; I broke my switch over its ears, in vain; I grasped one rein and at the risk of breaking its neck forced it to turn its head toward the road; but the mule, which had hurried along not to please its rider but only to get home, left me the control of its head and,

---

54. The Spaniard Tomás de Iriarte's *El caminante y la mula de alquiler (The Traveler and the Rented Mule)* is Fable XVIII of his *Fábulas literarias*, first published in 1782. It tells of a hired mule that sets off at a good pace but then balks and throws its rider. JP.

itself asserting that of its body, continued at a relaxed trot down the straight road to the corral gate, impervious to my kicks and abundant threats. While in this desperate situation, I had the misfortune of sighting two ladies who, seated on fine horses and in the midst of an elegant company, were galloping toward town. I gave it all I had, shouting, "Giddyap, damn it!" Useless! Kicks and the whip, even more so. In this dreadful situation, my honor and gallantry made me land so violent a blow on my stubborn mount's jaw that it staggered and made its rider lose his balance, earning him a salute of boisterous laughter. The hapless voyager, sending so discourteous a quadruped to the devil seven times, and its owner, thirty, began to discharge on the eyes and ears of the beast such a deluge of punches that if the mule had not responded to this justified burst of enthusiasm with the wildest of starts, he would no doubt be at it still, so great was the indignation produced in that honest gentleman and courtly gallant by the first noisy applause he received from the fair sex in Copiapó.

At nine that evening I reached Totoralillo, the first amalgamation works of the Empresa Unida, after following the left bank of the river, dry at the time because the water had been diverted to irrigate a farm farther up, and after passing through Tierra Amarilla and Nantoco, small villages that were centers of the trade in bootleg ore.

Although there were as yet no steam-powered machines in Copiapó, those there were, driven by water power, fascinated the first-time visitor. They were constructed with a view to solidity, economy of operation, and the principles of the new system of amalgamation used there for the rapid extraction of both pure and chlorinated silver. In the mining establishments of Freiberg[55] amalgamation is carried out by means of rotating barrels that mix the ground ore with mercury and water. This system was unknown in Copiapó, but its results were more than matched by large wooden vats with iron bottoms constructed around a sturdy shaft that imparted a powerful circular motion to the iron crosspieces within. The mills for grinding the ore were also made of solid iron; both they and the amalgamation machines would often be driven smoothly night and day by that amazing thread they call a river, which, thanks to the natural slope of the terrain, would no sooner issue from one machine than it could begin to drive the next, without any detriment to agriculture.

Let us be fair: as far as agriculture is concerned, and especially with respect to irrigation, we southerners must take off our hats to the farmers

---

55. A town in Saxony that was the administrative center for the mines of that kingdom and seat of a mining academy. JP.

of Copiapó. From Las Juntas in Potrero Grande, which is the best and most pleasant section of the department, to the point where the river disappears west of Copiapó, its sinuous course extends for at least two hundred kilometers. This water, which in the south, with its wasteful methods, would barely suffice for a single farm, was enough, thanks to carefully ordered distribution, to keep this long strip of land looking like a garden, with orchards and fields of alfalfa or grain everywhere. All this is even more astonishing when we take into account the very important service that this insubstantial stream also provides, as I have explained, to the processing of ore by driving the amalgamating machines installed on its banks.

The Empresa Unida had twenty-one amalgamating vats and two mills in constant operation at Totoralillo, and with great effort and expense was building another powerful machine, newly invented, to recover the large amounts of arsenical silver lost in the washings.

Beginning at the western edge of the city of Copiapó, and in the order of their location, the ore processing establishments that I was able to visit and for which, as for their mills, the creek provided power were:

> The machines of La Chimba, property of Messrs. Gallo and Montt, with 11 vats.
> Those of Subercasseaux, with 5.
> Those of Carrasine, with 3.
> Those of Empresa Unida in Copiapó, with 11.
> Those of Ossa & Co., with 11.
> Those of Abbot & Co., with 6.
> Those of Dávila & Co., with 3.
> Those of Cousiño, with 10.
> Those of Empresa Unida at La Puerta, with 24.

I omit those that I did not visit: those of Ossa in Totoralillo, those of Potrero Seco, those of Gallo, those of Zavala, and a few others.

Some day the power of steam will come to restore to agriculture what belongs to it, the river; in the meantime, the establishment for exploiting washings installed in Copiapó by Don Carlos Darlu merits our admiration. There a single mule, by means of skillfully designed machinery, imparts steady activity to a triple mill and its enormous vats.

Returning now to the account of my expedition to the mines, the day after my arrival at Totoralillo I set out at dawn for Chañarcillo, my head filled with those vaporous hopes that always arise in the mind of the man who has never been able to find anything, when he is heading for the place where others are finding a great deal.

I soon came to the crest that around here, for reasons unknown, is called "del Diablo." The pleasant part of the trip ends there; the road suddenly turns southward; and the traveler, regretfully leaving the valley, enters the harsh and empty mountains that lie between him and Chañarcillo. What solitude, what barren hills, what silence! Not a bird, not even a distant glimpse of a hut, not the slightest drop of water! The desert of Atacama showed its stern face here. The road, however, showed itself to be the work of man, for it was perfectly laid out and constructed, although, to avoid grades, it passed through the narrowest of gorges formed by enormous rocks whose walls seemed to have been chiseled smooth.

There are two such narrow passages on the way to the summit, and their smooth sides constituted all that was left of a free press in Chile. The narrowness, the majestic polished walls, and the need to pass through here on the way to the mines spurred idle travelers to exercise their various literary and artistic talents on these giant blackboards. One draftsman produced a chalk portrait of General Flores, beneath which he wrote, "This is Flores." Another drew a steamship, shaped like a grocer's scoop. Another, knowing that his lady love's brother was heading for the city, addressed these verses to her:

> Antonia, I ache for you,
> Your eyes are my lucky strike,
> Take my body as you like,
> With much love from you know who.

Then came the work of a political writer: "The intendant is a jackass. How long do we have to put up with this brute?" and, below that, "The judge at Chañarcillo is a thief." Farther on one could read, "Pay me my three *onzas*, Ramón," or "Don T. P. says he is not a mulatto," and right after that, "Don Z. J. O. was the first to bootleg ore out of here," and in several places, these mysterious initials: M. P. Q. M. L.[56]

Farther south and about four leagues from Totoralillo one comes to the first watering place, which they call El Ingenio (The Mill), because at one time there was one here, as can be seen from the slag that remains and from the total destruction of all the vegetation in the area. Here

---

56. *M.P.Q.M.L.* One possible interpretation: "Muy puto quien me lea" ("Whoever reads me is a big faggot [or pimp]." JP.

stood a wretched hut, a pool of water, and some small sheds to ward off the heat of the sun. From there I climbed a rather steep slope, so steep that when I reached the flat space at the top I had to stop to let my mount catch its breath. This height, from which one can also see the Department of Huasco, overlooks a great part of the lower end of the Department of Copiapó; from it one gets a clear view of the Andes, which, when covered with snow, delight the thirsty Copiapinos, of the famous Cerro del Checo, whose copper made the fortune of the Mattas, of the Cerro Blanco, rich in ore but abandoned, of the Cerro de la Plata, about which so many superstitious tales are told, and of all the other peaks and ridges that can bring to a miner's mind the memory of a find, a rich strike, a bankruptcy, or a bamboozlement.

I descended from this height down a long narrow canyon littered with mummified horses and mules, such as one finds on the high slopes of the Andes; and after another four leagues' journey I reached the mines of Chañarcillo, whose praises one cannot sing loudly enough.

The richness of the mineral deposits of Chañarcillo, which lie about seventeen leagues southeast of the town of Copiapó, on the southern mesa at the foot of Chañarcillo Hill, continues to be a source of amazement; and the fame of the department currently rests on their coveted silver ore, as previously it did on the gold mined in abundance at Las Ánimas and Jesús María. They were discovered by Juan Godoy, a simple woodcutter, in May 1832; since then this store of wealth has never ceased for a moment to be the most tyrannical and inexorable dispenser of fortune, of poverty, of hopes, of disillusionment, and of unexpected titles of nobility.

It would take more knowledge than that possessed by a simple tourist like myself to give an account of these deposits, appraise their possibilities through geological study, and decide whether or not they were being properly exploited. All I can say, basing myself on the attestations of the miners themselves, is that the operations were generally rather hit-or-miss, for not a single miner, while applauding his own methods, failed to condemn those of his neighbor.

To get a grasp of the countless efforts under way at Chañarcillo required the help of an expert, because even counting them would otherwise be difficult for the first-time, or even sixth-time, visitor to this labyrinth of mine entrances, paths, and endless rubble.

There were only two main lodes at Chañarcillo; together with the network of smaller veins and leaders on either side of them, they constituted what there they called *corridas*. The Corrida de la Descubridora, which runs north–south and about five degrees to the east and lies on the eastern side of the deposits, contained the properties called Manto de Ossa, La Descubridora, Carlota, Santa Rita, San Félix, and some others. The western lode, whose visible eastward inclination suggests that it must eventually join that of La Descubridora, holds Valencia, Esperanza, and Colorada, among others. In addition, both between the two main lodes and on their outer edges, the number of claims being worked more or less successfully in so favored a location seemed almost infinite.

There was neither water nor firewood at the mines; both of these commodities were brought in, the former from some paltry wells laboriously dug and maintained at three leagues' distance, and the latter from the country around the watering place, the only area, thanks to the long walk needed to reach it, that had escaped the miner's hatchet. Both were conveyed on the backs of donkeys; and so many troops of animals were employed in this traffic that no sooner did the sun rise than the roads around the hills and watering place were covered with donkeys, carrying either small three-gallon barrels to be sold at six *reales* per load, or bundles of twigs and poor wood, which cost eight.

On the average, the wages of a laborer at Chañarcillo were not less than seventy pesos a month. Payday was the first of every month, so from the twenty-fifth on one could see the mine owners in the city of Copiapó scurrying back and forth in search of cash, a commodity that was at times exceedingly rare in that place. On the twenty-eighth, twenty-ninth, and thirtieth you could see men rushing up the road into the mountains with this panacea, the sole means of reining in the turbulent miners, estimated to number a thousand and capable of smashing everything if not properly paid on the first day of the month.

The social and commercial center of this bustling hive was the town of Juan Godoy, named in honor of the discoverer of Chañarcillo.[57] It is situated on a level space right at the base of the mining district, separated by a wash from the Bandurrias deposits to the east, and by another wash from the Pajonales deposits to the west, so that this turbulent and hardworking capital of the true Kingdom of La Plata, or Silver,[58] could not have a better or more appropriate location. Its founder's imagination was not much troubled with the ordering of its streets, but there is perfect harmony between that original layout and the disorder that reigns in everything else.

---

57. Juan Godoy is now a ghost town. JP.

58. The author is apparently playing with the name of the Viceroyalty of La Plata, centered on the Río de la Plata, or River Plate (in Spanish literally River of Silver) in modern Argentina. JP.

In Juan Godoy comfortable dwellings were not in fashion. Those that composed its urban—and rustic—part, which were all jumbled together, large and small, huts, sheds, and canvas shelters, were so many centers of lively business dealings; and since a lucky miner is synonymous with a generous man and a free spender, it was not surprising to find select foods and the best wines in every lowly tavern. The market of Juan Godoy was the only one in the province that displayed, in the most unpretentious way and almost in the open air, the finest meats and the best and earliest fruits and vegetables to be had anywhere. Inns, steakhouses, *picanterías*,[59] and seven billiard halls in constant service gave evidence of the sociability of these wearers of caps and sandals. The supreme chief of the happy place was a subdelegate; a paltry drywall hut was at the same time city hall, courtroom, and jail, its entrance flanked by a flagpole and an inverted wooden crate that served as a sentry box.

For those unacquainted with a northern mining district, Chañarcillo and its charming capital would be worthy objects of study. If a Chilean unfamiliar with his country's geography, as so many are, were suddenly snatched from our bean-eating capital by a mysterious hand and mysteriously set down in the square of Juan Godoy, he would be hard put to say what part of the world he was in, because both at the mines and in town, everything would be new to him: customs, dress, aspirations, even speech. The Spanish spoken in Chañarcillo was, to be sure, the language of Cervantes, but dressed in a miner's *culero*.

The practice of religion had quite broken down. A chapel there was, but no one to say mass or hear it. Confession was something mentioned only by some sly miner who wanted a pretext for going down to the plain in search of some daughter of Eve, a commodity even scarcer in Juan Godoy than mass. No woman was allowed there without a special permit, ever since the fair sex began to hide the forbidden fruit of the mines, bootleg ore, beneath its skirts.

On Sundays, when the sun went down, the gentlemen of the hammer and pick would show off their picturesque clothes in the marketplace, clothes whose variety of colors imitated a veritable garden and that were even charming and elegant up to a point. A miner wears wide trousers reaching to his knees from a well-fitted waist, over them a broad *culero* that drapes halfway down the leg, and on top of everything else a long striped shirt that covers most of the *culero*, leaving only the edging visible. An enormous red sash winds about his body from the hips to the chest. From it, in front, hangs his tobacco pouch; behind, a

59. *Picanterías,* eating establishments featuring spicy foods. JP.

knife handle peers out. He wears black leggings and sandals. A black or red cap, with a large tassel that falls down over his neck or ear, adorns the head. The miner's greatest luxury and extravagance, however, is the poncho; he is prepared to pay any price for a good one, and he wears it with the greatest natural elegance. The dress of these men is very similar to that of modern Greeks.

As for the fair sex, in such short supply there, no one could say that quality made up for the lack of quantity. These negative beauties wore fine but filthy boots, elegant stockings filthier still, expensive dresses stained with grease, and precious embroidered silk kerchiefs whose colors, like those of the chameleon, varied with those of the mine where their man was working.

And that, I think, is enough about Juan Godoy.

I returned to my lodgings at the Esperanza mine, where good ham and delicious wines were awaiting me, because, though it is true that in Chañarcillo broken-down huts took the place of houses, it is no less true that not even a bankrupt miner lacked good food, champagne, brandy, or other necessities for making that desolate country bearable.

As the time for concluding this first voyage drew near I acquired a few specimens for my collection and set off to visit the mining districts of Bandurrias and Pajonales.

When one descends the slopes that form the southern part of the mining area and then climbs partway up the Cerro de Bandurrias he sees the hive that is the Cerro de Chañarcillo in all its glory; and when the newcomer beheld that jumbled mass of mine entrances, huts, wooden sheds, rock piles, stone walls, and laboriously carved out terraces, and observed the noise and constant movement of people and animals, all concentrated on that one point, a feeling of admiration and enchantment came over him, and visions of golden hope fluttered through his mind. Why should one not have the same good fortune as all the others? Bad luck could change to good with one stroke. And why only for others? The effect that Chañarcillo had was such that apathy itself would lose its composure.

Since the time of their discovery, these mines have exercised and continue to exercise dominion even over the rank and talents of those whom they have chosen to favor. They decreed that Godoy and the Bolados should be gentlemen, and gentlemen they became, followed by a great train of flatterers. To one they said, "Be like your betters, move in society, and take the places that are reserved to talent"; and he started to resemble his betters, he moved in society, and he took the places reserved to talent. To another they said, "Old and broken down as you are thanks to your vices, marry a tender young girl and be a solid citizen"; and he married a child and became a solid citizen. They told the mulatto, "You're white," and he believed it. The man who served others and accepted tips now has others to serve him and won't tip them. In short, whoever yearned for the waters of the fountain of youth and for the drugs that produce talent looked for them in the ore sacks and sashes of the mine workers of Chañarcillo, and there he found them.

A half hour's ride brings one to the ore deposits of Bandurrias. That hill, though only a dry creek bed separates it from Chañarcillo, is rather uninviting; its mines were few and widely scattered. Nonetheless, it had beautifully formed veins of ore. The Fuentecilla stratum was an enormous mass of ore, valued, though its silver content was low, for the ease with which it could be mined. The ores of Bandurrias differ from those of Chañarcillo, which in general yields little pure silver and a great deal of chloride, while the ores of Bandurria more frequently yield pure silver, ruby silver, arsenic, and galena than they do chloride. Its principal mines were La Descubridora, San Jerónimo, Solitaria, and El Manto.

Pajonales, though by no means comparable to Chañarcillo, seemed to be more substantial than Bandurrias; and its ores resembled those of Chañarcillo more than they did those of Bandurrias. It is situated to the west of Chañarcillo, separated from it only by the wash at whose mouth lies the village of Juan Godoy; and it had somewhat more working mines than did Bandurrias. Among the more renowned of these, also scattered here and there over the whole extent of its slopes, were Miller, Contadora, and a few others. The two days that I devoted to an examination of the surface of these last two mining districts were very tiring because of the bad condition of the roads, the burning sun, and the dearth of water. Since I had to arrive in Totoralillo by night, I left Pajonales at four in the afternoon, and after four hours of a steady trot I reached the longed-for river, where you can see water, see something green, and take delight even in the smell of the weeds that grow on the banks of that brook. Although the traveler from the south or from the pampas, where only the horizon limits his gaze, feels hemmed in by the long and narrow canyon they call the Valley of Copiapó, if he sets out from the mountains and reaches the river, which is the center of the valley, he receives an impression so pleasant that he comes to consider it not only beautiful but very extensive. The brook ceases to be a brook and, for the tired voyager, takes on the appearance of a river.

In the course of this rapid excursion I had the opportunity to study the character and inclinations of a new and unique being that followed me like my shadow everywhere. The prospector and the bamboozler live and reign in the towns and leave them only when their profession demands it; the bootlegger has his throne at Chañarcillo and every other place where silver is there for the picking. Himself the sire or at least the wetnurse of the town of Juan Godoy, the bootlegger recognizes as his father the itch for a collection of ores, which sooner or later pass from the splendid showcase to the rough wheels of the mill, and as his mother, the stinginess of successful miners, who would rather be robbed than show generosity. It comes, thus, as no surprise that the bootlegger is the darling, the sweetheart, and the mainstay of some smelting furnaces, some mills, and many eminent individuals.

All that this mine-less miner, who often strikes it rich and is not infrequently struck by the constabulary, has in common with the bamboozler is that both are thoroughgoing pagans, sacrificing to Mercury and worshipping as household gods their playing cards, their dice, their *mate*, and their little woman.

Bootlegging, like poetry, has irresistible charms. Who is the man that has not pinched even a tiny scrap of ore? Who has not tried his hand at making verses, even if he had to cheat a little in the meter? But just as not everyone is called to be a poet, so the title of perfect bootlegger is not for everyone. Unless he has a robust constitution, unshakable composure, sharp eyes, even sharper ears, astuteness, courage, and above all good legs, the bootlegger is doomed to fail. He is a genuine topographer; he knows every corner of these hills, has visited every narrow pass, and there is no cave so remote but that his prying eyes have penetrated it. He knows all distances, knows where he has to leave the road, where he must drive his mule more quickly, at what time he must reach a certain spot; and he calculates and carries out his movements with the regularity of a steamship.

When he goes into action the bootlegger displays true theatrical talent; his colors, like those of the chameleon, are so perfectly in keeping with those of the persons around him that it is hard to notice that the group has acquired a new member. Sometimes he appears in the shape of a prosperous miner, with great wealth in the north and extensive land holdings in the south and all the prestige of the riches of a Río Santo. At other times he takes the form of a person of modest means who, however, owns a mill as artlessly placed as is the fortress of Gibraltar at the entrance to the Mediterranean. He can also appear as an honest godly man—very well-off, because God protects the innocent—who does not buy but rather ransoms scrap silver from the hands of thieves, as captives used to be ransomed in olden times. Just as in the case of those unfortunates no one would ask where they had come from, because it was enough to know that they were Christians, neither does he inquire about the origin of what he buys: it is enough for him to know that it is silver. Every pound he ransoms at the rate of twelve pesos is a good deed he does for his neighbor, because if so much mischief can be done with twelve pesos, how much might not be done with eighteen, which is the value of the pound he has rescued from unclean hands? He can appear as a sickly old man from whom the world is slipping away while he struggles not to slip from the world; or he can play the role of an energetic, diligent young man who thinks nothing of enduring sun, darkness, or rain. On the market square he is the honest merchant and supplier; and everywhere he is subtracting, never adding. Where, indeed, can one turn one's eyes in this promised land without encountering this "gentleman of the night"?[60] Perhaps under a priest's cassock? That could be, because these folk form collections only for display. True, eventually their little pounds of silver are extracted from them, too—but only for display. So no scandal-monger should deduce from this that the clergy also bootleg. No, sir; they do, indeed, accept the nuggets that their penitents bring them and that these have bought from their washerwomen, who bought them from the miners, who got them from the negligence of their foremen. These, then, are sinful goods that end up in church, and that's all there is to it.

For the time being I refer to a brief work I shall shortly publish with the title, *The Perfect Bootlegger, or, The Art of Bootlegging Without Being Bootlegged*, with an extensive itinerary of all the watering spots where no beans are cooked, the convenient lodgings of Don Beno, the no less important and almost unsuspected ones of Agua de los Sapos, where, if the bootlegger can once reach them, he need not fear the snorting of his mule or the braying of his donkey, who, crushed under the weight of ore, not infrequently implores the help of meddlesome police patrols with his discordant trumpet. The work will conclude with monographic studies of the traveling outfitter who while working for others enriches himself; of the bootlegging peddler who—look out, miners and nonminers!—pays one man two for what is worth four and charges another four for what is worth eight and still manages to present his financial backer with accounts that while they have an exorbitant air about them do show a profit; of the tavern bootlegger who turns anisette into pure silver to the sweet music of harp and guitar; and, finally, of the petty bootlegger, who is more common than all the rest and without knowing it supports them all.

60. In English in the original. JP.

Once you have been tricked by the prospector, robbed by the bamboozler, and initiated into the mysteries of bootlegging, you can say with confidence that you are an experienced miner. If you can escape the clutches of all three, everyone will loudly bestow on you the weighty title of a man who even smells of the miner.

What I have written should not lead anyone to think that my activities in Copiapó were limited to sightseeing and criticizing. I renewed my old connections with La Rioja and Catamarca, I traveled throughout the desert, I worked mines there, I suffered hunger, and I suffered thirst, which rules supreme in those arid sands.

After three hours' trot north from Totoralillo on a decent horse, and after another three hours' ride eastward on a donkey, a traveler, having had his fill of sand, sweat, and exhaustion, can reach an old and little-known copper mine that has lain abandoned, and understandably so, for thirty years. In that remote place there remains the gaping mouth of a dark hole produced by the urge to get rich quick, in the midst of a group of isolated rocks that rise from the undulating surface of the desert like reefs above the moving surface of the sea. Not a drop of water is to be seen anywhere; no bird sings there, and not even that yellowish down that is the first sign of vegetation on rocks decomposing under the onslaught of time introduces a cheerful note in that purely mineral landscape, that baking oven baked by the burning rays of the sun.

Our chronicles tell us that about 1848, a worthy gentleman, tired of seeking his fortune on the surface of the earth and inspired by the devil to seek it below, decided to launch an enterprise at that sad and solitary spot, which was not then the venerable abode of any repentant sinner. He was a newly minted miner, that is, profoundly ignorant and convinced he knew it all, just as were most of the old-time miners who, in those happy times and like him, went looking for trouble beneath the surface of the earth. All he needed to join the guild of seasoned miners was the knack of feigning, the astuteness to deceive, deftness in getting his hands on bootleg goods, and the talent of selling them as fruits of his own labor, qualities that, to be sure, are most valuable, but that if I were a carpenter I should say did not join, dovetail, or overlap with the spirit of our novice miner, who, for his sins, was more inclined toward the pen than toward the pickaxe.

To save money, this entrepreneur lived in a tent, a portable oven that served him as lodging and as storehouse. His situation, therefore, was not enviable: he was alone; and inside his tent he had a view of sacks of toasted meal and bundles of jerky that hemmed in his bed, while through the triangular opening or door of the tent he saw the endless sands, the shimmering reverberation of the sun's rays, and the ears of the donkey who brought him drinking water and who, downcast and engrossed in thought, seemed, to judge by his trancelike stillness, to be searching his mind for some difficult rhyme.

They say that one afternoon, when our friend came to be heartily sick of it all, he heard the noisy chatter of his laborers and exclaimed, "Could it be that even my donkey is giving me practical lessons of philosophic resignation? Could it be that the gang of clods that I have here, just because they possess the negative virtue of never giving a thought to tomorrow, have the power to adorn their empty conversations with laughter and shouting, when I, who could silence them with a single word, don't have a moment's real pleasure? This is a phenomenon worthy of study; and to do so with solid documentation, now that they're so animated I'm going to make a shorthand transcript of everything I hear in an hour." No sooner said than done; and since he knew something about stenographic scribbles, he took pencil and paper, settled down as comfortably as he could on a sack of toasted meal, and patiently followed the conversation of his miners, who, sitting on the ground, were chatting in good fellowship as they cleaned off the tortillas they had drawn from the stirred-up embers in their midst.

I have before me the document produced by that solitary dweller in the desert, a document that, modifying only an occasional less than decorous word, I present to interested readers as a snapshot of the customs still fostered in the minds of our rustic peasants by the firm belief that a husband who lets his wife's sins in this world pass without thrashing her, whipping her, or at least pulling her hair will be responsible for them in the world to come.

The following, then, is the text of the manuscript.

DRAMATIS PERSONAE

A laborer from Gualinán, who, like a good Argentinean, thinks and speaks in sing-song.

Another from Elqui, an Indian who likes his pleasures and is not inclined to please.

An ore carrier, a Parisian *gamin* with a *culero.*

The worthy Velásquez, a native of Andacollo, a solid citizen whom his age (two hammers, or 77) has relieved of his role as a strong young laborer and placed in that of humble supplier of drinking water to the group.

The others, as many as nine, I list jointly as chorus or extras, that is, active listeners or passive actors.

ONE OF THE GROUP: And how about that punch of Don Campillo's? There was nothing wrong with that! Nice and clear, and strong, too!

ARGENTINEAN: Oh for a little anisette right now, eh?

VELÁSQUEZ: Just listen to these lazy bums talk!

ONE OF THE GROUP: Are you telling us a little anisette wouldn't hit the spot? It's the best thing there is for your stomach.

VELÁSQUEZ: The stomach, you say? Yeah, trying to get rid of a stomachache that way was the start of all my troubles. I wish I'd never heard of anisette! *(General laughter and shouts.)*

ONE OF THE GROUP: I bet! And what was it that happened to you?

MAN FROM ELQUI: He must have got in some scrape. Why even ask? He got into an argument, and his bad luck drove him on . . . . Right?

VELÁSQUEZ: I wish that was all there'd been to it!

ARGENTINEAN: Oho! Did they start shooting at you?

VELÁSQUEZ: Shoot, nothing! Worse than that!

ALL TOGETHER: What do you mean "worse"?

VELÁSQUEZ: They got me married!

ALL TOGETHER, *with raucous laughter:* Come on now! That's a new one!

ORE CARRIER: I'll be . . . ! That's all that happened to you? I'll drink a whole bottle of anisette right this minute!

VELÁSQUEZ: What do you know, boy? Bunch of know-it-alls! You'd be better off learning how to pray.

ARGENTINEAN: So they got you married, eh? Go on, tell us all about it. Here's a smoke for you, all lit.

VELÁSQUEZ: Thanks. They got me married, or I got married, it's all the same. Fact is, I was just a kid then, because if it was to happen again now . . . . *(He laughs.) Ave Maria,* what a temptation!

SEVERAL AT ONCE: Tell us, tell us about it, Velasquito!

VELÁSQUEZ: I must have been about twenty-one back then; I used to wear a good cap draped down over my ear, my *culero* hanging down, folded over, and my shirt—a shirt, my friend, that dragged behind me on the ground. I strutted down the streets, and the girls looked at me and said, "Now there's a miner!" and I wouldn't pay no attention to 'em, not for nothin', my friend.

I was going along, and I fell in with a bunch of *zambos,*[61] and every time we got to a tavern they'd open a barrel of punch for

61. *Zambos,* persons of mixed African and Indian descent. JP.

'em, and those *zambos* would get to drinking till they couldn't walk straight.

And one time when I'd come down from the hill to have a little fun, I got it into my head I wanted to eat some green watermelon, and if you think that didn't give me a belly-ache! All my guts was splitting in pieces! I was sweating away and I thought I was dying, when in comes a *zambo* even uglier than me and says, "Drink a glass of anisette, Señor Velásquez; just drink it, and you'll see how you'll feel better." And he hands me a glass that was right up to the brim, and I commended myself to Our Lady of Andacollo and kissed that glass so hard it flattened my nose.

ONE OF THE GROUP: All right!

VELÁSQUEZ: The pain was gone as if somebody'd just lifted it off me. There you see the power of faith, don't you? That Queen of Angels can really work miracles! So there I was, better than before, and my spirits perked up. Then we passed by a shack where things were so hot you could scorch yourself. Right there I downed another glass of anisette, and then, you know, I went over to where there was a black girl that was really something.

SEVERAL TOGETHER: Oho!

VELÁSQUEZ: Right away I started my attack, and there I was strutting around and pulling out a *real* that I had left, to treat her to something, when off she goes and disappears behind a wall. But she didn't beat me by more than a nose, because I was right behind her. "You there, miner," she told me all scared, "don't you see that *zamba* that's over there in the doorway all dressed up like a lady? Well, she's the one that brought me up; and since she sent me out to buy *mate* and I've slipped in here, she'll kill me." And I look over, and, you know, I see that *zamba* standing in the doorway so round and fat she looked like a well-stuffed sack with bug-eyes that poked into every corner; and meanwhile the girl stood behind me crying and said, "And all this happens to me because I haven't got anybody to speak up for me." "Wait here," I told her, "and don't move. You don't have to worry. Velásquez says so, and when Velásquez says something, it's as good as gold." And off I went to have a look at the old woman, and I come close, strutting along, and as soon as I see her I remember—how can I forget?—that we'd already had a little run-in between one glass and another. "Well, here goes," I says to myself coming closer, figuring she'd be a hard nut to crack. As soon as she recognized me, she ruffled her feathers, but I went straight for her. Right off I said I knew what she was after and told her all kinds of fibs and stories, and then I said, "I'm responsible for all this, and there's no reason at all to blame her; and if you want it and it's all right with her, I'd like to marry her. I'm not bad off, I've got a good outfit, I'm ready to work and I'm never out of a job."

SEVERAL AT ONCE: That's the way to tell 'em, Señor Velásquez!

VELÁSQUEZ: You should have seen the grin on that *zamba*'s face when she heard my declaration! Then I got her a glass of anisette and right there she gave me a big hug. "You're the man, sweetheart," she told me, "and I'm happy you're going to marry her and here's a rosary for you with gold beads . . . ." I don't remember what else she said, but a few days later we were married.

ORE CARRIER: That must have been hard to take! I don't see why you're complaining about the booze.

VELÁSQUEZ: Now listen to this guy! Always breaking in! It seems a man can't . . . .

A LABORER *(interrupting)*: Shut up, boy, stop bothering people. Don't pay any attention to him, Señor Velásquez, you just go on, let's get to the good part.

VELÁSQUEZ: As far as I was concerned the honeymoon was a bust; as soon as I saw that moon it had a *clipse.* Now that I was a married man and had some obligations, I went to town to look for work, and I even went into hock to get her a kerchief; and what do you suppose I found when I got home? Nothing, nobody! I go out and ask here, I ask there, and it turns out the tramp hadn't been around for five days!

SEVERAL AT ONCE: How about that? That's really something!

VELÁSQUEZ: So then, as soon as she found out I was looking for her, she sneaks back to our hut and comes up with the story that she was afraid of the souls in Purgatory that bothered her a lot when she was alone and so she'd gone to that old pimp's house to wait till I got back. Well, that was all over with now; but I had my experience and my suspicions, and so I pretended to be sick and got in bed. "Señor Velasquito," she asked me, "what's the matter with you?" And I didn't say a word, just laying there moaning and with my eyes closed. "Oh yeah, you redskin rascal," I was thinking, "you won't put one over on me that quick." Then I pretended to be asleep, and she, what do you suppose she did then? Very quietly she pulls out a little two-bit mirror, straightens out the wool on her head, pastes it down with a little spit, and stepping so lightly she wouldn't crack an egg goes over and opens the door, and she's gone!

So what do I do then? I get up, my friends, I take my lasso and braid it to twice double strength and sneak after her. And I hadn't gone far when I see her with a miner ugly as sin, and they're talking about going for a drink under the big willow tree. "And what about your husband?" asks the miner. "Never mind about him, señor," she answers. "I left him back there snoring and dreaming about the souls in Purgatory. I'll just go have a look at him and I'll be right back." "Just you wait, you tramp," says I while I was hiding in the foyer of a house, "you'll soon see whose hide is going to be burning." She walks by, and, whack!, I let her have it in the face with the lasso! "Help, murder!" the girl yells, and, whack!, I let her have it on her ribs. "So you were going for a little drink and you didn't even invite me?" Whack! And she dropped to the ground.

SEVERAL AT ONCE: I'll be . . . !

VELÁSQUEZ: "I'll teach you to trot around like some brassy flirt! Better stay with your husband, because he's afraid to be alone with those souls, too!" Whack! "Ay, señorsito!" "Ay, you say?" And in a jiffy she was home, with smoke rising from her back. There at home the other *zamba,* the matchmaker, was waiting for me, and she was ready to eat me alive, I'm telling you. And didn't I know that the girl was a lady, and so on and so forth. Now look who's a lady! I'm telling you, these *zambos* are getting out of hand. So that's the end of it for a while, and I go off into the hills again, and who would have thought that when I came back down there wasn't a trace of her to be seen. And what's worse, the *zamba* who'd defended the lady now told me that if I didn't rein her in, nobody'd be able to get any sense into her. Some luck I had! So off we go again to find the whereabouts of that no-good stray who used to get thrashed when she was single because there was nobody to speak up for her. Good-for-nothing *zamba!* Wouldn't you know it, I found her in a tavern dancing the malambo with a tall *zambo* and going at it so lively his *culero* was flapping in the breeze. As soon as she saw me she keeled over. Some said she'd been taken sick, others said she'd had a stroke. The guitar stopped playing and there was a big uproar, and I go over to her to take her pulse and I tell her, "Beat it home, you black rascal!" She got well in no time and went off home sniveling, with me going after her. "And what are you going to do with me," she kept muttering, "and let me tell you, I'm not your slave." I didn't say a word, my friends, and just kept fingering my lasso. As soon as we got home I strung her up and let her have it with the lasso, maybe fifty times. She went on with her stories, but I outargued her with my lasso and then I put her through her paces.

ARGENTINEAN: That's a bit much!

MAN FROM ELQUI: No, man, not at all. Can't you see that a man's responsible for his wife's shenanigans?

VELÁSQUEZ: That's exactly the way it is, my friend, and I don't want to be responsible to God for somebody else's sins just because I didn't punish her.

ORE CARRIER: Señor Velásquez, did you set out a candle so I can start carrying out ore in the morning?

VELÁSQUEZ: It's all ready for you.

ORE CARRIER: Well then, I'm going to bed. Your story's getting pretty silly.

VELÁSQUEZ: So now you think it's silly, do you?

ONE OF THE GROUP: So you put her through her paces, did you?

VELÁSQUEZ: Yes, and when that was over she was gentle as a lamb. She asked me to forgive her. "Sweetheart," she said, "I admit I didn't do right by you, but that's all over. I thank you for thrashing me, and I'll stick by you for the rest of my life." That made me happy, so I sold my stirrups and pawned my saddle and got her up prettier than ever, and off I went to the hills as cheerful as can be. Who could have told me what I'd find when I came back to look for my turtledove in her nest? As soon as I was gone, she acted worse than ever! When I saw that, I decided to get out of there, because I don't like for nobody to bring shame on me; and although I know that a husband has the right to let his lasso massage his wife's back, I don't like doing it, you know, and God and Our Lady of Andacollo know that it was only my Christian duty that made me give her one last punishment.

ARGENTINEAN: Do you suppose it's really true, Señor Velásquez, that a man has to answer for all his wife's shenanigans in the next world?

MAN FROM ELQUI: What a question! Don't you know, man, that the priest gives her to you so you two will be one and the same and so you'll defend her from the devil? All right, then, suppose she makes a mistake and slips: there she is in temptation and there you are to discipline her, so how can you not do it?

ARGENTINEAN: All right, then. So a man's got to be hanging on to his wife's skirt day and night, and if he don't, he's sinning?

VELÁSQUEZ: That's why the books say, "Watch what you're doin' before you go wooin'."

ONE OF THE GROUP: So is it better to stay single?

ANOTHER OF THE GROUP: Sure it is.

SEVERAL AT ONCE: Oh go on!

VELÁSQUEZ: Anyhow, all she was, was trouble, but I went off to look for her again, and she found out and hid, and I go on looking till I run into her, hiding in a corn field. The rascal barely gave a sign of life, but I told her very gently, "Come with me, it's for your own good." She got up and headed home, with me going after her, and she's not saying a word. We got home, I bolted the door as best I could and sat down to catch my breath. "A fine kettle of fish!" I said very mournfully. I took out my tobacco pouch and handed it to her. "Roll me a cigarette," I told her, and she did and handed it to me all lit. I was sighing, and she was feeling me out. Finally I got up and said, "God's will be done!" and strung her up tied tight and stark naked.

ONE OF THE GROUP: That's the end of that devil!

VELÁSQUEZ: "What are you going to do to me?" she kept asking. "Are you going to kill me?" And I say, "I don't know if you're going to live after I'm through with you." And with a good strap I had there, hidden, I lit into her till I got tired.

SEVERAL TOGETHER: Oh boy!

VELÁSQUEZ: That *zamba* was yelling loud enough to bring the house down, but she was a tough one, she didn't even sweat! And with that big b . . . of hers, so big it looked like an Inca drum, it was a real temptation. Meanwhile the old woman's outside banging on the door to beat the band, and I'm not paying no attention. "I beg you on my knees," she says, "that's enough now!" And I don't pay no attention. Then that old bag starts praying out loud out there with her arms held out like a cross, and I yell at her, "It's your fault! If you'd crucified her when she was little none of this would be happening to her now." And I keep at it, and she screams, "He's killing me!" and the old woman outside, "Holy Mary, Mother of God, pray for us . . . ," and I'm saying, "This one's for the soul of my father," whack!, "Lord help me!" the Indian cries, and by now, you know, she's hoarse, and I say, "This one's for the kid we should have had," whack!, and the old woman says, "Our Father, Who art in heaven . . . ," and I say, "This one's going to be for the travelers who have lost their way," whack!, "Gloria Patri," the old woman says, and I say, "This one's going to be for the soul of my mother, may she rest in peace," whack! "Heretic!" shouted the old woman, and I said, "This one's for madam out there," whack! and the old woman accompanied the lady's screams with *kyrie eleison* and *ora pro nobis* and all sorts of jabber every time I called on another saint. To make a long story short, after I'd called on every saint I could think of, and always afraid there might be one I was leaving out, mind you, I cut her down and she dropped on the floor without a peep. Then I sat her down on a sack and opened the door. I wish you could have seen the fuss the other *zamba* made when she started to look after her wounds. I was tired, so I sat down in a corner all bent over and sighing without saying a word, and as soon as I saw that devil coming to, I handed her my pouch for her to roll me a cigarette. And what do you suppose she did? Would you believe it, that nasty *zamba* threw it in my face and spilled all my tobacco! The nerve! I'm telling you, these *zambos* are getting out of hand! So what do I do then? "If you can't cure your trouble, get away on the double," is what I said, "and the devil's not going to carry *me* off on somebody else's account." Oh, that was a time I'd just as soon not remember! I grab my saddle and bridle, my razors that cost me a good quarter of an *onza,* I pile it all up next to her and I says, "All of this, that I've worked and sweated for, is yours. Here's my time sheet, that comes to twenty *reales;* you go collect it. Now kneel down here so I can give you my blessing." And down she went and snivelled, "Are you really leaving, Señor Velásquez?" And I gave her my blessing *(He is moved.)* and the tears came running down! "I'm going," I told her, "and I'm not taking anything with me, not even tobacco. Now we're separated. I hope God lets you live well and die easy. If you're ever in a pinch, I'll help you if I've got anything to do it with; and if not, God will look out for you." We embraced and cried a lot, and they tried everything to make me stay, but I didn't want to have to suffer for nobody. "Thy will be done!" I said, and out I went. So I left carrying my empty saddle bags, with no tobacco or even a skin to sleep on, but with a clear conscience. After that I never heard what become of my wife.

ORE CARRIER, *from his bed:* Señor Velásquez, what happened to you with the anisette?

At this point the stenographer grew tired.

When with a new supply of disillusionment I left silvery Copiapó to return once more to the business opportunities that beckoned to me from the free pampas of Argentina and the company of my *huaso* Rodríguez, the jewel and the terror of those desolate lands, the news of the awful death of this chieftain, softened by that of the golden wonders to be found in California, once again spurred me to leave my country.

XIII

General considerations on Upper California, its past and present. — Fortuitous events that hastened the discovery of gold in California. — Sutter's arrival in America. — Brief biographical sketch of this captain of Swiss Guards in 1830. — His model colony. — Sutter's hired hand Marshall discovers gold at Sonoma. — The effect that this news produced in Chile. — My voyage to California. — A rebellion on board, incited by Álvarez. — How later on I miraculously saved this same gentleman from the gallows. — Mishaps during our voyage. — The Golden Gate. — San Francisco Bay.

Twenty-nine years have passed since foreign immigration, with its usual accompaniment of enterprise, energy, and progress, began to reach the lonely and remote regions that today make up the flourishing State of California.

That hoard of natural wealth had lain under the rule of the Spaniards for two hundred ninety-five years without their even suspecting that

that corner of their enormous domain was one of the most precious jewels that could adorn the crown of their dour sovereigns. Another more enterprising and more daring race had to come and sweep away the rough surface of that land favored by nature before its inexhaustible riches, among which gold was by no means the most enviable, could astonish the world with their unexpected emergence.

Who ever thought of California before 1841? Only after the disastrous war that led to the definitive annexation of that part of the territory of Mexico by the North American Union in 1850 did it become apparent how much Mexico had lost by losing California, and how much California, mankind, commerce, and industry had gained from that loss.

In 1848 the population of Upper California only came to 20,000 souls, of whom 15,000 were of the native race and 5,000 of the Spanish. The official census taken after the definitive annexation and published in 1852 sets the population at 254,453 souls, composed on the whole of adults, whose incredible efforts, during only three turbulent and stormy years, had, as though by magic, produced the city of San Francisco, with 34,876 inhabitants, Sacramento, with 20,000, Marysville, with 7,000, and Stockton, with 5,000!

Five years before the abovementioned census, the modest and isolated village of Yerba Buena, today's proud San Francisco, whose harbor had been visited only by an occasional whaler, an occasional ship looking for tallow and fat, and a few small boats engaged in salmon fishing, suddenly found its roadstead turned into a forest of masts from which fluttered every flag in the world. A year after the discovery of gold, 650 ships were anchored in its fine harbor, representing 400,170 tons capacity.

It would, however, be a mistake to conclude from so extraordinary an accumulation of vessels that the countless bold adventurers whom they had brought had come only to get their fill of gold and then return to enjoy it in their native lands. No; not only simple miners came to California, but also merchants and manufacturers and all those men who had not found at home a field of activity that would reward the efforts of their individual enterprise and who rightly thought that in virgin California, in her fertile fields, and in the other natural riches of that unexplored region they would find the necessary ingredients that for a thinking man constitute what we call home and hearth. And so it was that in 1852 that small corner of the world, which had produced so little, poured into the channels of commerce, in raw agricultural products alone and as a sample of what it might produce later on, 33,995 hectoliters of wheat, 370,473 of barley, 12,574 of oats, and 174,143 of potatoes.

The crowbar, the pickax, and the sluice, which turn everything upside down to bring up gold from its subterranean bed, entered California along with the healing plow, which levels everything and smoothes it out.

In the first twenty-six years since its annexation—and apart from the value of its gold, which came to the enormous sum of 1.763 billion pesos—that marvel, one of the many of our century, has, according to official accounts, poured into the channels of world trade 360 millions in grains, 20 millions in wines and liquors, 76 in construction lumber, 63 in wool, 23 in coal, and 20 in mercury, apart from the value of the other ores exploited in that chosen land and that of its many industrial products. In 1878, 216 shipments of wheat, amounting to 8,069,825 hundredweight, left California for many foreign ports, representing a value of 14,464,166 pesos. California also exported 2,612,777 hundredweight of flour and 41,000,000 pounds of wool, all, it should be noted, at a time when that apparently inexhaustible source of production had fewer than a million inhabitants.

The Sacramento, the San Joaquin, and their numerous tributaries join to force their way through the coastal granite hills to form the imposing straits of the Golden Gate, through which they plunge into the Pacific. The valleys of those two splendid river basins, the gentle slopes of the evergreen hills that descend into them, the fruits and wildflowers that elsewhere are cultivated and that there seem to spring natively from the soil, the abundance of strawberries, raspberries, grapevines, and oats, the amazing vigor of the forests of pine, cypress, oak, and cedar, the bountiful mines of coal, iron, silver, and cinnabar, the wells of oil and of brine, the mildness of the climate, all show with eloquent clarity that gold, as I said, certainly does not constitute the principal wealth of that happy land.

It is a pleasure to trace, even if only sketchily, the progress of civilization and enterprise.

The soldiers of the immortal Cortés had visited California in 1533. Don Fernando de Ulloa sailed along its coast in 1539. Spain took possession of the entire territory in 1602, and only forty years later the Jesuits took it upon themselves to lay the foundations of civilization in that region. In 1790, 7,148 human beings lived scattered over the 406,000 square kilometers of land that make up Upper California; in 1801, there were 13,668; and in 1846 the sum of the inhabitants, both natives and foreigners, was barely 25,000. In 1848 California was annexed by the United States, and a year later its immigrant population reached 110,000!

That rugged and imposing land, whose mysterious silence was broken only by an occasional storm, by the harsh cries of the wild native celebrating his successful depredations on the fruit of civilized man's first steps in those lonely places, by the cawing of the raven, the howl of the coyote, the whinny of the deer, or the clamor of the wild birds — what had become of all this a year after civilization, enterprise, and work had begun to bring nature under their dominion?

A year later the navigable rivers and their harbors were full of vessels loaded with merchandise and passengers; a year later cities were springing up everywhere as if by magic to the noisy beat of the hammer and the saw; and the forests, whose shaded floor hindered the growth of annual vegetation, resounded to the crash of giant trees brought down by the steady blows of the axe, which always precedes the plow in mountainous country. Fires set by the hand of civilized man, while wiping out the plague of poisonous mosquitoes that infested the river banks and marshes, also destroyed the slimy deposits of grasses and reeds that had been accumulating for centuries and that infected the atmosphere with their harmful vapors. Roads were being built everywhere; the force of arms pursued the native who refused to work and left him no refuge anywhere; and the famous Rocky Mountains, whose precipices and barren ridges had never been visited by man, were on every side occupied by groups of laborers, caravans of travelers, and droves of mules loaded with tools, clothing, and food to provide for the needs of the bold adventurers who, standing in water up to their waists or sweating with the pickax on dry land, struggled to bring forth the gold from the bowels of the earth.

Individual initiative, the power of concerted action, the energy and boldness that determinedly and strenuously sowed in that region the seed of the material and intellectual progress of nations, were bound to produce what with astonishment we behold twenty-six years later, that is, the emergence of a mighty state that rightly bears the honorable title of second commercial center of the Americas.

Those twenty-six years have sufficed for hard work, manufacturing, and commerce, under the aegis of practical common sense, to produce within the borders of that youthful state all that the most demanding and refined man can desire for his happiness, because the very special efforts of the remarkable persons of all nationalities who came to California were coupled with the Yankee spirit, which never conquers for the sole pleasure of conquering.

The cart of the printing press was never absent from among the gun carriages of their armies; from every headquarters thousands of broadsheets issued every day, disseminating both the news of victories to inspirit the soldier and the anticipation of the benefits that immediate and peaceful annexation to the American Union would bring to the occupied country. Thus it was that barely had the intrepid Commodore John D. Sloat, encouraged by the victory of Palo Santo and Resaca de la Palma, taken possession of Monterey in the name of the United States, when the newspaper *The Californian* appeared in that town, while foundations were being laid for a church that gave evidence of the freedom of religion and two schools whose spacious and elegant construction contrasted sharply with that of the heavy buildings of Spanish colonial times.

Once annexation had been decided on, the first thing that Congress approved was the grant of half a million acres of land for the support of the schools; and each municipality, moved by the same spirit, reserved two acres of its most valuable downtown land for the same purpose.

A year after the appearance of the *Californian* in Monterey, the modest village of Yerba Buena, today San Francisco, had its *California Star*, and two years later, its *Alta California, Pacific News, Journal du Commerce, California Courier, Herald*, and *Evening Picayune*. The towns-in-the-making Sacramento and Stockton had the *Transcript* and the *Placer Times* in the former, and the *Journal Times* in the latter. Sonora, too, had its *Herald;* and even the tent camp Marysville had its publication with the same title. Twenty-four years later, in the city of San Francisco alone, whose population had already reached 300,000 souls, there were 16 daily newspapers, 43 weeklies, one fortnightly, and 15 monthly and fortnightly magazines. In the state as a whole, there were 239 newspapers and journals.

I repeat, however, that it would be a great error, as well as an injustice, to attribute the phenomenon of this transformation solely to the influence of the Anglo-Saxon race. It is also the product of the individual contributions of the most daring and enterprising elements of the superior strata of every other human race. Speaking of this miraculous transformation toward the end of '49, the learned writer S. C. Upham told me what many years later he expressed in writing, "Those who have immigrated here are the cream of the populace."[62] Men who in their native lands found no field in which to display their energy, boldly sought it on the virgin shores of America and found it there. The German, the Irishman, the Frenchman, the Italian, the Spaniard, the Chinese, and every other man whose heart does not feel his own worth and an energy sufficient to face trials and dangers far from home, does not emigrate, just as professional learning in the arts and sciences does not emigrate from the places where it can be utilized.

---

62. The quotation is in English in the original. The writer is Samuel Curtis Upham (1819–1885), author of several books on Gold-Rush California. JP.

As I said, then, today's California does not owe her population and her progress to any one race but, with a few exceptions, to the cream of the enterprising spirit of all nations.

As evidence of this truth a sense of patriotic pride obliges me to record here some instances of individual initiative on the part of Chileans that will show that that virtue is not native to any single land. The establishment of the town of Marysville is due to the efforts of the Chilean Don José Manuel Ramírez y Rosales. The first ship of deep draft that dared, without benefit of a pilot, to reach the port of Sacramento and proudly anchored there to the cheers of all the townspeople was the Chilean bark *Natalia*, belonging to the Luco brothers. The first charity hospital established in Sacramento sprang from the generosity, so rare at that time, of Don Manuel and Don Leandro Luco, who donated the bark *Natalia* and all her cargo for this noble purpose.

Many times we see that those events that seem least conducive to the achievement of some aim serve precisely to bring it about. Such was the case with the July 1830 revolution in France. The man who was to discover California's gold escaped, as though by a miracle, from the bloody hub of that revolution.

There is no doubt that in the hands of the Anglo-Saxon race this state, even without gold, would have been able to achieve at least the level of prosperity enjoyed today by the other members of the American Union; but it is certain that it owes its brilliant and accelerated entry into the ranks of prosperous and civilized nations to the July Revolution. The hand of fate saved the 6th Regiment of Swiss Guards, stationed in Grenoble, from the massacre that took place in the French capital during those July days and thus saved the life of the gallant Captain John Sutter, who commanded one of the regiment's companies.[63]

I remember that through the clouds of smoke produced by fires and gunpowder on the frightful twenty-sixth day of that terrible month I could see bloody shreds of military uniforms hanging from the ropes that held up the streetlights and that in the vicinity of the Tuileries I saw only uniforms of the famous Swiss Guards who, lacking more lucrative employment in their own country, sold their brawn and their blood abroad, risking their lives to defend that of the king of France.

When the 6th Swiss Regiment, stationed in Grenoble, was dissolved, as were all other mercenary corps in France, by direct and express order of

63. Sutter's military service in France was a fiction of his own invention, as he admitted in his last years. See James Peter Zollinger, "John Augustus Sutter's European Background," *California Historical Society Quarterly* 14 (1935): 28–46. JP.

Louis Philippe d'Orléans, captain general of the kingdom after the expulsion of Charles X, Sutter, the elect of fate, returned alive to his country.

The cast of soul that led those Swiss adventurers to rent out their lives to defend that of the tyrant who paid them best was certainly not of a kind that would lead one to suspect that among such fierce watchdogs there might be a man who, like Sutter, was not only upright, intelligent, and highly yet nobly ambitious, but also absolutely fearless and unshakably convinced of the marvels that always result from steadfastness and hard work.

Captain John Sutter was a tall young man, well proportioned, and of gallant and martial bearing. After the catastrophe of July he took refuge in his native cantons, where the density of the hard-working highland population, the extreme poverty into which he had fallen, and his eagerness to prosper and seek adventure soon convinced him that Europe was the least suitable place for profiting from an adventurer's capital, which is rarely anything but intelligence, courage, and the capacity to bear the reverses of fortune, no matter how hard and painful. Armed with his valor, therefore, and filled with hope, he set off for the plains of Missouri.[64]

But it was written that he was everywhere to meet difficulties in trying to reach his ambitious goal of becoming a leading figure in his place of residence. What befell him in North America was similar to what had happened to him in his native land. His lack of means in the midst of a dense hard-working population drove him away; the great energy and individual initiative of the Yankee forced him to leave this other country where he was bound to occupy a relatively secondary station, and so without further delay he sought in Spanish America what he had been unable to find in English America.

Accompanied by some adventurers as bold as he, Sutter left Jackson County in Missouri, set off to find the new region that was to satisfy his aspirations, and in August 1838, after many an adventure and travail, reached the pleasant country that lies between what is now the city of Sacramento and the famous American River of Upper California, at that time a part of the Republic of Mexico. The appearance of the place, the quality of the soil, the abundant vegetation, and the proximity of the navigable part of a great river captured the heart of that natural-born colonizer; convinced that in exploiting the riches of that wasteland he would meet no obstacles but such as his perseverance and proven valor

64. Sutter also emigrated to escape a warrant for his arrest on charges of defrauding the creditors of the dry-goods shop that he had been keeping in Switzerland during the years of his supposed service in the Swiss Guard of Charles X. JP.

could overcome, he asked the Mexican government to grant him land, undertaking to rein in the Indians inhabiting it and punish them if they persisted in their depredations against the civilized population on that most dangerous frontier.

Mexico granted his request gladly, as it had an earlier request by Russian immigrants who, at some distance from the land assigned to Sutter, were occupied in gathering furs and fishing for salmon. The presence of another colony as important as was the Russian, and so close to the one our adventurer planned to establish, was certainly a major stumbling-block on the way to accomplishing the many plans bubbling up in the imagination of the newcomer. Disregarding the cost, therefore, he not only bought from the Russian colony all its rights to the former mission at La Bodega but by means of skillfully calculated concessions succeeded in drawing the scattered members of the dissolved establishment into his enterprise and with their help laying its foundations by building a fort that might serve as a base for subsequent operations.

The former soldier of the Swiss Guards knew from experience that there are only two ways to dominate others: attracting them with kindness so that obedience is a pleasure, or forcing obedience on them so firmly that they will see all resistance to be useless. Until then the Mexican authorities had in vain employed missions and other means more sentimental than practical to modify the fierce character of the Indians of that region, so that the only civilizing method that remained was the use of force guided by knowledge. For more than three centuries we have used the same system as the Mexicans to win over and civilize our Araucanians; and only now, and then but halfway, are we beginning to obtain what with a little more energy and good sense we could have obtained long ago, because the wild Indian, stubborn or dominated by his bad instincts, will accept peace, work, and respect for the property of others only once he is persuaded that as soon as he comes within rifle range, if he comes with hostile intentions he will die or be enchained.

At the outset, then, Sutter was cruel; with no resources but his courage and that of his selfless companions, attending by turns to the sword and the plow, he fought, won, worked the land, forced the conquered to labor on it; and only when the treacherous and fickle tribes were fully persuaded that they had to choose between death and submission did our pioneer begin to set in motion all those civilizing ideas that do him honor. He distributed land among the natives of his district, gave them clothes, even gave them mattresses so that they would grow used to comforts they could enjoy only in union with civilized man; he built schools, he became the inexorable judge of their private disputes, and he protected them against distant free-roaming tribes, from which he exacted substantial tribute.

Next he taught them to farm the land, built them smithies and carpentry shops, purchased the fruit of their labor, and finally, to crown his work as a model colonizer, elevated the most deserving natives to the rank of his partners. By means of work, prudence, and steadfastness, this exceptional man thus came ultimately to merit the coveted title of father that, when the author of these lines was traveling through those lands, he still received from the same conquered natives in whom he had succeeded in inculcating the love of work along with that of home, which the nomad holds in such disdain.

To Sutter, then, belongs the glory of having established the first model colony to flourish in the western part of the American continent; and it is therefore not surprising that at the tempestuous meeting with which in 1846 Philadelphia celebrated the annexation of California to the Union, General Gibson should have addressed these well-deserved words to Sutter:

> The patriarch of California, the compatriot of Tell and Washington, pure and brave, noble of nature, kind of heart, benign and generous of character, father of each of his men and father of them all, deserves statues not of marble or of bronze, but cast from the very gold of California.

One of the busy enterprises of this tireless laborer for civilization and industry was a substantial millrace by means of which the swift water of the American River, a few leagues before its confluence with the Sacramento, powered a sawmill for cutting and finishing the valuable cedar and pine found in the woods surrounding that valley. Among the rustic laborers who worked on that ditch was one James Marshall, to whose stout pick we owe the first gold nuggets that were to exert such an influence on world trade and to which the but lately forgotten California undoubtedly owes the speed of its enviable progress.

The disastrous war between the United States and Mexico, which began in September 1846 as a result of the annexation of Texas by the great Angloamerican state, and which ended with the treaty of Guadalupe Hidalgo in February 1848, coincided with the discovery of gold in Upper California. The last volleys of the cannon fired in this war thus announced to our lucky adventurer that not only his fortune but also his adoptive nationality had changed.

Nuggets weighing one, two, four, and even six pounds soon circulated with lightning speed through all the markets in the world; and everywhere was heard the call of the trumpet that summoned men to the feast offering to boldness and hard work the enviable hope of sure and instant fortune.

How much was a modest bushel of wheat worth in Chile before 1848? Six, eight, twelve *reales,* two pesos at the most, depending on the distance between the point of harvesting and that of consumption. Back then, who even thought of exporting to Europe what is now one of the mainstays of our agricultural wealth? Only twenty-eight years after the time I am speaking of, the first cargo of wheat that in the way of timid experiment had crossed the Atlantic reached Marseilles, and in a Chilean ship. The wholesale price of yearling calves was three pesos. Cows ready for fattening could be bought for eight pesos; oxen brought as much as fourteen. Sheep were distributed at cost to our cowhands as food. A roasting turkey cost four *reales;* a whole load of alfalfa, another four; and in our good old Santiago apples were still being sold in the streets at half a *real* for a hundred. A capital of 25,000 pesos, a pittance nowadays, used to make its fortunate owner an enviable match for obtaining the hand of a desirable spouse; but how hard it was for an ordinary businessman, with the prices I have indicated, to amass those 25,000 pesos! It is, thus, not surprising that the news of the fabulous wealth discovered in California should excite the world of commerce, the waifs of fortune, and even those on whom she seemed most to smile.

Gold nuggets, convincing ambassadors of that wealth, hidden at first, were soon displayed among us for all to see. As their fame spread like calumny in *The Barber of Seville,* they produced in the minds of peaceful Chileans an explosion of feverish activity that, deaf to the voice of caution, led thousands of adventurers to the golden honeycomb where so many hopes were to perish.

For those who believed in the existence of California's gold, the only reckless fool was the man who did not dash off to share in it, and who can wonder at this when even now we are still lamenting much more recent illusions? Humanity seems born never to learn! Merchants prepared cargoes; the man of means who could not go himself organized expeditions; the poor man sold what he had, to pay his way; and the man who had nothing worked as a seaman or contracted out his labor in exchange for the cost of his passage to that El Dorado, those Thousand and One Nights turned reality.

With all this commotion, the author of these modest pages, used to the vicissitudes of an ever stormy and adventure-filled life, could hardly remain unmoved by such feverish activity.

Four brothers, a brother-in-law, and two trusted servants made up our expedition to California.

I shall indicate the stock of supplies with which we set out on an enterprise that took us more than 6,700 miles from our country and our loved ones, so that from it the reader may deduce the assets of most of the Chilean adventurers who, lacking our resources or anything like them, rushed off fearlessly in pursuit of fortune to a remote region where even the air they would breathe was totally alien to them.

The capital of our foolhardy undertaking consisted of:

6 bags of toasted meal,
6 of beans,
4 hundredweight of rice,
1 barrel of sugar,
2 of Concepción wine,
a small stock of shovels, hatchets, and crowbars,
an iron pot, gunpowder, lead for bullets,
250 pesos cash, plus 612 more for our passage.

Apart from linens, which we abandoned after our arrival because there was no one to wash clothes, only to wash gold, our individual outfits consisted of boots, a wool shirt that also served as a jacket, heavy wool trousers, a leather belt, a knife, a pair of pistols, a rifle, and, to top it off, a cloth hat that could double as a pillow. In addition, each of us had a small leather pouch for toasted meal, a fire-resistant tin jar or bowl, hunting equipment, and a flint and steel lighter.

If my memory did not vouch for their accuracy, I should not believe the notes that I took then and have before me now. For Chileans, California was an unknown country, almost a desert, full of dangers and prey to epidemic diseases. There were no friends or relatives there that one could count on; personal security could be found only in the barrel of a pistol or at the point of a knife, yet robbery, violence, sickness, death itself were secondary considerations when compared to the seductive gleam of gold.

As the nature of our baggage shows, we were not to begin our adventures until after we had reached California; but the case was different for those who paid for their passage by working as seamen and even more so for those who came from the Atlantic in pursuit of El Dorado. From Valparaíso to San Francisco we had to sail only some 6,700 miles, while from the eastern part of the United States there were at least 19,300, not to mention having to round Cape Horn. These travelers, then, began to suffer long before we did. All the more amazing, then, that neither struggles and sacrifices to pay for the passage, nor the well-known dangers of a voyage where deadly disaster was common, sufficed to temper their eagerness.

We ourselves barely managed to find first-class accommodations on the French bark *Staouéli*,[65] already packed with passengers, yet we had not wasted a moment between the announcement of her sailing and the payment of our passage. In order not to delay our departure we had to leave our supplies behind, to be forwarded on the *Julia*.

Finally, on December 20, 1848, we managed to leave Valparaíso, bidding farewell to a host of friends and curious onlookers who, downcast above all for having to stay behind, begged us over and over again to write them what truth there might be to the acclaimed wealth of the place where our good fortune was taking us.

Here, then, begins the account, in turn serious, ridiculous, and frightful, of that mad escapade.

At that time the harbormaster was Señor Orella. He ordered that all those who were not to sail should go ashore. When he repeated this order to an adventurer of the female sex, merely because she had taken out her passport under the name Rosario Améstica, when the word was that she had been born as Izquierdo in Quilicura, lived in Talcahuano as Villaseca, in Talca as Toro, and in Valparaíso, till the day before, as Rosa Montalva, this bold woman, still youthful and elegant, made such a row to stay on board that she almost caused the steerage passengers to rebel and toss the good Señor Orella into the sea. Poor little Rosario's glances and tears made witnesses to the spotless virtue of this chaste damsel spring up from between decks as if by magic. One had known her from infancy, another was her godfather, and all, in a word, had had dealings with her, and all to a man maintained that she was Améstica and nothing else; and so willy-nilly the harbormaster let her stay on board, to the delight of many a merry passenger.

The voyagers consisted of ninety men, three women, four cows, eight pigs, three dogs, seventeen seamen, one captain, and one pilot.

At the moment of departure no one gave a thought to the dangers and travails awaiting us. Unanimously we cheered the fresh breeze that was moving us along, and we lost sight of our native land without revealing with a single sigh or tinge of remorse that we understood the magnitude of our collective rashness.

65. The ship was evidently named after the French victory over the Algerians at Staouéli that the author mentions in Chapter VI. JP.

One of the passengers on the upper deck was a certain Álvarez, a Chilean by birth, skinny of build and so eccentric in character and apparently distrustful that although he was a rich man and could have traveled in first class, he refused to do so because, he said, the French, thieves that they were, would not there feed him any of the abundant good things he had in his crates of supplies. The first-class passengers were Boom, Pioche, secretary of the French legation, Bayerweck, our party, and, among our other merry companions, a Frenchman so wide in the hips that he had to pass sideways through the narrow little door that connected our cabins with the deck. We bestowed on him the nickname *Culatus*.[66]

To maintain the order of these recollections I shall copy some passages from my diary.

JANUARY 18, 1849. Our only distress up to now is an excruciating monotony and unbearable heat. The look of the sky and the captain's observations tell us that we are already crossing the Equator. For the last few days we have been noticing some discontent among the steerage passengers. Álvarez has quite a hand in this, because it seems that his mismanaged provisions will not last him through the voyage; we fear an insurrection on board.

JANUARY 19. The joyous shout of "Ship ahoy!" has cheered us all. At 9 A.M. the other ship's movements showed us that she wanted to speak with us; and at 10 we saw, with great excitement, that she was lying to and lowering one of her boats. Filled with curiosity, all one hundred twelve of us happily received the visit of the amiable and modest Yankee captain who favored us with his visit; the sailors who accompanied him almost fainted with envy when they saw the charming Rosarito in our midst.

During lunch we learned that the ship was called *American* and that her captain, Mr. John Perkinson, planned to stop at Talcahuano before continuing his voyage around Cape Horn and then northward. In feverish haste we all wrote to our families. The good Perkinson, after resignedly eyeing our fine table service, pronounced these words that I shall never forget:

After thirty-nine months of sailing without ever going ashore, this is the first time, gentlemen, that I have eaten at so luxurious a table. You have silverware, plates, good bread, and fresh meat. I had forgotten what these things are; worm-eaten biscuit, hard and black, and bad salt meat have been my choicest nourishment since I left my wife and children. You are very fortunate, because on top of all this you're on your way to look for

66. From *culo* (Latin *culus*), "bottom, butt." JP.

lots of gold in California. Still (he added with a sigh), I don't envy you your good fortune: I'm on my way to embrace my children.

This has been a very full day for us. We had not yet lost sight of the whaler when with a great deal of hullabaloo we managed to haul up a gigantic shark. After struggling to finish him off while he defended himself thrashing about with his tail, we found, in his belly, a seaman's shoe and two sardine jars that we had just emptied. The heart of this voracious animal, set on a plate, continued to give signs of life for three hours and leapt when touched.

January 30. It is 8 p.m. This has been a hard day, which could have been disastrous. I had been suspecting for some days that the peace and quiet of our voyage might at any moment be broken by the haughty way that the steerage passengers treat the crew, and my prediction almost came true.

We had just finished our dinner when a sailor rushed into the dining room and whispered something to the captain, who, with a suddenly changed expression, immediately stood up and, his voice trembling, told us, "We have a revolution on board! Álvarez is leading it; and if you don't help me, we're lost!"

Since this was the worst disaster that could befall us in view of the character of the rebels, everyone went to his cabin in search of weapons, while I dashed on deck in search of my servants, who, with the help of three laborers whom I had recently hired on board, managed to take effective countermeasures and hand the mad instigator of this senseless affair over to us, disarmed, before the rebellion could reach a dire pitch. We are fortunate indeed! The prisoner will remain under guard until we can set him ashore.

Here I temporarily interrupt the excerpts from my diary to devote a few words to this ingenuous madman, whom a few months after this episode I saved from a frightful death.

Having left the placers of Sonoma to do an errand for my partners, I came on Mr. Gillespie resting in the shade of a pine tree near Sutter's ruined fort, when our ears were struck by the shouts of a man whom some others were stringing up on top of a covered wagon. The voice of the unfortunate who was begging for help sounded familiar. I jumped up terrified and shouted to Gillespie, "They're killing a friend of mine; let's run over and save him!"

Fortunately we arrived in time. I can still see the hapless Álvarez with his neck tied to the stump of a branch and his feet tied with another rope to the top of a wagon ready to roll. He was going to be torn in two! In California people took me for a Frenchman, and I knew that the name of Lafayette was venerated by even the most rustic Americans. I invoked that magic name and said that Álvarez was the only protector the French had had in Chile, that he had saved my own life, and that I would vouch for his honesty. My companion automatically endorsed everything he heard me say, and with God's help Álvarez was respectfully lowered from that awful improvised gallows!

The cause of this act of hasty and barbaric justice was our scatterbrained countryman's meddlesome character. I never could find out what had led him into that encampment of traveling miners; but since a shovel had gone astray and the only likely suspect was that scion of Africans, which is what the Yankees called the Chileans and the Spaniards, the theft was attributed to him and without further ado those savages set themselves up as a jury and were about to do with Álvarez what was often done everywhere with known thieves. For the next five days the unfortunate gentleman was out of his mind, as though under the influence of a convulsive stupor. He left us after his recovery, and I never heard of him again.

I return to my interrupted diary:

FEBRUARY 13. We have now been sailing for forty-seven days. Sanitary conditions are perfect; only one poor sailor has died, and we had to throw him into the sea. According to what the captain has told me, in about four more days we shall reach the land of hope or of disillusionment. A fresh breeze; we are making eight knots; if we go on like this, the four days will turn into two. Dense clouds are all around us. All day long the captain has been lamenting the absence of the sun.

FEBRUARY 15. It is 11 P.M.; this tiresome voyage obviously does not want to end without a parting gesture. Only an hour ago we were about to perish, smashed against the string of well-known rocks[67] that rise from the water five leagues from the entrance to the harbor of San Francisco! Dense fog, calm, and currents have kept our captain understandably concerned since daybreak. At 4 P.M. he ordered the sails shortened and the anchors to be ready. Those of us who understood the reason for his precautions were uneasy; but for the rest of the passengers, who did not know the meaning of these measures, it was all cause for jubilation, and rightly so, because during any long voyage there is and can be no more pleasing sound than that produced by the anchor chain on the deck, always a sure sign of successful arrival.

---

67. The Farallones (meaning "rocks" in Spanish) or Farallon Islands, a group of steep rocky islands outside the Golden Gate. JP.

To keep us awake and alert without alarming us, the captain proposed a game of whist, in which he also took part, whispering to me as he sat down that he thought we were already very close to the rocks.

Everyone was in the best of spirits, some playing, others drinking tea, all talking at the same time, all blustering about what they were planning to do; and the worthy Culatus, who was more ready for sleep than for anything else, his mighty bulk placed on the first step of the ladder that led up from the chamber, was calmly getting a bit of fresh air there, when the captain, suddenly dropping his cards, rushed onto the deck. A moment later, and when we least expected it, the terrifying shouts, "Rocks dead ahead! The spar to windward! Set all sail!" struck us like lightning bolts.

Recovering from our initial fright, we dashed to the door, knocking over chairs and breaking plates; but since the door was blocked by Culatus, who in his alarm forgot that he had to go through it sideways, our collective push sent the stubborn bulk that blocked our way flying out on deck as though shot from a cannon, and we climbed over him. Meanwhile our fine ship, obedient to the helm, had skirted the danger, leaving behind an area of noisy white foam that signaled the base of the black rocks where, but for the alertness of our captain, we should all have lost our dreams of wealth and our very lives!

Since it was very dangerous to proceed and the sounding line had shown us to be in forty fathoms of water, we dropped anchor.

FEBRUARY 16. Calm, heavy seas, wet fog. No one slept last night. We are surrounded by a herd of sea lions or seals that slide off the rocks and drop with a crash into the water. The noise of the sea birds and the barking of the amphibians are deafening.

FEBRUARY 17. The distressing fog continued today, and it is raining hard. At midday, with a favorable wind, we raised anchor to move away from our dangerous neighbors; and at our first tack seaward, we were almost hit by a brig that passed by us in a flash scraping the bark's stern. It tried to tell us something we could not understand and disappeared into the fog. What a dangerous locality!

FEBRUARY 18. What contrasts mark life at sea! There we were, stretched out, half dozing, still fully clothed, in our cabins, when at daybreak thunderous shouts of joy made us leap on deck. What was going on?

Once we had passed through the thick low-lying fog that like a curtain almost always hangs over that place, between the coast and the ships heading for it, our eyes fell on the most beautiful view that could be offered them at so difficult a moment. To the south we saw the black rocks that had put us in such peril, and to the east, whither our bow was headed under a clear sky and with a fresh breeze, the straits of the

Golden Gate, which, glorious and imposing, seemed to be opening wide to receive us. We had reached California!

The Sacramento and San Joaquin, the mightiest rivers that pour their waters into the western sea of the American continent, have broken their way through the line of coastal hills that defend Upper California against the onslaughts of the Pacific and formed the picturesque channel that, since it leads to the region of golden dreams, has earned the name of Golden Gate. This major strait is six miles long and one to three miles wide, is accessible to every kind of vessel, and is the only entrance into San Francisco Bay. Its rugged shores, pounded day after day by the periodic fluctuation of the tides, rise perpendicularly on both sides of the channel, forming steep walls whose granite base, perforated by fascinating caves, support patches of fertile soil covered with trees and greenery.

Beyond this imposing entrance lies San Francisco Bay, which is without question the most beautiful, extensive, and secure of all those bathed by the waters of the Pacific. The significance of this bay can be judged both by its dimensions and by the excellence of its anchorages. It is 70 miles long, with an average width of 14 miles and an area of 275 square miles. It consists of two principal divisions, San Francisco Bay proper to the south and San Pablo Bay to the north. The former, on whose northwestern shore the town of the same name stands, is 41 miles long and contains some picturesque islands, among them Birds Island,[68] which seems to have been deliberately placed by the hand of nature to serve as both a lighthouse to guide ships and a fort to assert control over the bay. San Pablo Bay, which lies to the north, is 30 miles long and is connected through a narrow channel with yet another bay that is 15 miles long and bears the name Suisun.

Into this third bay flow, as into a lake that detains their currents, the two great rivers Sacramento and San Joaquin, whose united waters there begin, thanks to the effect of the tides, to lose their freshness, until they plunge into those of the Pacific Ocean, after having run a navigable course of more than three hundred miles for the Sacramento, from northeast to west, and a slightly shorter one from south to north for the San Joaquin. The bottom of the bay is sand and mud, and its shores are everywhere accessible. No bar offers any true danger to navigation at its mouth, although the tides are so high that as they enter and leave the narrows they form many small eddies that can prove disastrous to smaller vessels that might imprudently venture into that dangerous passage at the wrong time.

68. *Birds Island,* Pérez Rosales writes in English, for Bird Island, the former name of Alcatraz Island. JP.

X I V

Reports of the abundance and richness of the gold fields are
confirmed. — The harbormaster. — Rosarito Améstica. —
A tour of the town. — Contradictory reports about the mines
and the best time to start working there. — My mining
company begins its operations. — In the freight business.—
The company goes into the laundry business.

With most of our sails furled and our anchors at the ready we cautiously passed through the famous Golden Gate and soon, filled with excitement, we caught sight of the town that would, as though by magic, turn from the petty village of Yerba Buena into the rich and populous San Francisco.

To be sure, we had no very clear idea of what that town might be like. We remembered that the place had belonged to Spain and to Mexico, we knew that it was far from any major city, and on these grounds we believed that we should find a second edition of some Curacaví. We were quite mistaken; and great was our surprise when we rounded the headland that shelters the anchorage and, through the masts of the ships and despite the late hour, saw a pretty though irregularly laid out town that spread over the slopes of its picturesque site and contained some first-rate houses.

Thirty-four ships of all nationalities had preceded us, in addition to an American fleet composed of one ship of the line, three corvettes, and one transport. Since our *Staouéli* was the first French vessel to enter the port after the discovery of gold, the naval commander graciously replied to the salute of our flag by having his men, standing on the yards of his flagship, give us three cheers that roused the echoes of the bay.

Finally we heard the longed-for shout of "Drop the anchor!"; as a general "Hurrah!" accompanied the rattling of the chain, we were all on the point of embracing each other in celebration of our safe arrival, as if we had escaped from some imminent peril. It was a remarkable thing: I have made many sea voyages in the course of my life; at the age of fifteen I had already rounded Cape Horn three times, and two years later I had rounded it again and undergone, on the Atlantic, the dangers of the most violent winds blowing from Patagonia; I have crossed the dangerous Bay of Biscay at the time of the equinox, when the city of Bordeaux was overflowing with the victims of shipwrecks; but none of these dangers made so deep an impression on me as did those of this voyage.

A moment later we could see the lights of this infant town; as we gazed on it, with doubts in our heads and anxiety in our hearts, we waited, like the criminal waiting to hear his sentence, for someone to tell us whether the tales we had heard about this place were true or false.

One would have had to be in our situation and see the many and varied expressions on the faces of the passengers as fear and hope seethed in their hearts in order to understand the effect made on us by the arrival of the first boat to tie up to our side. At first we thought it was the harbormaster's boat or the coast guard; but since things happened in California that do not happen anywhere else, the boat that approached us belonged to the *Anamakin,* whose captain, Mr. Robinet, came to get news of Chile.

The arrival of this gentleman put us in a fluster. From his lips would come our sentence. All of us dashed toward him, all speaking at the same time; although each thought he was asking a question different from those asked by his companions, there is no doubt that all these questions could be reduced to one: "Is there really as much gold as they say?"

My party and I did not hear the answer. As though impelled by a mechanical force we had all clustered together against the opposite railing, because we wanted to prolong an uncertainty, which, cruel as it might be, was yet preferable to disillusionment. Finally, a charming young Frenchman, also traveling in first class, who four months later died of longing while calling out the name of Chile, rushed toward me overflowing with joy and shouting, "It's true, all of it! There's lots of gold, a huge lot of gold!"

The reader can judge whether this news allowed us to breathe again. Agitation and commentary were so general that no one seemed able to understand anyone else, while groups formed here and there and exclamations rose everywhere, some more, some less energetic. There were those who shook their fists in the direction of Chile; others raised their heads high; and not a few, savoring future felicity, sat down on a pile of rigging, apparently sunk in solitary and delightful contemplation.

For me good fortune has always been a delusion, but this did not keep me from sharing in the general happiness as I stood contentedly contemplating the scene. If an impartial spectator, however, had dropped at that moment from the moon, he could easily have read these inscriptions, or something like them, in each of those agitated hearts:

"My dream's come true! I'll be a banker in France!"

"Now Amalia will eat her heart out! And she turned me down because I was poor!"

"If you think you'll catch me now, Julia, think again!"

"If there's that much gold, I'm a rich man. That girl's pretty and good, but she's so poor!"

"If there's gold, there'll be idlers, and where there's idlers, there's gambling. Hurrah for my loaded dice and my pack of cards!"

"I'm a smart fellow now! Nobody's an ass in Chile if he's got money!"

As for Robinet, he told us that the stories being told in Chile couldn't hold a candle to reality, that the lowest bumpkin was tossing around gold as though he were a Croesus, since all one had to do to acquire this precious metal was to bend over and pick it up, that we had reached the land of equality, and that the noble and the plebeian walked shoulder to shoulder in California. In a word, the good gentleman dazzled us with so many wonders that when we shook his hand to say goodbye we seemed to be thanking him for the news more than for the visit.

Since by now it was very late, we all went to bed so as to be up at daybreak.

The sun had hardly risen when our ship was surrounded by boats and skiffs, some bearing merchants and onlookers, others in search of baggage and passengers. Everyone confirmed what we had heard about the gold; and many, though of poor and unimpressive appearance, poured part of the contents of the leather bags that they carried at their waists into their hands, displaying to our joyous eyes nuggets the size of hazelnuts and gold dust the size of lentils.

A crowd of acquaintances soon appeared, too; but we had to look at them long and hard to recognize, under the rags of threadbare trousers and a heavy seaman's jacket, the refined Santiago dandy or the Valparaíso merchant. Elegant young Hamilton was now a seaman and master of a skiff in partnership with a Negro, whose bed he shared because they had only one; wearing a frayed cap and a wool shirt soaking wet from the morning dew, he was looking for passengers to take ashore. Don Samuel Price, fat, happy, and busy, with his trousers rolled up, his hands calloused, and his coat and boots covered with mud, bombarded us with questions about the goods we had with us and answered the flood of our questions with tales of wonder. Mass, Sánchez, Cross, Puett, and many other gentlemen who called me by my name before I could recognize who they were, crowded into the first-class quarters. The appearance of these adventurers, all of them formerly wearers of frock coats or cutaways, was so grotesque that a glimpse of just one of them would have supplied Dumas with material for ten novels.

It was not only curiosity that moved these busy men to visit us. In California people did not waste time looking at curiosities; every man was intent on his business. Everything on board could have been sold at extravagant prices; but since the prices on land were even higher, it is not surprising that the apparent onlookers made such efforts not to let us disembark without first striking a deal. While Cross was negotiating with a passenger on the quarterdeck, another merchant, dashing after one of the just arrived marks, suddenly bumped into Cross and knocked his hat into the sea, without the one noticing it or the other even thinking of looking back. Concern for a hat or turning around out of courtesy were wastes of time, and the man who wasted time in California was wasting gold. Shortly after this, Cross left with a sailor's tarred cap, as proud and easy as if he had been wearing a bishop's miter.

About ten in the morning a tall, chubby, and determined-looking Yankee boarded us. One of his eyes was in good condition, the other blackened from a punch he had received during a drunken brawl the night before. This was the harbormaster, who, chewing tobacco and still smelling of liquor, was coming to station a customs guard on board to supervise the unloading of the cargo. Looking more like a cyclops than anything else, he jumped over the railing and, in a loud pleasant voice, said, "Welcome to gold country—lots and lots of gold!" The captain of the *Staouéli,* who knew no English, thinking we were being asked for our passports, immediately displayed them all, because we had handed them to him when we left Valparaíso. The expression of surprise and disgust with which the Yankee looked at the passports and stamped documents was worthy of a painter. He considered that by showing these papers our captain had offered the gravest possible insult to the Stars and Stripes; and so, raising his good eye from the contemplation of these frightful objects, he exclaimed, "To hell with travel permits! Let's not have any stamped papers or passports! That's highway robbery and stupid tyranny, and we won't put up with it here! I've come just to congratulate you on your arrival and to station this inspector on board to receive the landing permits you'll get from the customs house, and that's all." He was offered some wine and answered that he only drank champagne; after downing a bottle of it, he left us in good spirits, probably saying to himself that even if the newcomers did not quite understand republican ways, at least they drank very good wine.

Rosarito, dressed to kill in a magnificent silk gown, cape, and parasol, fawned and fluttered over by everyone who came on board, soon went ashore and, surrounded by a crowd of admirers, disappeared into the low fog or semi-drizzle that obscured everything.

The first passengers who, decked out in their finest, had gone forth to explore the lay of the land soon returned bearing good cheer, mud, and contradictory information; my friends and I, determined not to be left behind, also set out to see whether we could get something clear where so much was muddy.

At that time what you saw and heard in California was so exceptional and so outside the normal order of human affairs, and one event followed another with such extraordinary rapidity, that only if you wrote them down as you observed them and subsequently see the notes made in your own hand can you believe that it was not all a dream.

Full of determination we reached land, or rather mud, because the low tide had left nothing else from the point at which our boat ran aground to the edge of the slope of terra firma where the town began. To the right of the landing place there was a kind of board fence behind which some beef was being cut up and on top of which a row of ravens was cawing with delight at the smell of blood.

Some friends had impressed on us the need to go armed, and always at least two of us at a time. We followed this advice and saw that most of the local traders were also armed, displaying not only their goods but also a knife at their side or a revolver, a firearm that was then beginning to gain popularity. To find Price's place we had to walk through a great part of the strangest town imaginable. Its streets, arcs whose two ends touched the shore, were traversed by others that ran straight to the sea and ended in incipient docks that hindered more than helped the work of unloading. Some of the houses that lined both sides of the streets of this labyrinth must have been worth at least a hundred thousand pesos. There was no uniformity among them; by the side of a valuable, though simple rustic building stood rows of tents, tarpaulins, wooden sheds, and huts, some finished and others under brisk construction. The Parker House Hotel was leased for 175,000 pesos a year. There were no sidewalks or anything like them, and the middle of the street was a sump of churned mud whose most solid elements were the thousands of broken bottles thrown from the houses once they had been emptied. The inhabitants, of the most varied nationalities, came to 1,500 residents and that many more transients, and seemed to be celebrating an immense and boisterous masked ball, to judge by their exotic costumes, the variety of their languages, and the very nature of their occupations. Even the women seemed to have dressed as men, because no matter how much you looked for a skirt in that madhouse, you could see nothing like it to save your life. The fringed leather jacket of the tough-looking Oregonian, the peaked Chilean cap, the parasol-like hat of the Chinese, the huge boots of the Russians that seemed to be swallowing their owners, the Frenchman, the Englishman, the Italian disguised as a sailor, the yokel in a frock coat about to breathe its last, the gentleman with no coat, in a word, everything you might find in a gigantic carnival was to be seen there, and in dizzying motion. We were constantly forced to step aside and wade into the mud to give way to some former dandy in a wool shirt and rolled-up trousers who, sweating under the weight of some load, was making four pesos for each trip up from the beach, or to avoid being run over by a more fortunate carrier, owner of a hand cart, who marched along haughtily with no regard for obstacles, arousing the envy of those who lacked such a machine. The words "tranquility" and "idleness" held no meaning in San Francisco. Amid the echoing sounds of the hammers thundering everywhere, some were putting up tarpaulins, others sawing wood, one man was rolling along a barrel, another struggling with a post or thrashing wildly with his crowbar to force it into place. As soon as the tarp was up, the business was under way with an outdoor display of cheap clothes and boots, Chanco cheeses, bundles of beef jerky, piles of dried fruit, shovels, crowbars, gunpowder, and liquor, objects that along with toasted and untoasted meal were being sold for their weight in gold. Cheap Chilean liquor was bringing almost twenty pesos a gallon, and the sweetened soda water they called champagne, eight to twelve pesos a bottle. These prices were not determined so much by the scarcity of goods as by the need to save time, because no one wasted it in bargaining even if by walking a bit farther he could buy for less. Gold dust was the most common coin; the way it was handled to make payments testified to its abundance, because no one was much concerned with returning to the leather pouch the excess that might have fallen onto the scales.

We saw the luxurious brick and mortar house being built by Mr. Hawar, a common seaman risen to the rank of millionaire, and farther on, on the square, another being finished for an ornate café by another common seaman no less affluent than the former.

After a quarter of an hour's slow and tiring, but exciting, walk, we reached an elegant hotel that belonged to a Gringo who had served in the expeditionary force against Mexico. Just then one of the servants, who was nothing but a young gentleman converted into a café waiter, was standing at the door of the building and beating on an enormous metal cake tin that went by the name of Chinese gong, hitting it so often that he deafened all passers-by to call them to dinner. In the dining room we found Price and the elegant young Chilean J. L. C., who had started out in business by making leather sheaths for knives at two pesos apiece. A long narrow table took up the whole room, and around it sat no fewer than thirty customers of the most bizarre appearance, wolfing down their food with as much speed and gusto so as not to delay giving up their place to those who could not find an empty seat and were waiting impatiently for one to appear. At that time in California, the Yankee ate three times a day but limited himself to roast meat, fresh or preserved salmon, a stew of sorts, molasses, tea, coffee, and butter. He breakfasted at seven, dined at twelve, and supped at six.

The following were some prices: a beefsteak, 1 peso; coffee, 75 centavos; bread and butter, 50 centavos.

Lies and capricious, more or less poetic, conjectures reigned supreme in that promised land when we arrived. No one had any geographic knowledge of any place, no one knew the distance from one point to another and much less whether one ought to go by land or by water; but all to a man knew it all. The very few who had come back from the placers either showed little inclination to answer our questions or deliberately steered us away from those locales, apparently for reasons of their own. We were thus reduced to hearing the accounts of men who were perhaps in greater need of enlightenment than were we. What we heard everywhere was limited to:

"Don't go to Sacramento, there's not much gold there. Head for Stanislaus just as soon as you can."

"Don't even think about Stanislaus! Tom found so and so many thousand in just one day at Sacramento."

quiere dar el q. los tiene; por que el compra-
dor considerando q. el tiempo es oro en California con tal q. encuentre a la mano lo que
necesita no se para en tanto mas cuanto ni
se va a callejear a otra parte. La moneda co-
rriente es oro en polvo y la desembaltura
con que lo manejan p.a las compras o ventas da a entender lo poco q. les cuesta el adqui-
rirlo. Las calles estan empedradas de botellas
rotas y entre las muchas casuchas que se le-
vantan como p.r encanto a guisa de las ca-
yampas en los primeros aguaceros de Mayo se
ven multitud de ventas de licores y de casas de
juego. Cerca de la playa como en la mitad de
la poblacion se esta levantando una hermosa
casa de cal y ladrillo perteneciente a un tal
Passar marinero ayer, hoy millonario. En
la playa se construye con mucho lujo un in-
menso establecimiento p.a Café de otro marinero no menos rico q. el primero. Aqui la
mayor parte de la gente habla ingles bien o mal
pero p.r los trajes y el acento descubre V. al
lado del yankee flaco y de calzones cortos al
abultado john-bull

¿Qué me miras ...!!
¡Ah! don Chileno, Most...
¡qué ... payo!!!!
¡Porque tenía tu madre!!

al Chino, al bengala, al ruso y al californio tra-
tando de entablar una compania

al Chileno y al oregones mirandose de reojo

y al frances y al italiano guiñando a una india
Canaca coronada de flores de mano, vestida azul y zapa-
to colorado. Todo en fin cuanto puede verse de
raro y extravagante en los trajes de un baile de
mascara, se ve en esta tierra de promision
pero en proporciones gigantescas. Lo q. se extra-
ña mucho en este perpetuo carnaval son las
creaturas de aquel que unos llaman bello
sexo y otros hembras como los yankees (female)
y q. otra cosa han de ser las mujeres de estos animales

"The gold country's flooded; and Dick, who came back just yesterday, says he was standing there with the water up to his waist."

"What do you mean 'water'?" said another. "That area's drier in winter than in summer."

Why go on? Fortunately, a certain Mr. Prendergast hit upon the idea of gathering gold without budging from San Francisco by setting up a geographical office whose only member and collaborator was he himself. Somewhere he managed to find an old map of the viceroyalty of Mexico; and enlarging the part corresponding to Upper California as the spirit moved him, he flooded the city with sketches that, though badly executed and consisting of sheets of cigarette paper, brought a price of twenty-five pesos each.

Thanks to the kindness of Señor Price I was introduced to a friend of his who had recently returned from the gold fields; for the first time I could contemplate, next to an enviable collection of bags of gold dust, a solid nugget that weighed at least three pounds, which that good gentleman said he had found while taking a walk in the country before breakfast. Why should we not find some, too, even if it was after dinner? But we could not move, because of the accursed cargo that we had been forced to put on board the sluggish *Julia* in Valparaíso, and so we lost a day and a half, that is, thirty-six hours, which in California was a whole century.

Determined to make some use of our time, we set up a freight business until that tub might arrive. This company for land and water transport was composed of my brothers, Cassalli, a former opera prompter in the time of Pantanelli, young Huerta, and Clackston, a businessman from Valparaíso. The captain of the now empty *Staouéli*, eager to have us live on his ship, let us use his private boat; and so, some of us staying on shore waiting for cargoes and others setting out in the boat in search of them, we cheerfully and enthusiastically began our operations three days after dropping anchor in San Francisco.

It would be a long story to recount all the ups and downs of our company, the brave deeds and disappointments of the partners in the long space of eleven days that our business lasted. Finally the *Julia* arrived, and with her our fine supplies. We immediately dissolved our firm, whose distributable earnings came to twelve hundred pesos; and after bringing ashore our supplies, we deputized my brother-in-law Ramírez to hire a sloop in which to continue our voyage inland, while the rest of our company, reconstituted now as a laundry, turned to washing our remaining linens.

The boat therefore set out for a nearby cove northeast of the harbor, where there was running water; equipped with soap, buckets, a kettle for

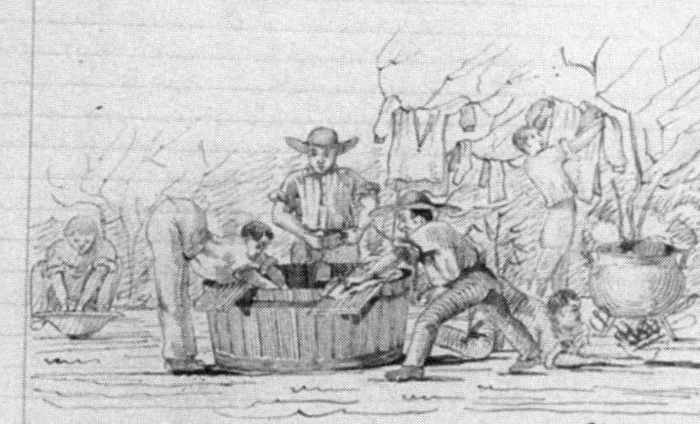

hot water and a second, smaller one for our beans, the gang of improvised washerwomen went ashore, each one carrying enormous sacks that contained the well-traveled clothes of seven individuals who had just come from beyond the Equator. This cove, which we shall call Laundry Cove and which is one of the lovely inlets within the great bay, is horseshoe-shaped and protected by great mounds of sand and soil covered with fine bushes of delicious raspberries. Around a small central pool of saltwater were traces of other innocents who, like us, had gone there to waste their time washing clothes. Without further delay we laid the foundations of our new enterprise there.

Kettle, pail, clothes, and soap were soon ready to commence operations. Our old Mama Borja and Ña Rosaura never in their laundering lives scrubbed so much and so vigorously as did Mama Ruperto, Mama Cassalli, and the other stalwart mamas who in turn and as required ran our operation at Laundry Cove, trading in their oars for stockings and the tiller for soap. This was our last grateful farewell to the comfortable white linen that had accompanied us all that way.

In Santiago there was at that time an amiable lady who was very fond of us and who, after she heard of our decision to leave for California, was forever telling her friends with great feeling, "Fine boys, my dear!" I mention this detail, which I have found in my notes, so that the effect that its repetition produced in us may show how the new circumstances in which we found ourselves shaped the character of each one of the Chileans who shared our foreign travails. After every disagreeable incident, "Fine boys, then, my dear!" was the refrain that preceded a burst of merry laughter. I remember that later, during the dreadful fire that destroyed the whole town of San Francisco, instead of lamenting the loss of our house and all our belongings, seeing that there was nothing to be done, we relaxed and decided to enjoy the spectacle produced on a dark night by that tremendous bonfire, so powerful that it lifted many burning boards into the air and kept them floating there. I remember, too, that when the day after the fire one of my brothers, trying to find the place where our house had stood, fell into a disgusting heap of garbage, he reappeared with the most comically pathetic appearance imaginable, saying, as he showed us his filthy figure, "All right, fine boys, my dear!"

In California there was at the outset no disaster that enthusiasm could not overcome; it was a different story later on.

X V

Our voyage to Sacramento. — The Dicey My Nana *and her Captain Robinson. — The sheltered bays of San Francisco, San Pablo, and Suisun. — The confluence of the Sacramento and San Joaquin Rivers. — Embryonic cities. — The town of Sacramento. — Brannan. — The first traces of gold. — In California, he who hesitates is lost. — Our voyage to the placers. — A dangerous encounter with the Indians. — Their method of panning for gold. — Our commercial transaction with them. — We arrive at the famous Mill.*

Our commissioner of transportation for the continuation of our voyage inland to Sacramento had completed his work, but in California individual effort and willpower were not always enough for carrying out even the best-laid plans; what we lacked was the sinews of war: money. Our disposable capital barely came to a thousand pesos; and since we figured that the voyage and its most immediate consequences would cost twice that, we set out to find a loan. With considerable effort we extracted a thousand pesos from a Jew, who as a good deed and favor handed us this amount upon receiving a guarantee from Sánchez and with interest at 5% a *month*.

Once our passage had been agreed on, the *Dicey My Nana*[69] made fast to the side of the *Staouéli,* the vessel that had brought us to California and been our home up to that point. The *Dicey* was a twenty-ton sloop built in prehistoric times, waterlogged and slow of movement, its rig in the form of a long pole that seemed designed to sweep away anything that might project above her gunwale, just as a miller's straight edge sweeps away all the wheat above the rim of his bushel measure.

After depositing what we could in the narrow and already full hold of this boat of mournful countenance,[70] we took our places, bringing the total of passengers to twenty-nine, all seated on sacks, crates, shovels, rifles, baskets of provisions, and thirty thousand additional bundles that awaited only the slightest rocking of the vessel in order to plunge into the sea, taking along all those resting on them.

At this point I must again be allowed to copy some pages from my travel diary, which have the advantage of having been produced right on the field of battle.

The new, considerably enlarged even if perhaps not corrected, edition of our company consisted of one Ramírez y Rosales, retired officer of the Chilean Navy; one Hurtado, a worthy young native of Santiago; one Clackston, a Chileanized Gringo in business in Valparaíso; one Cassalli, a former prompter in our municipal theater from the time of Pantanelli; three Solares y Rosales; one Pérez, half-brother of the foregoing; and three laborers from the estate Las Tablas.

No voyager could budge without stepping on his neighbor or lie down without encountering a pillow of knees and shoulders. In fact, we found ourselves envying the fate of sardines, because, while they are indeed tightly packed, they are at least lying down.

69. I write *Dicey My Nana* because that is how the owners pronounced the name of the Mexican sloop *Dice mi ñaña.* VPR. The boat's name means *My Honey Says.* I have emended for the English-speaking reader the author's transcription of this mispronunciation. JP.

70. *Of mournful countenance,* a reminiscence of Don Quixote, who at one stage of his adventures called himself the Knight of the Mournful Countenance. Pérez alludes to the boat's age and dilapidated condition. JP.

Our vessel was under the command of the memorable Captain Robinson, an irascible old Yankee, short, lisping, and habitually drunk. His crew was composed of a Scotsman with a nose like an overripe tomato and two Yankees who, lacking money for their passage, had just signed on as sailors. Trying to describe the banditlike appearance of my other traveling companions would be to bite off more than I could chew. All were repulsive to behold, and each was different from all the others. What they had in common was the indispensable equipment of the time: enormous boots studded with nails, knives at their waist, and rifles and pistols, which even on board they did not stop fingering for a moment.

At 4 P.M. on March 6, 1849, we bade farewell to the *Staouéli*, which had extended us such amiable hospitality, and began the difficult task of threading our way among the abandoned ships that surrounded us, of which there must at that time have been at least a hundred.

For our sins we had brought on board a demijohn of liquor and a basket filled with bottles of wine; when the worthy namesake of old Selkirk,[71] of Juan Fernández fame, saw all this, he remarked, much to our regret, that so delicate a cargo had to be transported under his immediate supervision, whereupon he took charge of it. Hardly had we got under way when the lightness of the breeze and the contrary currents, favoring the secret designs of the guardian of the bottles, deposited the vessel and all her passengers on a bank of mud and sand from which we could not get free, despite the solicitous help given us by the boat of a Russian ship anchored in the deepest part of the tidal channel. Curses and laments filled the air; some jumped into the water to push the boat, but in vain; and in vain did we ask for help from other ships: they paid no attention to us, and we had no choice but to stay where we were. Night was falling rapidly; and cold, drizzle, and discomfort were sure to wipe out the whole expedition if our brute of a captain, drunk by now, should by chance take it into his head to sail on in the dark with the rising tide. We therefore began to wonder whether we should go ashore and ask the owner to order the *Dicey My Nana* lay over till the next day, when lo and behold!, a snub-nosed little boat came up to our side with five more passengers whom our good Captain Robinson had lined up to embark behind the owner's back.

Frightened as we were by this invasion that was going to cram us in more tightly than ever, a committee set out in the Russian boat to inform

71. Alexander Selkirk was the Scottish seaman marooned on the Chilean island of Juan Fernández whose adventures were the basis of Daniel Defoe's *Robinson Crusoe*. His namesake, then, is Captain Robinson of the *Dice mi ñaña*. JP.

Brannan of what was going on. This gentleman was an important merchant, the chief or director of the Californian branch of the Mormon sect, and, furthermore, the owner of the famous vessel into which we had been packed. He was asleep at the time; we awoke him and, with considerable difficulty, got him to give us a slip of paper with the order we needed.

Once we came back on board all hell broke loose, because when Robinson threw Brannan's paper overboard without having read it, our companion Clackston shouted at him that he should not dare to move before dawn, because to do so would violate the orders of his boss. A most unfortunate choice of noun! The word "boss" produced an effect like that of a bombshell set off in the barrel on which Robinson was sitting.

"What do you mean, 'my boss'?" he shouted with the most frightful oaths. "I don't have any boss, and there aren't any bosses around here; and if you asked me, the first one to hang as a scoundrel ought to be that bum Brannan!"

This burst of brutal energy fortunately exhausted his strength, because he fell flat on his face on some bundles and could not get up till the next day.

What a night! All our fellow-passengers got drunk on our bottles and our demijohn while we stood guard to prevent excesses, for our damp and dismal lodgings were twice on the point of being bloodied. Finally day came, and our crew came to with the morning chill. Since there was not a breath of air and we had not a single oar, we had to allow ourselves to be dragged along by the tide to bump into the ships around us, using the strength of our arms to avoid crashes, until about eight o'clock, when the currents and the grace of God set us loose.

These iron men's capacity for liquor can be judged by our tomato-nosed Gringo, who found a bottle of purgative that by chance had been mixed in with those of our poor wine and, thinking it was port, drank it all down. I still cannot understand why he did not explode.

The trip has lasted seven days and seven deadly nights; all this time we have not been able to stand up, because even when we were seated the rigging of the lateen sails swept across our faces with each of the two hundred thousand tacks that the wind and tide forced us to make. Even in that extremely uncomfortable position, wrapped in ponchos and blankets that by dawn were dripping with the dew, battling against the tenacious swarms of poisonous mosquitoes that in those swampy regions fill the air as soon as night falls, our spirits were still capable of commenting on the beautiful panorama that unfolded before us as we traversed the poetic bay and the lovely narrows that lead to the mouths of the rivers flowing into it. What is more, there was no lack of jokes and laughter in that bark of Charon as we looked at each other's pained countenances. We were ready to bear everything with stoic resoluteness; the only thing we cursed was the boorish trampling of the Yankees, who, with their nailed boots, respected neither backs nor noses as the boat tacked along. One of them planted his big hoof right in poor Cassalli's face; when his victim grumbled threateningly, the Yankee merely responded with a loud "All right!" and went on his way as though nothing had happened.

Finally we reached Suttersville, where we said goodbye to our charming traveling companions on the *Dicey My Nana* of dreadful memory and to that awful Bacchus who, under the name of Captain Robinson, was also on his way to explore the placers.

Had not our voyage been so brutally uncomfortable it would not have lacked for charms. The traveler crosses the lovely bay, believing it to be one body of water, as far as the narrows of Dos Hermanos, formed by two very similar islets bearing the same name.[72] Anyone would think that this narrows is a river mouth and is therefore surprised when, after passing the two rocks, he finds himself sailing on another bay, also apparently without outlet and called San Pablo Bay. This new body of water has the appearance of a large lake surrounded by hills and fertile fields covered with woods and cattle. Ships of the deepest draft can navigate its waters and find coves and anchorages everywhere.

The effect of the tides reaches even farther inland. Long parallel fringes of agitated and dirty foam can be seen periodically rising and falling in the bays, forming bubbles and eddies that, as I said, can become whirlpools dangerous to smaller vessels in the last channel that leads through the Golden Gate into the waters of the Pacific. The periodic ebbing of the waters in the inland bays makes it necessary to employ pilots who know the depth of the river channels, the shallows, and the nature of the exposed banks, though that does not mean that navigation there is dangerous.

In San Pablo Bay you sail very close to land and through calm waters, constantly coming upon harbors, coves, and a multitude of ships and smaller vessels full of passengers and goods. No newcomer would suspect that there is any outlet until he reaches its northern end and sees before him the beautiful Benicia Straits, which connect San Pablo Bay with Suisun Bay. Midway along the northern shore of this impressive deep and rapid channel, which is about a league in length, the first foundations of the city that bears the name Benicia, in honor of the wife of Colonel Vallejo, are being laid. The harbor and the environs of the intended town were, to be sure, less than imposing. The land barely rises above the level

72. The Brothers are two rocks at San Pablo Point in Contra Costa County, California. JP.

of the high tides, there are few trees or shrubs, and the devilish mosquitoes exercise the most bloodthirsty tyranny over the whole region. A warship was riding at anchor there, and on land stood a flagstaff around which many people seemed to be bustling about.

In that place so inhospitable by its nature but so necessary by virtue of its very appropriate location for a shipyard, the walls of a church were beginning to rise, as were those of two schools, a large café and inn, a theater, and a mint.

The Yankee is a master in the art of colonizing and establishing settlements. He does not begin with programs or pompous promises that are rarely or never fulfilled, but by building roads, by making the place he wants to populate accessible, by public works whose cost and magnificence give the immigrant firm guarantees of stability; and as payment for the first lots that he distributes he imposes only the obligation of building or working on them. The day before yesterday, agents of Benicia residing in Sacramento offered me excellent sites in Benicia if I set my lovely tents upon them; but since we had come to California not to settle but to gather gold, we answered with a smile, "Sorry, that's not our cup of tea."

After you pass through the Benicia Straits, which seem more like a river than like straits, you enter another large navigable lake called Suisun Bay. The land around it is so low that it seems larger than it really is. Suisun Bay is full of banks that make navigation extremely difficult if one does not know the main channels perfectly; nonetheless, very deep-draft ships cross it now, and I am sure that in time captains will no longer see anything extraordinary in not having to wait, stuck in the mud, for the high tide in order to continue their voyage. As one proceeds inland, the banks, islets, and marshes become so numerous that one only leaves them behind when entering the labyrinth of channels that constitutes the mighty confluence of the San Joaquin and the Sacramento. Although from Benicia on you can drink the water if you must, once you come to the confluence of these two rivers you can consider it truly potable.

It required considerable skill not to miss the channel that leads through this labyrinth of more or less deep branches to the Sacramento, but the practical genius of the Yankees has made such games unnecessary, because we saw that another nascent town, called Moctezuma,[73]

73. Various places named after the Aztec ruler give evidence of Mormon settlement in California. The Mormon agent Lansford W. Hastings "laid out Montezuma [*sic*] City at the head of Suisun Bay in 1847. Although often mentioned in contemporary newspapers and books, the 'city' never seems to have developed beyond Hastings' own adobe." Erwin G. Gudde, *California Place Names*, 3d ed. (Berkeley, Los Angeles, London: University of California Press, 1969), 209–10. JP.

was already beginning to mark the route. Through the southern part of the labyrinth flows another channel by which the waters of the San Joaquin lead to the new city of Stockton, and at the entrance to which another new city was planned with the name of New York. We went by way of Moctezuma, left behind the labyrinth of the confluence, and soon found ourselves sailing on one of the most beautiful rivers of the western coast of America. Its current is slow and calm, its surface like a mirror, and through its clear waters you can see the bottom. The most luxuriant vegetation grows on the hills and valleys that line its banks; as one proceeds around its majestic curves, the trees shade one's vessel and the long branches stretching out over the river even tangle with the rigging of the sloops that draw closest to the shore. This fine waterway, whose depth easily admits the largest cargo vessels and which as far as Sacramento is not above half a mile in width, is not the main course of this river, but one of the branches that most directly leads to the town, where after six hours we landed with the hellish sloop that was our purgatory for seven deadly days.

The site picked out for the town of Sacramento was the beautiful oak- and cypress-covered valley that lies southwest of the American River's confluence with the Sacramento. Its designation as a place for settlement seems to have been made with an eye more to utility than to salubriousness, because with many sloughs, swamps, and marshes lying between that confluence and the town, agues and putrid fevers were bound to ravage it in time. Nonetheless, since convenience and commerce make climate and the most dreadful plagues seem but minor obstacles, the port of Sacramento was the favorite locality in that famous New Helvetia founded in honor of his homeland by the colonizer Captain John Sutter, whose life I have already sketched.

The nucleus of the town consisted of a handful of houses of rough boards with canvas roofs, a few shops, many awnings of different shapes and sizes scattered about helter-skelter, and a great many sheds made of branches.

Dressed for action, we pitched our tents by the side of this encampment and without further delay, as though we were quite rested, set about disembarking and dragging up our gear. Envy filled all who watched us when they saw us provided with all one could desire in that place where everything was either lacking or exorbitantly expensive.

Since all the inhabitants of this camp were on their way to the mines and none had been there, we were, with regard to news, as much in the dark there as we had been in San Francisco.

No sooner had we settled down than we were favored by an extraordinary visit from an agent or broker of cities, who, armed with a map of the future city of Sacramento, offered us fine lots provided we camp on them immediately; but even this gift could not bring us to tax our depleted strength anew for the promise of mere lots. We resolutely declined; and once our blankets were stretched out on the ground, we stretched our long-cramped bodies out on top of them and slept without interruption till the next morning.

At dawn we had the impression we were in the midst of a military camp where the alarm had sounded. No one walked, all seemed to fly; and among shouts of "Go to it!" "Forward!" "Steady there!" we heard the patter of curses blended with cheerful sounds of the popular song about Susanna, written especially for the gold seekers, with the refrain: "Oh Susanna, don't you cry for me, for I'm going to California to bring you bags of gold."[74]

We noticed a good deal more movement in this town than even in San Francisco, which is not surprising, since camps were born instantly every day and disappeared with the same speed. The arrival of twenty or thirty boats might flood the town with tents and people; the next bright morning swept them all away to the gold fields, leaving behind, for the next wave of travelers, a battlefield littered with clothes, saddles, torn sacks (many with dried peaches), empty bottles, and every other trifle that might slow or hamper the miner's march to the gold-bearing tributaries of the American River.

All went on foot, all looked like pack mules or walking storehouses, and all displayed their nationality in the very nature of the load they were bearing. Toasted meal, saddlebags, shovels and crowbars, a vessel for panning gold, a big knife, and a cow-horn scoop revealed the good Chilean from a mile off. A rifle, six-shooter, knives, powder flasks and canteens, big boots, and a load of brandy bottles, the rough and bellicose Oregonian. A parasol hat of varnished paper, a rolled-up mosquito net on his shoulders, a scimitar at his waist, shoes with thick cardboard soles, two bags of rice hanging from a pole across his shoulders, the son of the Celestial Empire. Only the outfits of the Yankees and Europeans, thoroughly intermingled, did not reveal the nationality of their owners.

Everywhere one heard nothing but rifle or pistol shots; everyone engaged in frequent target practice with no thought for where his bullet might land. These unexpected explosions were most numerous at nightfall, either as warnings that there were firearms handy or to clean and

---

74. This is evidently a Forty-niner version of Stephen Foster's *Oh Susanna,* but I have been unable to find its English text. I therefore translate what Pérez writes, at a loss for what might have been the appropriate rhyme. JP.

del Rio de los Americanos con el del Sacramento. Muchos bajos cubiertos de pajonales
y laguna[illegible] en donde hierven las tortugas
parece q. desean de hacer a este lugar poco
sano en los rigores del verano. Hay solo cuatro casas de mal dispuestas tablas con te-
chos de lona, alguna q. otra q. se principia
a trabajar, y un sin numero de carpas de
todas figuras y tamaños colocadas del modo
mas irregular. Nuestra primera operacion
al saltar a tierra fue la de reconocer el campamento y elejido el lugar menos humedo a
la orilla de la barranca q. determina la Ciudad
al norte, tendimos nuestras hermosas carpas.
Pronto y a pesar q. distaba nuestro campamento mas de dos cuadras de la playa, armados ya
de nuestros vestidos de guerra comenzamos el des-
embarco y acarreo de nuestros efectos. Cuantos
nos veian nos echaban miradas de envidia
al vernos llegar provistos de cuanto podia uno
apetecerse en un lugar en donde todo vale
un sentido. La mayor parte de esta gente
no ha ido aun a las minas asi es q. no tace-
mos a que atenernos aun sobre el objeto
unico de nuestro viaje.
La carpa grande de nosotros se ve desde
lejos sobre el promontorio de carpitas y to-
ldos q. nos rodean. Los habitantes de todo el
campamento q. llaman Sacramento City, no
andan, vuelan. Cada hombre parece un
almacen de guerra sustentado sobre las
hombreras de un gastador. Gorras chupin, pistolas, botas, butas de lana, puñal entero

y porras distinguen al aventurero [illegible]

Rifle, pistolas de seis tiros, puñal, navajas, polvo-
rines y carmañolas, botas granaderas y muchas
botellas de brandy, constituyen los instrumentos
menores del Yankee.

Hay aqui tres o cuatro carretones de alquiler pa. ca-
[illegible] bajos y piden un [illegible] por el flete de [illegible]

reload the weapons. When he is in the field, no Yankee goes to bed without first taking this indispensable precaution.

This contagious stir soon seized hold of our energies, once we recovered; but since the weight of our baggage allowed us only to keep time in this chorus but not to sing, we decided to lighten it. A Yankee told us he would lease us a wagon that was to arrive in another two days, that the wagon would hold twenty hundredweight, and that he would charge us only thirty-five pesos a hundredweight from Sacramento to the placers of the American River, a distance of some fifty-five miles. We accepted his offer and formed a committee to select the twenty most indispensable hundredweight and sell the rest, another committee to go to a ranch, which is what the Californians call what in Chile we call an *hacienda,* to buy two horses, and a third committee to build a cart with some wheels that we had brought by chance from San Francisco and load it with our tents and implements of daily use.

Up to this point the government of our little colony had been polycephalous; but since we had to be ready for concerted action, we decided to establish a single authority and proceeded to choose a monarch, whom we called our Elder. Once this was settled, each committee fell to its task.

We sold our clothes and tools at unheard-of prices, our toasted meal at forty centavos a pound, the remnants of Penco wine that survived at the bottom of the unforgettable *Dicey My Nana*'s hold at eighteen pesos a gallon, and the cheap liquor of Tiltil, at ten. The supplementary cart that was to be propelled by a combination of horse- and manpower was ready by nightfall; we fretted only at the delay of the horse buyers, when suddenly these arrived at headquarters, with empty hands and a surplus of hunger and exhaustion. When we inquired into why our valiant commissioners had failed, it turned out that on their journey Hurtado and Clackston had fallen under the spell of a siren, whose lethal eyes had made them quite forget their mission. Since we had lost sight of our Rosarito Améstica, neither they, nor we, nor anyone had again laid eyes on a skirt; and since the rancher unfortunately was accompanied by a girl, the committee had lost its head and, with it, the chance to keep other slyer foxes from carrying off the best horses, leaving only the most pitiful nag imaginable in the corral, though at a price of 250 pesos. They would have bought it for 150, Clackston explained, but the presence of the girl inhibited them from making so low an offer; and so, muttering that they would rather have paid 250 for her than for the horse, they came back with nothing. On hearing the word "girl," our Elder addressed the company; after a measured and sensible speech in which he explained to his audience what evils might befall the itinerant colony through the acquisition of goods other than those we had come to seek, he concluded his touching address by taking upon himself the charge of going to cope with the siren and oblige the extortive owner of the nag to let us have it at a lower price. When daylight came he therefore set off, accompanied by his whole general staff and even the troops, all fearful that some misfortune might befall our chaste leader in so risky an adventure.

For an hour and a half we walked westward through the green and pleasant valley of the Sacramento, close by the swift and deep waters of the American River. Tall pines, mighty live oaks, both in groups and scattered over a green terrain covered with spring flowers, gave the place the appearance of an endless English park. The only signs that we were very far from perfidious Albion were the solitude, the pleasant temperature, the cries of the flocks of wild turkeys constantly flying overhead, like parrots in our country, the songs, shapes, and colors of birds completely unknown to us, and the startling sight of more or less lethargic snakes lying across the road and waiting for the sun to warm them before going on their way.

About six miles from our camp we came to Sutter's famous fort. It consisted of one enormous building with thick cracked walls, rising from a moat half filled with rubble and weeds, and of a few rusty artillery pieces lying on the ground and overgrown with grass. We saw a rustic wooden cabin there, a few branch shelters, and a short way off, a large store with an enormous sign that read "Brannan & Co." The head of this commercial establishment was the ex-Mormon Brannan, owner, as I mentioned, of the awful *Dicey My Nana* and possessor of one of the most substantial fortunes in the California of that time. As leader or pastor of his sect on this side of the Sierra Nevada, he had succeeded in using the labor of his many parishioners to his advantage; once he had managed to monopolize a productive stretch of the banks of the American River, he quickly garnered great wealth. It seems that he had no sooner done so than he abandoned his religion and did without any, though gossip had it that to assuage his conscience he frequently prayed to Saint Polygamy.

The store, situated directly on the road that led to the placers, offered a wonderfully complete stock of everything one might want for work in the mines. I say nothing of the prices, since they produced for the seller only the paltry profit of fifty to a hundred times costs!

We had already gone for about two hours keeping the American River, at which we could slake our thirst, on our left when we learned from a native of Sonora that we might find gold right there, because although we were still seventeen leagues from where the river began to receive the gold-bearing streams known as its North, Middle, and South Forks, its current was powerful enough to drag gold as far as its own confluence with the Sacramento. Desirous of probing the veracity of the courteous Sonoran, we tested those mysterious sands with the Chilean miner's inseparable scoop; delighted at the sight of gold, though not much of it, we headed for the ranch buildings that were by now visible some distance off.

The place made us think we were entering a no man's land; not a soul came to receive us, not even a dog deigned to bark at us. Doors and windows stood wide open, and why not, since nothing worth protecting was to be seen. Not one flower, not one tree, not one bird! A traveler on the Argentine pampas, if suddenly deposited on a California ranch, would no doubt think he was changing horses at one of the post-stations of that wasteland. Finally a churlish face appeared above the brambles enclosing a silent corral, loudly asked, "Who's there?" and then turned away from us so as not to waste time waiting for our answer. We had arrived none too soon. The owner of the place was about to close a deal with a Yankee to sell him the unfortunate nag we had failed to buy the day before, and since in California time is gold, the competition forced us to hand over three hundred pesos for something that in Chile could only have been sold for the grease pots.

There was no sign of a siren, and none of us dared to inquire of the Cerberus as to the whereabouts of such a jewel; but since chance always favors worthy desires, and we had to pay in gold dust and not in coin, which we did not have, we were led to a wretched little room where, ah Heavens!, the living image of the goddess Astrea, scales in hand, was waiting for us, the only female creature worth looking at that we had encountered since leaving the Chilean shore. With her own innocent, or perhaps sinful, hands she weighed part of our poor treasure. She served us milk, a luxury item whose very name we had forgotten, she made eyes at us, and we should have yielded her our battered hearts had not the presence of Fierabrás[75] checked our natural impulses, which were and could only be to serve her. It pained us to leave that hospitable house; but hurrying to return to our camp, we reached it after nightfall.

Tumultuously we all gathered around our rickety brute, then tested it to see what it could pull and saw that it was good. Next we set to making knapsacks out of empty bags so that each of us might carry as much as he could in order to lighten the load for the nag. We fitted it with a girth and an improvised harness, loaded the rented wagon, which had been duly delivered, and the cart, ate a whole potful of beans, and stretched out on the ground, where we slept till dawn as though resting on a bed of the softest feathers.

75. *Fierabrás,* a fierce giant in romances of chivalry. JP.

At daybreak, as we were about to leave, two Garcéses, father and son, and one Herrera, all Chileans and also ready to go, joined the company. We all had some hot *ulpo,* or meal porridge; and after we had loaded on our backs all we could carry and had no further business in that place, our Elder gave the command, "March!"

Our marching order was the following: Cassalli and one Garcés in the vanguard, in charge of the wagon; then came my four brothers along with one laborer, helping the horse that was pulling the cart; Clackston, Hurtado, another laborer, and the Elder formed a reserve in the rear.

We had not been long under way when merriment gave way to imprecations, so much trouble did we have with the accursed horse and the vehicle. The animal did not seem happy with the burden that for our sins we had hitched to its cinch, and during a period of ill humor its bucking almost knocked our ill-fated conveyance to pieces. We had to help it by pushing while it pulled; after five leagues the hellish beast told us by very clear gestures of open rebellion that nothing, not even the whip, would budge it any farther. We had to pitch camp.

The tale of our adventures during five days' journey at forced labor until our battered bones reached the mines at Sutter's Mill can serve only to entertain the old men who took part in that dance. Suffice it to say, as proof of the moral energy that back then had laid hold of the most timid hearts, that not one of our adventurers failed to share hunger, discomforts, and toil with our beast of burden, and to do so with a smile on his lips.

Through beautiful meadows abounding in forage and good water and studded with cypresses and live oaks we made our way eastward on our first day's journey, until the plain turned into the first remote foothills of the Sierra Nevada. In some places broken terrain then made the passage of wagons difficult; elsewhere, almost impassable dunes forced the traveler to climb over piles of shattered rocks covering the road. But trees and bushes grew everywhere, as did, on the many level areas along the way, abundant forage and many of the bright flowers that at home we carefully cultivate in our gardens.

We always camped in the shelter of some mighty oak, around whose trunk we settled down like the spokes of a wagonwheel around its hub; and since at that time of the year California is blessed with dews very similar to downpours, our beds, reduced to the barest essentials, for they consisted only of a serape or Mexican blanket, which served as a mattress and cover, and of a bag of toasted meal, which was our pillow, were literally soaking wet every morning.

Our journey, leaving to our west in turn the dwelling of the enchanting deity whose memory was kept alive for us by the diabolical nag of so little use to us; the ruins of a costly mill built at the first violent rapids that mark the end of the navigable course of the American River, a few leagues before it joins the Sacramento; and the small but pleasant nameless valley where one necessarily camps and from which two roads set out, one heading west to the dry placers called *Dry-diggings,* the other east and leading to the wet placers of the mill, brought us to the first gold-bearing stream, called Weber Creek.

The riches of the sands of this first Pactolus,[76] though comparatively less abundant than those we were to encounter later, seemed to have been placed there to refresh the spirit of tired travelers; but the delight and encouragement that this herald of future wealth produced in us did not make up for the danger in which we found ourselves moments before we reached it.

We had gone astray about six hours before; not a soul was now to be seen on what we took to be the road, though the difficulty of advancing on it grew from moment to moment. Our Elder, a tracker with experience on the Argentine pampas, not finding the trail of broken bottles that the Yankee always leaves, became alarmed and called a halt. A frantic uncertainty was beginning to seize hold of us when, attracted by the unusual sight of people in that place rarely visited by whites, a mestizo peasant appeared before us and told us not only that we had lost our way but that we had unwittingly and foolishly entered the territory of a band of bad Indians who, though they had until then remained loyal to Captain Sutter, were now, thanks to the outrages committed by the Americans, going back to their old ways of robbing and murdering any whites they could catch alone. He added that although he had not, up to then, had any difficulties with these Indians, because many of them knew him, he had quietly sent away his family and had been heading into town when he had had the pleasure of meeting us.

This was not, to be sure, very welcome news; but trusting in the superiority of our firearms, we hired Santana, which was the peasant's name, as a guide, and leaving him with the Yankee wagoner and two others in charge of setting up camp and cooking our beans, we went off with our scoops and pans to pan for gold on the shore of a creek, as much at ease as if nothing could happen to us. After a few steps we met our servant Leiva, who was coming all delighted to show us the results of his work with a little hand pan, on whose bottom one could see about a sixth of an ounce of gold, which he had collected in an instant. At the word "gold" our kitchen was abandoned and everyone dashed to the

76. *Pactolus,* a gold-bearing stream of Antiquity, in Asia Minor. JP.

river by the shortest route possible. The result was that an Indian woman who with a child on her back was taking shelter from the sun among the bushes next to the river, seeing herself surrounded on all sides by white faces and thinking we were Yankees, went off running like a deer; when we, to frighten her some more, made as though to follow her, she stumbled, fell, and began to shout. Her cries for help, answered from afar by other voices that sounded like roars to us, soon brought a troop of Indians, who with yells and threatening gestures, drawing their poisoned arrows from the coyote-skin bags that serve them as quivers, seemed prepared to attack us. Our situation instantly lost its charm, and we quite forgot the gold in our hurry to take up our arms, when the shouts of Santana, recognized by some of the natives, kept both them and us from having to lament painful events that day.

Santana went over to them and let them know that we were not Yankees but Spaniards and friends of Sutter's, and that furthermore we were good people and were only planning to spend one night there and go on to the Mill without doing them any harm. A few of them cautiously came up to us; then others came, too, and soon our shows of kindness, reinforced by gifts of little cotton kerchiefs, worth pennies, in exchange for little bags of gold dust worth four or five pesos each, established the most cordial and perfect harmony among the belligerents. They offered us acorns, their sole and favorite food; in exchange for them and a goodly amount of gold, they received a few bowls of toasted meal.

These people are a little darker than our Indians and struck us as of a weaker constitution, with sheeplike faces. Their dress was an indescribable mixture of the savage and the European. Some of them had on nothing but a ragged and filthy frock coat, bravely worn over their bare skin; others, a knit shirt that barely reached to where our soldiers used to place their cartridge box; others, a simple loincloth. None displayed feathers or other typically native dress. The better-off women swaddled their waist in a kind of skirt of wool or esparto grass that hung down to their knees; others wore a simple loincloth; but none bothered to cover those appendages that in less liberal and less ingenuous regions are customarily kept rigorously cloistered. They tie their babies on a wicker frame that they lean against a tree when they are working and that when they travel they carry on their backs, held by a strap around their heads.

We urged them to continue their interrupted work of washing earth so that we might watch it, and they very readily obliged us and took us to the place from which our imprudence had brought them.

The system they used for washing soil is the same that our own miners have used for some time, but more methodical. Using fire-hardened

sticks or some battered European tool, the men would dig till they laid bare what we call the *circa,* which is an alluvial bed rich in sand and heavy objects. The children loaded these sands into baskets of tightly woven grass and carried them to the river bank, where a row of women with pans of the same material washed them. As they separated the gold, they parceled it out in little bundles of about a third of an ounce each for ease in trading.

In the evening the chief of the tribe visited us with fifteen young men, who responded to our hospitality by doing what they could to entertain us. They played a betting game that we might call *odd or even.* As they sat in a circle between two great fires, the dealer laid down four little sticks, each about an inch in length, and next to them a small quantity of dry grass thoroughly rubbed between his hands. After the other players had examined these objects, one of them picked them up and with both hands behind his back to hide what he was doing, formed two small packets of equal size with the sticks and the grass and then placed these on the ground for all to see. The players then called out "odd" or "even," after which they called over a boy to untie the packets. The winners bellowed their satisfaction three times, and the others hung their heads in silence. After a good while, during which many of them lost their bundles of gold dust, the chief suggested that they play the war game as a farewell. They all gladly stood up, and after the fires had been stoked, drew back from them twenty paces forming a single file led by the chief. At his command they lumbered toward us, accompanying each step with a guttural sound; when they reached the fires, at another command they all leapt with a shout and surrounded the chief, who then began to sing a kind of mournful song. At its conclusion, all clapped their hands and shouted at the same time and began a dance of the most violent postures of attack and defense, which lasted until the chief, with another command, once more removed them to a distance of twenty paces to begin the simulated combat all over again.

The next day, without waiting for the return of our friendly Indians, we undertook to find the way we had lost; and after many a climb and strain, we had the pleasure of seeing the famous Mill, the first goal of our voyage and our aspirations. We entered that pleasant village at sunset.

X V I

Sutter's Mill. — How gold was discovered there. —
Our situation and how we began washing for gold. —
Mining explorations. — The California gold country. —
Every known metal can be found in California. — Our mining
activities. — An ingenious and very useful pan or cradle used
in California for washing dirt. — An attempted native
uprising and its bloody failure. — How I drowned in
the American River and resuscitated.

As soon as we stopped at that wild but very pleasant spot we quickly
and noisily set up our camp, which caused universal amazement, as it
had in Sacramento and even in San Francisco, by the spaciousness and
comforts of our tent, since no one could bring himself to believe there were
men so thoroughly foolish as to haul such paraphernalia as far as the Mill.

This hamlet, which soon rose to the rank of city, is located in a charming little valley hemmed in by high pine-covered hills on the banks of what they call the South Fork, which is the first of the three mighty gold-bearing streams that descend from the Sierra Nevada and deposit their golden sands on the bottom of the great tributary of the Sacramento known as the American River. Here occurred that chance discovery that was to cause such a stir for so many, including ourselves.

The size and abundance of the gold nuggets released by the pick of Sutter's men, who were working to set up a sawmill by the side of the stream, was such that even those who saw the treasure came to doubt that it could be the king of metals. We know that before the news of this find reached Sutter, the workmen had jokingly divided some of the precious metal among themselves without even suspecting that it was gold; and not even Sutter could believe that the news of the discovery was true until the happy moment when one of his men deposited the first sample in his hand. Stunned by what they saw, he and all who were with him dashed to the gold deposits as fast as their horses could carry them. Meanwhile the report of this wealth reached the village of Sacramento and spread so rapidly that Sutter still had not realized what had happened to him when the populations of Sonora, San Jose, Yerba Buena, and Monterey, all astir, dropped everything and rushed madly to the promised land that offered fortune and felicity to all.

In no time and as though by magic, merchants and lawyers, druggists and sawbones, bricklayers and dandies turned into expert miners. The hands of country bumpkins soon clutched gold nuggets of colossal value; every common tatterdemalion lucky enough to be among the first to reach the golden fleece could go home with unassailable titles of nobility, youth, intelligence, and merit under his torn and filthy belt, all contained in stout and enviable bags of gold dust. How this news subsequently spread as far as Chile I have already related.

When we got there, the village at the Mill consisted of a store, two wooden huts, and many canvas and leaf shelters scattered hither and yon. It was, however, no longer considered the main mining site. What the miner looked for was an as yet unexplored place; and therefore many barely stopped here and went on to the Middle and North Forks, concerning which such wonderful tales were told. Still, there was no lack of gold at the Mill; if people had come to disdain it, it was because at that time nobody wanted to work at looking for gold instead of just walking up and finding it.

The day after pitching our camp, we all set out in a merry procession, each man carrying his pan, his scoop, his shovels, and his crowbars. After walking for a while along the river bank among the debris of recent excavations, we decided to try our hand as best we could, to get some experience in the use of the pan. For two hours we alternately scraped, hauled, and washed, and netted an ounce and a half of gold; whereupon, deeming ourselves sufficiently trained, we ate our tasty beans and then proceeded to choose a spot on which to set up our operations in earnest.

We found it on one of the steep banks carved out by the river, where an extensive bed of sand and gravel lay under a foot or so of soil. As soon as we scratched the ground next to the water, we saw to our delight that many bits of gold sparkled there; and after estimating how far that gold deposit might stretch, and in what direction, we immediately took possession of it, leaving two of our number to sleep there with their weapons as guards of this treasure.

The next day our Elder was invested with the twofold office of cook and controller of our treasury, and we went to work enthusiastically to pick at our bed of gold, which our good Cassalli named Cleopatra's Bed in memory of the sequins that sparkled on the one used by that queen at our Municipal Theater.

This undertaking occupied us for a whole month, during which none of us fell ill. Work was interrupted only at mealtimes and for sleep. At nightfall we returned to our abandoned camp, weighed the day's harvest of gold, and stored it in a kidskin bag that was our strongbox; then, after a little jovial conversation, we all stretched out and slept like so many logs.

The gold that we continued to gather at the Mill was heavily mixed with sand and iron pyrites, and occasionally we dug up handsome pieces of quartz that held from 25% to 70% gold.

We soon organized expeditions to more remote areas; these, along with some that I undertook on my own and the reports of the many adventurers with whom I struck up friendships on these jaunts, convinced me that pure gold, although so abundant, was not the only treasure that the generous hand of nature had bestowed on this region. I have seen rich mines of silver, cinnabar, iron, and coal, and in Grass Valley, a region that seems to have no limits, great veins of gold-bearing quartz with iron pyrites. In general, this last kind of ore, which at the time there was no reason to exploit, is so common in all the western foothills of the Sierra Nevada that it alone can account for the origin and existence of the great sediments of gold to be found at their base or carried afar by the streams.

I quote the following from my diary:

The gold country of Upper California, which currently attracts the attention of miners, lies between the mountain chain called Sierra Nevada on the east and, on the west, the Sacramento and San Joaquin Rivers, which flow down from it and join their waters in the swamps of Suisun. This triangle of mineral deposits, whose dimensions have not as yet been precisely established, stretches for about 135 miles from the Yuba River on the north to the Merced on the south, with an average width from east to west of some sixty miles, which means an approximate area of 8,100 square miles rich in gold-bearing sands. From the rivers that border it on the west, the terrain gradually rises toward the mountains, near which lie the richest deposits; these, however, and the abundant subterranean and exposed metallic ores, do not deprive it of an abundant vegetation. The improvised encampments of the miners follow the creeks and lesser rivers that descend from the Sierra along all of those 135 miles and divide the land into parallel strips until they merge with the Sacramento and the San Joaquin. Although reports of new discoveries arrive and circulate every day, so far the chief and most productive areas are: in the north, Yuba, Bear, North, South, and Middle Forks, Mormon, the Mill, and Dry Diggings; and in the south, Consumnes, Dry Creek, Mokelumne, Calaveras, Stanislaus, Tuolumne, Sonora, Merced, and some others of less importance.

The alluvial sands, one to six inches deep, that form the northern placers rest on beds of almost vertical sheets of slate; the depth at which one comes on this solid core varies between one and eight feet.

The southern placers or deposits are not so regularly distributed. Chunks of ore of extraordinary size, with gold plainly visible, have been found in various gullies in the Stanislaus hills. More or less rich pieces are constantly found in that area and thrown away as useless or objects of mere curiosity to avoid the expense of hauling them away. The last one I saw, which had been taken to San Francisco to decorate the table in a hotel, weighed over ninety-five pounds, including twenty pounds of pure gold.

The western part of the Sierra Nevada is crossed in every direction by gold deposits; yet future enterprise will find greater and more dependable sources of wealth in the valleys at the base of those mountains, because the loose gold to be found in this favored region is not as abundant as was suggested by the contradictory reports that reached us in Chile. I decided to augment the number of the Chileans who had come here because it seemed to me that even the average of what we heard would be enough to satisfy one's most exorbitant desires, and I was right: pure gold, as dust or in nuggets, abundantly deposited in gullies, in river beds, and beneath the very thin layers of soil that cover some of the flats, is waiting to be picked up with so little effort that if the situation were to continue, gold would undoubtedly come in time to be the cheapest of all metals. But to judge by what I have seen up to now, gold will some day be the least of California's riches, both because it will inevitably soon run out and because the industrious Yankees will wisely prefer the inexhaustible sources of agricultural and manufacturing wealth that have existed in this exceptional country since before it was discovered but were quite unsuspected by the Spaniards.

It is true that once the loose gold obtainable by simple washing is exhausted or greatly diminished, there remains the expedient of mining the veins of ore; but this approach will always be slow and far less productive, unless chance, as it often does, comes to the aid of the advances of science, because, in addition to pure gold, I have here observed pyrites that barely reveal the gold they contain, exploited by means of simple amalgamation; gray, almost lead-colored gold, which is gold alloyed with arsenic; yellowish-gray gold, which is alloyed with iron and is very abundant; blackish-blue gold, which reminds me of the samples of a type of Hungarian gold that I left in my mineral collection in Chile and that is called "lung-colored gold," samples that, were it not for the respect I owe to science, I might call petrified gold; and, finally, a kind of pyrite that is also found in Adelfors (in Sweden) and in Hungary and is known in the latter kingdom as *Gelfeft*,[77] a pyrite that does not display any gold and from which, nevertheless, the learned M. de Justi extracted as much as two ounces per hundredweight, despite the efforts of the distinguished pyritologist Heckel to prove the contrary.

Since I am writing only for my countrymen, I must here pause to draw the attention of both our government and our miners to the indisputable need to bring the study of practical mineralogy to the high degree of perfection that it has reached in Europe. Ores so poor that in Chile they are not even considered such are profitably exploited there. In Harz, according to Brongniart,[78] the pyrites of Rammelsberg contain only one twenty-nine millionth part of gold per hundredweight, and that suffices to pay for their exploitation.

For the time being the Yankee has no time for digging gold-bearing pyrites out of the bowels of the earth with pick and gunpowder, and even less for subjecting them to the laborious scientific treatment of heating and repeated smelting that in the form of vapors or slag expels the substances masking the gold and thus renders it, if not pure, at least more concentrated and more amenable to extraction by means of mercury or the cupel. He need only bend over and pick it up from the

77. *Gelfeft*. In the 1886 ed., *Gelft*. I have not found either word in any Hungarian dictionary or encyclopedia. I suspect that they are distortions of the German *Gelberz*, 'tellurium' or 'sylvanite,' a mineral containing gold, silver, etc. and named after the region where it is found, Transylvania, a part of Hungary in the nineteenth century. JP.
78. Probably Alexandre Brongniart (1770–1847), a French geologist. JP.

ground in merchandisable condition. But when the time comes when he will be able to devote himself to such labors, maybe—but there is no maybe about it!—his attention will already have been focused on the only mines that never run out, agriculture and industry.

The most productive gold deposits today are those of Siberia, in Russia, not so much, to be sure, because of the richness of the ores as because of their enormous expanse, which does not mean that one cannot sometimes find nuggets of surprising dimensions there. From the gold fields that lie to the south of Miass have come solid gold nuggets weighing from thirteen to twenty pounds each, and in 1843 one was found that weighs not less than seventy-eight pounds and is still preserved in St. Petersburg. Formerly nuggets weighing up to forty-five and even sixty-four marks[79] of pure gold could also be found in Peru, while until now none has been found in California that reaches the weight of twenty-five pounds.

In terms of purity, the gold of California is in seventh place among the known deposits. The following table shows the degree of purity corresponding to each of the most famous mining districts that play a role in world commerce.

COMPOSITION OF GOLD PRODUCED

PLACE OF ORIGIN	PURE GOLD	SILVER	COPPER	IRON
Siberia: Shabrovskoi (according to Rose)[80]	98.96	0.16	0.35	0.05
Siberia: Borushkoi (Rose)	94.41	5.23	—0.36—	
Brazil (Darcet)	94.00	5.85	0.00	0.00
Siberia: Berezovsk (Rose)	93.78	5.94	0.08	0.40
Siberia: Miass placers (1) (Rose)	92.47	7.27	0.18	0.08
Bogotá (Boussingault)	92.20	8.00	0.00	0.00
California (Warwick)	89.58	0.00	0.00	0.00
Siberia: Miass placers (2) (Rose)	89.35	10.65	0.00	0.00
Senegal (Darcet)	86.97	10.35	0.00	0.00
Siberia: Nizhne Tagil (Rose)	83.85	16.15	0.00	0.00
Trinidad (Boussingault)	82.40	17.60	0.00	0.00
Transylvania (Boussingault)	64.52	35.48	0.00	0.00
Altai: Siranovsk (Rose)	60.98	38.38	0.00	0.33

79. A mark is eight ounces of gold or silver. JP.
80. Gustav Rose, *Mineralogisch-geognostische Reise nach dem Ural, dem Altai und dem Kaspischen Meere*, 2 vols. (Berlin: Verlag der Sanderschen Buchhandlung, 1837–1842). The data for Russia that follow can be found in 2:412ff. I have corrected some misprints in the numbers and spellings, as well as adjusting as best I can the transliteration of the Russian names. JP.

The quantity of gold extracted from the Californian placers was such that some observers came to believe that this metal would soon be demonetized. Their reasoning was based on the fact that the gold produced by all the gold fields in the world at the time of Marshall's discovery did not exceed 22,300 kilograms a year, distributed as follows:

Russia	17,000
Hungary	725
Norway	75
Africa	1,500
North America	1,300
South America	1,700
TOTAL	22,300 KILOGRAMS

The gold they saw before them made them forget that from 1830, when the Russian gold mines were discovered, until 1842, their production had come to a value of 67,500,000 pesos, and that far from decreasing in productivity, they had produced twenty millions between 1842 and 1844[81] alone. If we were to add to these amounts, as of course we should, the yields of the gold fields recently discovered in the Urals, it becomes clear that in terms of gold production California must cede first place to Russia. Tomorrow or some other day Russia will have to cede it to another region, because great natural discoveries, just like the progress of the human spirit, are unstoppable.

As for potential demonetization, it is incontrovertible that until now there is not the slightest sign of a rival that might force the king of metals from his throne.

Thus far, from my diary. Returning now to the travails of our mining company, I must say that our harvest was exceedingly meager for the first three days, because we were panning by hand; but we soon acquired a California cradle, and, as we lovingly rocked our golden baby, we saw it grow prodigiously. This very simple but ingenious device, which has all the advantages of a gigantic miner's scoop, consists of an ordinary cradle about a yard and a half in length and half a yard wide, placed so that its head rests on a base about a span higher than that of the foot.

81. All the editions consulted read "1864," but if this date is correct, then not only was this part of the diary revised after the author's stay in California, but the expression "far from decreasing in productivity" is wrong, since 20,000,000 pesos in 22 years constitutes a far smaller annual production than 67,500,000 in twelve years. This would not be the only place where editions of Pérez uncritically copy each other's misprints. JP.

These bases, which consist simply of a quarter of a wooden disk, allow the cradle to be rocked. At its head there is a crude screen made of perforated boards; the foot stands open, and across the flat bottom of this unique contrivance little parallel strips of wood, a quarter of an inch by a quarter of an inch, are nailed at four-inch intervals to hold back the heavier matter contained in the mud that slips down over that inclined plane.

The method for using this primitive but most useful contraption is so easy and effortless that after watching it in operation for even a short while the most ignorant bystander can claim to be an expert. One man deposits gold-bearing soil on the screen, another pours buckets of water on it, a third rocks the cradle, and the last removes by hand the stones too large to pass through the screen, examines them, and if no gold is to be seen in them, throws them away. The water turns the soil on the screen into mud, which runs down the inclined plane; and the gold, along with other more or less heavy objects, is trapped by the wooden cross strips. The operation is interrupted every ten minutes to collect the gold dust and nuggets that, mixed with iron, have gathered in the angles formed by the strips; the yield is then deposited in a pan, to be further purified at night, and the operation goes on until day's end.

Once we began to use the cradle, our daily harvest varied between ten and twenty-two ounces of gold.

On three occasions my brother Federico skipped work to go, as he said, in search of excitement. After his first two absences he turned up with his pockets full of pieces of quartz studded with bits of gold, which we set aside for presents and the manufacture of buttons. After the third he surprised us with a solid gold nugget that he had found on the floor of a gully and that weighed 17¼ ounces.

Until then nothing had interfered with our peaceful work, but in early April we were on the point of losing everything and being lost ourselves if the natives had been able to carry out undetected their plan for a general uprising against the alien intruders who harried them everywhere. They had gone about it with such secrecy that, had they not been given away by a traitor, I should not now be telling the tale.

What happened was the following:

One morning we noticed that smoke was rising at various spots on the western slope of the lovely hills across the river from our disordered camp, and that because of the stillness of the air it seemed to form parallel lines whose whiteness contrasted with the dark green of the cypresses. We were all, however, much too busy to waste time trying to discover the meaning of such a trifle. At night the line of smoke became a long line of small lights that shone without going out and even without flickering despite the strong wind that had arisen. This did draw our attention; and since no one worked at night, we went to reconnoiter and found that the smoke and lights were nothing but the very clever telegraph used by the Indians to call a council of war.

The next day, while more or less alarming rumors awakened by these preparations ran through the town, my companions and I headed for the lights, which, in daylight, once more appeared as smoke.

To build this unique telegraph, whose message the experts read from the number and direction of the lights, the Indian forms jar-shaped holes in the ground, broad below and narrow at the top; then he fills the cavity with firewood, and the fire that produces smoke in the daytime produces steady gleams of light in the darkness.

When we returned from our expedition we learned that one Indian had betrayed the secret meaning of these mysterious signals and that the whole encampment, understandably alarmed, had called a meeting to adopt the appropriate measures. All the townsfolk gathered the same day and, in typical Yankee fashion, three hours had not passed when all of them left off their work to deal with the common danger and formed, ready to march, a body of 170 riflemen and eighteen of cavalry, with their respective improvised commanders.

Since I had not attended the meeting—something that seemed very odd in a Frenchman, which is what I was taken for at the time—a committee of miners came in search of me; I naturally received them with such demonstrations of being sick that when they heard me say that despite my ailments I asked them for only a few minutes to get ready to follow them, they heatedly rejected my "heroic sacrifice" and settled for letting the valiant compatriot of Lafayette help them with powder and lead.

Two days later it was all over and the successful expedition was back in town, with 114 captives, men, women, and children. The rebellious Indians had been surprised in their camp when they least expected it, and their desperate resistance was quite useless. They were overrun and mercilessly pursued, and only the desire to teach a lesson to the other tribes saved the few prisoners brought back to town from certain death.

For two hours these unfortunates stood waiting on a square that faced the stream, and those two hours were enough for an impromptu jury to reach a decision from which there was no appeal. The improvised leader, accompanied by some riflemen, then spoke to the hapless captives in Spanish, as follows:

"Now you've seen, you so-and-so's, what we can do and what we're ready to do. If you behave from now on, you'll have nothing to fear; but if you don't, what'll happen to you is what you're going to see right now before we let you loose to go back home with the news."

No sooner said than done: they fired on fifteen unfortunates whom they were holding off to one side, and left the ground covered with dead bodies!

I have recounted this bloody episode as rapidly as it occurred, because I saw in it a new and energetic expression of the Yankees' famous motto, "Time is money."

The impression that this terrible and very timely punishment made on the hearts of the bold adventurers in Coloma did not last even two hours, because we had not yet lost sight of the freed natives, who went off clamoring as they walked downcast through the pine woods on the surrounding hills, when the rumor of a new gold discovery on the other side of the stream gripped everyone. No one any longer spoke of anything else; and the whole population would have rushed en masse to get a share of that treasure, had not the means of crossing the dangerous intervening stream been so scarce. There were only two ways of overcoming this obstacle: either by wading across through chest-high water holding on to a cable fixed to both banks, or on a flatboat that might carry fifteen persons squeezed together. Still, after nightfall, we could see to our amazement, from the fires shining on the other side, that many people were already installed there.

Determined that we, too, should explore to see whether we might work to better effect elsewhere, we decided that the next day I should set out for that spot, leaving the kitchen in the charge of another member of our band. Early in the morning of April 11 they all went with me to see me cross the river.

I still shudder when I recall what was in store for me. I chose to cross on the boat. From the landing one could clearly see the plumes of foam that were rising from a cable whipped by the surface current about half a mile farther down the stream, which must have been about a quarter of a mile wide and a fathom and a half deep. So many people crowded on after me that although I saw the impending danger, since there was not even room to operate the tiller, I could not make my way off the boat.

Hardly had we left the shore when the boat, improperly laden and caught broadside by the current, capsized, plunging us all into the water while those who witnessed the catastrophe from shore screamed in horror. I used to swim in those days, and one might even say I swam well; but being a good swimmer is not always enough in such a case. Once the shock of the sudden dunking had worn off, I calmly recollected the cable that might perhaps save us; but I had just managed to make my way through the thrashing bodies that held me back, desperately bumping into me underwater, when something clutched my shoulders and dragged me once more beneath the surface. My efforts to shake it off were in vain; my breath was giving out and I was about to make use of my knife, when, before I could strike, God inspired in me the idea of making a desperate effort to reach the bottom. I recall that I was freed from the weight that was drowning me, that out of breath and with the water choking me, I felt a sudden sharp pain in my lungs, my eye sockets, my ears, and the base of my nose, and, finally, a furious thunder in my head as of many drums, which plunged me into unconsciousness.

Three hours later, our worthy Elder, stretched out on the sheltering blankets of his anxious partners, was telling them, in a voice half jovial, half pained, his impressions of his voyage to the next world, up to the point at which asphyxia had wiped away all memory.

They told me that as they all ran downstream along the bank they soon saw various human bodies clinging to the cable, and that one of them was I; and that after they had with some effort brought me ashore, where in their natural confusion they had let me drop face down to the ground, I had thrown up water and blood and then uttered the first moan that indicated to my disconsolate brothers that I was still alive.

The next day the controller and cook, though rather battered, was going about his culinary chores as though nothing had happened.

XVII

One of the partners goes to San Francisco. — The city of
Sacramento. — I save Álvarez from being hanged. —
Food poisoning in Sacramento. — Stockton. — San Francisco.
— The ups and downs of business life in San Francisco. —
The feverish activity of its inhabitants.— A judge judged by a
criminal. — Causes of the bad feelings between Yankees and
Chileans. — Brannan's timely intervention. — Expulsion
of the Chileans from the gold fields. — My hasty return
in search of my brothers.

Spring was coming in all its splendor, embroidering the green fields
of glorious California with its fair flowers, when we decided that
one of us should go to town, both to pay off our debts and to pick up letters from the devoted mother who in Chile was weeping for the absence

of her sons. The choice fell on the "Frenchman," who, recovered from the consequences of his hydropathic immersion, was continuing undaunted to carry out his functions as elder, controller, and cook of the itinerant company.

For us brothers, the morning of April 25 was sad, very sad. It was the first time one of us, alone and on foot, was to set out on a long journey through a country made semibarbaric by the exceptional circumstances it was undergoing. While we were together, dangers and travails meant little or nothing to us; but who could say what might happen once we were apart? We were more than two thousand leagues from home, property, and friends, in the middle of a country that had become a carnival of adventurers, among whom, along with fine upstanding men, there were swarms of bandits and a horde of those wicked hearts that the sea of humanity invariably casts up. On a journey among men who had no god but gold, no law but that of the strongest, no court of appeals but hot lead, it was clear that any assault, any sickness, wild beasts, poisonous reptiles, hunger or thirst in the open countryside, an ankle sprained by chance, might, jointly or severally, become deadly sources of irreparable harm for the lone traveler.

My silent brothers accompanied me for about a mile, after which it seemed to us that our sentimentality had exceeded what was allowed in the country where we found ourselves, and so we said farewell with a hearty handshake.

On my back, as my only bed, I carried a serape or Mexican blanket and a Chilean poncho, rolled up like a soldier's cloak, and, in the way of knapsack, a small bag with sixteen pounds of toasted meal with the usual tin bowl; on my left shoulder hung a rifle, and at my waist, besides my pistols and knife, a belt holding seventeen pounds of gold dust.

I was constantly obliged to leave the road to avoid meetings with small bands of adventurers who, some cheerful and singing, others cursing, were headed for the gold country. When I met a single traveler, the most courteous reciprocal greetings were the order of the day; when I encountered two or more pilgrims, only I had to do the greeting, because the others either ignored me or, if they looked at me, did so only to measure me from head to toe with a contemptuous smile. When night came, I would take lodging under the largest oak I could find, use my knife to remove the grass and trash that had accumulated around the trunk, sweep away the mud with a branch, and, after using dirt and dry leaves to stop up every crack that might hide poisonous insects or reptiles, build a fire with large pine cones. Then, dead tired, I would fall on my serape, not to sink into the deep sleep that my battered body was calling for, but to sleep as a soldier sleeps in the front lines on the eve of battle. It could not be otherwise, what with the frequent gunshots to be heard everywhere in the first hours of darkness, and, from then till the new day, the infernal howling of the packs of coyotes that, roaming the countryside in search of dead men and horses to devour, kept a constant watch on every encampment to take advantage of any distraction on the part of the exhausted traveler, forcing him not only to stay half awake but to tend constantly to his fire, the only barrier that could contain both the coyote and the bear, terror of those regions.

I walked thus for four days in a row, and on the morning of the fifth I arrived safely in Sacramento.

What material progress in so short a time! Sacramento was no longer what it had been only the day before. With the city plan laid out, many houses were already rising there at great cost, because boards, the only material used in construction, were selling at seventy-five cents a foot. Lots were no longer being given away, but sold, and sold dear; and the harbor held, in addition to smaller boats, the abandoned hulls and rigging of twenty vessels of over three hundred tons and some thirty brigs.

In the midst of all the bustle and the usual dashing about, I had no small difficulty finding the house, or rather tent, of Mr. Gillespie, an honest and phlegmatic American Gringo to whom, on our arrival in Sacramento, we had sold our wine and the Tiltil liquor. This man had taken a special liking to me. He was delighted with my unexpected arrival; and since our cordial handshake coincided with his getting ready to look over a lot that he was thinking of buying about a mile from town, he suggested I accompany him so that, as he said, he might have the benefit of my expert advice. I therefore rid myself of the tiresome weight I had been carrying and without further ado rested from my journey by setting out with him.

It was the saving hand of Providence that guided our steps on that excursion, because the frightful incident that placed my countryman Álvarez in danger of a horrible death occurred on our way back, just as we were resting in the shade of a tree. Fortunately we were able to prevent that savage murder, as I have explained in the first part of my account of this voyage.

Recently, after writing these recollections, there came into my hands a book by S. C. Upham. I have been amazed to see that his inclination to praise everything having to do with his country has so far blinded this learned author as to make him lend his respectable name to this sentence that I find on page 324 of his *Notes of a Voyage to California* (Philadelphia, 1878): "Yet paradoxical as it may seem, it is nevertheless true, that life and property are as secure here, as in the cities of New York, Boston, or Philadelphia." Voyagers to those centers of civilization and culture would be in a pretty pickle indeed if that was the kind of security that life and property enjoyed there! It is true that California's streets and beaches were piled with merchandise worth millions of pesos, apparently quite unprotected; but that should not be taken to mean that they were guarded by morality, because that apparent negligence rested on the owner's presence among the busy throng, or on the barrel of a rifle doing sentry duty some way off. Personal safety at that time of lawlessness did not and could not depend on anything but the number of those banded together for mutual defense or the superiority of the weapons carried by the victim of aggression.

We returned to Gillespie's place, where we put up the poor gentleman whose mind had been disturbed by the excitement; then, not long after we had chatted about our adventures and our hopes for the future, my friend's great kindness almost cost us both our lives.

My good Gillespie had a jar of oysters set aside for some great occasion, and since he firmly believed that my arrival was about as great an occasion as he was likely to see, out came the jar, and host and guest both fell to with a will to enjoy what in that part of the world was a rare delicacy. The pickling liquid seemed sweet to me at first, and its color milky; but I only began to be concerned when I started to feel violent stomach pains, and by then the damage had been done. My companion, who, as I learned later, had felt the same symptoms, found a pretext for leaving the tent, just as I, unable to stop myself, broke out in the most violent vomiting, accompanied by acute pain in my stomach. As fate would have it, I was able to drag myself, simultaneously burning and sweating, to a tent where I thought I heard French spoken; and when those men saw my contorted face and heard me beg them for water, they kindly came to my aid. I drank as though I would never stop, until my final heavings, which were of blood, began to relax me. I instantly begged these charitable people to go to the aid of Gillespie, which they did; and the next day that poor Gringo and I, now out of danger but as battered and bruised as if we had received the most awful beating, were recovering in his tent's only bed.

In California no one had time to get sick, so after two days of convalescence, a skiff belonging to Gillespie and supplied with everything needed for a voyage was carrying me down the Sacramento toward the city and harbor of San Francisco.

The Sacramento has branches that resemble the main channel of our Valdivia River, except for their depth and the absence of the beautiful *copihue* vines that festoon the trees on shore and are reflected in the tranquil waters.

Sailing along with the greatest of ease and with my head full of plans, I soon reached the vast expanse where this river and the San Joaquin join their waters to proceed together until they end in the Pacific. The sight of this fascinating confluence spurred my desire to explore in person at least part of the second waterway that serves the inland commerce of Upper California. I therefore turned the bow of my boat into what seemed to me to be the main channel of the labyrinth of sloughs and banks of sand and mud exposed before me by the low tide. The rise and fall of the tides daily transforms the appearance of the confluence, which now is a deep still lake, now a marsh covered by banks separated by waters of differing depth, so that at low tide it is very difficult to enter the main channel of the San Joaquin.

As I reached this place the tide was precisely at its ebb; and I was able to count nine launches, seven sloops, and a brig schooner lying in the fetid mud covered by rushes, among which, along with the colonies of turtles so motionless they seemed to be asleep, one could see groups of passengers standing in mud up to their knees and struggling amid curses and shouts of "All together now!" to push their vessels into deeper water.

This site, disagreeable as it must have been for those unhappily trapped in that infernal ooze, would not have lacked attractions for someone who, like me, was traveling in so small a vessel, if hordes of poisonous mosquitoes had not created above every voyager a living cloud that seemed determined to suffocate him. Forsaking, therefore, the contemplation of the poetic aspects of the place and quickly leaving for a future time the reflections it awoke in me, I gave the order to move on, and after only two brief struggles with the mud, we found ourselves in the middle of the main channel of the San Joaquin, out of sight of the unfortunate apprentice frogs whom we left behind us and beyond the reach of their shouts.

Ignorance about the channels of this confluence, and insistence on not hiring pilots, because every Yankee in whose hand chance has placed a tiller considers himself a second Nelson, were the reasons that it could take as many as five days of very tiresome travel to cover the 160 miles that lie between San Francisco and Stockton.

Except for its direction, the San Joaquin River is exactly the same as the Sacramento in the depth and gentle flow of its waters. After an agreeable journey, therefore, we soon caught sight of Stockton.

This small village, which by its location seems fated to occupy the third place among the chief centers of inland commerce, owes its existence to the adventurer Weber,[82] who was one of the favored foreigners to whom Mexico granted lands, and also one of the first to abandon the plow for the sword and serve under Commodore Stockton, whose name he gave to his beloved town.

In this budding village I counted sixty wooden houses, and a total of some one hundred eighty homes, including tents and shelters made of canvas or branches. The authorities told me that the resident population was at least a thousand, but that for the last month the transients had every day exceeded two thousand five hundred.

If you saw one new town in California, you had seem them all, because apart from its location and the occupations appropriate to that, the first thing you met with in every one of them were real estate agents or brokers with their maps, their sales talks, and their feverish activity. In every one you saw only men of strange appearance and wild dress, people who seemed to be busy and to sweep everything before them like hurricanes, and toughs armed to the teeth; and everywhere, to the beat of hammer and saw, you heard songs, curses, and the sound of gunfire. The streets were paved with the empty bottles that were constantly issuing like projectiles from the doors of the taverns, which, filled with merchandise salable or spoiled, were awaiting only the auctioneer to pass from one set of hands into another. Wherever you went you saw men who were bankrupt one day, rich the next, even more bankrupt the third, and finally millionaires, while in the cafés you saw pictures of naked women, for lack of the flesh and blood article.

In Stockton I saw what I had not yet seen in either Sacramento or San Francisco, a gallows solidly installed in the western part of town. Those generally used both in towns and in the country were supplied by nature herself, because a branch of the first handy tree sufficed to hang a scoundrel by the neck. That is why there is a certain humorous quality in the journalist Upham's reference to the Stockton gallows as "a mark of civilization."

Stockton was the commercial hub that supplied the miners and collected the gold of all the southern placers.

After a two days' sojourn in that place I again laid hold of my boat's tiller and headed for San Francisco, where I landed four days after leaving the gold fields,[83] battered and bruised, to be sure, but cheerful and resolute.

How different from what it had been did I find San Francisco on my arrival! Gone was the city of canvas sprinkled with the foundations of

82. Charles M. Weber, a German, for whom Weber Creek, previously mentioned, was named. JP.

83. That is, Sacramento, since the journey from the placers to that city took five days. JP.

more or less costly buildings. The tents and shelters had turned into rows of houses, albeit houses hastily and roughly built; the foundations, into luxurious hotels; and the streets themselves, which formerly ended in the tidal mud flats, now extended into the bay on piers supported by mighty redwood trunks driven into the bottom. Lots that previously were being given away in bulk were now measured by the foot, and their cost was higher than high.

The progress made by this town, especially surprising for men like ourselves, used to seeing our Chilean villages develop at a snail's pace, convinced me that we had made a great mistake in turning down the land offered to us for nothing if only we would set up our tents on it. Who could help regretting that he had looked down on something that so soon was to be worth so much?

Here, without wishing to offend anyone, it seems appropriate to remark that the only men to make a fortune in California were those who were not bold enough to set out in pursuit of fortune, disdaining hunger, toil, and danger, because by accepting free land, or by buying it at rock-bottom prices, or by lying in wait for fortune behind a rampart of merchandise that they had brought there more by chance than by design, such men found themselves from one day to the next in possession of substantial wealth.

The bay was crowded with ships, all abandoned. Their passengers and crews had brought the transient population to over thirty thousand, and the activity of transients and residents was so feverish that the city seemed to grow and be transformed as though by magic. Where each street met the shore, long piers resting on mighty redwood piles and still being extended, in addition to others half-built, were wresting space from the tidal mud for traffic and new structures. Here, for lack of building materials for new piers, boxes and sacks full of earth were piled up on the miry shore; there, so as not to waste time, piers, warehouses, and streets were improvised by running aground rows of ships that prolonged the streets and laying beams and planks from one to another as support for shops.

One of the first inventors of the transformation of a ship into a dwelling on terra firma was the young Chilean Don Wenceslao Urbistondo, who took advantage of an opportune full moon to turn his abandoned and useless bark into a prolongation of the street that runs along the foot of the hill bordering the harbor on the left. The masts became a bridge over the mud that separated the ship's stern from the street.

Sidewalks were being built even with bundles of jerky, which, for lack of cheaper and quicker paving material, were plunged into the mud next to the houses so that one might be able to walk without sinking in up to one's knees.

In that city, commerce underwent the same periodic fluctuations as the tides. Sometimes all was flooded, and abundance wiped out the most solid values; at other times all was dry; and not even the most far-seeing could escape the ruinous surprises brought about by the unexpected ebb and flood. One man grew rich without knowing why, and another was ruined despite the most cautious calculations. I remember that in view of the scarcity of building materials, prefabricated houses were ordered from Chile, and that by the time they arrived, materials were so abundant in San Francisco that those who had ordered the houses were forced to pay someone to take them over and unload them. I speak as both witness and victim.

Still, no one was daunted, because even the least needed goods could recover their value by means of the most opportune sudden fires that daily sprang up everywhere, threatening to wipe out everything.

On the stage of this most raucous international fair in human memory, no actor played the part that had been his lot in his native land. The master became a servant; the lawyer, a freight agent; the physician, a longshoreman; the seaman, a clodbuster; and the philosopher, abandoning the regions of the ethereal, became the steadiest laborer in the realm of the material. Without surprise, but with rightful pride as a Chilean, I have seen the tender and effeminate Santiago dandy, with a smile on his lips and the seawater up to his waist, the gold chain that used to adorn his vest at the balls of the capital still hanging from the buttonhole of a sweaty woolen shirt, haul the belongings of a brawny tar-smeared sailor, receive his wages, and immediately offer his helpful services to another yokel.

Pretentious signs sprang up everywhere. Above a makeshift hut you could read, *Hotel Fremont*. Above the flapping canvas of a tent, the property of one who may at the most have been a gravedigger: *John Doe, Physician and Surgeon*. Above the shed of a man we all knew as an insurance agent in Valparaíso: *Robert Roe, Attorney at Law*. Signs of *Doe & Co., Commission Brokers* were everywhere. And on the shack of a Santiago hairdresser: *Hotel de France*. Chileans were doing it, too, and few of our leading families escaped having their names displayed in California.

The multitude of men — and always men, because women were not yet in fashion there — had made it necessary to establish at least some facsimile of government in that Tower of Babel; in fact, something of the sort was set up with the title of mayor, an official whose powers perfectly paralleled those of our former subdelegates. The only difference between the two was that the orders and decrees of our Chilean subdelegates, whether or not just, were obeyed, while those of the Californian or San Franciscan mayor were heeded only when it suited his subjects.

Drawn by the hubbub produced by a mass of people, by some shouts, and by not a few curses, I saw that a fellow was being pushed and shoved, much against his will, into the presence of the mayor. I let myself be carried along by the crowd and with it entered the courtroom, which was a large warehouse with a door at one end and a low window at the other, where the mayor sat. Since "time is money," this official, after a brief interchange with the accusers and the accused, decided that he knew enough, stood up, and said in a loud voice, "Hear ye, hear ye! I sentence the accused to fifty lashes, to be laid on right now."

This sentence was no sooner pronounced than another voice was heard, drunken and punctuated by hiccups but also proclaiming its "Hear ye, hear ye!" We all looked over toward the source of that bellowing, and to our surprise saw that it was coming from an Oregonian, who, swaying atop the shoulders of two husky companions now transformed into a dais, repeated the requisite "Hear ye, hear ye!" and proclaimed, "Citizens! Since the mayor is for applying fifty lashes to this citizen of the United States, I'm for ten of us kicking the mayor in the . . . till he's a mile away from here!" "Hurrah!" they all shouted at once; and the accused and all the rest were about to fall on the mayor, when he, faster than a jackrabbit, jumped through the window and managed to make himself scarce among the surrounding streets!

With judges and litigants like these, it was no wonder that trials and appeals were decided by the pistol or the knife.

The relations between Chileans and Americans were far from cordial; and the decree issued by General Persifer Smith in Panama declaring "that effective this date all foreigners are prohibited from mining in California" put the finishing touch to the abuses committed against the peaceful and defenseless Chileans.

Alarmed at this development, the authorities and the merchants proposed that all foreigners should declare themselves citizens of the Union, a status that they offered to confer for a mere ten pesos. But this safe conduct was halfway useful only in the place where it was obtained, because everywhere else it was more jeered at than honored. Shortly after this the provisional state government in San Jose declared mining to be open to foreigners, provided they paid twenty pesos a month in advance. The receipt was to serve as sufficient authorization for working, but how many clashes arose from this agreement between tax collectors and tax payers!

The hostility of the common run of Yankees toward the sons of other nations, and most especially toward Chileans, had intensified. Their argument was simple and conclusive: the Chilean descended from the Spaniard, the Spaniard had Moorish blood, therefore the Chilean had to be at the least a Hottentot or at best something very much like the timid and abased *Californio*. The boldness of the Chilean had stuck in their craw, because, though submissive in his own country, he is very different abroad, even with a pistol pointed at his breast, as long as his hand can reach the handle of his knife. The Chilean, in turn, detested the Yankee, whom he constantly declared a coward; this mutual hostility explains the bloody calamities and atrocities that we repeatedly witnessed in the land of gold and hope.

A gang of bandits called the Hounds soon formed in San Francisco, composed of vagrants, gamblers, and drunks united in the fellowship of crime and under the motto of *We always get our way*. The disgust and fear inspired by their impudent presence preceded them everywhere, just as brawls and violence followed them wherever they went.

Since they did not always *get their way*, the miscreant Hounds, as they were roaming around the headland on the right, where a kind of Chilecito had grown up set apart from the center of town, decided to give it a good hard thrashing; and since in California "time is money," a large number of these brutes fell upon the unsuspecting Chileans with their sticks and revolvers. The uproar produced by so brutal and unprovoked an attack is easily imagined. Once the Chileans had recovered from their surprise they began to rain stones on their attackers. A respectable Chilean gentleman, unable to flee through the door of his tent because it was blocked by several Hounds who were assailing him, laid the first comer low with a pistol shot and, slashing the canvas of his tent with his knife, managed to escape through that improvised door and rejoin his companions unharmed. Brannan, the ex-Mormon and owner of the unforgettable *Dicey My Nana*, informed by some Chileans of what was going on, rushed onto the roof of his house filled with just indignation and shouted to the people to gather below, declaring in succinct but energetic terms that it was time to make an example of the perpetrators of such outrages against the citizens of a friendly country that every day sent to San Francisco, along with the finest flour, *the world's best adobe cutters!* "To make the fullest amends," he added, "I propose that some Chileans of good will, led by citizens of the United States, proceed immediately to arrest these disturbers of the peace."

A general shout of approval resounded through the assaulted district, and the almost instant appearance of the impromptu protectors of law and order put an end to an outbreak of savagery that could have had the most disastrous consequences. Eighteen bandits dragged from their lairs were handed over as prisoners to the corvette *Warren* of the United States Navy; with this, peace and quiet returned to the infernal scene.

Three days later, when I was hastening my preparations for returning to my family and friends, I was startled to read the following alarming news in the San Francisco paper: "American blood shed by vile Chileans in the gold fields! Citizens beware!" By the next day the news had grown out of all proportion; by night it was rumored that not only had the Chileans been violently expelled from the San Joaquin, but that the same band of outlaws that was pursuing them intent on robbery and vengeance was also heading for the other Chileans who were working on the tributaries of the American River.

Imagine my plight when, as I was still vacillating about what to do in so difficult a situation, an acquaintance passed on the wildly exaggerated news that the most dreadful atrocities had just been committed against the Chileans at the Mill! I confess my sin. Neither the distance between the Mill and San Francisco, a distance I knew so well, nor the clear impossibility of the news arriving with such speed, were sufficient to make me doubt what I had just been told. My brothers were involved, and I was bound to lose my head! My brothers, my poor brothers alone up there, without my being able to share their misfortune! In a frenzy, with no baggage but my weapons, with no hope but to avenge them, I paid two hundred pesos for a boat that was to take me to Sacramento; and without heeding the voice of prudence or daring to let it sound, I yielded to the power of my fate!

Where was I going? What did I plan to do? I have no idea. All I can remember is that everything seemed possible to me, everything easy, except returning to Chile without my brothers!

We traveled day and night without stopping; when we reached Sacramento, I leapt into the water without waiting for the boat to tie up, and with an agonized heart I ran to Gillespie's place.

Imagine my surprise! God had not forsaken me! My brothers, who had reached Sacramento the day before, poor, robbed of all their possessions, but unscathed, were just consulting Gillespie about how to join me in San Francisco as soon as possible. Getting there, seeing them, counting them, and collapsing under my emotion were all matters of an instant! Ah, to understand my situation you must have experienced it! Despair, anger, perhaps the spirit of revenge, would have continued to infuse my feeble body with the strength and vigor of which an excess of joy deprived me at that moment!

That afternoon, as we all sat together under a modest covering of serapes and exchanged news of our adventures, good cheer soon returned to our hearts and made us understand that all that had passed was and could be nothing but an absurd nightmare. After all, we were hale and hearty and all accounted for. What more could we ask? The Yankees had not had need of much violence to expel the Chilean intruders from the Mill. To be sure, they were robbed of all they possessed; but in California that was a matter of no consequence.

Our other companions had scattered. That same night we declared ourselves a committee to decide what we were now to do. No one favored returning to Chile; instead we unanimously resolved to struggle anew, though with a different method of attack, against a hostile fate, until such time as we should conquer it.

XVIII

We go into business. — What business we go into. — We buy a boat. — Legal difficulties in the way of river navigation and the less than honorable way to overcome them. — A voyage on the Impermeable.*— California's snakes and mosquitoes. — The death of young Martínez.— Tertian fever in Sacramento. — The Chilean hospital of the Luco brothers. — Establishment of a hotel in San Francisco. — Don Juan Nepomuceno Espejo's well. — We become waiters. — The milk adventure. — My voyage to Monterey. — Reputation of the Chileans in California. — Monterey. — Its hospitable inhabitants. — A soirée. — A valuable gift, and my return to San Francisco. — Arrival of the first women in San Francisco. — Repulsive* tableaux vivants *in the cafés. — Women are auctioned off on board the ships.— Gambling. — Elections for the convention in San José. — A fire destroys San Francisco. — We become sailors. — Our return to Chile.*

The mines were not the only opportunity open to enterprise in the California of that time. After they had become inaccessible to foreigners, there was still trade, which was flourishing. We knew from experience that retailers and idlers made more money than did hard workers and entrepreneurs on a larger scale; this fact, after some brief consideration, led us to erect altars to Mercury, the god of thieves. To be sure, we lacked the proper accouterments of this soul of commerce: the traditional sack, little wings on our feet, and the caduceus; but my brothers were not that easily held back. They made a sack out of several small bags for gold dust that they had miraculously managed to salvage by tucking them under their belts; as for the wings, I was to buy them in San Francisco in the form of a boat; and we forgot about the caduceus because we could see no practical use for it. The day after our reunion the happy Elder, now made head and general manager of the firm Pérez Bros., was sailing down the lovely estuary that leads to San Francisco.

The circumstances under which we changed course to enter the path of commerce were exceedingly favorable. Since the frenzy to gather gold with their own hands had set all heads spinning, no one paid any attention to the fact that what was sold inland for a hundred was being practically given away in San Francisco. The number of new arrivals was so great and the goods they had brought with them were such a hindrance to further movement that in order not to waste time, what could not be sold, and sold cheaply, was thrown away.

The number of Chilean acquaintances landing in San Francisco seemed also to be constantly increasing, and they came with such eagerness that they looked down on any Chilean who had not become a Croesus. Only slackers and incompetents could be poor and downcast! After answering the volley of questions they threw at me, I let them strut and swagger while I kept on quietly collecting on the beach the bundles of worm-eaten jerky I had just bought at two pesos a bundle, saying to myself that these babes in the woods evidently had no idea which end is up. They found out soon enough! And how many a brave boast turned into laments once they did!

One of the countless acquaintances and relatives whom I was constantly running into was Don Miguel Ramírez, who, when he heard me say that I was going to buy a boat, offered to sell me a twelve-tonner that he had just bought for seven hundred pesos and that he would sell me for three hundred, since he no longer needed it, having decided to work as a sawyer. We struck a deal.

With the help of three young Chileans turned sailors to work their way to Sacramento, the captain and Elder, ex-cook and ex-controller of the mining operations at the Mill and now merchant and shipowner, soon made up the cargo of the *Indefatigable,* which was the name of his enviable boat. This cargo consisted of eight bundles of jerky considerably lightened by the despoliations of worms; twenty hundredweight of pieces of Chanco cheese, carefully cut into cubes to separate the sound parts from the rotten; four bags of dried peaches; two four-gallon kegs of *chivato* liquor; a small crate of jars of preserves that I had received from Chile; and two sacks of toasted meal.

I was about to go on board when the devil—because it could have been none other—almost sank my whole business. A customs agent ordered me not to move, because my boat was not American made and its keel was not of American wood, two absolute requirements for trading on the rivers. Being in a country where "time is money," I cursed this setback. Then, however, it occurred to me to invert the order of these two nouns, saying to myself, "If time is money, then of course money is time, and not only time but everything else in the world"; and without further delay I ran off in search of an insurance agent from Valparaíso, now transformed into a lawyer, or attorney at law, to quote the sign on his house. He pretended not to know me or even speak Spanish. "Short time in Chile . . . " He told me that my boat was well known, that there was no need to tell him where it was, but that my problem was a very ticklish one, though not insurmountable.

"Ask what you want," I replied, "because if I can't get out of this I'm going to hell in a handbasket."

"All right," he then said very gravely, "you can start by paying half of my professional fees in advance, and we'll go on from there."

I handed him 450 pesos in gold and was already out the door when he shouted to me, "It's a small boat, right?"

"No, sir," I answered with some irritation, "a large boat, twelve tons, named *Indefatigable!*"

And this rascal said he knew her, and that he had been in Chile only a short time, when he had grown gray there!

Four days later, which was a century in California, this attorney at law turned up with a stack of papers full of scribblings that held unassailable proof that the lumber of my vessel had been cut in a certain American forest and that the very builder who had laid her keel happened to be right in San Francisco, on his way inland. Furthermore, it turned out that not only was the vessel a purebred, but so was its name, because instead of *Indefatigable,* which was how the Mexican barbarians who don't know English pronounced it, it was *Impermeable!*

What could I do? Owner, lord, and captain of an American vessel, with a surcharge of nine hundred pesos for this favor, I proceeded to prepare for departure.

The crew of this expedition consisted of five persons, from captain to cabin boy: two Velásquezes from Chiloé, one Valdivia from Casablanca, Martínez, a young man from the south, and me.

Martínez, who was about twenty-two and whose pleasing appearance and refined manner I had found engaging, was suffering from tertian fever, which, when it attacked him, did so with such force that after alternating throes of feeling hot or cold he would lie for more than an hour in a kind of stupor very much like a prolonged faint. How I wish we had never allowed him to come on board!

Since the violence of the ebb tide had caused two skiffs to capsize that morning in the eddies or small whirlpools of the channel that connects the bay with the Pacific, with loss of their entire crews, including three Chileans, I determined not to move except with the incoming tide; while waiting, I had occasion to observe with horror the fever's effect on the wasted body of my poor companion Martínez.

The gallant *Impermeable* sailed for three consecutive days with favorable winds and tides, exchanging cheers with every vessel we passed, until we entered the waters of Suisun, where the wind dropped and the tide began to run against us. Toward midday, as we were immobilized, tied to a half-submerged tree trunk covered with turtles, the heat obliged us to go ashore in search of some shade and to await the rising tide there. Unfortunately Martínez had just suffered another furious attack of his cruel illness. We made him as comfortable as we could beneath a canvas awning, set a dish of sugar water by his side, and, leaving him in his lethargy, went ashore feeling sorry for him but little suspecting what we should find on our return.

I have already mentioned the vast swarms of venomous and tenacious mosquitoes that plagued the swampy banks of the Sacramento and San Joaquin Rivers, at whose confluence these annoying insects made their headquarters. Defending ourselves as best we could by thrashing about us with our handkerchiefs, we took shelter under some bushes that faced a small level space devoid of grass and covered with small burrows like those made by our *cururo* rats in the dry country beyond the Maule. We spent about an hour there without quite understanding the significance of the many dry sticks, about three inches long, that seemed to be deliberately planted in each of the holes in the ground. No sooner, however, had curiosity led me to approach them than I drew back in fright, crying out, "They're snakes!"

In the course of my life I have traveled in many desolate regions, and I recall none that had more snakes than do parts of the golden soil of California. The coral snake and the rattlesnake are found everywhere, among a multitude of other ophidians of differing kinds and sizes that, though not always poisonous, always frighten the traveler and cause him to step aside when he finds them stretched out across the road in the sun. There was nothing suspicious about the snakes before us. None of the many we killed had a scaly head; they rather resembled our Chilean snakes, which instead of small scales have shells like that of a tortoise.

Who knows how long we entertained ourselves decapitating snakes by striking at them with switches and throwing stones at the many rows of turtles that swelled the tree trunks resting on the water, all the time under constant attack from swarms of mosquitoes so dense that they obscured our vision while tearing us to pieces with their stings, and against which smoke, slaps, and waving branches were equally useless defenses. Evening was coming on when we returned on board.

There are certain impressions so intense that they are never forgotten. Martínez lay motionless, monstrously bloated, his covers bunched at his feet, no doubt as a result of some convulsive movement, his body, including his head, covered with a bloody and disgusting shroud of mosquitoes that, sated and lethargic, formed on their luckless victim a layer that in our shock we estimated to be more than an inch thick. No sooner did we see this than we rushed toward our poor friend, called him, and shook him, thereby crushing thousands of mosquitoes that drenched our hands in blood; but our help came too late. Martínez was dead!

We had no tools with which to dig a grave there; there was no sense in taking him to Sacramento; dumping him on the ground to be eaten by coyotes was out of the question. The next day, therefore, after a dreadful night, the waters of the Sacramento received, along with our tears, the inanimate body of that unfortunate youth, who only the day before had been our companion and our friend!

The life of a miner in California at that time was very similar to that of a soldier in the field. A tear will dampen the dour soldier's weathered cheek at the last touch of his dead comrade's hand, but that tear is soon dried in the face of new dangers or with the elation born of victory.

The cool morning breeze, the disappearance of the mosquitoes swept away by it, the impressive sight of the tranquil waters of Suisun Bay, that of the forests and delightful hills on its farther shores, the joyful clamor of the birds, the constant encounters with innumerable vessels full of merry passengers, and perhaps the thought that a tear shed over an irreversible calamity is a wasted tear, soon restored our downcast spirits to their original vivacity.

When we reached Sacramento two days later, I showed my invoice to my brothers, who received it enthusiastically, because the goods I was bringing them were just then experiencing one of those periods of high demand and high prices that were so astonishing in California. We consequently proceeded without delay to unload them and prepare them for sale.

We no longer had a tent; such luxury was a thing of the past. A scrap of cotton cloth atop crude stakes was the roof of our home and storehouse, and walls made of branches formed a modest semicircle that protected us from the wind. A crate set upside down in the opening that served as our door was baptized as counter; and since the whole shipment did not fit inside our walls, the name of storehouse was extended to where we kept our surplus out in the open. On top of the crate we installed the indispensable scales for weighing gold, standing next to a slice of cheese, a pile of dried peaches, and two fine glasses backed by a bottle, the vanguard of the barrels of *chivato* that we kept inside in reserve.

The sight of these offerings soon attracted some interested potential customers, and everything was selling like hotcakes, with the exception of the jerky, which could not decently be exposed for sale. Not knowing what to do with it, because the worms, for lack of better nourishment, might start on us, the directors of the company decided to restore the appearance and solidity of the jerky by plugging its holes with tallow. After we had undone the bundles, the jerky, which looked more like shreds of a sieve than like jerky, was shaken and stretched out on the grass, where, after applying hot tallow to both its sides, we left it a short while in the sun. The day before, Federico had brought us a bag of cumin seeds that some Chileans had abandoned at the base of a tree; and since there is nothing that human ingenuity cannot put to some use, we took advantage of the incident and poured that devilish condiment on the heated jerky, after which we formed an artistic Egyptian pyramid with the whole.

The aroma rising from this bizarre merchandise attracted two wealthy men from Sonora, who asked what this fragrant foodstuff might be; we assured them that it was the most select jerky, a staple on the tables of the nobility in Santiago, and that we had been unable until then to sell it because in California people seemed, in spite of the gold, to be more interested in bad and cheap merchandise than in good and expensive. We lied like veteran shopkeepers who assure some charming housewife that they're losing money on the deal, that just for her they'll sell at so low a price, that she shouldn't tell anyone, etc. Those abominable scraps sold by the pound and, what is more, they sold out. The *chivato* was sold at six *reales* per glass, because it was what the Duc d'Orléans drank; the same method worked for everything else.

While this was going on, Sacramento kept filling up with Chileans, who, driven from the placers by the lack of security, came grumbling and dispirited to seek refuge there; and as though the new laws and Yankee hostility were not enough to destroy the accursed race, the climate decided also to take a hand in the matter.

The effect of the heat on the mudbanks and marshes formed by the confluence of the Sacramento and American Rivers began so to corrupt the purity of the air with putrid vapors that these soon produced violent tertian fevers, very debilitating for some and even deadly for others. My brother César almost lost his life, and our newly founded enterprise had several times to abandon its merchandising activities for those of the undertaker.

This is not to say, however, that the climate of California is inhospitable. On the contrary, since it lies between 32° and 42° north latitude,[84] a location that in our country would correspond to the region between Coquimbo and Valdivia, the climate, instead of being what is called extreme, falls into the category of temperate. But the western part of the American continent, in all its great extent from north to south, offers so many sharp changes of elevation and, consequently, so many factors that contribute constantly to interrupting the regularity of the isotherms, that the traveler can at one moment find himself subjected to tropical heat and, a short way farther on, surrounded by polar ice. California can consider the cherry and the apple native to its soil, as well as cotton and pineapples — and putrid fevers, too, where the full impact of a burning sun strikes as yet undeveloped areas.

In summer, as in spring, the mornings and afternoons are cool, and midday is very hot. The dews of spring, summer, and autumn are abundant; the winters, despite their torrential rains, are mild.

To my late lamented friend Dr. Pretott[85] I owe the following thermometric observations corresponding to the year 1849:

AVERAGE TEMPERATURES
(FAHRENHEIT)

Spring	66°
Summer	70°
Autumn	67°
Winter	61°

The hottest month reached 74°; the coldest, 48°.

---

84. In the text: "entre los grados 32, 28 y 42 de latitud norte," but this makes no sense unless "32, 28" be taken for the very precise "32.28." The corresponding passage in the author's *Diario de un viaje a California (1848–1849)* (Buenos Aires and Santiago de Chile: Editorial Francisco de Aguirre, 1971), 137, reads "between 32 and 41½ degrees north latitude." JP.

85. I have never before seen this name and have not found it in any materials dealing with the California of the Gold Rush period. Perhaps this friend's name was really Prescott, though I cannot identify anyone by that name either. JP.

Returning now to the thread of my narrative, from which I have momentarily strayed only to comply with the traveler's duty always to tell the truth, the tertian fevers and others equally pernicious caused such ravages among the Chileans and other foreigners residing in Sacramento or passing through there that I was astonished to see that the authorities, on which in Chile we always rely for everything, did not at least set up some kind of shed as a minimal hospital for the needy who were dying bereft of everything, after wandering about emaciated and shivering, begging for the help that the selfishness of the times denied them.

The Yankee authorities saw the spread of that dreadful epidemic quite unmoved, convinced as they were that charitable works are the province of the individual and not the government, which ought to participate in them only once individual initiative has proclaimed its inadequacy. It fell to Chileans to perform deeds of this kind. Two noble and charitable hearts, Don Manuel and Don Leandro Luco, were in Sacramento in charge of the Chilean bark *Natalia;* like so many other Chileans, they had come to El Dorado only to find ruin, for all their enormous efforts. These two worthy youths, with a selflessness unheard of in those times, turned their *Natalia* into a hospital and place of refuge for their needy compatriots; to this act of extraordinary generosity many Chileans owed their lives, among them two of my brothers, a brother-in-law, a young Sepúlveda from Santiago, and several more whose names I omit.

In this distressing situation, we put everything aside to help the Lucos in their philanthropic enterprise. It fell to me to play the twofold role of physician and priest, insofar as a layman can exercise this ministry. The Lucos were nurses and cooks; my other companions served as aides and gravediggers, the former staying up all night and the latter digging graves in which to bury those of our countrymen who were leaving us forever.

Once the epidemic began to ebb, we decided to leave Sacramento as soon as possible and therefore sold all we had, along with our vessel, to be delivered in San Francisco; and with a capital of six thousand pesos, the result of our original investment, which did not exceed thirteen hundred, we set sail for that place.

What had we done since the rightly joyful day that had seen us arrive in California? For a while we had been in the freight business; we had been miners, and things had gone badly for us in the mines despite our strenuous efforts to avoid such an outcome; we had been merchants, and while going at it with every deceitful trick of the trade we had made lots of money but lost time, which in California was worth more than our profits; we had become Frenchmen, drowned, been poisoned, and been both doctors and gravediggers, professions that, although they go hand in hand, had profited us not at all. What was there left for us to be? By now we were starting to believe that if we founded a hat factory our bad luck would see to it that men were born headless, but then the sight of the gold dust scattered around the floors of the cafés gave us the idea of setting up a hotel.

In California the sharply pointed legs of a compass never measured anything but a straight line between the conception of a project and its immediate implementation. For our new purpose, therefore, we entered into partnership with two sons of General Lastra, who, like us, were trying to make a go of it in those parts. For three thousand pesos we bought a lot on Dupont Street[86] that two months earlier we had turned down when it was offered to us gratis, because it seemed to us dear even at that price; and supplied with lumber and carpenter's tools, which we knew how to use, we began with the help of a Yankee to cut, plane, and chisel so determinedly that within days—because in California a month was a century—we raised our splendid pile, composed of a lounge and three bedrooms on the ground floor, four bedrooms upstairs, and a privy, which was a luxury then in San Francisco and which we placed like a sentry box at a prudent distance from the palace itself. I mention this chamber because many Chileans, and among other gentlemen our dear compatriot Don J. M. I., spent many a night, for lack of more comfortable accommodations, resting there, as the King of Spain might have done in the softest bed.

At the same time we dug a well for drinking water; this work was entrusted to Don Juan Nepomuceno Espejo, who, instead of wielding his accustomed light pen, worked with the heavy iron of a rough crowbar in a way to rival the huskiest yokel. He would dig on the bottom of a pit and dump the soil and stones into a bucket that I would then haul up with a rope. I remember that when the water came to his knees he called up to me in a sepulcral voice, "Vicente, do you suppose this is deep enough? You know, I'm working my . . . off." And the only answer he received was, "Just keep at it, my friend. No work, no pay!"

We hired a famous French cook called Monsieur Michel, who, in addition to his room and board, worth two hundred pesos a month, received a salary of five hundred, for a total of 8,400 pesos a year, which is a good deal more than a cabinet minister makes in Chile. On the door of the new establishment we placed a large sign reading *The Citizens' Restaurant,* and in midsummer of 1849 we began our operations.

86. *Dupont Street,* now Grant Avenue, largely in Chinatown. JP.

Needless to say, business was excellent at the start, because in California everything was excellent at the start and only foundered at the midpoint. We owned the restaurant and served in it, too; and except for a few forgivable occasions when we forgot our role, we did not serve all that badly.

One of our regulars was a mulatto, recently elevated to the rank of gentleman but not yet cured of his rustic habits. When he ordered, he did so in a tyrannical way and with a very unpleasant demeanor. Milk was still the height of luxury in San Francisco; and since I had not drunk any since the siren from whom we had bought the horse in Sacramento had so kindly offered us some, one morning the devil tempted me, and in two swallows I almost drank up all I had set aside for our gentrified customer's breakfast. I made up the shortage with water and went about my usual tasks.

I was just serving what the Gringos call a *cock's tail*[87] to a casual patron when I had to drop everything to attend to the stream of curses that Mr. Fatlips was directing at my brother Federico because of the sort of milk he was serving him. The manners of that would-be gentleman had made Federico forget his role as waiter, and he had reached the point of clenching his fist when I arrived in the nick of time to intervene and save the reputation of the restaurant. With a great deal of bowing and scraping I removed the filthy water from the sight of the offended patron to whom it had been offered as milk, took it to the kitchen, poured it into another pitcher, and hurried back with this new container to the scion of Africa, who exclaimed, "That's more like it!" How many might there not be among the high and mighty who have been brought to swallow millstones by a little courteous deference!

After closing late at night, we would all sit on the floor to wash the dishes, then appoint someone to get up early the next morning to sweep and wash the floors and get everything ready for the day, and finally go to bed as happy as every other innkeeper.

Such was our life during the short time we were partisans and agents of *restoration;* but since the business did not require so many hands and I was unable to forget the incident with the milk, on pretext of extending our sphere of action I obtained my partners' permission to make a journey to Monterey.

I confess that my only real aim was to drink milk there to my heart's content. To achieve this I had to climb the coastal hills on foot and in the same way cover the ninety-five miles that lie between the two towns; but what was all that for a veteran of bodily travails, compared with a

---

87. In the original, *"cola de gallo."* JP.

few days' relief far from the strenuous masked ball in which he had been dancing since his arrival in California? What was all that, compared especially with the hope of raising to my parched lips whole jugs of pure, white, foaming milk?

It may seem trivial, but I remember that when in 1828 some Indians of the Osage tribe of North America came to Paris, they began, despite being lodged in the palace of Charles X, to waste away with homesickness; they would have died had the smell of whale oil, which was then used for illumination, not made them exclaim, "Bring us barrels of this nectar, which is more precious to us than the curtains that are stifling us and the damned fancy stews with which these European natives delude their stomachs!"

In the cool of a beautiful July morning, therefore, with my rifle slung over my shoulder, my pistols and a slim belt stuffed with gold at my waist, a filthy felt hat, and a serape, I boldly set out on foot through the hills that lie between San Francisco and the former capital of Upper California.

In the company of some Sonorans who were heading home in disillusionment, I passed the first hills, which they call the Coastal Range, and then entered an extensive valley covered with grass and flowers and crowded with birds and especially with so many squirrels that these nimble and engaging quadrupeds seemed to be sprouting as though by magic from beneath our feet. Herds of deer came to look us over, as do our guanacos, and dashed away at our least movement, only to stop suddenly and come back once more. In this valley, as everywhere, one is surprised by the number of very useful trees. The live oak, the pine, and the ash seem inexhaustible. The land across the bay from San Francisco is covered with redwoods very similar to our larch, and these trees certainly rival the giants of our southern forests in size. On my previous excursions I had the opportunity to marvel at the splendid grove at the Mariposas gold field. There I saw trees that were from ninety to a hundred yards tall, and from twenty-eight to thirty-one yards in circumference at their base, and, what is still more surprising, with lateral branches, three and a half yards in diameter, growing out at a height of forty-five yards. These wonders of the vegetable kingdom, which science calls *sequoia gigantea,* have so many names in California that the traveler is at a loss for which to employ. Some call them *grizzly giants;* others, *red woods;*[88] the English call them *Wellingtons,* the Yankees, *Washingtons,* and we might call them *San Martíns.*

We camped under a live oak; and all night long we were disturbed by the visits of the coyotes, who approached us with hunger and evil intentions.

88. "Pino colorado," i.e., "red pine," which I have translated above as *redwood.* JP.

Fear of coyotes is what drove Señor Ortiz A., a dainty Argentine dandy well known in Santiago, from California. He was trying to do as others did and ventured out on a trail by himself, where they relentlessly pursued him until they drove him screaming back into town. These accursed animals plundered our larder by dispatching, almost under our very noses, the remains of a deer that was to serve as our next day's breakfast.

As during my earlier encounters with Sonorans and Spanish Californians, I now again had occasion to marvel at how naively these poor people view the invasion and conquest of their homeland by the Yankees. They believe themselves incapable of expelling those whom until now they rightly consider tyrants; but, having seen how vigorously the Chileans have resisted brutal persecution by the Yankees, they are also firmly convinced that the Chileans could expel them if they wanted to. In my company, therefore, they seemed to feel as safe from all possible harm as if under the protection of some formidable Fierabrás; but when it was time for us to go our separate ways, the Fierabrás was no less frightened than they at seeing himself alone.

By the afternoon of the third day I was half ruing my escapade, when I was cheered by the not too distant sight of one of the towers of Monterey; and I happily pressed on to reach the town before nightfall.

The harbor of Monterey is one of the best on that coast. The town of Monterey, which until then had been considered the capital of Upper California, was a village similar to our Casablanca in 1840; its population did not exceed fifteen hundred. The country around it and, in general, the whole district, along with Santa Cruz, are the best and most fertile land I have found in the state of California.

The outskirts of this pleasant place were graced by numerous country estates boasting fine groves of trees; although the buildings were of the same style as our massive rural houses of half a century ago, their broad porches facing the road revealed the hospitable character of the Spanish race.

Night was coming on rapidly; and since neither my general appearance nor my far from respectable clothes would allow me to request indoor lodging, I thought I might sleep on the porch of a house whose closed windows and half-open door suggested that its owners were not at that moment in residence. As I drew near, I noticed that the door slammed shut.

"This is a bad sign," I said to myself. "They must have seen me, so why are they slamming the door?"

Nonetheless I stepped onto the porch, knocked softly three times in the Spanish style, and since no one answered, remembering that I was still in California, I gave the silent door two blows with the butt of my rifle that brought an immediate response.

"Who's there?" said a decrepit old woman's voice from inside.

"Praise the Lord, Señora," I replied. "I'm a peaceful traveler, and all I want is permission to lay my serape on your porch floor for the night."

Then I heard people scurrying around inside and a woman's voice that said, "But he's not a Yankee . . . He's Spanish. . . ."

After a belated "Forever and ever, amen!" as reply to my salutation, the door cautiously opened halfway and I saw a gentleman of about forty-five, simply and correctly dressed, who greeted me and asked me what I wanted.

When he heard me speak, he exclaimed with the most unadulterated joy, "God forgive you the scare you've just put us through, my friend! When we saw you coming, we thought you were one of the many rogues that infest our roads and towns, ever since the peace treaty gave us new masters. Come in, sir, please come in!"

And he had been right to take precautions. Only a Californian landowner could know to how many outrages, from which there was no appeal, he might be subjected since the start of the invasion by those they called barbarians from the north.

That charming and hospitable family, composed of a gentleman, his beautiful wife, and two sisters-in-law who could pass for pretty with anyone but seemed like angels to me, was overjoyed at seeing that they were dealing not only with a respectable person but with a Chilean. For Californians, a Chilean veteran of the diggings was the symbol of personal security, the scarecrow to ward off the outrages of the Yankee, and the brother toward whom one's hand should always be outstretched.

Frank cordiality soon reigned between the newcomer and his kindly hosts, who never tired of asking about Chile, about the Chileans living in San Francisco, about my misadventures, and about my objectives in coming to Monterey; they almost split their sides laughing when I told the ladies that the main purpose of my voyage to Monterey was to get my fill of milk there.

Don Juan Alvarado,[89] which was the name of the owner of the house, took me by the hand and led me to his private bedroom; making me promise to stay in his house as long as I could, he succeeded by means of entreaties and even of angry outbursts in making me accept a linen shirt and a jacket, so that my appearance would not be constantly reminding

89. One is tempted to identify Pérez's host with Juan Bautista Alvarado y Vallejo, a former governor of California. The ex-governor, however, seems to have moved from Monterey to San Pablo shortly before Pérez came to California. Furthermore, I should think that something as significant as being an ex-governor would have been mentioned by Alvarado to his guest and reported by the latter in his memoirs. JP.

him of the intruders he so loathed. He left me by myself; and like a second Don Quixote changing clothes in the palace of the duke, after a thorough washing and a bit of trimming of my sideburns, I felt the incomparable delight produced by the delicate coolness of a starched linen shirt against a skin toughened by so prolonged a use of woolen garments. That night I slept in a bed with sheets and a pillow! And the next morning, next to a porch that opened onto a beautiful grape arbor surrounded by gardens, two splendid cows awaited me to fill me with milk, which glass by glass passed to the tireless consumer through the attentive and delicate hands of my host's kindly sisters-in-law. If there is a Seventh Heaven, as they say, I was in that Seventh Heaven!

There is nothing like weariness to teach you to appreciate rest, just as you had to have been an adventurer in the California of those times to appreciate what is meant by comfort.

Through Don Juan I contracted with a rancher to have twelve milch cows and eight oxen delivered in San Francisco; and thinking that a week's easy living was more than sufficient vacation, I informed the family of my impending departure. I was met with entreaties of the kind with which only the Latin race knows how to ply its guests; when they told me that they wanted to hold a party in my honor on the evening of the next day, I gladly yielded to the wishes of these kind people.

A goodly crowd came for this occasion, and the fair sex of Monterey reminded me of that of Chile: refined, charming, and always eager to please. The not-so-fair sex had many of the traits that characterize the frank and easy ways of the merry people of our Elqui: if there's an earthquake, let's have a dance to get over the scare; if someone dies other than a friend or relative, everyone's calling for another dance to wipe away the impression left by the funeral procession; and if there are reasons to be joyful, by all means let's have still another dance! The rooms were decorated in a rustic but bright and cheerful fashion; and it was a pleasure to behold the porches and passageways next to the parlor, adorned with green boughs and flowers forming arches and borders, all illuminated with wax candles, the height of luxury at that time. In each corner of the outer rooms stood small baskets with aromatic bouquets and boxes of cigars of different calibers, in the midst of which burned an elegantly placed spirit flame.

At first I thought that this was for men only; but I was mistaken, because in Monterey, even if a lady does not smoke herself, she gladly puts up with the smoking of others. After the contredanse played on the piano by the sacristan of the nearby chapel, the ladies went out in pairs to walk along the porches; as they passed by the baskets, they took a cigar, lit it with aplomb, and returned to the parlor only after they had thrown away the butt. The mothers had the privilege of smoking in the parlor, but with the very remarkable peculiarity of carefully covering their mouths with their shawl while inhaling, and uncovering it when exhaling.

The Chilean guest of honor was the topic of all conversations; and when toward 2 A.M. the others said their goodbyes to him, they did so as cordial good friends.

The next day I put on my miner's clothes and got ready to leave. The whole family of my genial host accompanied me as far as the outer porch, where to my surprise I found waiting for me, to make my trip more comfortable, a superb mule with the most splendid Mexican saddle I had ever seen, adorned with gold-embroidered velvet and, on the saddle horn, a beautiful eagle's head of solid silver. It was impossible to turn down Don Juan's insistence that I accept that present, that trifle, as he said; and after an effusive and fond farewell, I left that oasis in my journey across the desert of cold selfishness, mounted on my fine mule and trotting with a head full of hopes along the old and only road to San Francisco.

It seemed an age since I had left that extraordinary town, so much had it grown by the time I returned! I have already mentioned that there was hardly a well-known family in Chile that did not have its representative in California. Those few days of absence sufficed for me to find the place full of new faces belonging to compatriots of mine, though almost all of them seemed lost and even rueful of being there, because the enterprise that only yesterday had seemed like a surefire success had now become a synonym of ruin.

Amidst the laments of the disillusioned, many of whom had to pay more to unload the goods they had brought with them than they were worth on land, my partners and I continued to make futile efforts to struggle against the tide of discouragement that was tugging at us. I sold my mule for six hundred pesos and my splendid saddle for seven hundred. My brother-in-law Felipe Ramírez went to work delivering firewood to hotels; my brother César, milking cows and selling the milk on the streets; we deputized Federico to return to our dear mother; and I and the remaining partners ran the restaurant.

In San Francisco everything became special, because everything was carried to extremes. Only a timid soul would settle for the middle ground.

Until then we had evidently had to do only with men, because in the famous capital of El Dorado, women, as the French say, shone by their absence until halfway through 1849. Awareness of the need for the presence of the fair sex arose as soon as gold fever began to subside; and since half a loaf is better than none, the spirit of enterprise, which seeks to profit even from the corruption of morals, suggested to the owners of gambling halls the bizarre idea of decorating the walls of their rooms with a repulsive display of naked women. These daubings, produced with the coarse brush of the house painter, would anywhere else have put even the most shameless satyr to flight; but there they lined the unscrupulous pockets of the owners of such treasures with gold. Good business sense, concluding from this evidence that if so much money can be made off shadows, the original that produces them ought to yield at least twice as much, set off without further ado in search of flesh-and-blood women.

On its first voyage the Panama steamer brought two daughters of Eve, of the kind they call ladies of easy virtue. When the men who had gone to the western headland to see the steamer come in spied parasols and women's bonnets, they became so enthusiastically agitated and so eager to reach the pier that, sweeping along all whom they met on the way, they formed a group of well over a thousand at the water's edge. Once the anchor had been dropped, a most original dispute arose on board between the two damsels errant and the ship's purser. The pair wanted to land before anyone else; the purser objected, saying that the agreement was for them to pay their passage on reaching San Francisco; and the bolder of the two women, on the grounds that "time is money," was already threatening to sue the frightened purser for damages with interest, when two onlookers, tired of waiting in a boat, climbed on board, flung a bag of gold at the obstinate fellow's feet, and took both newcomers ashore amid general jubilation. The happy throng parted; and on the arms of their fortunate saviors, scattering salutations and receiving cheers, the ladies soon disappeared among the huts that lined the streets, followed from afar by the lascivious and envious glances of those who had failed to show due regard for the maxim that "time is money."

It was to be expected that the owners of the steamer, pleased with the high transportation charges that female merchandise could pay on reaching San Francisco, would try to load, as indeed they did, as many bales of this sort as possible. Seven more came on the next voyage and were received with the same gallantry as the first, while still more reinforcements were under way.

The café owners were alarmed by the competition posed to their ill-painted gargoyles by the more substantial gargoyles that were arriving, and so they thought up and put into effect the most grotesque and obscene scheme that human brazenness could invent in such a case. They hired those disgusting persons at their weight in gold to form *tableaux vivants* in the cafés; they set up pedestals on both sides of their rooms, on which, totally nude and in indecent postures, they placed those images of Californian modesty and decorum.

At 8 P.M. and to the sound of music, the door to the exposition opened. The curious, after leaving at the entrance a good part of the gold dust in their pouches, would barely begin to look things over when, pushed by those coming after them, they were forced to leave, cursing, through the door opposite. I remember that a respectable Chilean, Don J. E., whose name there is no reason to make more explicit, told me, "The devil tempted me, pal, and they've almost cleaned out all the gold I had in my pocket, half a pound! I was pouring the price of admission onto the scales when a push from behind made me spill almost everything I had in my bag and move on cursing without being able to go back to collect my overpayment!"

This business, however, only lasted a little over a month, because the steamers no longer came with a few but with whole cargoes of women, all of them under obligation to pay their fare on board one day after arrival. The accelerating pace of this process was such that what at the outset had come by the dozen, later came by the gross, until in 1853 the arrivals totaled 7,245, at which point the lucrative business began to founder.

If the scenes I have just described were repulsive, those that I shall now recount before putting aside this part of my notes will be equally astonishing.

At night, outside the door of the room occupied by each of the first Messalinas to arrive, those who wished to be the first to enter and greet them would have at each other with cudgels and pistols; the women, who knew very well that no gold was to be gotten from the defeated or the dead, would rush out to pacify their suitors, making use of arguments that modesty forbids my repeating.

Once the demand for women had somewhat abated thanks to the many shipments that the steamers were bringing, the captains, in order to protect their profits, decided to auction off the price of passage. The highest bidder would carry off the prize, and the captain would apply the amount bid against the charges due. Thus the strangest and most grotesque scenes would take place. With the objects to be auctioned off standing on the quarterdeck tricked out in all their spurious adornments, the auctioneer, taking one of these hussies by the hand and singing the praises of her form, youth, and beauty, would call out, "Gentlemen, how much would you be prepared to pay right now to have this beautiful lady come from New York to pay you a special visit?" The bidding would begin at once; the highest bidder, as soon as he heard the hammer fall, handed over the gold dust and took possession of his goods.

But it is time to turn this page. May the charming sex that makes up the fairer half of the human race forgive me if, to designate these vile mammals in skirts, I have been forced to name them with the name with which we designate the angels of our homes. Even among the chosen of the Lord there was a Lucifer.

Vices of this sort were not by any means, however, the only kind of muck beneath which the foundations of what in time was to be a rich and sovereign state were then being laid. Theft, murder, arson, and gambling also had a prominent part in it.

Every night the sound of music in some gambling dens, or that of the drum or the Chinese gong in others, called the faithful to be fleeced amid the inebriation produced by drink and dancing. Every night there were injuries, fisticuffs, and thrashings; and every night new bankrupts would go out to recoup their losses through theft or robbery.

I had occasion to witness a card game in which a wily Oregonian took part. This man stepped up to the table and without saying a word set a small bag that might have held about a pound of gold dust on one of the cards, and he lost. Just as silently and gravely he set down another bag of the same size and lost it, too. Unperturbed, he then removed from his waist a slim belt, which must have contained about six pounds of gold, set it on a card, drew his revolver, cocked it, and pointing it at the dealer, quietly awaited the result. He won!

"So I won, did I?" he said sarcastically, calmly picking up his winnings. "That's a lucky break!" And he left. He had won because the shrewd dealer knew very well that the matter could have cost him his life.

But it is only fair to confess that not everything was disorder in San Francisco. In the midst of all that commotion people were also thinking of the political future. The military government had long since been rejected by the resolutely libertarian spirit embodied in each one of the adventurers who planned to settle in California. These men also wanted the new territory to be raised, and soon, to the rank of a sovereign state. To add weight to this legitimate aspiration, which had lately reached the point of imperious demands and caused many a step in this direction to be taken in Washington, it was proposed to choose delegates to a convention, not in Monterey, as had been suggested earlier, but in San Jose, where the governor was to have his capital.

Public meetings were consequently held for this purpose everywhere, and the candidates for the office of delegate began immediately to mobilize their respective connections. Large groups with flags and impromptu bands marched up and down the streets, each accompanying its favored candidate, who, carrying a large portfolio containing his political platform, would go from house to house in search of support. If the man approached was willing to grant it, he gave his name; otherwise, he simply said that he was already committed to someone else. In the former case, three cheers accompanied by music and even by some gunshots in the air celebrated the future vote; in the latter, the candidate settled for saying, "I'm sorry; maybe another day," and the procession went on in silence to the next house.

Each candidate chose a color for the ribbons that were to adorn his supporters' hats on election day, and the town's taverns and hotels raised their candidates' colors and provided free food and drink to all who came with the appropriate ribbon.

Once the voting stations had been set up under the vigilant eyes of as many groups of beribboned poll watchers as there were candidates, the latter, on horseback and accompanied by some friends, trotted along all the streets of the city calling their supporters and turning up at every station, where they were received with wild cheers by their political coreligionists. The speeches of the candidates, always from atop their four-footed dais, filled the air, along with answering shouts from the supporters of their rivals. The barrels and tables on which these hecklers climbed so as better to be heard were overturned. Circles of onlookers formed and dissolved around those who discussed their preferences with their fists. But not one gunshot, not one injury! That day all weapons fell silent. How different from what happens in other countries! What is more, once the election was over, all the voters adopted the color of the winner and forgot their private preferences to cheer the choice of the majority, with as much jubilation and thoroughgoing enthusiasm as if they had themselves had a part in his triumph.

In terms of the business opportunities that had attracted so great and so varied a mass of speculators to it, California had in the meantime, ever since the orders or disorders of the worthy Governor Smith, lost almost all the charm it had held for the foreign adventurer. The need now, as everywhere, was not simply for foreign labor that would successfully work on its own account, but for hired and taxpaying labor. It was therefore not surprising that those who did not possess ample capital should beat a discouraging retreat. We were already planning to do the same when fortune, which had treated us so badly, gave us the coup de grâce that sent us packing from that once-promised land or land of promise, one of those frightful fires that wiped out everything in the final months of 1849.[90]

90. Every edition of Pérez's work consulted gives this date as 1850, but this must be either a slip on the author's part or another faithfully repeated misprint. Pérez says that he started his restaurant business in mid-summer of 1849 and continued in it for a "short time," which

We had gone to bed about two hours before, having decided to sell everything and return to Chile, when a flickering red light came through the panes of our window to illuminate the room in which we were sleeping. The fire had been deliberately set, according to rumor, in the hotel with the abovementioned famous *tableaux vivants.* Since this establishment was more than three blocks from ours, it never entered our minds that the fire could reach us. We were already celebrating the misfortune of those miscreants and calculating our splendid profit from the rise in the value of houses, when, an hour and a half later, fate came to prove to us that the gleam of a liquidation, while it may indeed gleam, is not always profitable. The fire spread in all directions with the same sickening speed with which we sometimes see it spread in Chile in some of our wheat fields at harvest time. In the midst of that immense roaring bonfire, stoked by the explosion of barrels of gunpowder that filled the air with sparks and flaming timbers, everything was soon invaded by burning boards carried by the wind. The fire surrounded us on all sides, and like everyone else we saved ourselves only by the speed of our flight.

A week later, the bustling freight agents, the modest launderers of not very clean clothes, the voyagers on the *Dicey My Nana,* the tireless miners with pick, shovel, and pan, the defeated in Sonora, the owners of the *Impermeable,* the charming and, like so many others, crooked merchants in Sacramento, the doctors and gravediggers, the carpenters and builders, the innkeepers and waiters, now converted, some into sailors, others into expert pilots, were setting out for the Southern Ocean in an abandoned bark that, for lack of a crew, had been left to rot in San Francisco. After an unenviable odyssey of two-and-a-half months spent hauling on cables, furling sails, and guessing latitudes, miraculously saved from crashing against the headland of Piñón del Gallo, they tenderly embraced their weeping mother in peaceful Chile.

We went for wool and, like so many others, we came back shorn, but satisfied because we had steadfastly stood our ground till we had fired our last shot.

hardly suggests a year and a half. Other events he mentions in these pages leading up to his return to Chile also belong in 1849: the arrival of women midway through that year, and the elections (August 1, 1849) for a constitutional convention. This convention met in Monterey (though San Jose was to be the capital thereafter) in September and October 1849, and the resulting document was approved by the voters in November of the same year. News of California's admission to the Union reached San Francisco on October 18, 1850, an event that Pérez Rosales would certainly have mentioned had he witnessed it. Finally, several of the dates given in subsequent chapters are inconsistent with that originally given here. The author must thus have left California toward the end of 1849, reaching Chile, after a journey of two and one-half months, in early 1850. The surviving text of Pérez Rosales's *Diario de un viaje a California* (*1848–1849*) breaks off before reaching the conclusion of his California adventure. JP.

X I X

*A tempting invitation to write a vitriolic newspaper.— I am
appointed an immigration agent in Valdivia. — The civil
servant and the personal servant. — Corral.— The town of
Valdivia.— The province of Valdivia. — What immigration
meant for many people. — Unjustifiable encroachment on
public lands and means for gaining ownership of them.*

They say that as soon as poverty comes in through the door of a house,
virtue escapes through the window. There is a good deal of truth in
that, though not because there are no remedies against the disease poverty,
but because of the patient's ridiculous reluctance to take them. A distinguished name, a former position in society, and our national concern with
"What will people say?" are the worst enemies of the benefit that modest
labor always yields to those who seek it. In his own country, no one dares to
be a shopkeeper after having bought box tickets to the theater. In California, how many would have starved to death or turned to banditry if concern for their name had kept them from being stevedores or bootblacks?

On my downward path I had reached the lowest rungs on the fragile ladder of fortune; in California I had reached what seemed to me the lowest rung of all, that of personal service as a waiter, and it never occurred to me that an even lower one remained for me to tread, that of a minor civil servant! Because I did not know that there are more than enough jobs everywhere for servants, while everywhere there is a lack of jobs for the rest of us.

The servant, either out of his own ingratitude or because of some brutal offense he has suffered, cheerfully leaves his master, because he knows that next door, even if his situation does not improve, he will at least have what he had before, while the civil servant who leaves his post, willingly or not, instead of finding a similar position elsewhere finds only disillusionment, hunger, and poverty, unless he's willing to come down a peg or two.

I had lost everything, except honor; but honor alone was not going to keep the wolf from the door.

I was mulling this over one morning while casting an expert eye on a pair of coach horses that a sister of mine was to buy, when two well-known individuals, whose names are not to the purpose here, came into the stable in search of me and initiated the following dialogue:

"Here's the Californian, Don José, wasting his time looking at horses."

"Good morning, gentlemen; at your service. And you're right, I was having a look at these horses."

"They're fine horses, but it's odd that a man like you should spend his time on something like this."

"And what should I be spending my time on now? As you know, after California, looking is all I can do, and so I look."

"Always our cheerful Pérez! And wouldn't it be better for you to spend your time on something that brings you some profit, without investing any capital other than what you have? On something like . . . writing for a newspaper, for example?"

"Writing for a newspaper? I of all people should start that all over again?"

"Yes, you, and don't laugh."

"And who'd be so rash as to give half a *real* for my scribblings?"

"We would," said the two at the same time.

"You? How's that?"

"By paying you good money for whatever you write in keeping with our suggestions."

"Well, if that's the way it is, I'll take up my cross, provided that the topics I'm to write about are ones I know a little something about and that your suggestions are in keeping with those of my conscience."

I noticed that they were as pleased with the first part of my reply as they were displeased with the second, and this made me begin to have my misgivings. They walked around and looked over the stable, talking to each other in a low voice; then, resuming our curious conversation, my interlocutor continued as follows:

"To write in opposition to a bad government is an obligation that rather than trouble the conscience soothes it, and we only want you to write against the government and nothing else."

"You've come to the wrong man! It's been ages since I knew what a government is, or whether the men who rule us now are Moors or Christians, or what they're doing or have done or failed to do. With that kind of preparation I'd be in big trouble if I started to shoot my mouth off, or my pen! Besides, I don't understand. . . ."

"My dear Don Vicente," interrupted the second tempter, a short chubby man with a smug round face, "you are a liberal, and you only stopped fighting in defense of your party when you thought that its permanence was assured by the marriage of the hero of Yungay with the daughter of the father of all liberals.[91] You have been deceived, as have we. The conservatives and the tobacco monopoly are ruining us, and there's no hope they might reform the iniquitous Constitution of 1833 and give the country back what it ought never to have lost, that of '28 . . . Am I making myself clear?"

"I think I'm beginning to understand."

"Splendid, and let's leave it there. We have a meeting at two this afternoon. I'm going to announce that we can count on you; this evening, at seven, so as not to arouse any suspicions, we'll be waiting for you, along with some other friends, on the oval of the Alameda."

Evening came, and with it came to the designated place this new political Adam who still did not see how he could bite into an apple so long forgotten; but fifteen minutes later, there he was, surrounded by tempting serpents, chatting with them amicably while sprawled on a comfortable park bench.

The suggestions of the governing board soon became clear to me. There was no talk of infringement of rights, nor of violated laws or damsels, and even less trumpeting of principles, because what these men were after was not principles, generally of a vaporous sort, but their own selfish ends.

Their project was to found a scorpion of a newspaper, with a deadly sting; its ink would be petroleum, and its words, fire. The aim was not

91. General Manuel Bulnes, President of Chile from 1841 to 1851, married a daughter of General Francisco Antonio Pinto, a former president and a leader of the liberal party. EOV.

to leave a governmental bone unbroken, and the plan was to be against everything. At times I suspected they might be tanners, so determined did they seem to skin everyone alive; to be sure, they were prepared to pay handsomely for the job, because when they bestowed the position of chief skinner on me, they offered me thirty gold *onzas* a month for the fruit of my labor. What a letdown! . . . There I was, facing them alone, and not answering them while I hastily leafed through the dictionary of my memory in search of one of those resounding Spanish exclamations to throw in their faces. They took my silence for consent and were already talking about distributing far and wide one of those inevitable circulars that always hide a nest of vipers beneath the plumage of a guileless dove, when instead of the "yes" they were so sure of they found themselves listening to a few unvarnished and unflattering truths.

Two days after our negotiations had come to this crashing end, and when I was least expecting it, I was called into the office of Señor Varas, who was at the time Minister of the Interior. To this day I cannot explain why I was thus favored, since I knew Varas only by name, and the government offices only from the outside. Two weeks after my interview with the minister I had been given the title of immigration agent and was sailing toward Valdivia to oversee, on behalf of the government, the work of settlement in that remote province, where expeditions of German immigrants were expected at any moment.

I reached the very important and very neglected harbor of Corral, or Coral, as some who prefer a more refined language usually call it,[92] on February 12, 1850, after sailing past the abandoned fortresses that in Spanish times defended the quiet and picturesque mouth of the lovely inlet of Valdivia.

The town, or rather the scattered poor huts of this harbor, for whose defense Spain had invested millions, consisted of twenty-eight badly placed dwellings, some facing the shore and others, for unknown reasons, facing the surrounding wooded hills.

From Corral on, the extremely dense vegetation that covered most of the province made it very difficult to travel from one point to another, no matter how close. The sturdy trees that overlooked the harbor and the even larger ones that bordered the river seemed to be rivals for the right to bathe their robust roots in those salty waters. Since there were no usable paths along the riverbanks, the only practicable route between

92. I presume that this means that some considered "Corral" to have too much of the barnyard about it, while "Coral" is more decorative. JP.

the port and the provincial capital, Valdivia, was the river; it took four hours to go from one point to the other by small boat.

One would think that our little Valdivia River, which we consider gigantic, would offer nothing to attract the attention of one who has sailed the imposing rivers of California; but in fact, all the beauties of unspoiled nature, all the magnificent views scattered along the banks of the latter are also to be found along the Valdivia, painted on a smaller canvas but none the less complete for all that.

We reached Valdivia. Good Lord! If by some magic or diabolical cunning the founder of that town could have accompanied me on this trip, he would certainly have turned back cursing the negligence of his descendants. I still possess an oil painting that shows the sad appearance of that collection of huts three days after my arrival, a most lifelike product of the skillful brush of the late lamented Simón, now much sought after by some honest old Valdivians who want to seize it, throw it into the fire, and thus make ashes of that irrefutable witness to their hometown's backwardness.

The layout of this town, which was very regular for the time of its founding, had over the years deteriorated to the point that the sidewalks were no longer parallel and the streets no longer of a uniform width. The houses, all very low and generally with a porch facing the street, had walls of oak logs, roofs of larch boards covered with moss and volunteer plants, and barred windows, some of which had glass panes.

Since carts were quite unknown there, deliveries of firewood were made by dragging enormous tree trunks down the streets with oxen and leaving them in front of the houses where they had been ordered and where each day's supply would then be obtained with the kitchen hatchet. On the western side of the Plaza de Armas, the town's only square, stood an unfinished wooden church, where everything was lacking with the exception of two very high towers, which for no known reason rose proudly, if disproportionately, over the entrance. The Plaza de Armas served not only as a drill ground and a place to take a stroll, as in some of our other towns; the inhabitants of Valdivia knew how to get more use out of that four-sided piece of public urban real estate. On it, if not in the middle of the streets, they staked out the hides of the cows they killed for food; garbage was dumped there; and, lacking an appropriate place in the jail, the prisoners were constantly coming out to do on that long-suffering square what cannot be mentioned in polite language. Soil from the square was hauled off for use in the construction of private houses. I remember that so much filth was dumped beneath the rickety wooden box set on posts that served as courthouse that the judge, who at the time was the modest and upright magistrate Don Ramón Guerrero, was forced to issue a heated demand for an end to so foul an offense.

This is the origin of that story of the famous vessel bought by the municipal authorities for the use of prisoners, a story that I told in my *Sueños que parecen verdades y verdades que parecen sueños,*[93] and that many people have considered purely fictitious or a mere literary exercise.

This matter of the chamber pot was typical of everything. The spirit of local improvement, the urge to learn something, the common natural desire to ameliorate conditions through enterprise and work—all were asleep, vegetating. Buildings, like imaginations, were peacefully overgrown with that moss that only appears and spreads on the bark of neglected trees or of those that are in the throes of the final decay that turns them into earth. No traveler, Chilean or foreign, came to Valdivia but he exclaimed, "All the works of nature here are as great, as imposing, and as beautiful as the works of man are mean, unkempt, and disagreeable."

Far be it from me to seek to offend the inhabitants of those remote places with my tale. I simply tell the unvarnished truth of what then struck my eyes, as it did those of anyone who came from outside to settle in Valdivia.

The spirit of progress was only dormant, not dead; if I now preserve this wretched picture, my aim is rather to use its darkness as a foil for the bright colors of one that could be painted today, than to satisfy some foolish appetite for baseless calumny. The spirit of progress existed even then, and so much so that the presence of a foreign element, even on a very small scale, has sufficed not only to awaken the province of Valdivia from the stupor into which neglect had sunk it, but also to make it fully equal to its proud northern sisters in terms of its material and intellectual conditions, its commerce, and its special industries, which brook no competition in domestic or foreign markets.

Be all that as it may, leaving California to move directly into the Valdivia of that time was to leave the region of the most feverish activity to enter that of the deepest and most peaceful slumber. The relatively well-to-do sought nothing from work but what was strictly necessary to maintain the middling standard of living with which they appeared to be quite satisfied. The farmhands, because of the low wage offered for their labor and the abundance of foodstuffs, worked a little only to get drunk and

93. *Diccionario de "el Entrometido": Sueños que parecen verdades y verdades que parecen sueños* (*The Busybody's Dictionary: Dreams that seem true, and truths that seem like dreams*). JP.

sleep a lot. The former, like the latter, lacked the stimulus that only foreign immigration can supply to a society stupefied by inertia.

But I do not want to get ahead of myself.

Once the clamor and natural enthusiasm provoked among the northern population by Cochrane's glorious seizure of the mighty fortresses of Corral had faded away, the province of Valdivia, better known in Spanish times than after independence, remained for more than a quarter of a century, if not wholly forgotten, then at least as a simple and rather unimportant territory trusting to the natural effects of time to merit, sooner or later, the same solicitous attention that the government bestowed on the central provinces. The very title of garrison, by which it was still known, seemed to condemn it to perpetual oblivion; but the Intendant Cavareda, despite the guarded style of writing then in fashion, published a brief tract that partially lifted the veil hiding the skies and natural riches contained in that distant corner of our mainland provinces. To the amazement understandably produced by the revelations of this official, the province of Valdivia owes the importance of the political position that it now occupies by the side of its sisters and the degree of relative prosperity that it now enjoys.

A temperate climate; absence of dreadful diseases, as well as of hostile natives and dangerous wild beasts; abundant and in general uncultivated land; arable soil, in many places very fertile; plentiful raw materials for manufacturing and industry; inexhaustible forests of excellent timber for construction, shading the deep, tranquil, and navigable system of the tributaries of the Valdivia, a waterway that after traversing an extensive territory flows gently into the sea in one of the most secure and accessible harbors on the Pacific coast: what more could forgotten Valdivia need in order to be forgotten no more? Population! But not a population born among riches, feeling no urge to better its condition, not even suspecting the existence of the comforts that grace the life of a cultivated man and that agriculture, commerce, and industry daily satisfy and increase, but a population that the spirit of enterprise or of the liberal ideas of our age drives from the great centers of civilization to come to virgin America, both to enjoy the tangible benefits of liberty and to garner in abundance the riches that we, ignorant of their value, disdain.

A country like ours absolutely requires the active collaboration of the foreign element, a powerful factor that, as it tries to enrich itself, enriches the country offering it shelter, that turns wastelands into populated regions, and that forms states that, even if called mere colonies, astonish even their homelands by their industry, their commerce, and their prosperity.

Once our government was persuaded of this truth, it fell to the administration of the illustrious General Bulnes to lay the base for foreign immigration to Chile by promulgating the law of November 18, 1845, a law that, adorned with the signatures of that warrior and of the wise statesman Montt, who was then his minister, lays out in clear and generous terms the manner in which we must receive, accommodate, and stimulate this element of life and progress in our country.

The sound of the word "immigration" had set everyone to assess the benefits and evils it might bring to Chile according to his own way of understanding the matter.

The Catholics feared it would destroy our religious unity.

The owners of rural and urban real estate applauded enthusiastically, believing the nonsensical notion that immigration depresses wages, something that has never happened.

Many apparent philanthropists, speculating in fact with the ignorance of the poor masses, took what was being said by the landowners and other such learned men as reason to pity the country's industrial and agricultural workers for the impending competition of cheap foreign labor. Both the landowner and the philanthropist forgot or pretended to forget that if immigration harms anyone temporarily, it is the landowner or the man who can prosper only by paying the lowest wages, but never the laborer, for the simple reason that newcomers from abroad are not and cannot be farm laborers because of the low daily wage that we pay to the ones we already have; since it is not this kind of labor that comes from abroad but persons who give employment to our workers, increased demand will obviously force the level of wages upward.

The merchants of Valdivia thought that with an increase in population the prices of their merchandise would increase.

The owners of uncultivated lands that produced nothing and that they had not even visited because they were kept from doing so by the dense and gloomy forests that hid them even from the light of the sun, were now convinced that in each parcel they had a treasure that the government or the newcomer simply had to buy.

The speculators who seek only the most advantageous placement of their capital saw future immigration solely as a splendid opportunity to increase it and wasted no time in starting to buy up all the land in the province that might be suitable for settlement.

Following the example of these gentlemen, many more or less well-to-do residents of the province did the same thing, without realizing that this eagerness for premature and ill-considered gain was in effect digging a ditch next to the foundations that the law had laid for sheltering the immigrant, a ditch that would cause the entire building to collapse, along with the bright hopes the law awakened in sensible men.

In vain had the government, to avoid this evil, commissioned the energetic and intelligent sergeant major of engineers Philippi to explore and survey the public lands that were to be distributed among the immigrants, a most laborious task in which he was succeeded by the modest and intelligent engineer Frick, while he was sent to Germany and worked tirelessly there to foster immigration to Valdivia; as the arrival of the first expedition became ever more likely, the number of those fraudulently claiming possession of lands justifiably considered vacant became ever greater, so that on the eve of the arrival of the first ship that, trusting in the government's promises, had set out from Hamburg in 1849, one could say that in the whole area to be colonized there was not a single inch of land without some imaginary owner.

The news of this boldfaced pillage, a term warranted by the manner in which these scandalous acquisitions were made, soon reached Europe.

The messages sent to the government by Don Bernardo Philippi during that period are truly distressing. In them he insisted on the urgent need to repossess those lands whose occupation had become common knowledge in Germany, and to do so as soon as possible, because little or nothing could be done in the way of sending emigrants while the government's clear title to the land it was offering was in question.

This is the state in which I found the immigration project when fate brought me to Valdivia, and not because of any neglect on the part of the government, for when I received my letter of appointment I was also given a thick file of official letters, directives, and decrees that made it crystal clear how hard the higher authorities were working to help their agents to overcome the difficulties with which a misguided zeal for profit threatened to destroy immigration in its infancy.

At that time the vast fog-shrouded region of Valdivia, boasting lakes, primeval forests, two beautiful navigable rivers, and abundant vacant land that was thought available for distribution among the immigrants whose arrival was deemed imminent, contained only three hamlets, which, thanks to the isolation produced by the bad condition or total absence of roads, led the life of genuine hermits: Valdivia, which we already more or less know; La Unión, a half-executed sketch of a town; and Osorno, with a stone church, a convent, and heaped rows of overgrown dirt whose regular arrangement showed them to be the ruins of some building.

Before I came to Valdivia, people in the north had such a low opinion of the agricultural production of this province that they believed that not even wheat could be grown there, when in the granaries of La

Unión and Osorno the weevils were eating the wheat, because what little was grown was more than enough for local consumption and there was no way to export the surplus.

Except for the apple orchards that for some reason were to be found everywhere as though lost in the woods, and for plots so close to town or so small and clearly defined that their legitimate or alleged owners could occasionally watch over them, pretty much all of those fields, so productive now and so little prized then, were held in common, whether by the descendants of the Spaniards or by those of the natives, who still considered themselves the legitimate owners of everything. From time immemorial the very neglect in which they lay exposed them to the rapaciousness of the sparse settlers who, simply because they had occupied the clear bank of a river or the seashore, even without being able to penetrate further, considered themselves owners of what they still call *centros.*

If this was the way things were done before anyone thought of immigration, it is hardly surprising that the voice of the government's agent in Europe should inspire many Chileans with an urge to monopolize land, to the point that for many leagues around Valdivia, where the first immigrants were expected, not a span of arable land was left available.

When a citizen wanted to become sole proprietor of some communal land, all he had to do was look for the nearest Indian chief, get him drunk, or get his agent to get drunk along with the Indian, and supply the chief and his people cheap liquor and an occasional peso; that was enough to let him appear before a notary with a seller and witnesses, or declarations under oath, to certify that what was being sold lawfully belonged to that seller. No one objected to this manner of acquiring property, the proceeds of which were amicably shared among the supposed owner-seller and the venal witnesses who accompanied him, on the well-known principle of you scratch my back and I'll scratch yours. The only difficulty that always arose in this smooth and simple maneuver lay in describing the boundaries of the land conveyed, because there was no way to do this in the middle of forests where even the birds often found no soil to land on. But since there is a remedy for everything but death, behold the antidote employed by some to sell what was not theirs and by others to acquire for a pretense of a price what they neither could nor should have bought. If the land sold bordered somewhere on a river, a creek, a chance clearing in the forest, a road, or anything that might be designated with a known name, the problem was as good as solved. This base was measured as far as possible; if it lay to the west of the tract, the latter was declared to extend, with the width so determined, as far as "the high mountains," without taking into account that this might include whole cities; if the accessible border lay to the east, the western edge became the Pacific Ocean; and if it lay to the north or south, sometimes they would say "from there to the Green Forest," as though there were forests other than green, and at other times they would name no limits, as happened with the deeds held by a certain Chomba, which bestowed on their fortunate owner the rights to a broad band of terrain that began at the waters of Reloncaví Bay, and modestly ended in the desert of Atacama.

Do not for a moment think that I am exaggerating. The public records of Valdivia and even of Chiloé are full of such extraordinary property deeds, which each buyer kept like a treasure in his trunk and which gave rise to complicated and interminable lawsuits.

I have dwelt on this matter so that the reader will see what sort of difficulties hampered the work of the government agents charged with distributing unoccupied land to the immigrants, land that they were unable to find anywhere, and what were the unfortunate reasons that the residents of Valdivia and the outside speculators initially had for taking a dim view of the presence of the first foreign immigrants: these land thieves were planning to sell for its weight in gold what had cost them so little, and it was clear to them that as soon as the government learned from its agents what was happening, there would be countermeasures that would affect them for a long time and that would demolish all their fond hopes.

In vain did I travel throughout the province to find some land good enough to please the first immigrants to arrive, knowing that in undertakings of this sort it is absolutely necessary to insure the success of the initial phase. I was troubled on the one hand by the attitude prevailing in the place and on the other by the justifiable fear that if there were no public lands available for immediate distribution, this would be, for the immigrant who had left home and hearth trusting in the government's promises, clear proof that he had been deceived and lured into a wicked snare; and I was preparing to set out for one of the many deserted beaches of Carelmapu, when the commendable attitude of some honorable and discerning public-spirited Valdivians dissuaded me from my plan by helping me to combat the effects of unthinking selfishness with their generous offers. Some cheerfully volunteered to shelter the immigrants in their homes; others, to lend them land near the town for their first plantings; still others, even to lend them oxen—all of it with no remuneration whatsoever.

X X

Arrival of the first immigrants at Corral. — The questions they put to the government agent. — Lessons to be learned from this interview. — An act of generosity by Colonel Viel in support of immigration. — Isla de la Teja. — Additional groups of immigrants.— The sort of people they were, a real treasure for Valdivia. — How Chileans understood immigration. — Advice on this subject pours in to the government. — Muschgay's settlement, sponsored by Domeyko. — Muschgay, the archbishop, and the Larraín family. — The arch-Catholic Muschgay adopts the Araucanian religion. — The dreadful Cambiaso in Valdivia.

As I have had the pleasure of noting at the conclusion of the last chapter, not all Valdivians sacrificed the future well-being of the province to petty immediate profit; but their offers only halfway met the aims of the government and the true interests of the country.

This was the state of affairs when somnolent Valdivia was roused from its habitual lethargy by the news that the bark *Hermann,* proceeding from Hamburg, had reached Corral after a one hundred twenty days' journey, with eighty-five German passengers on board: seventy men, ten women, and five children. These immigrants, who had paid their own passage, came less as a first contingent brought by a firm expectation of gain than as a scouting party eager to learn how much truth there was in the offers that in the government's name Major Bernardo Philippi of the Corps of Engineers was making in Europe to persons who might want to go to Chile. The greater number of them were reasonably well-off men, and some of them had been commissioned by wealthy firms to approach the government with immigration projects that they would underwrite in exchange for more or less extensive grants of vacant lands that they would undertake to populate within an agreed-upon time.

It was thus most imperative that the first impressions received in Chile by this very important vanguard of the future progress of Valdivia should correspond to the hopes as to the hospitality awaiting them among us that they had conceived as they left their homes. I consequently lost no time, upon receiving news of the *Hermann*'s arrival, in setting out for Corral.

After I had boarded the vessel, I introduced myself and explained to the newcomers what was my mission with respect to them, thereby wholly dissipating the natural fear of men newly arrived in a foreign country with no guarantee, beyond a simple promise, of finding there a friendly hand to guide them in their first steps. Timid apprehension was succeeded by the liveliest satisfaction. All crowded around me, all interrogated me most pressingly; their tumultuous questions about our government's sentiments toward them, the eagerness with which they listened to my replies, and the sincere thankfulness with which they received each one of them, all made me suspect that some malicious person had sown distrust in the spirit of these intrepid voyagers.

I immediately arranged for refreshments to be sent them, I indicated to them the provisional lodgings they were to occupy, and after having strongly urged the authorities at Corral to look after them, I left for Valdivia, telling them that since it was my special duty in that province to convey their needs, their first recourse with regard to any problems they might have should always be to me.

Two days after my return a committee composed of six of the most consequential passengers came to Valdivia and asked me to meet with them, which I did on the evening of the 17th. All of them were special agents, some from Hamburg, others from other parts of Germany, sent by emigrant societies for the express purpose of investigating the lay of the land and reporting to their principals detailed and reliable information concerning both the country that would become their home and the privileges conceded to them by the government that was to rule them. I was handed a list of questions, to which I replied as unequivocally as I could, in keeping with the instructions given to Señor Philippi by the government, their further elaboration in subsequent messages to that commissioner, and the applicable immigration law.

At the head of the list appeared a compliment to the Chilean authorities for the cordial reception, and an expression of the immigrants' most sincere gratitude for the kind efforts to mitigate their misfortune in leaving their native land. After this prologue came the following questions, most of which applied to the settlers who had paid their own passage.

1. What measures must the immigrant take to become a Chilean citizen?
2. How long after his arrival can he expect to be naturalized?
3. Can he vote in elections?
4. If there were Protestants among them, would they be obliged to give up their ancestral religion?
5. Could Protestants marry each other?
6. In such cases, what steps must be taken so that the marriage would be considered valid and lawful?
7. Must the children of Protestants be baptized according to Catholic ritual?
8. If not, what must be done to provide proof of the legitimacy of these children?
9. If the settlers should find it expedient to establish villages, can they expect one of their number to be named judge?
10. May they enlist in the militia?
11. Can they count on the cooperation of the government in building public roads?
12. Are the contracts and agreements entered into by them in Germany for implementation in Chile firm and valid here?
13. What are the maximum and minimum values assigned to public lands?
14. If they buy land from private parties, will they have to pay tax on the transaction?
15. How many acres of land can each settler buy from the government?
16. Must payments be made in cash?
17. If they should be unable to pay at the stipulated time, may they pay the normal rate of interest until such time as they can pay the principal?

18. Can the government of Chile give assurance of land for a thousand families?

This curious and interesting questionnaire, drawn up in Germany with a thought for privileges to be preserved if already enjoyed, or sought elsewhere if not, should be consulted whenever one tries to attract voluntary immigration to an unfamiliar region.

It becomes immediately clear that the first aspiration of the emigrant whom necessity, misfortune, or the pursuit of gain obliges to break the bonds linking him to the land where first he saw the light of day is to forge new links to his adoptive country. The second is the free exercise of the religion in which his parents raised him. The third, founding a family; and the last, becoming a landowner.

Nothing gives a man a greater appreciation of life under a free republican government than having been born and being obliged to continue living under the more or less despotic tyranny of a monarchical one. It is consequently not surprising that the emigrant's first aspiration should be to realize the idea of being a citizen of a republic where the words *master* and *serf* have no meaning, where virtue and work constitute nobility, where there are no taxes to be paid but those mandated by laws in whose imposition those who are to bear their effects have a part; even less surprising is it that once he is enabled to found a family and protected in the free exercise of his religion, he should aspire to no more than the for him indispensable title of landowner, be it only of an inch of soil. For the European, whether proprietor of a modest fortune, farm laborer, or simplest farmhand, the certainty of becoming a proprietor, no matter how remote the region that offers him this gift, is the fulfillment of a dream that, though almost never realized, follows him from the cradle to the grave.

It is because they have not ascribed to this aspiration the great importance it has for the immigrant that many of the great landowners of the north have until now failed to understand the unconquerable resistance that even the poorest immigrant in Valdivia opposes to forsaking his not very productive property for the high wages and easy life they offer him on their estates.

One can well say that if you deny the emigrating farmer the chance at once to become a landowner, you deny him everything.

The respectful committee was extremely satisfied with the tenor of my replies; and the worthy and learned Professor Don Carlos Anwandter, its chairman, stood up and, choking with emotion, pronounced these heartfelt words:

We shall be Chileans as honest and hard-working as the best of them. In the ranks of our new compatriots we shall defend our adopted country against any foreign aggression with the resolution and firmness of men who defend their fatherland, their families, and their interests.

When the immigration agent could not immediately fulfill his obligation of conveying to the newcomers the land promised to them, his situation was evidently grounds for despair, just as the immigration project ran an obvious risk in the absence of this basic requirement; but fortunately this situation did not last, thanks to the hand of Providence, which, when stretched out to Chile as it always is, unexpectedly placed in my hands the most felicitous way out of this difficulty.

At that time there lived in Valdivia, as military chief of the province, a worthy old man, Don Benjamín Viel, a former soldier of Napoleon I and a colonel in our army. This delightful and enthusiastic officer, whose head held as much poetry as his selfless heart did generosity, had just secured his future and that of his children—because he was very poor— by acquiring, on good terms and at a low price, the important island of La Teja, formerly belonging to the city and located opposite the town at the confluence of the Calle-Calle and Cruces Rivers, which join to form the Valdivia. When he learned what was happening, Viel, like the best and most patriotic Chilean, did not hesitate a moment in ceding to his adoptive country his rights to a property that was allowing him and his children to enjoy a modest but secure subsistence; and with this act of generous selflessness he saved the day.

The island of La Teja or Valenzuela is the largest and most important of those bathed by the waters of the Valdivia. Its length is 4.82 kilometers, and its maximum width, 1.8 kilometers. Like most of the countryside thereabouts, it is covered by beautiful forests and groves of wild apple trees; the quality of its soil and its proximity to the city, of which, though lying to the west of the river, it is in effect a part, made this the ideal property for our purpose. Once, therefore, that the island had been returned to the city by the generous annulment of Viel's contract, the municipality proceeded at once to assign it to the immigrants, selling each family a suitably sized parcel at a reasonable price, with payments to be made annually in perpetuity.

Joyful enthusiasm reigned before its new owners took possession of this small territory, on which the future of the province would perhaps rest; and the city council saw an unexpected increase in its funds.

The settlement of Valenzuela Island, so close to the city, immediately produced two priceless benefits: first, the moral and material effect that the example of German energy, laboriousness, and enterprise would produce on the apathetic and melancholy population; and, second, that in a place so close to where they were to land, future immigrants would meet with dependable support and with the cordial hospitality that obtains among compatriots when they find themselves in a country where for the newcomer everything is unfamiliar: language, laws, and customs. This development also gave me the time to explore the province and regain possession of the public and vacant lands so brazenly occupied by unscrupulous individuals.

While I was engaged in this effort at repossession, whose only result was the acquisition of the mission of Cudico and Pampa de Negrón in the Department of La Unión, and of the banks of the Valdivia between Niebla and Cutipai, lands linked by wretched roads and only amounting to some 2,500 acres, another group of immigrants arrived aboard the *Susana* to make the situation even more difficult than it had become thanks to the speed with which the Valdivians had tired of the acts of generosity that, after much urging, they had begun to display toward the newcomers.

As soon as the *Hermann* had left, selfish interests regained their sway; the immigrants, cooped up on the island, were viewed as so many mines awaiting exploitation. Lands that before their arrival had lain abandoned as uncultivable suddenly had owners; each owner either refused to sell or raised the price from the nominal one *real* an acre, at which there had been no buyers, to the outrageous one, in the vicinity of the city, of one peso the yard; and land that shortly before had been bought in bulk, so to speak, for a hundred pesos, was sold to the Germans, and as a favor, for as much as two thousand. The difficulties increased when they tried to acquire property in town; its owners held it in reserve to sell at a higher price to future immigrants, as though receiving the present ones badly could raise a reasonable hope of the arrival of others. They assumed that each property was a treasure, while destroying the very cause of its value; and as far as they were concerned, anything that tried to get them to insure abundant harvests by not eating their seed was sheer nonsense.

Bear in mind that they began to experience the benefits of immigration the moment it began in Valdivia, because, since those who came on the *Hermann* were not all farmers, but also artisans and manufacturers, no sooner had they landed when Valdivia could begin to buy, at good prices and good quality, what days before it had to buy elsewhere with all sorts of chicanery, of low quality and at high prices.

With the help of God and some good citizens I found what lodgings I could for the 102 immigrants that came on the *Susana*, so that they might be more comfortable while waiting for the distribution of those promised lands of which only traces were to be found in the environs of Valdivia.

The immigrants who came on the *Hermann* and the *Susana,* as well as those expected on the *Sankt Pauli,* the *Adolf,* and other ships sent out by the Hamburg firm of Godeffroy were not Japanese coolies drawn to leave their country by the wages we paid our day laborers; quite the contrary, they and their successors were all more or less well-off tradesmen who were not seeking favors but granting them, asking, in exchange, only that with their money they be allowed to buy lands that before their arrival had been considered totally worthless.

The records of property transfers prior to the arrival of that handful of Germans brought by the *Hermann* consisted only of simple transactions with supposed native proprietors, all of them carried out by means of liquor, an occasional peso, some trinket, or some shed to which a high value was ascribed to make the acquisition seem more legitimate; but no sooner had the immigrants arrived than exchanges began to be regulated by money and enterprise began to take root.

In the four short months from December 1850 to March 1851, eight German houses were going up in the village of Valdivia on lots bought at inflated prices; and two rural properties, equally bought for cash, were receiving the baptism of European cultivation, the first to do so in the vicinity of the town.[94] The poorest of the newcomers, a certain Kott, who died en route, had been able to pay his passage and that of his wife and two children, bring a modest supply of household goods and tools, and even to have some surplus for the initial expenses of settlement. Among the immigrants came men of the caliber of Philippi, Schneider, and Anwandter, tradesmen and manufacturers such as had never come to Chile, and many capitalists, who on their own account or in the name of European companies came to acquire lands on which to establish colonies. Immigration was, thus, for Valdivia a beneficent visit from learning, arts, and material wealth, coming to rouse it from its stagnation.

We Chileans are convinced we know it all and are just itching to criticize whatever does not agree with our universal erudition. If you want to discuss economic policy, Chile is swarming with economists; if your subject is war or naval affairs, we are all generals, or at the very least ad-

94. The first proprietors of lands acquired without previous government assistance were Ebner, Lechler, Kayser, Ribbeck, Hornikel, Hoffmann, Haebler, Yneffer, von Zusch, and Krugen. VPR. ["Yneffer" seems like a deformation of a German name, but I cannot guess of which. JP.]

mirals; and so it is no wonder that when the subject of immigration arose, everyone became a specialist in colonization.

The people of Valdivia wanted immigrants to whom they might sell for ten what had cost them one; the northern landowners wanted farm laborers that would drive down the wages of their tenants; for the wealthy residents of Santiago, anything that did not encourage the coming of coachmen and cooks was a waste of money; for the mine operators of the north, immigration was useless if not made up of pick and shovel men; and, finally, even an exaggerated zeal for religious unity came to play its part in this general tumult.

From among the absurd events that occurred constantly in the early days of our colonizing efforts, I shall relate only one, which can serve as a lesson and example, not only to future colonizers, but to every religious man whose guileless virtue puts him in danger of accepting appearance as reality, the habit for the monk, the hypocrite for the true servant of God.

The well-known naturalist Domeyko,[95] a man of sincere faith and a zealous observer of the precepts imposed on Christians by the Roman Catholic Church, also had his say on the topic of colonization; and since in all the writings on this important subject each author looked out for his own interests and intent, this one asked that only Catholics, and no Protestants, be recruited for our settlements. As proof of the importance of this recommendation he included in his text the letter that a certain Muschgay, a Catholic from Wurttemberg, had written to "Her Excellency Chile," requesting concessions and lands to found a Catholic colony in our country under the aegis of the government.

That letter, whose submissive style and pious aims provoked such sincere eulogies from honest Domeyko, said, in sum and among other things, the following: that thirty Catholic families would come, that none of their members had been involved in politics, that all enjoyed a good reputation, and that as for moral conduct, all undertook to be responsible for each, and each for all; but that in exchange they demanded that their settlement be placed near some Catholic church.

In another letter in the same style, but more explicit and dated on April 10 of the next year, that reached the same *Excellency,* the plain and modest forest warden of Wurttemberg appeared magically converted into a skilled miner, a great agronomist qualified to run trade schools, and above all a teacher of the Catholic religion. This arrant scoundrel, who thought that in Chile he would find only fanatics or fools to be hoodwinked, took care, in

---

95. Ignacio Domeyko was a Polish immigrant to Chile who distinguished himself in science and education. EOV.

order to add weight to his epistle, to sign it. . . . Where do my readers think he might have signed it? In a monastery! His brazen signature, "O. Muschgay," was preceded by these very words: "Monastery of Zwiefalten, in the Kingdom of Wurttemberg, April 10, 1850."

Muschgay reached Valdivia on the brig *Susana,* not in the company of the twenty pioneers who, according to his letters, were to form the vanguard of his Catholic colony, but with only fourteen individuals, who perhaps were the only participants in his project he could find before embarking. He immediately asked to meet with me, a request that was at once granted. He was a robust man, rather tall than short, with heavy sideburns and black hair. He rarely looked me in the eye, no doubt because modesty made him lower his glance. I noticed that with a degree of sly affectation he took care to let me see the metal crosses that served as buttons on his shirt and his cufflinks in the form of ivory skulls.

In spite of the bad impression made on me by this visit, I fulfilled, though under protest, the commitments that the government, impelled by Domeyko's writings, had made to this herald of model Catholic colonies. To the detriment of the other immigrants, I put the best land I had at his disposal; and he never even visited it. I gave him a place and equipment for a school, and neither he nor any children appeared there. The companion of the monks of Zwiefalten, in the Kingdom of Wurttemberg, was after bigger game. Instead of busying himself with carrying out his commitments, he spent his time thinking up the wildest plans and projects; in one of them, which I have before me, he proposed to the government the boring of a tunnel through the base of the Andes to shorten the voyage to Buenos Aires.

But since everything in this world comes to an end, the immigration agent, fed up with Muschgay's daily notes and projects, ordered him to attend to his business and to cease forthwith, in his notes, to attach the appellation "Catholic" to "Muschgay," which he never failed to do, as though this were a regular part of his name.

From that day on Muschgay disappeared from Valdivia, where he had not found dupes on whom to practice his chicanery; and with Domeyko's paper in his hand, he threw himself at the feet of our good prelate the Archbishop of Santiago as a victim of the animosity of a heretical immigration agent who persecuted him merely for being a Christian. He found his way into the heart of that honest and modest prince of our Church, and, equipped with this key, into the hearts of the prelate's friends; and a few months later we were astonished to see him return to Valdivia transformed into a haughty merchant, master of a steamboat, and endowed with full powers to acquire vast territories on behalf of the wealthy Santiago family Larraín y Gandarillas, with no recommendation or guarantee but what he had himself managed to extract from his enviable title of persecuted Christian.

The result was inevitable. After the scoundrel had squandered the money entrusted to him and turned his boat into a brothel, he managed in his drunkenness to send back such drafts on his frightened partners in Santiago as to force them, albeit tardily, to come to Valdivia and seek the help of the heretical immigration agent in prying the remnants of their ill-employed fortune from the grasp of his alleged former victim; to make matters worse, the innocent backers and partners of honest Muschgay had the misfortune of seeing one of their brothers drown in the Valdivia River.

What did the Catholic entrepreneur do then? As a full accounting for the funds that had passed through his hands he presented the Larraíns with a sheet of paper on which, over a confused mass of different-colored boxes, were seen scribblings and numbers that no one could understand; and while his partners were cursing themselves for what was happening, Muschgay, who had let his hair grow long, moved in with the Indians of Pitrufquén. Confident that there he had found a safe shelter, he declared that the Araucanian religion was the most perfect of all, proceeded to marry as many women as he could, and was never heard from again! Poor religion, how often are you the victim of abuse! Just as the Devil usually lurks behind the cross, so the word "virtue" almost always cloaks the falsely pious man.

Before beginning the account of my excursions through the interior of the province, I must here, because this is the right place for it, write of something having to do with the barracks rebellion at Magallanes led by the savage Cambiaso on December 21, 1851, which horrified the whole country and deprived the Chilean navy of one of its brightest hopes with the treacherous murder of Muñoz Gamero.

That year I was intendant of Valdivia, and my political obligations and those concerned with immigration were unfortunately such that the government had been forced to separate the duties of the military chief from those of the intendant. At this point a government transport ship anchored in the port of Corral on its way to the prison at Magallanes, bearing a number of convicts and a squad of artillerymen commanded by the notorious son of Chiloé, Lt. Miguel José Cambiaso. I have said "unfortunately" because if my authority as intendant had not been counterbalanced by that of the military chief, Cambiaso would have spent a long time shut up in the jail of the fortress of Nieblas, and the bloody pages of the annals of crime would not, as they now are, be augmented with the account of the atrocities whose beginnings, which I witnessed in Valdivia, I shall now recount.

Cambiaso made such good use of the transport's short stay in Corral that by the day after his arrival, Valdivia, where he seemed to have resided previously for some time, was filled with enough reports of the disturbances he was causing to alarm me and make me ask the ex-intendant Don Juan Francisco Adriasola whether he knew anything about this madman. Don Juan Francisco answered me with bitter humor, "You call him a madman, but he's more of a rogue than a madman; he's a thoroughgoing scoundrel, and the least of his sins have always been gambling, wheedling loans he never repaid, drinking, and chasing skirts, all of it in the most brazen and unrestrained way imaginable—and ask me no more. If this fellow, for reasons I'll never understand, weren't in charge of a squad, he'd be going to the proper place all right, provided he was well tied up."

The day before the departure of the transport on which this model of virtues was to continue his voyage, and when I was least expecting that anything would interrupt the dull monotony of my daily office hours, I suddenly heard violent screams, whereupon a poor woman burst into my office in tears and told me in an agitated sorrowful voice, "Sir, I was away from my home, and Lt. Cambiaso has taken advantage of that to carry off my only daughter and hide her on board the ship, along with my trunks of clothes and what little I've been able to save to live on."

After I had calmed the unhappy woman, and eight hours after I had thoroughly informed myself about what was going on, the innocent dove that had planned to fly off to southern climes had been returned to the maternal nest, and her seducer, shackled in the Nieblas fortress, was awaiting the beginning of the criminal proceedings that I had set in motion against him.

Seeing what lay in store for him, Cambiaso invoked his military status and appealed to the military chief, who at that time was the honorable and trusting Colonel Don Benjamín Viel; and that frustrated my plans.

Why reproduce the arguments about jurisdiction that this incident produced between Viel and me, arguments whose originality would make me enjoy the recounting were it not for the fact that my losing them led to the catastrophe at Magallanes. Among other things, I remember that Viel, after showing me that as the matter stood it was now beyond my obligations as a mere intendant, tried to make me forget about what had happened by telling me that the word "abduction" is a two-edged sword. "And if you don't believe it," he added with a smile, "tell me, my good Vicente, when an abduction occurs, who's carrying off whom? Is the man carrying off the woman, or is it the woman who's carrying off the man?"

Cambiaso evaded the charge of theft by blaming the deed on the girl, and that of abduction by blaming his youth! Thanks to Viel, this blackguard continued on his way; it was he who led the mutiny during which blood and liquor flowed alike and during which he murdered the brave and gallant Commander Don Benjamín Muñoz Gamero, one of the brightest hopes of our navy. When he received news of this catastrophe, Viel, who loved Gamero like a son, rushed to find me and, embracing me and weeping, said, "I'm the only one to blame for this calamity! I should have made that villain spit blood before I ever let him continue on his voyage!"

X X I

Voyages into the interior of the province. — Lake Llanquihue.
— We burn the forests of Chanchán. — I am shipwrecked on
the lake. — The settlements fall into dangerous disrepute. —
The way out of these straits. — Exploration of the Chacao
channels and Reloncaví Bay. — Cayenel.

The uncertain situation in which I found myself absolutely had to be
resolved as soon as possible, because the attitude of the squatters
on public lands was making it questionable whether Valdivia would become the first immigrant settlement in Chile. I therefore set off for the
interior without further delay, leaving the newly arrived immigrants
lodged in the vaults of the old Corral castle, after having allotted to
some of them the wretched lands of Cutipai and a few isolated stretches
of the banks of the Valdivia River, banks that were so useless no one laid
claim to them and that I took care to award free of charge, so that the
recipients might more cheerfully await the appearance of those lands
that they had been told were awaiting them.

This was a purely exploratory expedition. Like other northerners, I had no clear idea of what the blessed province of Valdivia was at that time, except for the generalized belief that it was large and very thinly populated, and that it rained there 370 days out of the 365 that make up the year. So widespread was this ignorance that just as I was about to set out I received a message from the minister, Don Jerónimo Urmeneta, who told me that since he had, to his regret, learned that wheat would not grow in the province, he thought he should tell me that it would be desirable to take prudent measures to transfer the immigrants to the territory of Arauco.

On this expedition I was accompanied by the modest and very competent engineer Don Guillermo Frick, a German and a former resident of Valdivia, commissioned by the government to inspect the public lands of the province, and by two of the recent immigrants.

We set out from Valdivia by boat, since the river was then the only road to Futa, a kind of way station where the Futa River, one of the tributaries of the Valdivia, ceases to be easily navigable. During this short journey, the traveler marvels at the clear and placid waters of the river, the exuberant vegetation that begins at the water's edge without leaving an inch of shore on which one might step, the shade of the colossal trees that bend over the river festooned with garlands of *copihue* vines that sway to and fro above the boat, and the many groves of wild apple trees that, though overrun with burdocks, seem to rival the forests in their vigor.

Once in Futa, we continued on horseback, struggling with the roads, or rather with the most tortuous and pitted paths imaginable, always in the shade of the dense forest that separates the coastal valley from the central one. Shortly we came on a major incline whose clear center displayed a great deposit of coal, which, I was told, was not exploited for lack of labor and of roads, two difficulties that in my opinion could easily have been overcome.

A newcomer's first sight of Valdivia tells him very little about the beauty of its inland valleys and their value for agriculture and manufactures. The impenetrable forests that cover two-thirds of the land display their marvelous vigor only at the coast and at the foot of the Andes. Everywhere throughout Valdivia, between these two shaded zones lies clear land exposed to the beneficent influence of direct sunshine, the southern tip of the central valley that stretches uninterruptedly from the rampart of Chacabuco to the waters of Chacao. With the exception of the vine, every product of the temperate zone is raised in Osorno; if, as I said, wheat was not exported at that time, it was because it was more profitable to take it to Corral by sea from Valparaíso than by land from Osorno and La Unión, so wretched was the condition of the roads.

After we left the dense coastal forests we were able to gallop through the lovely open plains of the central valley until we reached the small village of La Unión, which at that time boasted the title of capital of a department.

The governor of that hamlet was Don Eusebio Ríos, a fine energetic countryman who tolerated no obstacles when it came to carrying out the orders of higher authority. He heard me complain about how the newcomers had been treated in Valdivia, and instantly we had more than enough lands at our disposal in his department, though the state of the roads unfortunately did not allow me to make use of them.

I left the two German immigrants in Ríos's care in La Unión and continued my way to Osorno. We soon came across the waterway, impressive for Chile, that bears the name Trumag. The effects of the tidal action in this beautiful estuary can be felt far inland in the central valley; although the seawater does not penetrate there, the tides hold back the river's flow, and its waters rise to such an extent that vessels sail over the tops of submerged trees when the moon's alignment with the sun produces the highest tides.

I paid no attention to Osorno, a historic town worthy of study. My mind was wholly occupied with acquiring public lands to meet the government's obligations and thus rescuing the immigration project; and so I dedicated the days spent in Osorno exclusively to getting my hands on all the land I could, taking advantage of the happy circumstance that the idea of challenging the government's rights to it had not yet taken hold there. Yet this was not enough, because the lands I acquired were too scattered to form a significant settlement. To make use of them, furthermore, roads had to be built; and the acreage was not extensive enough to justify such costly improvements. A methodical investigation convinced me that I should find what I wanted only in the very heart of the immense virgin forest that begins at Ranco and covers the extensive base of the Andes until its roots plunge into the salty waters of Reloncaví Bay.

Only the Indians could supply any significant information about this dark region, since it was quite impossible to enter it other than on foot, clearing a narrow path with a machete through dense foliage, only to have it soon wiped away by the vigor of the vegetation and the falling of dead branches.

Having learned that a little to the southeast of Osorno I would run into the western part of that forest, in whose center lay Lake Llanquihue, I set out for that fearful place accompanied by Frick and two Indian scouts, despite the governor's efforts to dissuade me from my intention of penetrating there.

We spent the night in a place they called El Burro; and at dawn of the following day we penetrated on foot, and more by dint of determination than of physical strength, into a five-league wide strip of forest so dense that in its shade we could not even read our maps. Tangled roots, thorny bushes, thickets of *quila* shrubs joined to the tree trunks with mighty lardizabala vines, and the muddy ground where we constantly sank into puddles camouflaged by decaying leaves, all offered determined resistance to our advance; but finally, after seven hours of hellish struggle, we reached our goal, though battered and almost ruing our arrogant intrepidity.

All our discomfort and exhaustion, however, turned into joyful enthusiasm when we suddenly left the dark domain of the forest and without any transition saw the most splendid panorama stretch before us. It was as though a curtain had been raised on a stage, transforming a dungeon into a bit of heaven.

To my astonishment, I suddenly found myself on the western shore of the great Lake Llanquihue. As with a sea, mists hid the northern and southern limits of the clear calm waters that seemed to be playing at my feet among the roots of the sturdy trees that bordered the beach where we had stopped. In the pure air to the east, the most delicate traces of the last snows that crowned the heights of Pullehue, Osorno, and Calbuco contrasted with the blue of the sky; these volcanic cones, westerly continuations of Tronador, seemed to be standing in a line admiring their reflections in the waters of the lake.

Although much of the territory had the appearance of a marsh, the thick muddy humus that covered all the land I had been traversing so clearly showed the benefit that agriculture could draw from this place that despite tiredness and lack of provisions, I determined not to return without first exploring this interesting country for at least another couple of days.

I was accompanied by one Juanillo or Pichi-Juan, a drunken native, celebrated for his knowledge of the most hidden forest paths and also as a genealogist ready to declare which of his ancestors had been the owners of the lands that the Valdivians used to purloin. Pichi-Juan assured me that we should not die of hunger; as soon as he had made me a comfortable shelter of boughs with his machete, he built a fire and went off, returning a quarter of an hour later with a great quantity of hazelnuts and five delicious honeycombs that he had extracted from hollows in the trees. The ground around the lake was literally paved with hazelnuts, and honey was to be found everywhere.

The large Chilean bumblebee that we so often see buzzing among the flowers in our gardens does not fabricate wax as does the European bee. The honey that it stores up is transparent and liquid, and the vessels where it deposits it are symmetrically placed cells made of vegetable fibers so tightly joined that not a drop of the honey deposited in them can escape. This interesting insect, which can perhaps be domesticated with time and skill, defends its property as does the European bee; when it cannot protect it with the violence of its stings, it does so with its astuteness. Tired as I was, I had left two full honeycombs near the place where sleep overcame me; and when I awoke I found not a drop of honey in them. The hemplike walls of the combs still maintained the delightful aroma of flowers. To determine whether they contained any wax, I boiled them in a tin pan; since the boiling produced not a trace of wax, I squeezed them dry and placed them in an envelope in my coat pocket, to be examined eventually at my leisure.

I remember that two years later, as I opened a trunk where I kept old clothes, I was surprised by the smell of flowers that rose from it, and that when I tried to find the cause of this unusual phenomenon I saw that the odor came from the forgotten honeycombs. Also remarkable was the fact that no trace of moths was to be seen on the woolen clothes.

Since we could not walk even a hundred meters along the lakeshore because of some steep banks and especially because of the forest that in the shallow areas grew far out into the water, we made a canoe out of a rotten tree trunk by simply hollowing it out and closing off the two open ends with sod; and provided with pieces of bark to serve as oars, Guillermo Frick and I set out in this vessel the next day, delighted to be able thus to bypass the formidable embankment that blocked our explorations.

At first everything favored this madcap adventure. The morning sun was shining in all its splendor and not the lightest breeze ruffled the mirrorlike surface on which we sailed, so that, although fatigued by propelling our hollow trunk with our fine oars, in two hours we had successfully rounded the point that had blocked our way and hidden from us the most picturesque and wild harbor of that small inland sea. The depth of the water seemed to us—for we could take soundings only with our bark oars—adequate for vessels of some draft, and the configuration of the wooded shores seemed suited to protecting an anchorage against winds from any direction; but the narrowness of the beach between the water and the thick forest soon convinced me that any exploration by land along the lakeshore would for the present be impossible. We thus busied ourselves collecting a large number of eggs that we found among the rushes of some islets that graced the waters of the harbor, and as the sun began to set we headed back toward our camp.

But what was peace and quiet within the harbor was strife and storm outside. A wave raised on a lake by the wind is always dangerous; but since we only discovered our rashness in leaving the harbor when it was no longer possible to return to it, we had to resign ourselves to hoping that chance and the mercies of the wind would grant us what we could no longer expect from our useless efforts. Night came on us there, darker than ever. Soaked by the waves, bailing with our hats, and anxiously trying to keep the ends of our trunk from becoming unstopped and thus keep it afloat, which was our only hope, we were beginning to despair when a bursting wave whose roar we had failed to understand overturned the ill-fated trunk and rushed with its hapless passengers onto the rocky shore.

A cruel night, long to be remembered, lay in store for us; we spent it wet, without fire or shelter, because we were between a bank and the water, unprotected from the wind that blew from the mountains, with no bed but some *nalca* leaves placed on the sharp pebbles of the beach.

The leaves of the *nalca*, or *pangui*, as they call it in the North, reach an unheard-of size at Llanquihue. I watched Frick measure those that we pulled off a *nalca* that grew at the foot of the embankment where we had capsized. To be sure, in our camp we had no yardstick but our arms, but one of the leaves measured three yards and almost a span in diameter. Later, as I was describing it, my kind listener, not daring to call me a liar, opted for the word "poetry."

The same holds true for the extraordinary dimensions of some tree trunks, and anyone wishing to see such "poetry" need only travel a short way from Puerto Montt on the road to Arrayán and he will see the most poetic garden growing on the raised cross-section of a larch.

At daybreak we learned from an Indian who was looking for us that we were not far from our first campsite; cured of our exploratory ardor, though with our heads filled with schemes, we once more got under way until we reached El Burro and then Osorno.

As I traveled I offered Pichi-Juan thirty days' wages, which at the time meant thirty pesos, to burn the forests between Chanchán and the mountains; and then I returned to Valdivia to soothe the discontent that was beginning to come over the immigrants, who did not know what to do with themselves in the provisional lodgings where, lacking lands, I had left them.

Immediately on my arrival I distributed the vacant lands of Osorno and La Unión, which cheered them all. I was also pleased to see that many of the wealthier immigrants had bought lots and farms in the neighborhood of Valdivia and that, encouraged by my reports, they were preparing to do the same farther inland, trusting that the roads I had promised them in the government's name would soon be built.

Valdivia is one of the regions of Chile with the most frequent rains, which does not mean that the rainfall totals exceed those of Colchagua; yet the sun comes out there every day of the year, even in mid-winter—an unusual phenomenon that constantly offers the landscape painter and the observer of the beauties of nature incredible contrasting effects of light and shade. There are times when it is pouring on one half of a tree while the other half is gleaming in the sunlight.

The sun's disk, always unclouded when it appears there, had now been veiled for three months, which is how long Pichi-Juan had been burning the forests that covered a great part of the central valley to the southeast of Osorno. The fires simultaneously set by this tireless Indian at various points spread with such unexpected speed that the poor man, trapped by the flames, saved himself only by taking shelter next to a rotten *coigüe*, among whose damp and decaying roots he was able to dig a dangerously exposed trench. That frightful blaze, which neither the greenness of the trees nor their ever dark and dank bases nor the almost daily torrential rains could contain, had carried on its work of devastation for three months; the resulting smoke, driven by the south wind, shrouded the sun, which during most of this time could be viewed in Valdivia with the naked eye.

As soon as the fire had died down I had to undertake another and more leisurely exploration of the area that it had laid open in the department of Osorno, and I therefore made a delightful expedition through all the land that lies to the north of Lake Llanquihue. The average width of the burned area was five leagues, and its depth, fifteen. All of it was level and of the best quality. The fire, which had so long devastated those impassable thickets, had whimsically drawn back from some stands of trees, as though the hand of Providence had deliberately spared them so that the settlers, in addition to clear soil, might have wood for construction and the necessities of life.

Once arrived at the district, I tried to push on as far as the lake; and unable to do so from the north because of the denseness of the intervening forest, I tried again from near the Maullín River.

The land around the lake was composed of three concentric zones of clearly differentiated nature. The outermost, some five leagues across, measured along the radius, was qualitatively inferior to the other two; its uneven, rocky, and sometimes very shallow soil, resting on an extensive sandy bed, was covered with great forests and such dense thickets of *quila* that it could be crossed only on foot while carving out a narrow and almost lightproof vault with the machete. This land improved noticeably as one drew closer to the lake; its vegetation was more luxuriant and its grasses more moist. The intermediate strip, which here they call *Ñadi*, is a beautiful meadowland, treeless and covered with dwarf *colihue*, *coirón*, and other excellent grasses that in springtime could offer long-lasting pasture to cattle. It might be about a league wide, and as it stretches around the lake it is interrupted by several wooded hills. The soil, heavy with clay in the lower areas, is excellent in the higher. These lowlands, like all others throughout our country, were extremely well suited for grazing in summer but less suitable at that time for agriculture, since there was insufficient drainage in winter; but once the area was settled, this drawback turned out to be easily remedied. Beyond this meadowland comes the level and fertile higher region that surrounds the water to the width of three leagues.

If the lake's circumference is, then, as is generally said, thirty leagues, and the average width of the public lands girdling it is five leagues, one could say that at that time the state held, in those surrounding lands and those cleared by the fire, more than two hundred leagues of level and virgin arable terrain that it could distribute among the immigrants.

I shall not enter into the opportunities offered to the farmer by that lead-colored plain, above whose ashes still rose an occasional gigantic survivor of the charred vegetation that the flames had almost wiped out. On the north it was bordered by virgin forests of tall oaks; thick *lumas*, massive bay trees, and dense growths of *quila* enclosed it on the west; and on the south, cypresses and larches, the giants of our southern vegetation, were only awaiting the hand of man to reward his efforts with their wealth. And since trees are not always an infallible proof of the excellence of the soil that sustains them, nature seemed to have made a special effort there to demonstrate this excellence by turning into giants those plants that in the North are notable for their smallness. The *ñilhue*, which grows to the height of a mounted man, boasts a tender and juicy stem two inches in diameter; the myrtle, that pampered shrub of our gardens, competes in height with the tallest oaks, and boards as much as a yard in width can be cut from its trunk. By the picturesque cascades that fall into the lake, Don Guillermo Frick and I, as recounted earlier, measured *pangui* leaves ten yards in circumference.

But that source of riches, left to its solitude and isolation, would remain useless without a convenient and inexpensive connection by road to a seaport attractive to shippers, because a new settlement—and this is a truth ever to be borne in mind—can grow only from the outside in. Suddenly to plunge an immigrant into the midst of an empty stretch of land, no matter how rich and fertile, without having first taken costly measures to avoid the disastrous effects of isolation, is to kill his selfless spirit of enterprise, or at least to make it useless. The immigrant must establish his first residence in a port of the land he is to settle and not move one foot forward without having the other firmly planted on the ground.

In pursuit of this goal and despite the inclement season of the year, I again visited the burned-out area, carried out some surveys with the help of Moraleda's map—the only one then available to me, because those by King and FitzRoy showed only the coast—and gained the welcome impression that at least the sea, if not a good harbor, had to be very near the southern part of the lake, whose surroundings were so well suited to serve as the foundation for the settlement that was the golden dream of the late lamented Philippi and, at the time, of the government as well.

Since mere impressions, however, can only suggest but not decide a course of action, I resolved, as long as my health held out, to continue in my difficult task of more or less haphazard probings before communicating anything to the government, and since the forests seemed to have been placed precisely where open ground was needed for a survey, I decided to seek it at the northern end of the lake. Finding none there, either, I was forced to climb along the steep western slope of the mountains that seemed to rise from that small inland sea, in order to gain at least a bird's-eye view of the lay of the burned-out lands and of the shape and location of the lake in relation to accessible sites. I gave orders to have a boat built by the shore; and while this work was going on, two companions and I headed for the symmetrical cone of the Osorno volcano, which I set out to climb with no less effort than determination.

If travel in an unexplored region brings its torments, it also has its charms. A clement sky had wiped away its frequent rain-bearing clouds, so that when I reached the second resting place of my laborious ascent, with my eyes free to explore the horizon, I experienced contradictory impressions beyond what I have found on any other voyage. Our country's central valley seemed to me there to be an endless string of great lakes separated from each other by equally great stretches of impenetrable forest; and south of Lake Llanquihue, which I saw below me, appeared to lie another equally extensive one, and not the open sea I was looking for, a fact that demolished the reliability of Moraleda's map and, along with it, my hope for a nearby seacoast, without which it was quite impossible to establish settlements in the place we had worked so hard to explore.

The heavens seemed to be testing my perseverance by prolonging the disillusionment that had laid hold of me as dense clouds continued to block my view of the south, which I was anxiously searching with my eyes. I confess that my spirits, which were usually aroused rather than overcome by difficulties, were beginning to flag, when a propitious ray of sunlight, striking the waters of what I had taken for another lake to the south, allowed me to see the gleam of the white sails that were traversing it! What I was looking at was no lake, but the ocean I was so anxiously seeking, the Bay of Reloncaví, whose waters, from the elevation at which I stood, seemed to blend with those of Lake Llanquihue, for only a narrow stretch of forest lay between the two. I am sure that good Vasco Núñez de Balboa, when from the mountains of the Isthmus he first saw the waters of the Pacific, felt no greater joy than did I when I learned that the apparent lake that had just demolished my fondest dreams was precisely what was to prolong them and make them into realities.

Happy as a child, because only children and madmen take pleasure in the services that they themselves perform and for which they receive no thanks, and with my head full of plans, I spent the most enviable and refreshing night in the rustic shelter offered to me by the hollow trunk of a gigantic *coihue*. Dawn, which beautifies all things, piqued my curiosity with the picturesque appearance of a spit that seemed to extend the base of the Osorno volcano into the waters of the lake. Since so clear an observation point was not to be disdained, I made my way toward it.

Nature has her whimsicalities that sound like the stuff of dreams and yet are firmly anchored in reality. That spit was in fact the tip of a massive ancient lava flow, which had spilled into the water and built up from the bottom to form a vast natural pier whose steep sides indicated great depth. The glowing liquid lava seemed to have hardened into the most distorted shapes as it entered the water, forming the most fantastic figures as it suddenly cooled. That splendid pier had the appearance of ancient ruins worn down by the action of time or broken up by the roots of the powerful vegetation with which they shared the spot. Here and there it gave the impression of demolished arcades, among which stood ghostly blocks of lava covered with moss and ferns, which the imagination easily transformed into broken statues. A good many leafy *coihues,* though worn by age, gave clear evidence that the eruption that had created so picturesque a landscape must have taken place more than a hundred years earlier.

To have tarried in that charming spot would have required a mind untroubled by the pressing thoughts that then occupied mine; and so I put poetry aside and, since midday was well past, continued my way to my improvised shipyard, which I reached well after nightfall.

The next day we all worked to finish building the rough canoe whose construction had begun before I had set out on my excursion, for without it or some other floating device that would overcome the impossibility of exploring the shores of the lake by land, there was no way to determine whether all of the plots that I planned to lay out around the lake for subsequent distribution could communicate with each other by water.

My exploratory expedition consisted of four Germans and five peaceful natives who, though still subject to their chiefs, lived near the town of Osorno among the white population. Our camp was located on the northern shore of the lake, about a mile and a half to the east of the cove that today, for some unknown reason, is called Puerto Octay.

Once our absurd vessel, hacked out as best we could, was finished, and we had made a pair of paddles that looked more like baker's shovels than like paddles, we fitted our craft with a kind of sail fashioned by joining two ponchos and launched it without further delay and amid general rejoicing.

We decided to set out the next day; and to make good use of what was left of the present one, I sent Señor Foltz with his Germans on some preliminary explorations in the neighborhood and set to putting my notes in order, watched by my Indians, who amused themselves by eating roasted hazelnuts sweetened with the fragrant honey that our bumblebees produce in abundance in those regions. About an hour after I had finished my work, and when I was most occupied in sketching the fine panorama in my album, a tempting breeze rising from the north began to ruffle the smooth surface of the lake in so gentle and charming a way that I could not refuse the invitation and the chance to test the seaworthiness of my clumsy oaken turtle. I therefore boarded her, along with a nephew of the famous Pichi-Juan; and since another chubby Indian from my band said that he, too, knew about boats, because he had twice crossed the Futa River by boat, I took him aboard as well. Poor fellows! Neither of them knew how to swim.

Gently borne along by that deceptive breeze that barely filled our ponchos, and without any effort beyond an occasional use of our baker's shovels to steer our vessel, in less than a quarter of an hour we found ourselves some four hundred meters from shore. Having so easily come so far, it seemed to me that I was so close to the cove now called Octay that it would be a sin not to visit it forthwith, especially since doing so now would leave less work for the next day. I therefore headed for it and arrived very late, and none too happy, to be sure, with the navigational qualities of my wretched tree trunk, which moved well enough when pushed by the wind from behind, but which no force on earth could bring to haul the wind, much less to sail against it.

I made a sketch of the little harbor, which I baptized with the name of the unfortunate naval officer Muñoz Gamero, a name with which I honored it because its location suggested that in time it might become the best spot at which a road might connect the town of Osorno with the future settlement.

As it was getting late, we once more set ponchos, not to say sail, to return to camp; but as soon as we came out from the shelter provided by a bank and the mighty trees growing on it, my antediluvian vessel became totally ungovernable. I tried to turn back so as to spend the night on shore, but I tried too late; I struck the ponchos and made use of the shovels, but in vain, because my crew did not know how to row and I was not strong enough to manage alone. The force of the wind was pushing the accursed trunk ever farther from shore. To make matters worse, night fell. To my consternation, I saw the rough waves splashing against us and soaking us; just as I was beginning to have a presentiment of a catastrophe like that which I had experienced not long before while sailing on a similar trunk and with a similar lack of prudence with the engineer Frick, one of the furious waves that the wind so often raises on Lake Llanquihue caught my bark broadside and plunged us into the dangerous cold waters. Once the first shock of cold and fear had passed there was nothing for it but to try by might and main to reach the nearest shore, because to hold on to the violently pitching capsized canoe would have entailed the risk of being knocked out by it. I reached land where the waves cast me, exhausted, but alone! My poor Indians did not know how to swim! What a night! The rest of its story I learned only a week later in Osorno.

My companions told me that alarmed by my absence, by the account of my imprudent expedition given to them by the two natives I had left in my camp, and by the dangerous state of the waters of the lake, they had built bonfires and shot off their guns all through that worrisome night and then at daybreak had made their way westward, opening a path with their machetes along the dark and densely overgrown shore, until they had found me lying as though dead on the sand at the foot of a steep bank. On an improvised stretcher made of their own clothes those good and kind friends transported me on their shoulders to Osorno, where, they told me, my violent delirium abated; if I am alive today, I owe it not only to my poor Germans, but also to the incomparably kind efforts of Dr. Juan Renous, who did not leave my bedside until he saw me restored to health.

At the very time of this misfortune the enemies of progress, hard as it may be to believe, were waiting in the comfort of Santiago for the chance to prove the disadvantages of foreign immigration by slanderously accusing the agent, as a good Mason, of carrying on bacchanalian orgies with naked women even in sacred places! But this is not the occasion for an account of this inconceivable aberration of mindless and almost always ill-intentioned fanaticism.

After regaining my health in Valdivia I returned to my interrupted work with renewed enthusiasm.

From the outset two grave doubts seemed to block the project of establishing settlements in such remote places: first, whether the northern channels in the Ancud Archipelago would allow the easy and safe passage of deep-draft vessels; and second, whether, if this difficulty were overcome, a safe harbor could be found in Reloncaví Bay close by the lands that were to be settled. How little I could learn from the many reports I received on both these issues can be deduced from the text of paragraphs 2, 3, 4, and 7 of the written instructions that I gave Don Buenaventura Martínez, captain of the *Janequeo,* when he was ordered to explore the channels and Reloncaví Bay. They read as follows:

2. On reaching San Carlos de Ancud, he will communicate with the intendant of that province, and after such steps as he may deem necessary to acquire information about the channels leading to Reloncaví Bay, he will take on board the best and most experienced local pilot and commence the exploration with all the caution that his prudence may call for.

3. He shall not fear to proceed slowly and methodically; what is wanted is correct information.

4. The captain shall not expose the schooner to known dangers, but neither shall he hold back on mere hearsay; and he shall desist from his enterprise only when he is persuaded by his own observation that to continue would risk the lives of his men.

7. In general, the captain shall ever bear in mind that the successful conclusion of the expedition entrusted to his diligence and patriotism is the basis of the future well-being of our southern settlements, and that the honor of having undertaken it will accrue to him and to his brave seamen.

This was the state of affairs when a conjunction of events extremely unusual in Valdivia, though very common everywhere else, seriously endangered the reputation that this province was beginning to enjoy abroad. Brutal acts of violence against the honor of the wife of a recent settler had occurred in La Unión. In Osorno the body of a German who had imprudently been buried with his gold rings had been disinterred and exposed to the voracity of the dogs; to make matters even worse, in Valdivia a fine young German who had just built one of the first and most comfortable houses of the many that German industry was building in these wastelands, and who furthermore had sent to Europe for his parents and his betrothed, was murdered by one of his best laborers, who killed him with a hammer just as he was receiving an advance that he had requested of his master.

These unfortunate events came to my notice along with a letter whose text was as follows:

Dear Sir:

If all Chileans were like you, Valdivia would be for us a true paradise; but unfortunately this is not the case. In La Unión our wives are being raped; in Valdivia we are murdered; and in Osorno we are denied even the repose of the grave, since our bodies are exhumed to be fed to the dogs!

Since the imagination can easily foresee the effect that so concise and painful a letter might produce in Germany on anyone planning to emigrate to Chile, I spared no effort or sacrifice to keep such news from reaching its destination without some palliation; while steps for the punishment of these crimes were being taken, expecting that the first letters to be written were bound to be profoundly discouraging, I let it be known that an opportunity for direct communication with Hamburg had arisen and that I wanted any correspondence to be handed to me as soon as possible. This was done; a great bundle of letters passed from the hands of my worried children—because the settlers called me their father—into one of my bureau drawers, where I left it to await a more suitable occasion for forwarding it to its destination.

This occasion soon presented itself. The murderer was arrested, convicted, and immediately sentenced to death; the rapist turned out to be a German; and the exhumation was shown to be the work of some wretched natives, who, merely to gain possession of a gold ring, had committed this foul offense behind the backs of the authorities.

The return of the expedition to Reloncaví Bay, the success of that exploration, and the hope for prompt distribution of the famous lands in the interior that were as close to the sea as Valdivia itself, combined to hearten the disconsolate Germans, who, learning from me that there was another chance to write directly to Hamburg, made use of it enthusiastically to urge their relatives to join them. I desired nothing better. I joined these letters filled with hallelujahs to the tearful ones still stored in my bureau and deposited them all in the mail pouch.

The diligent commander of the *Janequeo* had in fact discharged his commission with great skill and good fortune. His explorations showed that the Chacao Channel and its tributaries, through which flow the tides that swell and diminish the waters of Reloncaví Bay on the west, were safely navigable by deep-draft vessels; that the bay itself, sheltered from the north winds, was a calm, smooth body of water free of any hidden dangers; and that at the northwestern end of it, sheltered by the picturesque island of Tenglu, lay one of the safest harbors of the countless ones bathed by the waters of the Ancud and Guaitecas archipelagos. This harbor, which at the time I called Cayenel, because that was the name of the place, and which, according to the map prepared by Ensign José de la Moraleda and published in 1792, seemed to be about five leagues distant from the southern shore of Lake Puraila or Llanquihue, not only solved the principal difficulties that until then had impeded the utilization of those vacant lands for settlement, but also provided the rich department of Osorno with the accessible and profitable market for the export of its products that it had previously lacked.

In fact, my repeated excursions into the interior and the diligent work of the engineers that the government had placed at my disposal soon showed that a road 21.5 kilometers in length through the dense stretch of forest that separated the lake from the sea, and another, 48.8 kilometers in length, between the northern end of the lake and Osorno would suffice to link, respectively, all the products of the vast perimeter of the lake with the seaport, and all those of the rich but isolated department of Osorno with the harbors of the lake.

With this question resolved, it remained only for energy and hard work to carry out these projects; and so as not to permit a moment's delay or neglect, after having the public lands at my disposal in the environs of Osorno and La Unión surveyed and distributed among some of the immigrants, I gathered an engineer and various German workers and set out from Corral for Cayenel, the salvation of my projects, foundation for my future efforts, and first settlement of what was to be the colony of Llanquihue.

X X I I

The settlement at Llanquihue. — Early stages in its
development. — Its enemies. — The acting immigration
agent is arrested. — Progress of the settlement.

I n Chile there is a great difference between the climate of the northern regions and that of the southern ones. The former are plagued by
extreme dryness; the latter, by its opposite. In the north, roads are the
arteries of communication; in the south, rivers and channels. It comes as
no surprise that just as the north breeds men who, as we say, live and die
on horseback, so the south produces the hardiest and boldest seamen.

Nothing could be easier, safer, and more pleasant than navigation on
the channels that connect San Carlos de Chiloé with the calm waters of
Cayenel: they are wide enough and more than deep enough for every
kind of vessel, with regular tides and a constant succession of harbors, or
rather a single continuous harbor where one need only drop anchor to
be secure. In the Chacao Channel there is a single threatening rock at
the strait of Junta Remolinos; but since it is clearly visible and lies almost a mile off shore, it offers no danger whatsoever. Anyone sailing on

these and the adjacent channels for the first time finds it hard to believe that these narrow and calm waterways are arms of the sea and not deep navigable rivers subject to the direct action of the tides. The picturesque islands that modify the channels' width and shape have the appearance of colossal treetops half submerged in the deep waters. They are covered with tall dense forests; only along their edges does the traveler observe isolated huts, an occasional barely cultivated field, and a few small boats that provide the means of communication among the inhabitants of those humid places.

Especially noteworthy is the location of the village of Calbuco, the capital of the department of the same name. The Spaniards, who when establishing their cities never sought places suitable for commerce and industry but those fortified by nature, chose for the site of Calbuco a petty islet separated from the mainland by an arm of the sea that seems more like a moat than like anything else. This hamlet, poor and un-kempt, was the first sign of human life that presented itself to the voy-ager after he had passed through the dangerous strait of Puruñún, astonishing him with its display of wretched poverty in the midst of so rich a natural setting. When one leaves this town, kept alive only by the agents of the timber exporters of San Carlos, who stayed there to gather boards cut from the larches of the east coast of Reloncaví Bay and store them in the open air, one enters the beautiful bay itself, which resembles a lake thanks to the configuration of the mainland that borders it on the north, east, and west, and to the picturesque islands that on the south seem to block the passage to the waters of the ocean.

This was the bay I had seen from the slopes of Mt. Osorno after my visit to the scorched lands of Chanchán, and its proximity to Lake Llan-quihue encouraged the successful explorations that led me to locate the first establishment of the planned settlement on its shores. I have every reason to be satisfied with the results of my thorough investigation of the importance of this valuable bay. At its northern end, called Cayenel, amid the silent forest of Melipulli, chance had placed one of the safest and most practicable harbors in the country. Bountiful nature, when she formed that anchorage, seemed to have taken care to endow it with every convenience that in other harbors can only be achieved through human effort, and then at great sacrifice and over a long time. In addition to the imperturbable tranquility of its waters, protected against winds from every direction, it of-fers the great advantage of forming a natural drydock from which, when the tides are lowest, the water is completely drained, gently leaving even the largest keels exposed, only to return six hours later to submerge them once more and allow them to float without ever losing their stability.

This important place, situated at the precise spot where settlement was to begin, was designated as the center and permanent point of departure for all subsequent operations. The mighty forest that entirely covered it left man no foothold except for the narrow strip of sand and pebbles exposed twice daily by the ebb tide. Hatchet and fire soon cleared space for a crude shed; and that, in 1852, was the cornerstone of the splendid edifice viewed with patriotic pride by all who know what the place was and see what it is today.

To that lonely improvised shelter, hemmed in between the sea and the muddy floor of a great forest, we transported without further delay the immigrants who were crowded into the dank vaults of the fortifications at Corral, as well as others who just at that point arrived from Hamburg.

The census of those few first settlers deserves mention here. It consisted of forty-four married couples and was composed as follows:

Married men	44
Married women	43
Single men	14
Single women	8
Males 1 to 10 years old	31
Females 1 to 10 years old	28
Males 10 to 15 years old	24
Females 10 to 15 years old	20
TOTAL	212

These first immigrants still gratefully remember the generous and brotherly welcome given to them by the enthusiastic inhabitants of San Carlos when they passed through that town. The local merchants sent boats to bring them ashore; the intendant, along with the other local authorities, came out to receive them on the beach; and Señora Alvaradejo, whose marriage to a Sánchez combined two of the most highly esteemed families of Ancud, lent her beautiful country house, where, under her supervision, the attentive and delicate hospitality of the fair sex of the islands' capital provided the emaciated travelers with an abundant dinner. This was exactly the kind of demonstration we needed; those voluntary emigrants required something that would restore their almost lost hopes of being able to accomplish something in Chile, and so the next day they came to Cayenel with renewed enthusiasm and cheerfully took possession of the unenviable shelter that awaited them there.

Subject to every kind of privation and constantly exposed to an inclement climate that only the gradual destruction of the forests has eventually been able to modify, those first settlers were an example of what man can achieve in his struggle against nature when he is supported by faith in the future and by abnegation and hard work, the natural companions of that faith.

To bring even an acre of land under cultivation in that region did indeed seem to be a task far superior to the means employed for the purpose. The whole of that vast territory was covered with the densest forests, which seemed to spring from the perpetual snows of the Andes and march down uninterruptedly to the very waters of the sea. There grew and flourished those giants of our vegetation whose straight trunks still yield more than two thousand boards;[96] there ancient trees invaded the domain of the waters, sinking into them their mighty roots, to be exposed at ebb tide covered with seaweed and shells, their vigor not in the least impaired by the brine; there thorny bushes and dense *quilas* enfolded by the twisted cables of the supple *lardizabalas* that pressed them against the trees blocked the rays of the sun, and the damp miry soil on which they grew was hidden under impenetrable jumbled piles of rotting trunks. In those perpetually moist places, even fire lost much of its destructive force.

This description of the coastal forest of Melipulli, in which there is not the slightest exaggeration, could, with only a change of names, be applied to any other part of the region as yet untouched by the axe.

An account of one of the many painful episodes that occurred during the first stages of settlement in the midst of those forests will serve better than any description to show the nature of those places where not even birds could penetrate and where, if they managed to do so, they could find no soil on which to land, because the earth lay from one to six meters below an apparent surface consisting of piles of vegetable debris in a state of constant decomposition.

The settlers who had been brought to Llanquihue from the vaults of the castle of Corral were tiring of the vexing situation in which they found themselves because the lack of roads had made it impossible to place them on their assigned lands; and so no sooner did they see the return of the first pioneers who with hatchet and machete had just opened a tortuous and very narrow path between the harbor and Lake Llanquihue, than they asked the agent for permission to explore it. The agent in

---

96. The larch, that mighty tree more than half of which is wasted in the felling, has long been and still is that region's greatest source of wealth. VPR.

person set out with thirty-two of the most stalwart settlers; a moment later, proceeding in single file, they all disappeared on a path that might well be called a dark tunnel five leagues long, dug through dense moist brush growing from a muddy floor of half-rotten roots, trunks, and leaves. We stopped frequently to take count, for since the branches laboriously pushed aside by each traveler instantly closed again behind him, it seemed that each was walking through that forest alone. When after half an hour of very tiring advance we rested and once more counted, we noted, at first with surprise and then with horror, that the heads of two families, Lincke and Andrés Wehle, were missing. We called them, we fired our weapons, we turned back to see whether we could find some trace of where they had gone astray, so as to help them. In vain did we send out parties of local men spurred on by the hope of rewards, in vain did we repeatedly fire the cannon of the *Meteoro;* all was in vain: those two unfortunates had disappeared forever!

Seventeen years later, in the cheerful picturesque town of Puerto Montt, I met a young man of twenty-six who had come from Copiapó to claim the possessions left by his father Andrés Wehle, a man lost in the forest, dead of hunger and despair along with his companion Lincke, in the first days of the settlement.

When we laid the foundations of that community, the region was still exactly what it had been sixteen years earlier and could therefore be described only as it had been then by the distinguished English voyagers whom their government had sent to explore our coasts.[97] These energetic explorers were so unfavorably impressed by the gloomy and inhospitable coast that to describe it they chose to use italics, perhaps in the belief that this was the only way to win the reader's assent to their peremptory judgment. Their description is in fact such as to make any future hope of using those wastelands for the benefit of mankind quite unimaginable. Let us hear what they have to say:

> Western Patagonia is much like the worst of Tierra del Fuego. . . . Every inch of land, every tree, every bush is a sponge saturated with water. . . . In the twelve months of the year there are probably only ten days exempt from snow and rainstorms, and never as many as thirty free of hurricane-force winds. . . . One can truly affirm that in the south of Chile there is not a *single* place suitable for settlement by civilized man. . . . The climate of Valdivia is exactly the same as that of Chiloé, which in general is certainly an obstacle to the cultivation of those lands.

97. "Sketch of the surveying of His Majesty's ships *Adventure* and *Beagle,*" 1836, *Journal of the Royal Geographical Society of London.* VPR.

We see, then, that these distinguished navigators apply their reproof even to Valdivia.

What could men afraid of mud and rain tell us about a place where mud and rain abound? Only a farmer, when he examines a recently planted field that for the layman is nothing but the debris of trees and grasses among bare clumps of turned-up earth, can see in the midst of this destruction the seed that a few months later will transform the scene into a carpet of golden grain. To judge aright of material undertakings that require vigorous and steady personal effort; to face imposing difficulties head-on; to suffer hunger, weariness, and harsh weather; to condemn pain and danger while appraising the benefits that will one day flow from the lands that lie before one—these are not tasks for the fainthearted.

I have briefly commented on hasty judgments because these were not the least pernicious among the settlement's foes in its early days. This inoffensive and singularly useful enterprise had attracted the most absurd combination of enemies. The authorities in the neighboring provinces, infected by the groundless hatred that many of their citizens felt toward the foreigners, were constantly impeding the activities of the immigration agent in their respective territories. The vexing problem of public lands raised its unwelcome and shameless head in Llanquihue as well; there, too, every piece of land suddenly had an owner. When the press dealt with the matter it was only to fill some space or satisfy some petty slight. Very few journalists knew where the settlement was, which did not stop them from writing about it and criticizing its location, confusing Valdivia with Llanquihue and the meaning of *emigration* with those of *immigration* and *settlement,* thereby obliging me to compose the paper on these three words that I submitted to Don Antonio Varas in December 1854. There were articles that took the government to task for the "huge" sums wasted on such an establishment and asked with smug stupidity what benefit the country was deriving from it. Such talk was repeated even in private conversations. An infant in swaddling clothes was being criticized for being as yet unable to pay for the milk that nourished him! Why recall now the accusations invented by irrationality and stupid ignorance to fill the not always well-intentioned columns of the *Mercurio* and the *Revista Católica?* Political considerations on the one hand and sordid selfishness on the other, but not a trace of reason, led the former, in its No. 8001, to make hasty and unfounded attacks against the benefits of immigration in order to discredit the government that was encouraging it. The *Revista,* driven by shortsighted sectarian interests and material gain, enthusiastically sounded the same note; neither paper, to achieve its aim, failed to give a strangely cordial welcome in its columns to every despatch sent from the south by those who were unlawfully occupying public lands.

These enemies, however, did not suffice, but had to be joined by dark fanaticism, which, to the shame of mankind, still flourishes in our century. This implacable foe of progress and of whatever is divine in the human heart soon found, in a Minister of Justice for whom clothes make the man and in a university dean of the kind the Spaniards call half-baked, the instruments it needed to harass the settlement.

No matter how painful it may be for me as a Chilean to recall these events, I must make mention of them here, so that the low opinion in which immigration was then held may be clear, as well as the insouciance with which the most ill-considered measures were adopted, as long as they were designed to harm it.

On the lands of an abandoned old mission there was an apple orchard, as there are throughout the forests of Valdivia. The public road passed through this orchard, travelers camped under its trees, and for safety they shut their mounts up in a corral made of tall posts that according to tradition had served as the walls of the former mission church. Since this was land whose public ownership no one disputed, it was distributed in small portions to several immigrant families; and so that these might be less troubled by the rains while getting settled, the agent had the unfortunate idea of having the posts restored to an upright position and covered with a wooden roof, thus turning this shelter for animals into one for human beings.

The priest could not accept the loss of his apples, which he considered natural perquisites of his office; and to recover them he saw to it that some Indians should appear to request either the reestablishment of the mission or the return of the lands that their ancestors had ceded for it. What ancestors were those, and what heirs were these? No one had the slightest idea, but why be troubled by such trifles? Maneuvers of this kind were repeated daily to produce alleged owners for lands that were about to find firm buyers. A carefully coached delegation of Indians therefore left Valdivia and complained of the agent before the Minister of Justice, who, by the way, was so enamored of immigration that without calling for any reports or even calculating the possible effects of a rash decision, he drew up an order to the agent in the following terms: "Regardless of such importance as the settlements may have, you will proceed immediately to return to the Indians the lands of Cuyunco Mission, improperly distributed among the German families."

These families had already begun to build their houses and to make many other improvements on their land and had already written to Europe, sending maps and calling on their relatives and friends to join them. What would have become of the faith and credit accorded the government's promises had not the agent declared his intention of disobeying so unthinking an order?

If this was the behavior of the higher authorities, what was to be expected from the lower ones when selfish interests dictated their intervention in the affairs of the settlement? At times they supported the usurpation of public lands, insisting on their return to their supposed owners; at others they used foolish pretexts to prevent the settlers from hiring laborers to work on the roads without which no lands could be distributed; at others they complained of violations of their jurisdiction, paying not the slightest attention to the decree of June 27, 1853, which placed the area of settlement under the special and direct authority of the president of the Republic, to the exclusion of all others. The government's immigration agent served as governor of the settlement, and the subdelegates and inspectors of the area of settlement were appointed by him, subject only to the approval of the president.

I refrain from repeating the causes of this vulgar hostility and specifying the deeds that arose from it, limiting myself to the account of a single incident that will exemplify the outrageousness of all.

I was obliged to go to the capital on official business; and as I departed, I informed the authorities on Chiloé that I was leaving Don Santiago Foltz, a well-qualified immigrant, prudent, and enthusiastically devoted to the progress of what he delighted in calling his new fatherland, as my substitute in the settlement. Imagine my surprise, then, when upon my return I found the settlement abandoned, the wretched settlers, so as not to perish of hunger, digging up the potatoes they had planted, and my substitute held as a criminal in the foul jail of Calbuco!

This is what had happened: The governor of that town, who, like many others, dealt in lumber, had ordered the acting agent to send him, as prisoners, those sawmill workers who were working on the roads for the settlement and therefore not fulfilling their contracts in Calbuco. Foltz had answered that the settlement had its judges, without whose decision he would not allow any affront to the men whom I had hired to build the road and who were so sorely needed where they were. This refusal infuriated the governor, who then ordered Foltz himself to appear before him forthwith; and since he could not achieve this either, he sent soldiers to arrest him and imprisoned him in the Calbuco jail. Such an outrage would not seem credible had I not preserved, as proof of the incredible, the following document, which I copy to the letter:

Calbuco, September 1, 1853

Upon receipt of this order, Inspector Toribio Pozo will order the German Santiago Foltz to embark on the sloop I am sending to fetch him, and should he refuse to obey or try to resist, read him this order before witnesses and warn him to obey, but if he should persist in not obeying, then you and the men I send with you shall seize him by force and place him on board under restraint. Inform him that when he gets here he will have to pay the expense of bringing him. Signed,

Ricardes.

Yet even this was not enough. The onslaught against the settlement was to come not only from unthinking authorities, and a successful effort was mounted to elicit slanderous screeches from the very bosom of a body created to direct education and promote morality.

Nature is so fond of contrasts that even in that emporium of knowledge that among us bears the name of University, a name that would make one believe there is nothing it does not know, she mischievously placed, by the side of the great Bello, a great . . . fool, who, realizing that he had managed to become a dean, suddenly hit upon the idea of presenting to the eyes of his learned colleagues so dark and mournful a picture of what the settlement was doing to the country that the frightened savants immediately brought the matter to the attention of the Minister of Education, Justice, and Religious Affairs.

Their frightful scribble asserted that Protestant propaganda was spreading everywhere, that the teachers in the schools were Protestants, the seducers of women were Protestants, and that these Protestants were being protected by the agent, who, Mason that he was, had spent St. John's Day profaning churches with scandalous orgies! The document ended with a whole sheet of reflections, from which I copy the first lines: "In view of these events, how right were our good citizens to fear the establishment of this settlement, and how rightly did they foretell and lament these and other evils," and so forth.

What would foreigners think of us if they read such a document? And what will my readers think of the truthfulness of the attacks against the settlement when I tell them that on the very St. John's Day chosen by the slanderer for his defamation of the agent's conduct, that poor functionary lay in bed suffering the cruel consequences of another shipwreck in which he had almost perished while seeking for the new settlers lands distant enough and unencumbered enough by apple orchards to be safe from the encroachments of usurpers, priests, and university deans!

· · ·

Not everything, however, was cause for despair. Montt and Varas watched over the fate of the settlement, and with such protectors it was bound to succeed.

The settlement at Llanquihue was inaugurated on February 12, 1853, a day chosen by the agent so as to add another grain of sand to the pedestal of the great and glorious monument symbolized for us by that day;[98] and as the foundations of the town that was to be the center of the settlements were laid out, it was baptized with the name Puerto Montt, a small homage that its founders paid to the author of the law of November 18, 1845, whom the Chilean people had now elected to execute it.

As a legacy of colonial days, we Chileans have the abominable urge to bestow the same name on a multitude of different things. Thus we speak of the province of Aconcagua and the Aconcagua River; the province of Santiago and the city of Santiago; the province of Valdivia, the Valdivia River, and the city of Valdivia. Now, because some people have heard that a town was recently founded in the territory called Melipulli, they want to call it Melipulli, too, although no such city name is found on any map whatsoever, instead of Puerto Montt, a name known for some time even in Europe. Melipulli is the name of an area located on the northern shore of Reloncaví Bay; Cayenel is one section of that area, and in Cayenel were laid the foundations of that town whose name it is now proposed, in vain, to erase. If the Spanish system is to be preserved and what is Caesar's is not to be rendered unto Caesar, then call the town Cayenel and not Melipulli.

Now let us for a moment follow the development of the settlement. The same year it was founded, the wooded lands whose frontage on the road could be measured were distributed among the settlers; and by decree of June 27, 1853, the region between the northern shore of Reloncaví Bay, including some of the islands there, and the burned-out area in the central valley of Osorno, as far as the charred remains of its trees stretched, was declared a territory of settlement subject to special administration. The borders of this territory were the Andes on the east and, on the west, imaginary lines running through impassable and uninhabited forests.

The harsh winter of that year destroyed all the work that had been done and put the settlers in danger of starving to death. The winter of 1854 was equally cruel, and the fertility of the recently plowed virgin soil frustrated the cultivation of cereals by smothering them in their own excessive

98. Chile declared her independence from Spain on February 12, 1818. JP.

growth. In 1855 the government was obliged to grant more assistance to these unfortunate settlers, on whose fields a plague of all-devouring birds had descended. In 1861—that is, six years after such cruel reverses—the settlement had, thanks to the presence of that handful of immigrants, achieved such importance that it was made the capital of a province formed of the former departments of Valdivia and Chiloé, Osorno, and Carelmapu.

The dates speak for themselves. We shall not, however, follow the settlement's history as a political unit, but simply as a territory of settlement established in the province of Llanquihue.

The liveliness, energy, and happy inhabitants of the cheerful and picturesque village of Puerto Montt, born so recently from the mire and forests of a remote wasteland, contrast with the gloomy silence and neglect that are the rot affecting the prematurely aged surrounding towns.

What could have caused the untimely decrepitude of those towns that were once considered important? In my opinion, the answer is simple: in the time of the Conquest, the Spaniards simultaneously waged war and founded cities; and since they were at the same time pursuing new victories and turning back to protect their first settlements threatened by the Indians, they clearly paid attention, in founding these towns, only to their strategic importance, not to whether their location was suitable for commerce or whether the troops that gave them life could be withdrawn without placing the settlements' very existence in danger. Nowadays everyone knows that there are necessary towns in the world and unnecessary ones. A great many of the towns founded by the Spaniards in Chile belong to the latter class; doomed soon to disappear, they owe their precarious survival only to our habit of considering them necessary and therefore incurring fruitless expenses on their behalf. If, without offending racial sensibilities, I were allowed to add other reasons to that of a bad choice of location, I should only point out that our blood, more than anything else, is to blame for all our neglect and backwardness.

Puerto Montt is a necessary town, because it is part of a safe and convenient harbor placed by nature in the midst of abundant forests of larch, halfway along the seacoast of the settled area, and very close to the farming and manufacturing centers both of that area and of the rich department of Osorno, which formerly had no way to export its copious products.

The modest but comfortable and handsome buildings of this new provincial capital follow a layout far superior to that of any other Chilean town in the breadth and perfect grading of its streets, the relative smallness of its blocks of buildings, the spacious sidewalks, and the location of its public edifices, which, without leaving any empty spaces, takes into account all future needs of a modern municipality. There you will not see the harsh jail occupying the principal spot on the main square and displaying its bars and its repulsive fauna for the eyes of the merchant and the visitor. The town has its special places for soldiers and for punishment, just as it does for commerce and recreation. The first public square in Chile to have a park was that of Puerto Montt, embellished, to be sure, not only by the exotic trees so much in vogue now, but by the splendid evergreens and unusual flowers that have always adorned our forests. A huge and beautiful parish church is currently under construction; and meanwhile two chapels are in operation, one Catholic and one Protestant. The hospital, also under construction, is already noteworthy for its spacious and practical design; and despite their dreadful purpose, the two cemeteries, one for Catholics and the other for Protestants, are so located and adorned that they, too, constitute authentic parks. The market is also noteworthy, and even more so the National Guard barracks, which joins the spaciousness of its courtyard and the commodiousness of its interior with an elegant and meticulously constructed exterior. The notary's office, the jail, the departmental library, all have their own buildings, as do four schools, two public and two private.

The latest census shows that this village has 2,500 inhabitants; yet it boasts a perfectly organized choral society, a volunteer fire department with two pumps—an institution that the foreigners brought to Llanquihue, with no need of a frightful conflagration like that of the Compañía,[99] which produced the definitive establishment of Santiago's volunteer fire department—and, finally, the best-stocked departmental library in the country, which Minister of Justice Errázuriz commended as follows in his report for 1865: "This is a most well-ordered and thriving establishment, thanks to the enthusiastic support of the citizens and especially that of the Germans."

Every house, no matter how modest the means of its inhabitant, is endowed, even if on a small scale, with every comfort known to Europeans; all are kept absolutely neat, and there is not one that even though lacking more elegant adornments does not display large pots with select flowers behind the clean glass of the windows facing the street. Their furniture, all made of local wood by first-rate cabinet makers, is both comfortable and ornamental. In Puerto Montt it is unheard of for anyone to build without first planning for a garden. Every garden, along with flowers and

99. *Compañía,* the Society of Jesus. The author refers to the fire that in 1863 destroyed the Jesuit church in Santiago and killed some two thousand persons, mostly members of the country's leading families. EOV.

early vegetables, contains fruit trees the possibility of whose cultivation is only now becoming apparent to the older inhabitants of the region. Mills, tanneries, breweries, distilleries, excellent bakeries, every kind of artisan, and in general every resource and convenience to be found in a large city, with the exception of a theater and a printing press, are found in that model community, where, characteristically, begging is prosecuted as a crime.

The sight of that infant town, surrounded by neat and carefully cultivated hills, and the memory of what it once was, are a good indication of what it is destined to be, since in so short a time what was once despised has come to amount to so much.

The distance between Puerto Montt and Lake Llanquihue, whose picturesque shores are the chief site of the settlement, is a little more than four leagues from south to north. A costly and well-maintained wagon road spans this distance, replacing the primitive muddy path where the unfortunate Wehle and Lincke perished. For the first two leagues this route, solidly compacted, passes over a stretch of dunes and tangled roots that the local people call the Tepual. In this area, as yet unsuited for farming, the traveler's attention is drawn only to the distant view of the dark forest driven from the road by fire and the axe, the many charred tree trunks barely held up by their wasted roots, the skeletal remains of the *coihues,* the gigantic stumps of felled larches, so far impervious to flame and axe, and an occasional solitary hut, a storage place for the lumber elaborated in the interior of the forest and carried by hand to this loading point. December, January, February, and March, the season for the cutting and preparation of the lumber, are also noteworthy for the multitudes who come here from the farthest islands of the archipelago. They all work at the same time, all barefoot; and all — women, children, and old men — carry boards, girders, and heavy beams on their shoulders, by the side of the wagons that the Germans use for the same purpose.

The Tepual ends at a long stretch of scrubland, called Arrayán, that forms something like a street among the thick stumps of what was once a stand of larches. This Arrayán is composed of two long rows of huts, one more uncomfortable and less attractive than the next, inhabited by employees of people in town and by the numerous agents of businesses in Calbuco and Ancud, who come with abundant merchandise to be exchanged for lumber and carry on a lively trade during those months in that strange encampment in the middle of a forest. These people disappear with the first rains of winter; and that bustling place then becomes, for eight months, a wasteland with houses.

Beyond the end of the Tepual and of that small settlement, the countryside acquires a wholly different appearance. Untouched nature, with all its impressive solitude, is left behind, and the fertile settled lands that surround Lake Llanquihue begin. On stepping out of the forest the traveler's eyes cannot but fall with pleasant surprise upon a remarkable garden filled with bright flowers and planted on the stump of a felled larch. The German settlers make use even of those difficulties they cannot overcome. This great stump stood in the courtyard of one of them; more time was to be lost in demolishing it than in adorning it, and without further delay that obstruction was turned into a most whimsical garden.

Every quarter mile between this point and the clear waters of the lake two pretty houses stand facing each other across the road. Each farm has a frontage of a quarter of a mile, and each, with its dwellings, its barns, its stables, gardens, orchards, corrals and fields, machinery, hothouses, and specialized workshops, constitutes a complete, though modest, agricultural establishment where many of our wealthy landowners could find much to learn. One hundred forty farms of four hundred acres each, and eighteen of two hundred, lie on the northern, western, and part of the southern shores of beautiful Lake Llanquihue, which is fairly regular in shape and some forty leagues in circumference; and on the fertile banks of the Chamiza, whose irregular shoals stretch more than a league into the sea, you will also find, at intervals of a quarter of a mile, fifteen fine farms with docks for river navigation on the premises.

The farms of the settlement differ among each other only in the exercise of some new craft suited to the nature of the soil or in the degree of wealth or knowledge of their owners. Thus in Puerto Octay (Muñoz Gamero)[100] linseed and turnips are favorite crops, to be turned into oils for shipment to Valparaíso; in the eastern zone you will find fields of pearl barley along with the corresponding machines; along the Chamiza, mills for the production of pure linens and linen blended with cotton or hemp; in one place potatoes are grown, to be turned into spirits; in another, flour

---

100. I have been unable to discover the meaning or appropriateness of the name *Octay*, which has now replaced that of Muñoz Gamero, a name that appears in official documents since the founding of the settlements. To this worthy and lamented officer of our navy we owe the hydrographic maps of Lake Llanquihue and Lake Esmeralda; the ideas he conveyed to the immigration agent were the cause of that official's determination to build a road from the harbor to the lake, a road that opened thousands of acres of excellent land for settlement. Puerto Octay, when the agent chose it as the obligatory landfall for vessels connecting the northern and southern shores of the lake, had no name whatsoever, and neither did the coast on which it lay. The then recent catastrophe at Magallanes and the memory of the services rendered by the late officer led the agent to give his name to that picturesque little port. VPR.

or tannin mills are built; and wherever a visitor goes, he has the pleasure of observing not only activity but also well-being and contentment.

As many as six thousand acres are now clear of trunks and stumps and under intelligent cultivation; and to appreciate this achievement, we must remember that only in 1856 did some additional immigrants come to swell the number of the founders, and that it requires more time and money to bring an acre of this forested land under cultivation than it does to buy one at a high price in the north of the country, between Molina and Carelmapu.[101]

By 1858 the colony was beginning to be self-sufficient; although the number of settlers of all ages and sexes came to only 789, they already had a thousand acres under cultivation.

To be sure, one cannot expect much in the way of industries from agrarian settlements as small as ours; nonetheless, the little that can be expected and that is already in existence is destined, because of its unquestionably sound basis, to take an honorable place alongside what the vine, the bee, and the silkworm have already contributed to the Chilean economy. These industries, all new and also originally viewed with the sarcastic contempt with which complacent ignorance views whatever it does not understand, have already achieved what few had imagined they would achieve. With justified pride have we seen the first of them contribute its products to our wine country and win prizes for their excellence, while the second frees us from the importation of wax and honey and even competes abroad in quality and price with those who used to supply us. Finally, because of the interest in silk, silk producers everywhere are forced to have recourse to Chile for the excellent breed of silkworm that today is improving the quality of European stocks.

In the settlement, the cultivation of linseed and the establishment of industries that utilize it have quietly proceeded without begging the government for any special privileges, an approach that guarantees excellent results. Seccative oil, used for oil painting, is shipped and sold far more cheaply than what used to be imported through Valparaíso. Many families wear clothes made of linen cloth, and the wealthier among them use domestically produced tablecloths of damasked linen.

In the immigrants' homeland, potato production required the existence of an industry that could utilize the annual surplus of that foodstuff; and this important need has been filled here by two factories that are operating most successfully.

101. A laborer's wages are never less than fifty centavos a day and often reach seventy-five. VPR.

The barley crop sustains two important industries, that of pearl barley and the breweries, whose products our northern brewers strive in vain to imitate.

Curing plants, tanneries, tannin mills, wickerwork factories, all have been in existence in the settlement for some time, and apiaries are now beginning to appear in that land of flowers.

Along the road from the headquarters of the colony to the most remote German farms there are six flour mills, each of which, though having but a single set of millstones, is equipped with all the machinery necessary for the production of perfect flour. There are also a mill with three sets of millstones, four sawmills (three powered by water and one by steam), eighteen winnowing machines, all of local construction, and a steam-powered threshing machine. As for the small trades inseparable from great centers of population, such as tailors, carpenters, cabinetmakers, etc., I have already had occasion to say that none is lacking.

This rapid glance at the agriculture and nascent industry of the settlement naturally leads us to examine, even if only superficially, its still embryonic commerce. One could say that before the establishment of the settlement there was no commercial activity in the isolated coves of Reloncaví Bay other than the summer trade in larch timber cut in the forests closest to the shore, and even this trade was beginning to decline for lack of roads that might have facilitated the exploitation of trees growing farther inland after all those along the coast had been cut. In small boats and launches held together by straw ropes instead of nails, this timber was conveyed to the well-known old fort at Calbuco; and this hamlet, which had become a market for the lumber trade because it was halfway between the place of production and that of shipment, San Carlos de Ancud, was eking out a most precarious existence.

The employees and branch offices of the Ancud merchants operated in Calbuco; and since money was unknown in those happy places, the inhabitants, in order to facilitate their retail trade, had invented a currency, the *tabla* (board), which was their unit of exchange and had the official value of one *real* of our old coinage. In exchange for some hundreds of *reales-tablas*, a seller received flour, salt, peppers, much liquor, and the other provisions necessary to satisfy the modest needs of men who regularly went barefoot and lived much as did the Indians.

When the settlement was established at the same spot from which the lumber was shipped to Calbuco, everything changed. The branches of Ancud firms that had been operating in Calbuco now left that unnecessary place to set up operations in Puerto Montt; many lumbermen, delighted to see a town that from its very beginnings gave signs of life, moved out of their camps in search of a more civilized existence; and the rope-tied boats and launches gradually gave way to fine sloops and then to great ships, both foreign and domestic, that came from many points to load lumber at Puerto Montt.

I have already said that until 1855 the settlement needed supplementary shipments of food; its members were then too busy with the hard work of getting it under way to think of the timber resources, which were exploited exclusively by the islanders of Chiloé. In 1856 the spirits produced by the settlers began to compete with those brought in from elsewhere. In 1860 immigrants first entered the lumber trade; and according to official figures, commercial activity in 1861 amounted to 284,759 pesos.

Power saws are now beginning to obviate the destructive effects of the axe in those valuable forests; and the roads constantly being built farther into the forest, along with the four-wheeled wagons used on them, have created a trade in valuable lumber, most of which was formerly wasted in the felling.

The agricultural and manufactured commodities that we have spoken of and that we now see appearing in trade are grain and potato spirits, beer, tanned hides, seccative linseed oil, salted meats, butter, oats, and rye, apart from the wheat, flour, and pearl barley that are already being shipped out, as well as the linen cloth, wickerwork, and products of other small industries that for the time being are barely able to satisfy local demand.

This was the origin of the settlement at Llanquihue and these, as has been explained, the reasons for its removal from its original location near Valdivia. A handful of settlers scattered over the little regarded shores where they were taken by necessity had there worked miracles that by 1860 were already amazing those familiar with the geography of the country. Never a discouraging word was heard from those models of selflessness, steadfastness, and hard work, despite the travails that beset them from the moment of their reaching Llanquihue. There they had settled, pushing difficulties aside more than overcoming them, when a harsh winter came upon them and forced them to eat their seed grain, dig up the potatoes already planted, and even kill their draft animals so as not to die of starvation.

At that time the immigration agent wrote the following to his immediate superior: "They have undergone deprivation, hunger, and travail without flagging; the harsh test to which the steadfastness and faith of these unfortunates have been subjected during the past winter gives us every reason to hope. With people of this kind, if, as is to be expected, their number increases, I see the future prosperity of the settlement assured, let its unjust and shortsighted detractors say what they may."[102]

Sordid egoism, fanaticism, and defamation harassed it in its remote haven; and when these hostile forces began in the north to damp the temporary enthusiasm for the settlement, the agent buoyed up the spirits of its leaders with these words of consolation: "With persevering faith and steadfastness, this infant establishment will before long become the southern jewel of our country."

Seven years later, the aged Chilean now writing these lines experienced the pure satisfactions of patriotism on seeing his prediction come true.

102. Communication from the immigration agent, December 1853. VPR.

XXIII

Immigration. — The German population at Llanquihue and
Valdivia in 1860. — Its level of education. — Its influence on
native Chileans. — Unfortunate loss of public lands. —
Personal sacrifices made by the agent to provide land for the
immigrants.— Ways to prevent abuse in these matters.

Perhaps not one of the countless colonies founded yearly in the world's wilderness by the dynamic sons of Old Europe has required seventeen years to accumulate so insignificant a number of foreign settlers as has our settlement at Llanquihue; and that is certainly not because our government lacks practical knowledge after so long a period of timid experimentation, but because immigration is still viewed as a luxury and not a pressing need. In our country immigration takes second place to everything else, including a public building, no matter how unnecessary. While bewailing the lack of public funds, we budgeted additional thousands to continue building what here we call a university. Thousands were spent on providing comfortably for a factory of required textbooks, but there was no money for immigration. Half a million pesos were voted for a project to settle our Araucanian provinces and additional thousands for the support of troops whose presence there, if temporary, is useless, and if permanent, exceedingly costly; once again foreign immigration, which alone could incorporate the natives into society without exterminating them, was passed over.

With that half a million pesos we could have brought two thousand families, approximately eight thousand persons, from abroad and settled them among the Indians, with 50,000 pesos left over to supply them with modern arms. Nowadays an emigrant, to go to a country where property close to established towns is practically given away and where he is furthermore offered not inconsiderable privileges and concessions, asks only that his passage be paid. So substantial a group of foreigners would not flinch before the natives. No matter how bold and brave he may be, the Indian is not likely to get in the way of a rifle that will wound or kill him as soon as he comes within range, even if he has lost some of his former fear of firearms.

I have given a rapid sketch of the progress of the settlement, which would have been even more notable if the immigrants who have joined it over the years had been there from the outset to work at utilizing its resources. The following figures for immigration show how slow its growth has been:

1852	212	1861	11
1853	51	1862	32
1854	35	1863	12
1855	—	1864	155
1856	460	1865	—
1857	180	1866	36
1858	9	1867	—
1859	70[103]	1868	—
1860	93	1869	7

A pitiful total of 1,363 immigrants of all ages and both sexes! Seventeen years to bring in a number of immigrants inferior to that often reaching the harbors of the United States in a single day!

It is painful to look at this list and see how slowly, how reluctantly, and with how many interruptions our wastelands have been fecundated

---

103. I use the figure given by the Havana edition. The others consulted read 11, but with that number the total falls short of 1,363. JP.

by that stream of population and wealth that has worked such wonders everywhere else and that in our present condition, as we must never tire of repeating, is the only means of quickly rising to an enviable level among civilized nations.

Should we wish to make even plainer the benefits of sacrificing to maximize this important inflow, we need only glance away from Llanquihue and at Valdivia.

Very few immigrants remained in that remote province when the settlement was transferred to the wastelands of Llanquihue. Those few industrious foreigners had barely managed to build their dwellings when they laid the foundations of the different industries that Valdivia now proudly displays to the astonished eyes of those who knew it as a garrison town where even bread had to be brought from the outside. In June 1866 the intelligent chief of that province, in his report to the Minister of the Interior, already wrote, after referring to the lamentable backwardness and poverty of the unpopulated areas of his province, the following noteworthy words:

> Since the gradual natural increase of population cannot fill this unfortunate gap as quickly as is required, we must have recourse to the most efficient and, indeed, sole remedy, immigration. Such immigration as the province has received since 1859, though consisting of only 405 men above the age of fifteen, is already demonstrating the benefits that it could bring us. . . . Nothing is more obvious than the change that the German immigrants have effected in this province. Those few individuals have sufficed to produce in a few years a remarkable expansion of business and of the comforts of life, and even a pleasing change in the physical appearance of our towns. Thanks to their influence, not only have most of our established industries grown, but other new ones have been created, have flourished, and now annually export more than four times the value of our total exports before the immigrants' arrival. At that time the province of Concepción supplied us with flour; now the mills built by the settlers satisfy our local needs and compete with our former suppliers in other markets, even though the wretched state of our roads makes it difficult to reduce the cost of transportation. Meager harvests of grain that found no buyers because of the limited consumption and the importation of flour are now sought after by millers, distillers, and brewers, who turn them into products that were formerly brought from the outside.
>
> Instead of having to drive animals across Araucania, a difficult and risky undertaking, we now have meat processing plants that benefit both the cattlemen and the owners of these new establishments and that have

also given rise to the breeding and fattening of hogs, which were very scarce in former times.

Also due to the German settlers is the considerable development of our tanneries, whose products find no suitable market in our cities but are shipped to Europe, where they are eagerly bought up. Finally, a hundred other industries, embryonic or small in scale, will eventually grow and make their contribution to the progress and well-being of the province.

The educational and moral level of settlers like ours is in full keeping with the degree of intelligence and enterprise that they display in their work. The immigrants' most pressing concern, after assuring the sustenance of their children, is to provide them with education. Far from keeping them from attending school, therefore, they compel them to do so; and they always consider it a special benefit when an educational institution is established near their home. Thus education is not a mere adornment for them but, on the contrary, a pressing need, an indispensable requirement for not losing respect in the eyes of others.[104]

Two years after the establishment of the settlement a thorough census of the native and foreign inhabitants of its territory showed the number of Chileans to be 3,579 and that of immigrants, only 247. Among the former, 872 persons could read, or read and write, meaning that there was one who could read or write for every 4.1 who could not even read. Among the latter, that is, among the Germans, out of 247 persons, 181 could both read and write, meaning that all those old enough to read and write could do so, as can be seen in the following figures:

181	who could read and write
45	under the age of five
20	between the ages of five and ten, and attending school
1	woman who could not read
247	the total population

Neither does the German learn reading and writing only to go on to forget about it. Here is what Minister of Justice Errázuriz wrote on August 14, 1865, about the settlers' reading habits:

104. In Puerto Montt there still lives a German woman, poor at one time, who refused to marry one Romero, a well-to-do merchant of Calbuco, only because at the very moment of the ceremony she discovered that he could not read. VPR.

In Santiago 20 to 23 persons a day visit the National Library, with 8,000 to 10,000 readers a year. . . . As stated, 2,123 readers visited the library of Puerto Montt in the first three quarters of 1854, even though that period included the time that the establishment was closed for vacations.

A rapid comparison: wealthy Santiago, with its population of over 100,000, its superior educational institutions, its cultural incentives, and its superbly stocked library, can count eight to ten thousand readers in a whole year; Puerto Montt, with 2,500 inhabitants, in substantially less than nine months, has 2,123 readers in its modest library.

In school, even as they learn to read, children are taught the rudiments of music; and from earliest childhood, singing develops in them that spirit of fellowship and that appreciation of the need for sociability that we admire in the German people wherever we find it.

If the high morality of the southern settlers were not common knowledge, a glance at statistics of crime would suffice to convince us of it. But fortunately fanaticism and its inseparable companion, ignorance, have tacitly come to grant not only that the immigrant's moral standards are high, but that if one had to seek similar virtue elsewhere it would be a waste of time to do so among his unjust detractors. Happily the time—not so remote—is past when university deans marshaled their forces against the settlement, shouting in public assemblies and then forwarding their foul rantings to the government, that the immigrants were all Masons, that on St. John's Day they celebrated orgies in churches where they defiled all the Indian women wearing European dress, and more jumbled nonsense in the same vein. To date the courts of Valdivia and Llanquihue have reason only to be pleased with the conduct of the immigrants; for my part, not to waste words, I shall mention but one example of the religious respect they all have for the property of others. In every town throughout our country, large and small, people fit iron bars to the windows that face the street if they wish to live in security. In Puerto Montt and in the immigrants' farmhouses, no matter how remote and solitary, such bars are unnecessary. Although the windows of the Germans are decorated with flowers and with all those pretty trinkets so dear to the heart of woman, burglaries are unheard of, for a thin pane of glass suffices to deter them.

The same qualities are seen in the influence that contact with the foreigners has had on Chileans raised in squalor amid the forests, in whom the spirit of petty larceny had taken such deep root. Most of the inhabitants of Puerto Montt are Chileans, as are the day laborers and the servants who reside there on a temporary basis; and the example of the immigrants has almost completely banished that vice among them.

The immigrants are to date few in number, to be sure, too few for us to be able to demand much of them, yet the mere example of those few missionaries of labor and enterprise, and contact with them, are producing such changes in the habits and customs of their Chilean neighbors that they leap to the attention of even the most stubborn enemies of the settlement.

And what sort of people, after all, were the inhabitants of those little known places, before the foreigners came to modify their way of life? The isolation in which they were forced to live, scattered among the forests along the solitary coves of Reloncaví Bay, did not allow them even to suspect the benefits of life in society. The abundance of foodstuffs, the total lack of incentives and of those needs whose satisfaction produces the well-being of man in civilized places, had accustomed them to idleness, vice, and their disgusting consequences.

The few families who lived in those places, almost lost in their isolation, had sunk into a shockingly abject state before the immigrants' hustle and bustle came to interrupt the torpor that was undoing them. Each family's dwelling generally consisted of a one-room hut, dirty and sooty, with the hearth in the middle of the floor. Whenever chance had caused some wild apple trees to grow nearby, the hut, which evidently served simultaneously as kitchen, dining room, and bedroom, was augmented with another structure where, next to a few barrels, stood hollowed-out logs for crushing the apples and making *chicha*. Behind these dwellings one always found a small plot of cultivated land, where fire-hardened sticks, always handled by the women, served as hoe and plowshare for the sowing of potatoes and beans, the only vegetables anyone was concerned with in those times. It was a rare homeowner who thought of sowing wheat. By the door of the hut and facing the seashore, small half-submerged enclosures formed of stones and branches served to trap such fish as the high tides might by chance bring there. These and the inexhaustible banks of every sort of delicious shellfish exposed by the tides were, along with the beans and potatoes, the larder that sustained these people. Even their method of preparing this food was purely Indian, from the time of the Conquest. A hole was dug in the ground and filled with stones heated on the spot in a fire; then the fish, shellfish, meat (if there was any), cheese, and potatoes were piled in and immediately covered with enormous *pangui* leaves, over which were laid bricks made of earth and knotted roots, to keep the steam from escaping. A quarter of an hour later, the whole family, with the obligatory accompaniment of dogs and pigs, would be gathered around that steaming horn of plenty, into which each member in turn would plunge his hand and, blowing on his fingers, eat his fill. When night came, father, mother, brothers, sisters, visitors, dogs, and pigs would huddle on the floor by the fire and sleep till the next day, on which the activities of the previous one would be repeated.

To satisfy their minimal needs in the way of clothing, *mate*, and tobacco, and the pressing one of liquor, they would take their axes into the coastal forests and stay there for as long as strictly necessary to pay off a small part of the debt they had contracted with the shopkeepers of Calbuco in exchange for the merchandise supplied them. There was not a single lumberman but he was deep in debt; and every purchase meant a new burden for the buyer, while the large sums due his creditors remained unpaid. Finally, let us take note of the following fact: in those places the only persons to be married in church were those who had grown tired of their other arrangements and wanted to legitimize their children. Otherwise, all that was needed was for a man to tell his beloved's parents that he wanted her to be his "missus" and for her to declare that she accepted this suitor as her man, and forthwith they were considered lawfully married. This unflattering description shows the culture and the way of life of the local people living by Reloncaví Bay.

How different is their present condition! Once the hurdles that nature initially placed in the way of the immigrant's agricultural and manufacturing enterprises had been overcome, he soon displayed before the astonished eyes of the Spanish-speaking inhabitant of southern Chiloé and of the native Huiliche of Osorno the advantages and comforts of life in society and the benefits that hard work could expect from a rich soil that until then they had been content to tread heedless of what it could yield.

It is a pleasure to repeat it: the influence of good examples has produced and continues to produce in the original population the good effects that were to be expected, and the settlement has become a magnet that has drawn in and absorbed hundreds of families that now not only enjoy a less isolated form of existence but try as much as possible to imitate the newcomers after having spent some time in their employ.

Immediately after the establishment of the settlement, very few local people were to be seen there; and to obtain labor for the initial projects we had to send boats in every direction, which even at a wage of a peso a day barely managed to bring a few laborers to Puerto Montt. Two years later, the number of Chileans in the territory of settlement came to 3,520, and ten years later, to 6,464. These are the figures of the official census, but the very thorough census privately ordered by the intendant Ríos shows 11,242 inhabitants for the same period. Whatever the number, large or small, it is fair to say that if the settlement should disappear, its Chilean neighbors could not go on living without practicing the habits they have contracted, and even less go back to their previous isolated state.

The government admits, although it does not fully understand, the need of bringing as many immigrants as possible into Chile as soon as possible; and so, even if it is unwilling or unable to fulfill this need, it still has the pressing obligation, for a more favorable occasion, of protecting the public lands that, if I may say so, are currently being stolen left and right.

The pace at which such land as we still have in the south is being sold; the manner in which property deeds are drawn up; the lack of a strict law to put an end to the effects of declarations under oath in places where not only is it known that there are gangs of men called *jureros*,[105] but where the obligations entailed by an oath are taken very lightly; and above all, the fact that there is no one to represent the public interest, be constantly on the alert, investigate deeds of sale or mortgage, and prosecute squatters—all of this, without exaggeration, will very soon leave the state without a foot of land at its disposal. What would then become of immigration? It cannot be denied that the government has done something to avoid this evil; but if this insufficient something is deemed to be enough, it becomes detrimental. The decrees to which I refer are the six issued between March 1853 and March 1857. These decrees, which at Llanquihue and other places where there are public lands are wrongly believed to empower the intendants and governors to act as notaries and draw up deeds for the sale, lease, or mortgaging of Indian lands, are having the most disastrous effect on the public interest. They may serve a purpose in protecting the native from the snares and trickery of civilized man; but they suffer from an enormous defect, which is that they do not defend civilized man, and above all the state, from the snares and trickery of the native, who is no less a man for being uncivilized and no less inclined than his civilized counterpart to make use of snares and trickery when they are to his benefit.

The snares and trickery of the civilized man and those of the Indian are in conflict when matters between civilized men and Indians are at issue; but in matters concerning the public treasury, the snares and trickery of the one form the closest possible alliance with those of the other in order to rob the state of all it has, taking advantage of the absolute lack of any special defender who might hold them in check.

---

105. *Jurero* is the name given in the south to the man whose profession is swearing under oath. There is always a hidden hand that governs the activities of this infamous gang. VPR.

The path they take, which has been taken from time immemorial to get title to land that has no known owner, is the easiest and quickest imaginable. The point is simply to find a piece of land that has no owner but the state and, once it has been found, to arrange with the most appropriate local Indians to have them sell it as something inherited from their ancestors. The natives, induced by bribes and especially by drink, crowd into the courts to declare under every oath imaginable that those lands belong by inheritance to the Indian who is trying to sell it. The transfer tax is now paid, unless it is dispensed with, and a bill of sale is drawn up. By this time some absurd notices have been posted that no one reads, or if anyone does read them, he will certainly not allege any rights to a property he has never heard of. Besides, if the land to be sold belongs to the state and the state has no one to represent it in the very places where it is being robbed, what claims, timely or not, can be lodged?

It comes as no surprise, therefore, that when the immigrants came to Valdivia in 1850 there was not a scrap of halfway usable land that could be offered to them within many leagues of that town. This misfortune was about to be repeated with the settlement at Llanquihue and could be prevented only in part, since before the settlers could take possession of land where Puerto Montt now stands, a multitude of squatters had already gathered in that remote corner to speculate with the sale of property that was not theirs and never had been.

My annoyance and surprise were therefore considerable when, just as I thought that leaving Valdivia had made me immune from such thievery, I found a letter from the governor of Calbuco, Don José Ramírez, in which I was informed that if I wanted to found settlements in Cayenel I had to begin by buying that land, because all of it had lawful owners. Under the circumstances, if I hesitated I was lost; requesting funds from the government meant delay and no assurance of success, and bringing suit meant entering into a world without end. I thus resigned myself and began by buying the site of the future town and the immediate surroundings out of my own pocket; and taught by example and experience, I fought the squatters with their own arms by setting up simulated purchases from the Indians, the presumed owners of the vast territory of Chanchán. These purchases and another levy of six hundred *duros* extracted from my puny purse allowed me to calm the storm.[106]

106. See the letter from the governor of Calbuco, Don José Ramírez, dated September 24, 1852, and also, among the public records in Osorno, the deed to which I refer, drawn up the following year. VPR.

· · ·

For some time, and surreptitiously, the extensive shores of Reloncaví Bay and their capriciously delimited and unexplored "interior"[107] have similarly come into private hands. At the gate to the governor's residence at the fort of Calbuco one could frequently find announcements that were to be read by persons who could not read or who neither came to that town nor had any reason to do so. These announcements would declare that such and such a piece of land, lying between such and such accessible points along the coast and including the interior as far as the highest Andes, the property of John Doe, was being sold, and so that all concerned may have due notice thereof, etc.[108]

Beginning in 1850, and without having sufficient authorization for it, the authorities began to raise obstacles to the acquisition of property whose sellers could not show reliable written proof of ownership; and this was one of the principal causes of the bitter hostility that many residents felt toward immigration. In the absence of immigration, no one disputed their claims to public lands; with it came an effort to despoil them of what they already considered to be theirs.

If we examine the method of defining property lines, we see at once that these greedy usurpers, instead of bequeathing a respectable fortune to their children, leave them nothing but a source of endless future lawsuits. None of these alleged proprietors knows the approximate extent, not to mention the ultimate borders, of properties of which only one side is known.

To give a more concrete example of the absurdity of each of these countless deeds with their mythical "interiors," allow me to postulate that the well-known valley of Santiago is covered by impenetrable forests and that its topography represents the thinly populated southern regions. Those who own lands on the shores of the Mapocho know that the Maipo River forms the valley's southern border. Those from the San Francisco del Monte River or Santa Cruz know that the high Andes form the valley's eastern border.

Those along the Mapocho present their claim as follows: on the north, a line originating at the source of the Mapocho in the Andes and following its course as far as Lake Pudahuel, and as interior all the land contained between these two points as far as the Maipo River. Those from

107. *Fondos* ["interior"] are all the lands contained between the parallel straight lines stretching for an unlimited distance from each end of the line formed by some accessible side of a property as measured on the accessible bank of a river or on the seacoast. VPR. [A little later, the author further explains this system of delimiting property. JP.]

108. There are many announcements after this fashion, and they never explain from whom the alleged owner obtained his title, and when they do explain anything they only succeed in making the spoliation more obvious. VPR.

Santa Cruz or from the banks of the river until it joins the Maipo explain their borders thus: following the course of the river from Lake Pudahuel until it joins the Maipo, and as interior the lands lying between these two points as far as the Andes. Which of these two groups owns the land?

I have before me a deed just like this, whose claims begin at the northern shore of Reloncaví Bay and stretch to the Bolivian border. Another claim begins at Río Bueno and extends its inexorable interior to precisely the midpoint of the base line of the first deed.

Everyone knows that the government issued the decree of December 4, 1855, not so much to defend the Indians as to defend the public lands, and that this is the reason for the grant of powers to intendants and governors. But turning these officers into notaries and agents of the treasury while they lack the responsibilities of the former and the obligations of the latter is a monstrosity that does more harm than good to the interests it is designed to protect. Why not restore to the notaries the full powers that article 6 of the aforementioned decree seems to place in question? Why not appoint special treasury agents for each sector of public lands, agents whose sole and special mission would be to watch tirelessly over the preservation of this property and to clarify for the courts the true rights of those who present invalid claims?

To make the intendants and governors into agents of the treasury and notaries free from responsibility is to create a set of public records not subject, like a notary's, to judicial inspection and monetary accountability, and, further, to undermine the purpose of the decree and to increase the number of those who pilfer from the public treasury by giving them legal accomplices. Each scrap of paper that they honor with the name of deed of sale, mortgage, or lease, brings in ten pesos to the authorities. I mean no offense to anyone, and I shall be very sorry if my ideas on this matter are interpreted or described in any way other than what their good intentions merit.

Neither is it my wish in any way to exclude intendants and governors from intervening in these contracts; but I should like their intervention, once they have heard the opinion of the treasury agent, to be limited to a simple veto if they suspect fraud, and to approval in other cases. The presence of such treasury agents and the consequent difficulty of maintaining fraudulent rights would stem the abuses I have been pointing out, and everyone would in future know where he stood with respect to the validity and firmness of purchases of land that are later to be the patrimony of his children.

The longer we delay in taking this measure or another serving the same purpose, the more valuable will those wastelands become, the more difficult will it be to define property lines, and the even more difficult will it be to assert rights that time and uncontested possession may have caused to lapse.

X X I V

A voyage across the pampas to Buenos Aires. — The road to Uspallata. — Rosario. — The Paraná River. — Buenos Aires. — The ex-dictator Don Juan Manuel Rosas.

When you leave foggy Llanquihue and its damp forests and travel to the northern regions, everything there seems drier, more arid than it really is; and so, when I suddenly found myself on the road from the town of Santa Rosa de los Andes to Mendoza, knowing that to the north of me the mountainous region became more barren by the mile until it turned into the sands and rocks of Atacama, I came to think that in all of Chile there could be nothing more useless to mankind than these vast highlands that separate us from the Argentine Republic. But even in the mind of one who has grown up in the forests, this unfavorable impression cannot last once he learns that these arid lands contain mineral wealth matching the agricultural wealth of the mountains of the south.

The road between Santa Rosa and Mendoza was so neglected and so bad when I found myself on it for the sixth time in early April 1855 that I could not get over my astonishment at how a route so important and so easy to build and repair could be allowed to remain in so pitiful a condition, in both its Chilean and Argentine sections.

It is depressing that when it comes to roads and public works, to creating sources of wealth, to anything having to do with demolishing or diminishing ancient and ill-advised burdens of taxation, our governments are as fearful of spending a few thousands that industry and commerce will soon requite with interest, as they are veritable spendthrifts when it comes to many other matters, even fratricidal wars in which they squander millions that, once spent, are gone forever.

The wealthy province of Mendoza and that of San Luis had at that time no port for shipping their products other than our Valparaíso; one could be sure that they, or at least Mendoza, would have none for many years to come, in spite of railways that might link Mendoza to Rosario, if the road across the Andes ever became what it should have been long ago, a good one.

According to the Spanish itinerary as corrected by Rivarola, the distance from Mendoza to Buenos Aires is 293 leagues, and that between Mendoza and Santa Rosa de los Andes, 80 leagues. Of these eighty, 54 lie in Mendoza and 26 in Chile. Of the 54 leagues in Mendoza, only those between Uspallata and the summit, which come to 24, require repair; and of the 26 leagues in Chile, only the 13 that lie between the summit and the customs post need work. Could these two neighboring states be driven to ruin by the expense of opening and maintaining a good road where goods valued in millions currently travel despite having to do so on a wretched path?

For ordinary travelers, however, this road is far less dangerous than many people think. Once over the summit, the climb to which, though short, is the most difficult part of the trip to Mendoza, the rest of the road may seem long but can at worst be called tiresome.

After leaving behind the famous Bridge of the Inca with its well-known hot springs, we reached the customs post of Uspallata, where we sought lodging.

Uspallata was one of the oldest and richest mineral deposits worked by Chileans when the great province of Cuyo formed an integral part of the so-called Kingdom of Chile. This colossal lode, considered to be one of the world's largest, appears, according to experienced and perspicacious miners, with the name of Potosí in Bolivia, with that of Famatina in La Rioja, with that of Gualilán in San Juan, and with that of Uspallata in Mendoza. Mendoza, one might say, owes its early development to these ores, because when the miners sent from Chile to work in the mountains came down into that small town, they were so delighted with its mild climate and fertile soil that they settled there.

In 1836, eager to find out the facts about the reputed wealth of the deposits at Uspallata, I had occasion to make a thorough exploration of the municipal archives of Mendoza; and the result of my investigation was the following: According to mining records, in 1660 there were 319 mines worked by 300 men. The wealth derived from them must have been considerable, because the inspectors' reports showed that the leaders yielded 800 marks[109] a cartload, the smaller veins, 40, and even the poorest ores, from 10 to 12.

Along this well-known old road I traveled, no longer free as in times past, but a slave to the obligations imposed on me by my appointment as consul general of Chile in Hamburg, where I was to foster German emigration to the settlement I had just founded.

Mendoza had progressed and prospered and was no longer the Mendoza of the despot Aldao. Seventy-six leagues farther on, San Luis de la Punta, was, except for the way in which it was governed, still the San Luis of the famous Lucero. There is nothing noteworthy about the other towns through which the road passes and in which the enormous Noah's arks that convey passengers between Mendoza and Rosario stop only to change horses.

Rosario is another matter. Before you reach this pretty little town recently founded on the banks of the giant of South American rivers, the domain of the pampa ends, and along with lively commercial activity on land and water, there appears in all its splendor a vigorous and rich vegetation that testifies to the fertility of the soil from which it springs. In Rosario the tired traveler boards the steamer that conveys him, amid the delights and charming panoramas offered by navigation on the Paraná, to the great city of Buenos Aires.

Nothing, however, could be more monotonous and more tiresome than the voyage across the Argentine pampa from Mendoza to Rosario. On that waterless ocean neither the tiniest tree nor the most remote fence rises between the eye and the farthest horizon. Just as the traveler is lost on the real ocean without the aid of a compass, so he goes astray on the pampa, and if no scout or wagon trail aids him, he often dies. They call this "dying *empampado.*" The stagecoaches in which one traveled were, except for comfort and elegance, almost like the horse cars of Santiago in shape and size. In them the traveler had to carry everything with him, including water if he wanted good water, because at the poststations nothing was to be found but a shelter for the man charged with supplying horses and a crude corral surrounded by prickly pears, the

109. A mark is about eight ounces. JP.

only vegetation planted there by the hand of man and the only obstacle, along with the shelter, that would now and then meet the traveler's eye on that eternal surface of the pampa, on whose earth, and under the open sky, he would spend the night.

But all the strains and discomforts of the voyage are, as I said, forgotten when you reach Rosario and when the impressive panoramas offered by the Paraná refresh the imagination and the eyes fatigued with the glare of the pampa.

Compared with this beautiful river, which, though five hundred leagues long, is but one of the tributaries of the great estuary of the Río de la Plata, the combined extent of the San Joaquin and Sacramento Rivers of California counts for little, and that of our Valdivia, for nothing at all, since in size it could not match the most insignificant of the countless affluents that nourish this colossus, pouring their waters into it as though into a true sea. Navigable by large vessels for hundreds of leagues, the Paraná is a source of riches for those fortunate enough to possess it. The numerous islands that divide it into a multitude of erratic channels are veritable forests of wild orange trees, which fill the air with their perfume when they flower and later fill thousands of boats that carry piles of oranges down the still waters toward the towns along the banks. Above the tops of these lovely evergreen trees the traveler sees, their whiteness contrasting with the dark green of the forests, the topmost sails of the ships proceeding in the opposite direction; and whenever he rounds the point of some island he sees whole flotillas of brigs and sloops that soon disappear, to be replaced by others from among the many that constantly sail back and forth along the channels.

As I traveled on this river, my memories of a voyage to Uruguay and the Chaco blending with the impressions of the moment, I would ask myself, "In all this vast territory one sees only an occasional herdsman, living well enough, thanks to the natural richness of the soil, but in the most pitiful isolation. What valid reason, then, can the Argentineans have to seek further expansion, when it will take centuries properly to settle the many millions of men who could live rich and happy on the land they already hold unchallenged and without the least expense? How many countries would consider themselves great and rich if they but possessed the Argentine Republic's share in the Río de la Plata and its mighty tributaries, or in the territories that are today its undisputed possessions?"

The Río de la Plata is thirty leagues wide at its mouth, fourteen at Montevideo, and an average of eight leagues as far as the confluence of the Paraná and the Uruguay.

Although the foundations of its buildings are washed by the Río de la Plata, Buenos Aires is not a port. Between the town and the anchorage lies a league of tidal mudflats, so that the loading and unloading of goods and passengers entailed serious difficulties. It was accomplished with carts on which the passenger stood, holding on to the stakes that formed the sides; the vehicle would then enter the river, drawn by horses with the water up to their chests, until one could transfer to the boat waiting offshore.

In those days there was nothing about the town to distinguish it from other large towns in America: its houses were low, none was architecturally interesting, and its streets were on the whole neglected. Nowadays, despite the great growth of this city, whose population some estimate to be as much as 300,000, and despite its proximity to Europe, it still has nothing to compare with the architectural magnificence of the principal churches and buildings of Santiago or with any of the beautiful public promenades that adorn that capital of the Latin American west.

On my excursions through the town my guide was my kind and distinguished friend Don Domingo Faustino Sarmiento, who delighted in pointing out to me the progress of every kind that had taken place in the country since the fall of Rosas. When I asked him why men so distinguished as he held so insignificant a place in his now regained fatherland, he immediately replied, "Because revolutions, Don Vicente, just like Saturn, always devour their children."

The date of this my third visit to Buenos Aires, May 3, 1855, came only three years and three months after the remarkable event that had forced the dictator Rosas, defeated at Monte Caceros, to seek in far-off England the safety he could no longer find in his own country.

I know of no statesman who has aroused in the literature and the press of America so violently partisan a reaction as has Rosas. The real or alleged deeds attributed to this remarkable man, who challenged France, spat in the face of England, heaped scorn on Brazil, and managed at the same time to struggle against his implacable domestic enemies and maintain his extraordinary power, have been sung in every tone employed by eight of the nine Muses of Parnassus. Only the ninth Muse has remained still—stern History, who, because it is not yet time for her to speak, has until now maintained the most absolute silence. And indeed, in the face of the reports that circulate and of the many contradictions they entail, the impartial outsider, if he is to be fair, must suspend his judgment until he is better informed.

These are the bare facts so far denied by no one and admitted by Rosas's bitterest enemies: both because of the great distances that lie between one populated area of the huge Argentine state and another, and because of their love of self-government, the majority of Argentina's inhabitants did not and do not want to live under a centralized authority. Merely because he wished to establish a centralized administration in the Argentine provinces, the enlightened statesman Rivadavia, but recently named president of the republic by the constituent convention on December 16, 1826, was forced to resign his office on July 5, 1827. From that day on, each province governed itself; and that of Buenos Aires chose as its governor the unfortunate Dorrego, who was then the leader of the Federal Party. Dorrego was not very popular with the army, which rebelled; the revolution of December 1, 1828, obliged him to take refuge in the countryside.

In order fully to understand what happened next, let us hear the account of these events given by the commission for the Philadelphia Centennial Exposition on page 20 of its work, *República Argentina,* published by the state in 1876:

> There [in the countryside] Dorrego found support from the commander of the troops in those districts, Juan Manuel Rosas, and formed a small army with which to march on Buenos Aires; but Lavalle defeated him, captured him, and had him shot without trial on December 13, 1828.
>
> Lavalle later repented of his haste because Dorrego, who was well thought of, was chief of the Federal Party; and the latter, because of the violent death of the former, which it saw as an abominable crime, decided to repay the Unitarians in kind. Not only did all the country around Buenos Aires, with Rosas at its head, rise up against Lavalle, but so did a great part of the other provinces. Considering this action as a declaration of war, the assembly, meeting at that time in Santa Fe, declared Lavalle's government to be unlawful.

Despite the wretched prose in which these paragraphs are written, a little good will suffices to let us understand what these Argentine men of letters tried to say in composing them.

I continue my recital of indisputable facts: After a fierce struggle, the provincial assembly of Buenos Aires, in December 1829, made Rosas governor of the province with extraordinary powers. Three years later, in December 1832, he refused the reelection he was offered. He retired into the country, and only in March 1835 did he accept the almost unlimited dictatorship that he was offered and that he continued to exercise until the revolt in Entre Ríos led to his defeat at Monte Caceros on February 3, 1852. He then withdrew to an English warship, which carried him to

England, where "he was received by the English authorities with every mark of honor."

From these facts it follows:

1. That two parties that hated each other fought for the triumph of their respective ideas.
2. That Dorrego, lawful governor of Buenos Aires and head of the Federal Party, was overthrown by rebellious troops under the command of General Lavalle, who at the time was head of the Unitarian Party.
3. That after he was defeated and taken prisoner, Dorrego was shot without any trial by Lavalle; and
4. That this savage murder in effect proclaimed the law of an eye for an eye and a tooth for a tooth.

Now then, the question is: supposing that all the dreadful deeds attributed to Rosas were factual, which is by no means the case, why should not the blame for them fall in part on those who initially and without any prior justification provoked those deeds with the murder of Dorrego? If Rosas, as is said of him, killed all enemies who fell into his power, taking pleasure in their suffering—which is untrue—what would the Unitarians have done with Rosas had he fallen into their hands?

Once we are in the presence of the utmost savagery, of the bloody horrors of a war to the death, neither one of the two beasts that are tearing at each other has the right to blame the other for the blood spilled, unless one of the two, with its unspeakable actions, has obliged the other to make use of reprisals, in which case the Unitarian Party should hold its tongue. Furthermore, how can we fail to withhold our judgment and delay pronouncing a definitive sentence on the actions of a man who has not yet been heard in his own defense, actions that his critics have sought out in the hearts of tigers before attributing them to him and that are represented in such paintings as that of a man squeezing the blood from a human heart with his own hands into a cup that he will then proceed to drain! The very nature of such exaggerated or atrocious accusations obliges prudence to withhold judgment until it is better informed.

What is true and well known, among many other things that I omit, is that Rosas chose his friends very badly, for those on whom this extraordinary man lavished the greatest affection and confidence eventually became his most dogged detractors. We have seen the examples of that in Chile, because while rumor and the press were brazenly declaring that the daughters of General Lavalle, tied to a post and with their eyelids cut off by order of Rosas, were exposed by the sun's rays on their defenseless retinas to the worst torments that the most barbarous and deranged mind could devise, these fair victims of the tyrant were happily dancing at the balls of merry Santiago.

I knew all this from the beginning and had on repeated occasions felt as secure in Buenos Aires as in our capital; and so, moved by curiosity, I asked Señora de Mendeville, a respectable and respected matron of Buenos Aires's high society, in whose home I was received with the most open and cordial hospitality, whether after Rosas's departure any members of his family were still left in the city, because I wanted to meet them. Her sole reply was to send a message to ———, a close relative of the dictator's, telling her that she awaited her visit.

Before long there appeared, dressed with the simplest elegance, one of the most lovely women I have ever known. Youth, beauty, a frank and open manner, good breeding, and refinement of manners graced that exceptional being, who, when she heard me say that I wished to pay my respects to Don Juan Manuel on my passage through Southampton, was so kind as to hand me one of her cards, on the back of which she wrote a single word with a pencil. I subsequently had occasion to see this lady twice at the theater and to observe how cordially other spectators greeted her from their boxes.

A few days later I was talking in Montevideo to Señor Mendeville, a prominent merchant in that affluent city, and he raised the possibility of our being able in no time to pocket a few pesos if I decided to write a pamphlet about Rosas and send him ten thousand copies. He assured me it would sell out at once and at a very good price, provided that it contained a moral analysis of the ex-dictator's heart, his current inclinations, and the basis of his hopes for returning to power in Buenos Aires. "Pay close attention," he told me, "to his facial movements, observe whether acts of human kindness are indifferent to him or sadden him, follow him to the theater when horrible dramas or tragedies are performed and take the most careful note of the expression on his face at the moments of catastrophe, describe, as you know how, the gleam of joy in his eyes at such moments, and how any expression of sorrow for crimes committed arouses his contempt."

It seemed to me that the instructions that this honest merchant of picturesque Montevideo was giving me were a trifle slanted; and they seemed to me a good deal more so when I showed him that famous *Catalogue of Crime*[110] that Rosas's enemies had spread throughout America

110. *Catalogue of Crime* (*Tablas de sangre*), a list of Rosas's alleged victims, totaling 22,030, with an appendix titled *Es acción santa matar a Rosas (Killing Rosas Is a Good Deed)*. The author of this work, published in the early 1840s, is José Rivera Indarte, formerly a fanatical supporter of the dictator. JP.

like wildfire as proof of the offenses attributed to the dictator, because when I asked him some questions about it, I noticed that he avoided like hot potatoes many an allegation that, without telling him so, I knew to be false.

When I reached Southampton after a smooth voyage, I asked my innkeeper whether he knew where Rosas lived and, when he answered that he did, whether he knew what Rosas was doing in that city, to which he replied exactly as follows:

"That gallows bird is certainly up to no good; and if he's not killing people here the way he did in Buenos Aires, that's because in England it's just a step from murder to the gallows."

Shocked by such an opinion, I tried a little to find out what it was founded on and soon discovered that the man did not know Rosas even by sight, and that if he had heard that there is a Buenos Aires in America, it was more because of the steamship line that ran between there and Southampton than from any geographical learning he possessed. His unthinking judgment had no basis more solid than what he remembered of the more or less partisan gossip of the Argentineans who, like me, had lodged in his inn.

Whatever was said of Rosas was evidently bound to pique my curiosity; and so, as soon as I had settled into my lodgings and taken a stroll around the city, which I was pleased to revisit, I set off for Rosas's domicile. He lived on the second floor of a modest five-story house, a building of the same height as many others in that town. I knocked at the door and handed my card to the answering doorman, a boy whose complexion led me to think him a native of the New World; and soon thereafter I heard the firm voice of a man who seemed to be accustomed to command, ordering that I be admitted.

A moment later Rosas in person came forth to receive me. He was at the time a man of about sixty-two, above medium height, and sturdily built. His complexion was white and ruddy, and in his face one saw two beautiful blue eyes, an aquiline nose, and thin, but perfectly marked lips. There was nothing remarkable about his dress, which was that of an honest and modest Englishman of the middle class. I saw no trace of the *chiripá,* or of the heavy trousers bordered in red, and even less of the red woollen vest and emblem that he wore in Buenos Aires, both when reviewing his troops and on the battlefield, all of which I had been assured in America that I should see on the ex-dictator here.

He received me with affectionate courtesy, without forgetting that prudent reserve that necessarily accompanies a man of the world in his first contact with a stranger; but this reserve was of short duration, for as soon as he had received his relative's card and read what was written on the back of it, he rose from his seat and stretched out his arms to me, calling me his *paisano* or countryman.

I spent six days in Southampton; on one of those six days I had occasion to lunch with him, and on the others, to join him in drinking *mate*, which he took without sugar and which seemed to be his favorite drink.

In my conversations with this singular man I noticed that he had become rather obsessed with his belief that it was impossible for the Argentineans to live in peace except under an absolute government, that he was the indispensable man who could rein in the passions so characteristic of those madmen whom, without knowing why, he continued so to love, and that it was impossible that the little good sense with which he was still willing to credit them would not force them at any moment to call him back. He expected this call with every steamer that reached Southampton, and with every steamer he was disillusioned anew; but this disillusionment inspired in him more pity than anger, because, according to him, their loss in not calling him was greater than his in staying where he was.

He spoke heatedly about the atrocious nature of the crimes attributed to him; and I remember that the day before I was to continue my voyage he walked about in agitation, took my hand, and led me to a room full of open crates and bags of papers, saying, "Do you see all this, *paisano?* Well, these are the private archives of my government. Here you can find not only the documents that vindicate my conduct, but also many of those that prove the perfidy of my enemies, some of whom are ingrates and almost all of whom are wicked men. One day all these documents will be made public, and that's what I'm working on now," he added, pointing to a mass of papers lying on his desk and covered with scribblings. "I understand it all, *paisano,*" he added resentfully, "because I know what schemes I foiled; but what I don't understand, what I've never been able to understand, is that without even hearing my defense the Chileans should have swollen the ranks of my enemies, when a glance at the behavior of the gang of savages—excuse the expression— that took refuge in Chile was more than enough to show the kind of witnesses that were appearing against me."

When I asked him why he had done nothing to establish a newspaper in Chile that would rectify the slanders of his enemies, he replied, "Because I had bad luck with my first attempt along those lines. . . . I took steps to set up a paper in Valparaíso, whose editor was going to be a certain Señor Espejo. . . . I remember he was called Don Juan Nepomuceno. But I got nowhere, because the Chilean papers were all in the hands of Argentineans. Then I sent a young man whose family was under obligation to me and who up to then had given me to understand that he was an ardent supporter of mine; and no sooner did he reach Chile than, under the influence of his father, he turned his back on me. And besides that, Don Vicente, let's speak frankly: I didn't try any more because I was silly enough to trust more than I ought to have done in the Chileans' ability to deduce, from the conduct of my calumniators and from the very exorbitance of what they said about me, how little stock was to be put in their stories."

X X V

*Government of the state of Hamburg. — How the 4% tax on
personal property is collected. — The kindergarten. —
Emigration agents and emigration. — What different nations
do to foster it. — The Chilean agent in Hamburg encounters
serious difficulties in sending emigrants to Chile. — His polemic
with the* Allgemeine Zeitung *of Augsburg. — The necessary
bases for an immigration project. — Spain. — The legendary
accounts of the Gran Capitán. — The waters of Franzensbad.
— The Russians. — Francisco Javier Rosales. —
Abd-el-Kader. — The End.*

O n September 9, 1855, at a season of the year when tender shoots on
our trees proclaim the arrival of our joyful springtime and when
nature begins to put away her finery so as to bear the harsh winter of
northern Europe, I arrived in the beautiful, rich, and free Hanseatic city
of Hamburg. This ancient and formidable fortress, the strength of whose

arms once made it the key to the Elbe, is now a peaceful center of wealth and commerce and the trusty intermediary that serves German industry by both distributing its products to all the markets of the world and receiving the abundant returns that stimulate its activity.

At that time Hamburg, as its title of Free City showed, was not merely a city incorporated in the great Germanic Confederation; though small, it was a true independent state, a republic whose political, civil, religious, and tax policies were worthy of study.

Writers on constitutional theory are anxious to divide the powers of the state in order to establish among them the yearned-for, reciprocal, and necessary independence that, since it is impossible to set indisputable limits to the authority of each, has so far eluded their grasp. In the constitution of Hamburg these powers are vested in a Senate that functions as the executive and the judiciary—there is nothing like a chief magistrate—and in an Assembly of diligent citizens that enacts the laws in collaboration with the Senate. Thanks to the wise arrangements that govern it, this apparent confusion of powers has not, until now, interfered with the normal functioning of the state or with the calm and peaceful discharge of his duties by every public official.

What here we call political factions are almost insignificant in Hamburg, because, since the desire for power is always in direct proportion to the greater or lesser profit to be had from its exercise, it is hardly surprising that in a town where the remuneration of the highest functionaries barely suffices to cover their office expenses, there is no sign of that screen of deceit behind which lurk those craving power. In terms of the luxuries they confer on the employee, public employments there are very similar to those of our subdelegates in that they are unremunerated. That is why an appointment as subdelegate produces as much terror in Chile as one as magistrate does in Hamburg. In Chile the citizen who refuses to serve as subdelegate pays a fine; in Hamburg the citizen who refuses to be a senator, or a judge, syndic, or president, which comes to the same thing because all those officials are chosen from among the members of the Senate, is punished by banishment and, in addition, by the loss of the tenth part of his fortune, which is forfeited to the public treasury.

How many aspirants to public office would take hold of the plow, how many eternal orators would fall silent, how many political factions and cliques dedicated to seizing power would melt away, if public service were made, as far as possible, obligatory and unpaid!

In our country we do not blush to employ intrigue, corruption, deceit, and threats to gain even membership in a city council; we freely spend money that we begrudge education and the relief of poverty and suffering, and we do not shrink from shedding blood as long as we gain the longed-for title of "illustrious," which even the most opaque minds modestly bestow on themselves in the council chambers. And all of this, to what purpose? To receive certain emoluments, to sit in the theater, to have a place of honor at public festivities, and above all, to have the right to take part in future elections that will elevate one's sympathizers to parliament and prepare them to scale the heights of profitable power. If our Chilean councilmen had no part in elections and if, like the ancient Romans, they were obliged to pay out of their own pockets for all the perquisites that they now enjoy so arrogantly, men would undoubtedly flee from the council chamber just as in Hamburg they flee from that of the Senate.

The taxes that support Hamburg's treasury are few and fair. What especially drew my attention was the method for collecting the 4% tax on personal property, because the 4% tax on the value of real estate is only collected in great emergencies or very unusual cases. In the Hanseatic cities the tax on personal property is called a "patriotic tax of honor and conscience." It is always paid in secret, and the amount that each taxpayer is to pay is left to his conscience. To collect it, four senators and twelve public-spirited citizens serve for a whole month in a room where a coffer is set up. Each taxpayer comes to this room on a day of his choosing, deposits in the coffer what he believes he ought to deposit, and then leaves; the commission, which witnesses this act at some distance, without inquiring into the amount deposited, simply writes down the taxpayer's name, followed by only these words: "Satisfied the legal requirement."

The local taxes paid by property holders are so directly linked to the satisfaction of their needs that their burden goes unnoticed. The city serves as an insurer with whom every owner is obliged to insure his property, which does not preclude his also insuring it elsewhere. The city is the exclusive purveyor of drinking water as well as of street lighting, and, as in every German town, there is a lottery.

The public charitable institutions are so numerous, so well endowed, and so well run that I know of no town that can rival Hamburg in this respect.

The schools are noteworthy, too; but what most attracted my attention among this sort of establishment were the schools for children between the ages of two and seven. They call them *kindergartens,* and they originated exclusively in Hamburg. These very interesting establishments, under the direction of very competent teachers, are designed for the twofold purpose of serving the child as a second mother when his real mother has to leave him alone while working outside the home, and of seeking, by means of ingenious methods, to change the destructive instinct so characteristic of that tender age into one for conservation, order, and even productive work. An institution where such tender creatures take in, so to speak, along with the milk that nourishes them, the seeds of such important habits is bound to produce excellent offspring for the country that maintains it.

I paid a leisurely visit to one of these establishments, where eighty-two small children were receiving motherly care. Everything in the place was designed to make it appeal to the pupils: gardens, shady nooks, baths, swings, trapezes, toys, small plots for cultivation and planting flowers. Every toy had a scientific name and something about it that would be a source of both pleasure and instruction. Balls took the form of geographical globes with varying degrees of detail. Some showed only the lines of latitude and longitude; others displayed the continents in beautiful color, and these were given to the child only once he could give an explanation of the simpler ones. The blocks with which they played were cylinders, squares, cubes, ellipses, etc. Every child old enough to play with the soil was in charge of a miniature garden half a yard square and had tiny farming tools with which to cultivate it; the teacher, as she put these tools in his hands, not only taught him their names and how to use them, but inculcated in the mind of these farmers the sacred spirit of competition in labor. No violence was used to control a child's more or less headstrong character; no activity concentrated the pupil's skittish imagination on the same object for more than six minutes at a stretch; and the children, far from resisting their mothers when it was time to go to school, were begging to go as soon as the time came.

A working mother would only pack a modest lunch in her child's little satchel and then go off to her employment, leaving him happy and learning effortlessly what she herself could not teach him, until she would quit at one o'clock. The children were taught to pray and sing. Their memory was trained by learning short and lively fables. As they sat around a table, each was given as many blocks as he could count, up to ten. With an equal number of blocks the teacher would form some regular figure, which each child then tried to imitate; and it was amazing to hear from the mouths of those small creatures words like triangle, square, polygon, etc., etc., and more amazing yet to hear how readily each child could count from one to ten and from ten to one, while the teacher added a block to the figure the child had just imitated or removed one from it.

I have seen straw objects skillfully manufactured by those miniature artisans, and every time a piece stood out for its relative perfection, it was framed with the name of the artist, who was praised and pampered by all who visited the place.

I omit additional details, since those I have noted suffice, I believe, to suggest the importance of these interesting establishments.

The propagation and conservation of the kindergartens were at that time in the charge of a society of philanthropic ladies, who took turns supervising them for a week to remedy their defects or provide whatever they lacked.

The city and port of Hamburg, capital of this small republic whose territory consists of only 157 square miles with a population of 200,000, of whom 160,000 live in the town, is one of the most beautiful in Germany, despite its irregular shape. It is picturesquely situated between the mouth of the Elbe, always covered by a forest of masts flying every flag in the world, and the Alster, a beautiful lake surrounded by promenades and elegant buildings that penetrates the city to mix its waters with those of the Elbe by means of splendid canals. Formidable old moats, forty meters wide, transformed into gardens and promenades that surround the town with flowers and monuments, and the contrast of modern edifices with those in the Teutonic style, survivors of the raging fire that in only three days in 1842 destroyed 1,992 buildings, made of this emporium of commerce and wealth one of the most desirable places of residence, both for the simple businessman and for anyone else who might wish to enjoy an affordable, comfortable, and pleasant life in peace and order.

Every state desirous of fostering German immigration must bear in mind that Hamburg is one of the indispensable locations for its immigration agents, an important channel where year after year the great tide of emigrants coming from all parts of Germany crowds in before fanning out, more or less abundantly, to all those unsettled lands that need additional human resources to assure their material and intellectual progress. In the year before my arrival, during the months that the Elbe was free of ice, Hamburg had sent out 163 vessels with 32,310 emigrants destined for various transatlantic ports.

This does not, however, mean that German emigrants should be sought only in Hamburg, because Bremen and Antwerp often challenge its primacy.

When one first arrives in one of these places and learns how many thousands of emigrants come there annually in search of a new homeland, it initially seems easy and simple to direct that stream to any one of the special regions clamoring for it; but such is not the case, because the operation is a good deal more difficult and more time-consuming than it appears.

At Hamburg, Bremen, Antwerp, Liverpool, Le Havre, and every other port where emigrants come to book passage, there have been, ever since the onset of transatlantic emigration, agents especially accredited by their respective countries to see to it that the emigrant should head for this or that region in preference to any other of the many that simultaneously offer him a home and hospitality. As soon as they hear of the appearance of some new plan of settlement that might interfere with their monopoly on the shipment of men, these assiduous agents, though each works for himself against all the others, not only join to combat it but do so with the most underhanded methods. The semibarbaric state of the Pacific regions; the degradation and imminent extinction of the Latin race; its religious intolerance; the daily and bloody revolutions; the deadly climate of the Isthmus of Panama, which they present as extending as far as Cape Horn; invasions by cannibalistic Indians; snakes and other poisonous reptiles—all these are so many instruments with which, for their own purposes, they exploit both the simple credulity of the would-be emigrants and the fears of the mothers who witness their departure.

As soon, therefore, as my preparatory activities revealed the purpose of my coming to Hamburg, the emigration agents already established there, through newspapers in their pay, let loose such a flood of lies about Chile and false reports about the new champion who was entering the lists to maintain the matchless beauty of his peerless settlement at Llanquihue over every other settlement present or to come, that they soon taught me what great difficulties my undertaking would face from its very outset.

Among other things, it was reported that a gentleman had just come to Hamburg offering pie in the sky to anyone wishing to emigrate to Chile, and that their love of humanity compelled the writers to warn the unwary, who should remember that dealer in human flesh called von Schutz and the no less celebrated Rudolf, who had come with much ado and many a sham to recruit victims to go to Peru, and so forth.

The number of interested parties who took a dim view of my plans seemed to me to be growing by the moment. The states of the American Union, Quebec, Brazil, the Cape of Good Hope, and Australia all had their agents in Hamburg; and these had their sub-agents at the most important points in the interior of Germany. Brazil alone had seven special immigration agents stationed in various towns to provide manpower for Rio de Janeiro, Pernambuco, Bahia, Rio Grande do Sul, Santa Catalina, Victória, and Santos, in each of which places a settlement had been established.

Alone, unknown, with no visible qualifications but my title as consul general, insufficiently competent in the language to be able to defend myself, unable to subsidize newspapers that might stand up for my country, I should have found myself in a most unenviable situation had my knowledge of how much honorary titles mean in enlightened Europe not come to my aid. I persuaded the government of Chile to enhance my title as consul general in Hamburg with additional appointments as consul general in Prussia, Denmark, and Hanover; and selecting among the leading men of science and commerce of these kingdoms those who seemed to me most likely to assist me, I had each of them appointed Chilean consul in the place of his residence. I donated to various learned societies the specimens of natural history that I had brought from Chile, accompanying them with the appropriate treatises; and turning to the customs brokers and other dealers in this and that, I suggested to them the advantages of an appointment as Chilean consul and even the possibility of replacing me with all my powers once I had successfully directed the stream of emigrants toward Chile.

And so Chile found zealous champions in Karl Andrew of Leipzig, in Wappaus and Ausmann of Göttingen, in the Baron von Bibra of Nuremberg, in Karl C. Rafn of Copenhagen, in Gulich of Berlin, in the wealthy Rossi of Vienna, in Pöppig of Leipzig—all of them esteemed men and scientific luminaries in enlightened northern Europe; and in addition to these there were many speculators of less account who, even if they did not promote emigration, did nothing to block it, because their hands were tied by the hope of coming to seem like somebody through appointment as Chilean representatives.

This plan was so successful that those learned individuals whose occupations made it impossible for them to accept the honor of being Chilean consuls were so kind as to point out to me others who might undertake this charge. By unquestioningly accepting their candidates, I succeeded in having in every town two persons to speak for Chile instead of only one: the proposed consul and the appointed one.

The learned Guerlin wrote me a letter dated June 24, 1858, from which I am pleased to copy the concluding sentence: "Nothing will ever diminish the intense interest with which I shall always seek the progress and prosperity of your virgin homeland." The no less distinguished naturalist, the Baron von Bibra, president of the Natural History Society of Nuremberg, which subsequently honored me with the title of honorary member, never failed to say "my beloved Chile" whenever he wrote me. In each of the present members of the Royal Society of Antiquarians of Copenhagen, to which I belong, I had an apologist for Chile; the same was true of my fellow-members of the Prussian Society for the Moral and Material Advancement of the Working Class.

By actively cultivating these new friendships and making Chile a topic of conversation everywhere, I soon achieved the expected results. I began to receive many letters bombarding me with questions about Chile. What is Chile, they asked. Where is it? What sort of government does it have? What religion? What natural products are found there? What kind of manufactures might profitably be established there? What is its climate like? What kind of epidemics or diseases threaten the foreigner there? And so on.

Such detailed interrogation is by no means to be wondered at, because it can never be repeated often enough that, outside those commercial firms that trade with it and the foreign offices of the maritime powers that are in the habit of forcing it to pay indemnifications, our Chile is as well known among Europeans as are the mountains of the moon among us.

This mass of inevitable inquiries, each of which called for at least a volume in reply, was the occasion for my *Ensayo sobre Chile,* a work that I wrote with the scanty information I had at hand and in the brief intervals between my duties, and that I mailed as my reply to my many questioners.[111]

These were the exertions initially required by my delicate mission until March 31, 1856, when I sent the first direct expedition to Puerto Montt on the *César Elena,* before making firm arrangements for the others that, come hell or high water, as they say, subsequently sailed for Puerto Montt and the settlement at Llanquihue.

After this I had more free time at my disposal; and attempting to make use of it, thinking as always of my country, I published, in Spanish, the *Manual del ganadero chileno,*[112] a microscopic atlas for use in the Chilean primary schools, and the *Cuadros cronológicos*[113] of the ancient and modern history of Chile and Peru.

At that time the *Eco de Ambos Mundos* of London, with reference to emigration in general, said, among other things, the following:

> According to the latest official data published by the Prussian Statistical Office, 227,236 persons emigrated from that country in the years 1844–1860, bearing with them a capital of 45,269,011 Prussian thalers.
>
> Until now Chile is the only Spanish American state that has made a serious effort to promote German immigration and that has seen its efforts in

111. Pérez Rosales wrote this work in French and published it in Hamburg. JP.
112. *Manual del ganadero chileno,* "The Chilean Cattleman's Handbook." JP.
113. *Cuadros cronológicos,* "Chronological Tables." JP.

this important enterprise crowned with success. Thanks to the favorable conditions offered by the soil and climate of that country, to the sacrifices it has made, and to the measures taken from 1850 to date by its successive immigration agents, emigration to the ports of Chile rests on a very solid basis.

On the other hand, what did the German papers not write about Chile? What did the Chilean papers, which I am ashamed to name, not have to say against what our government was spending on our southern settlements?

The matter is too important not to be considered for yet another moment. Sooner or later Chile will come fully to realize the advantages that promoting foreign immigration must bring her, and whatever might be said along these lines now should not be considered as idle chatter but as a seed that will eventually produce abundant fruits.

On October 17, 1856, an association of influential men called the Central Colonization Company was established in the capital of the Empire of Brazil with a fund of a thousand *contos* for paying the passage and initial expenses of German immigrants, despite the fact that in August of the same year the parliament of the empire had already authorized the government to invest six thousand in the same project.

The *Hansa* of April 22, 1857, announced the establishment of an English emigration society under the presidency of the Duke of Wellington, who had subscribed a thousand pounds to pay for the passage of emigrants to the English colonies, each man being granted very liberal terms for the eventual repayment of the expense incurred on his behalf. At the same time the British government was offering extremely generous rewards to emigrants choosing to go to its colonies at the Cape; and while Brazil and England, both privately and officially, spared no expense to augment the population of their settlements, many Chilean writers, instead of encouraging their government to continue along the line of the first steps it was taking in so sensible a direction, seemed to be taking delight in hampering them, simply because they could not immediately see fruit on a tree so recently planted.

The German publications seemed to be working hand in glove with the Chilean ones, the latter because of the money fruitlessly spent on the newborn southern settlements, the former because, according to them, the agent's promises were false and the territory being settled was nothing but a place of wretched exile inhabited by a perverse race of degenerates.

The most prestigious paper in the Germany of that day, the *Allgemeine Zeitung* of Augsburg, had for some reason decided to echo all the falsehoods that were being spread about in response to my efforts. I was forced to engage in a vigorous polemic with its writers; and the following paragraphs that I quote from my replies (which, incidentally, the paper was courteous enough to print in its esteemed pages) will give an idea of the charges that were being levied against Chile and the Chileans. To my malicious antagonists I addressed the following:

If all I had to contend with were a continuation of the unthinking criticism of my government's noble aim of populating the well-known fertile lands whose abundant vegetation adorns the southern part of virgin America, I should have kept quiet, as I have until now, because only a blind man cannot see the light of the sun, and especially because we have the printed reports of the world's most respected voyagers, who extol the excellence and riches of those regions and grant them the due importance that only ignorance or bad faith can dare to deny them. When slander does not stop at this, however, but goes so far as to fill the pages of so respected and widely read a journal as the *Allgemeine Zeitung* of Augsburg, where the humanitarian goals of my government are called puerile, and the noble and hospitable race of inhabitants with which the Republic of Chile is blessed is called degenerate, then silence would mean complicity in such intemperate nonsense.

Valdivia, for the information of the ignorant, is not a place of foreign settlement. Valdivia is simply a thinly populated province, as are the other provinces of Chile; and consequently it has room for additional inhabitants. The first immigrants to reach Chile arrived at Valdivia; and since there was no land locally available for them, the settlement of Llanquihue was founded at the southern edge of this province, not with "the puerile aim of scattering the immigrants so as better to keep them in submission," as some dare to assert, but in order to settle them in greater proximity to each other and thus improve their circumstances. . . .

It would be interesting to know to what purpose the author of the article, when comparing the Latin race with the Saxon, seems to lament that the latter will degenerate in Chile by mixing with the former, which, according to him, does not even maintain its original purity, since it is blended with weak-minded Indian slaves. What, in the view of this learned phrenologist who employs so much time and paper in writing against a country he does not know, makes for the superiority of the Saxon race over the Latin? Could it be that the latter, which has ruled the world with its learning and its arms, does not count among its sons such bright stars of the human intellect as Cicero, Tacitus, Horace, Vergil, Tasso, Dante, Raphael, Michelangelo, Murillo, and a thousand others?

Could it be that the race that my worthy opponent seems so to despise has not created monumental cities where to this day and without exception all nations come to drink, from the purest sources, the basic notions of art and good taste?

Let me remind the learned disparager of this race that after its victorious armies had marched through all of Europe it was the Latin race, and none other, that undertook the conquest of America, and that the race with which it has blended in Chile is that of the free Araucanians, the only one in the annals of human history that has given us the example of a three hundred years' struggle in defense of its fatherland against the most famous soldiers in the world, and this in a region whose geography multiplied the occasions for conflict and for meeting with bare breasts the swords that conquered at Pavia. If the Chilean people owes its existence to the mixture of such pure and noble blood, why need it fear comparison with the world's most select?

As for the advice that the Germans should make use of the generosity with which Chile receives them in order to proceed to its conquest, I leave it to the sensible sons of enlightened Germany, a country for which I have the highest esteem, to accept or indignantly reject the ridiculous compliment of suggesting that they are like the serpent in the fable.

These excerpts from my communications to the press show the sort of weapons employed in the campaign against the humanitarian cause that had brought me to Europe; and I gladly omit what was said of the poor battered Chilean immigration agent, so as to state, before going on to other matters, the main precepts that in my opinion, based on eleven years' uninterrupted experience, must be observed by any nation that, poor in men and rich in land, should wish to increase its population with the assistance of a foreign element.

The Earth is the common homeland of man, as of every animal dwelling on it. The interests, or rather the well-being, of each one of these living creatures is the only motive that impels them to join together, to separate, or to scatter over the face of both hemispheres. This readiness to pursue well-being is what we call emigration, and the being who emigrates we call an emigrant.

The European swallow emigrates when the winters of the land of its birth deny it the warmth and nourishment offered by the coasts of Africa. The barbarians of the north, as they used to be called, invaded the lands of the semibarbarians of the south not only out of a lust for conquest but also because of their need to better the conditions of their life by seeking in the temperate southern regions space for expansion along with those food products that the harsh cold of their native clime denied them. Distance, the risks of a voyage, and even the diseases endemic to certain parts of the world are minor obstacles for a hard-working man, provided that as he leaves his native land he does so with the hope of finding in those other regions a better life than what he leaves behind.

From this it follows that there is no nation on the surface of the globe, no matter how rich and favored, that is not subject to the diminution that emigration entails, because if a man cannot find in his own country the prosperity that awaits him in another, nothing can tie him to the former except being too poor to travel or not knowing for certain whether he can better his condition in the latter. To attract emigrants to underpopulated regions, therefore, the following precepts must necessarily be obeyed:

1. Make the country to be populated well known.
2. Once it is known, prove with irrefutable facts that the man invited to leave his country for the new one offered to him will improve his condition.
3. Once this important aim has been achieved, make it possible for the emigrant to reach his new country.
4. The establishment, administration, and promotion of immigration and settlement should not be under the direct control of government, which is always subject to disturbances caused by changes in the ministries, except only insofar as governmental participation can give the immigrant serious guarantees that the promises made to him will be kept.
5. In any state that desires to increase its population by means of the immigration of foreign labor, the direction of this source of wealth and progress should be in the sole hands of a philanthropic society composed of select individuals, both native and foreign, provided with the necessary authority, with a budget fixed in the sense that it cannot be reduced without a year's notice, and with a certain freedom of action to invest the money entrusted to it without any restriction other than the obligation to render an account of its investments in keeping with the norms that the government may establish at its foundation.

These five precepts are of the utmost importance. The means for putting them into practice will arise from due study and meditation on each one of them; and although these means may come to be very important, I refrain from specifying them, since they are sure to be as varied as will be the places to be settled.

As for the nationality from which one should recruit settlers for remote wastelands, between the Saxon race and the Latin, or rather, between the northern European and the southern, one should generally prefer the northerner. The southern races, pampered by the mild climate with which they are blessed, leave their homes only temporarily, as do the birds that emigrate in winter only to return to their native soil in spring. The northern races, which owe little to their climate and all to their energetic devotion to work, rarely look back if they find their wellbeing elsewhere. The exception to this general rule is the Basque, who is an excellent colonizer everywhere, and in Chile the best possible.

Since I have come to mention Spain, I do not wish to go on without evoking those special memories that our ancestral homeland merits, beyond many of those others that anyone who travels in Europe is bound to cherish.

After a visit to the recently bloody field of Solferino, my duties took me, for the second time, to Spain. Who, after he has studied the ways of most of the great cities of enlightened Europe, where the head reigns supreme, does not, on reaching Spain, think that there he has found the throne of the heart? Open and cordial hospitality is the daughter of the Peninsula; and if the word "loyalty" was not born in Spain, it seems to have been created for her alone.

We are the offspring of that homeland of which we know so little; and when, after traveling through Europe, seeking instruction more than amusement, we come to Spain, we feel as though we have come to Chile. The climate, the natural products of the land, the language, the customs, everything strikes us as our own. Twice have I been in the Peninsula, and both times I have left it with genuine regret, something that has not happened to me even when leaving France, in whose language I still think.

At that time it was not possible to travel from France to Madrid by rail; one traveled in dreadful exceedingly uncomfortable coaches drawn by mules, which, spurred on by the whip and the coachman's curses, flew from Irún to the royal capital.

Madrid is not large; but it is a handsome town that at that time had more than 300,000 inhabitants and everything that a civilized man could desire for his comfort, his instruction, and his amusement.

Among its many public establishments, my attention was drawn especially to the National Library, which consisted of more than 200,000 printed volumes and countless manuscripts; the Natural History Museum with its splendid mineralogical collections; the Art Museum, which, though a good deal more modest in appearance than many other European museums, is excelled by none either in the number or in the artistic quality of the original canvases it contains. The Michelangelos, the Raphaels, the Titians, the Rubenses, the Van Dycks, the Murillos, the Velázquezes, and the prized canvases of so many other princes of painting are not pointed out in the Madrid Museum, as in those of the rest of Europe, as objects of recognized rareness, because they are to be seen there in abundance.

Noteworthy, too, and full of treasures, is the Royal Armory, where every offensive and defensive weapon used by the heroes of martial Spain ever since the most remote times is religiously preserved and displayed in the most artistic and beautiful manner imaginable. The center of the great hall is taken up by a row of powerful horses, perfectly stuffed, on each of which rides the striking image of one of Spain's heroes, with his appropriate armaments; against the walls one sees nothing but splendidly mounted trophies of historic weapons. On a table near the entrance I noticed a box of jacaranda wood that contained the tattered but revered flag carried by Cortés during the conquest of Mexico; a little farther on, under glass held by a gilded frame, the famous accounts submitted by the great Gonzalo Fernández de Córdoba, which many of us Chileans consider mythical, though their appearance here might lead one to think otherwise. I, however, despite what I know of the customs of those times, continue to believe what I always have believed, because it could never enter any head, no matter how empty, that in the time of that famous warrior a Spanish subject could present so insulting and bizarre an accounting to his sovereign.[114] If any proof is needed, here are some entries from these accounts, which I copied into my travel notebook and still preserve:

200,736 ducats and 9 *reales,* for monks, nuns, and the poor, so that they might pray to God for the success of Spanish arms
100,000,000 for pikes, shovels, and mattocks
10,000 ducats for perfumed gloves to protect my troops from the stench of the bodies of our enemies stretched out on the field of battle
170,000 ducats for replacing and repairing bells damaged by constant daily ringing in celebration of new victories won over the enemy

114. Gonzalo Fernández de Córdoba (1453–1515), called El Gran Capitán, conquered the Kingdom of Naples for Ferdinand the Catholic, who, however, subsequently removed him from his governorship there and asked him for an accounting, to which, according to legend, the hero replied with deliberately absurd figures. *Las cuentas del Gran Capitán* has become a proverbial Spanish expression for an absurd or exaggerated account of expenses. JP.

100,000,000 for the patience that I exercised yesterday when I heard that the King was asking for an accounting from a man who had given him a kingdom

At the far end of one hall, inside a case holding many feminine jewels, lay a splendid sword whose golden hilt represented a cross. One of the attendants of the museum, who without knowing me was kind enough to serve as my guide, saw me stopping to observe the inappropriate placement of that weapon and said, "That is the royal sword of our Catholic sovereign Doña Isabel I."

I confess that I was moved by this information. I saw before me an object used by that exceptional being to whom, one could say, we Americans owe our existence; and this thought made me exclaim, "I should like to pay my respect to that relic with a kiss!"

When my interlocutor, to whom I gave my card, heard this, he begged me to wait a moment and then left me. He shortly returned in the company of an elderly gentleman, who, after greeting me, said, "It is forbidden to move this royal relic from its place, but a request from an American as distinguished as you seem to be cannot be left unfulfilled." And he handed me that martial treasure, which still seems to me too heavy for a woman. After kissing it I handed it back, saying to these courteous gentlemen, in explanation of my act of respect, "But for the lady who wore that sword, you would have had no occasion for your courtesy toward me, nor should I have had the honor of your granting me this distinction."

How many pesos the satisfaction of this wish would have cost me outside Spain, and especially in England, where a simple salute costs one pound sterling!

I frequently visited the National Library and the remarkable cigarette factory with its eight workshops, in which 3,048 women worked at the same time. Among other public establishments, the Madrid of my time also had a university and various academies, an astronomical observatory, a botanical garden, a school of arts, normal schools for the training of teachers, forty-four free schools for boys and forty-six for girls, in which three thousand pupils received instruction, three orphanages, and eighteen hospitals, and for the recreation and enjoyment of the inhabitants, four theaters, an immense bullring, and lovely public promenades both within and without the city.

In the home of the munificent Osma and in that of the very kind and affectionate Duque de Medinaceli I had occasion to make the rather close acquaintance of the distinguished authors Vega, Güell, and Renté.

. . .

As I headed north from this hospitable land par excellence, I had the serious misfortune of falling ill with cholera in the vicinity of Magdeburg, where this Asiatic plague was at the time wreaking havoc. I escaped as though from a shipwreck, battered but alive; and since, whatever the learned doctors may say, cholera can be contracted more than once, I subsequently asked Dr. Zaleta whether science might not have found some medication that, if taken regularly, even if it had to be for years on end, might protect one from so dreadful a disease, to which he replied, "The only medication against cholera is to be forty leagues away from it!"

The state of my health led me, for the third time, to the baths at Franzensbad, where I had previously had occasion to establish contact with many of the most distinguished defenders of Sebastopol and to realize how mistaken are the ideas that we Chileans harbor about the educational level of the Russian Empire. All I met, great and small, surprised me with their fund of knowledge, the refinement of their manners, and the extraordinary ease and facility with which they spoke foreign languages.

The Russians, then, were my most charming and assiduous companions at Franzensbad, for the surest way to win the esteem of an educated Russian is to be an American. There I met and enjoyed the company of the Princess Dolgorukaya, a beautiful lady who was cousin to the tsar and who spoke Spanish like an Andalusian. I recall that one afternoon, after having peevishly dismissed the small court of ladies and gentlemen that surrounded her, she turned to me as amiably as could be and with a pleasant smile spoke precisely as follows:

> I expect, my dear consul general, that you have been surprised at the somewhat haughty fashion in which I have sent my people off to leave me alone; but this is the way it has to be done, because what would become of us once we ourselves let them understand that there is no distance between us? I should take good care not to deal similarly with the children of the American republics. With them, an unreserved manner is considered a merit. Tell me, if you have any doubts: isn't it true that you could become president of Chile? Well, I could become empress only by the most unlikely accident.

In my honor they gave a sumptuous dinner, which I mention only because of the noteworthy comments made there on our virgin America. At the head of the table sat the governor of the Ukraine, and around it, placed according to their rank, sat many of the officers who had so distinguished themselves in the defense of Sebastopol. I remarked in them as much aversion toward the Austrians, whom my neighbor, in a whisper, called *outrechiens* ("ultradogs") instead of *autrichiens,* as I discerned fondness for the French, with whom sooner or later they were sure to be fast friends. As for the peoples of America, only good things were said. One of the guests could not quite understand how friendly relations could exist between an autocratic government and the system of liberty enjoyed by the American republics; when another of the merry assembly said, "The extremes meet," I was surprised at how quickly and energetically he was interrupted by an officer still convalescing from the serious wound received at Sebastopol, who exclaimed, "No, sir, it's not the extremes that meet but the middles. America is a new and virgin world, and so is Russia. Europe is finished; the future belongs to America and Russia."

If I had been guided by the ideas that my good uncle Javier Rosales held about the Russians, I should certainly have thought, while in the company of the Russian colony at the baths, that I was a thousand leagues distant from those alleged barbarians of the north. The Russians of a certain class, as we should put it, are fully deserving of the respect with which we always treat the finest, best educated, and most courteous men on earth; as for the ladies, many of the most sociable and educated among those I have known in the various countries I have visited would be quite content if, in addition to the general and special education received by Russian women, they possessed the natural charms that adorn those daughters of the colossus of the north.

We who are now born à la française, who savor French bonbons, who dress in the French style, and who no sooner learn to spell than on our storefronts, on our walls, and even on the very asphalt of our sidewalks we see nothing but *French Hairdresser, French Fashions, French Tailor,* etc., and who, to top it all off, as soon as the first downy growth appears on our cheeks have devoured French literature or its translation into Frenchified Spanish, as well as world history and especially French history as written by Frenchmen—what wonder is it that we should become Frenchified to the very marrow of our bones? That is why during the Crimean War France found in us those sympathizers that every gallant and well-bred youth finds when he valiantly struggles against men who are monstrous brutes, bigmouthed, hairy, low of forehead, and incapable of noble and lofty sentiments, which is how here and in France their enemies depicted the Russians at the time of the glorious and unexpected defense of the latter-day Troy, more fortunate than its unhappy predecessor, that bears the glorious name Sebastopol.

If Chileans who had been conditionally baptized as French in our homeland were so hostile to the Russians, what wonder was it that those of us whose baptism had been confirmed no less than in Paris should have seen everything à la française? Don Francisco Javier Rosales, a Chilean like us and, thanks to his long residence in Paris, even more hostile to the Russians than we, engaged me in acrimonious discussions concerning the Russia that he did not know in comparison with the France that he thought or believed he knew. These arguments became so heated that when news arrived that the Crimean War, which brought such glory to the arms of France, had ended and we heard the vendors grow hoarse advertising their papers with shouts of "Extra! Get your paper, gentlemen! Two *centimes!* Two *centimes,* peace at Sebastopol!" he refused to speak to me because I told him, "There you see what your peace is worth!"

And since chance has led me to chat about my good uncle, a man misunderstood by his acquaintances, it may not be out of place, at least for his relations if not for the history of a faithful servant of Chile, if I here sketch two aspects of his character.

Javier Rosales was so fanatical a Frenchman and so absolute a Parisian that for him the world rotated on but two poles, the Barrière du Trône and the Barrière de l'Étoile, which did not prevent his assigning to Chile, in his heart, the title of preferred satellite of that favorite world of his. His love for his native land and his desire to see it advance steadily on the path of progress, a goal to which he dedicated several publications, led him, in his conversations with Chileans—and only with Chileans, in whose company he was always to be found—to adopt the peculiar method of disparaging Chile, so as to derive pleasure from the heated and often even insulting defense that his visitors made of their fatherland.

He served his country zealously as Chilean minister in France, and in his private capacity served Chileans traveling in Europe with the same zeal; but lacking the prudence to contain his sarcastic bent even while rendering them unpaid services, he succeeded in making these services appear to be sold at an exorbitant price. These two habits of his, neither of which involved the least desire to offend, have been the chief causes of the mistaken opinion of Rosales's character and inclinations that has prevailed until now.

Turning our attention once more to the Russians, since these are even now so little known among us, I recall that their diplomatic agents so rigidly observe the protocol that governs their every least action abroad that they would be capable of letting themselves be hanged rather than give the slightest hint of admitting the existence of any nation but those recognized by Russia. My good uncle Rosales would grumble and curse every time he was visited by the Russian ambassador in Paris, who would neither call himself an ambassador nor address my uncle by any title other than *Monsieur Rosales*. I initially had the same experience with the Baron Freytag, Russian minister in Hamburg, whenever social intercourse brought us into contact; and this situation would have continued with no complaint from either Chile or Russia, had not chance decreed otherwise.

Some Chileans wishing to visit St. Petersburg came to me for the passport without which no one could then move from one place to another in Europe. To comply with their wishes but not daring to promise them anything for fear of exposing the arms and seal of our Republic to rejection, I held two lengthy meetings with the baron to see how Chilean citizens could go to Russia with a passport from the consulate general. During these meetings I pointed out how the good name of Russia would be enhanced if she allowed the Chileans the opportunity to visit and know a civilized region of enlightened Europe of which we children of the Pacific had only the erroneous news purveyed to us by France and England; I added that although it was true that we had not been officially recognized as a nation by the Empire, one could argue that we had been recognized de facto, since Chilean products shipped under our flag were provisioning the Russian colonies in Alaska, since an officially appointed Russian consular agent resided in Valparaíso, and since whenever Russian naval vessels visited our ports, they saluted our fortresses and were saluted by them in turn. The baron listened to me without interrupting, and after a moment's thought, as though searching for something that might satisfy me, said, "If the Chileans were to travel in Russia, not with passports issued by their own authorities but as citizens of Brazil, there would be no problem."

When I heard this reply, I picked up my hat to take my leave; without allowing the slight to my patriotic feelings to keep me from honoring the obligations of courtesy, I said to him, "My dear baron, for no purpose whatsoever would any Chilean be capable of renouncing his nationality even for an instant."

Four days later the baron came to see me, bringing along one of his little sons to demonstrate all the more clearly that this was strictly a visit from one private individual to another. As he chatted with me about our interrupted conversation, he said, "Please don't think, Señor Pérez, that Russia has the least objection to recognizing your beautiful country as a nation; but ask yourself: would you extend the hand of friendship to an individual, no matter how respectable, if another friend, or that individual himself if no one else was available, had not introduced him to you in keeping with the rules of polite behavior? I am instructed especially to tell you that your passports will be respected and honored by the imperial authorities, provided that your signature is certified by the representative of a friendly nation."

As a result of my having later sent my *Ensayo sobre Chile* and some other literary productions to the Russian imperial libraries and geographical societies, I had the pleasure of another visit from Baron Freytag, this time without the accompaniment of the boy and without that plethora of unspoken reminders that it was not the Russian minister who was visiting me but simply one individual who was visiting another of the same rank and sort. This charming diplomat had been ordered to deliver into my own hands a courteous communication to me that the Baron Korff, Imperial Councillor, had signed on September 20, 1857; and he did so with the affectionate smile of a man who says, "You won't be annoyed any more or distrust a country that by instinct and for solid reasons is the friend of Americans." The communication merely contained eulogies of my writings; but the envelope, which I still have and which was covered with great official seals, plainly read: *To the Consul General of the Republic of Chile in Hamburg.* "Well, well," I said as I read this. Shortly thereafter, to confirm my exclamation, I received another communication, dated October 22 and sent to me by the secretary of the Imperial Geographical Society of Russia with the same splendid display of seals and titles.

It therefore seems to me that nothing would be easier than to settle with the Russian government the more imaginary than real difficulties that until now have kept us from jointly entering the community of recognized nations.

Every year the health-giving waters and marvelous mud baths of Franzensbad draw to that resort in the mountains of Upper Bohemia a multitude of persons who come there from different parts of the globe in search of health. Only war or the rigors of winter can temporarily make a desert of that picturesque small region, where good health, good cheer, and well-being jointly reign. And so hardly had the cannons of the Crimea fallen silent when it seemed as though all the sick and curious of the best-known nations on earth had agreed to meet at Franzensbad. The enormous and luxurious inns of that charming village, set in extensive and beautiful gardens, were full of visitors, among whom the Russian, the German, the Turk, the Arab, the Armenian, the Tyrolean, the Greek, the Frenchman, and the Spaniard all displayed their national dress.

In the room next to mine lived three Arabs who had already aroused my curiosity, both by the dress and affected gravity of one of them, and by the innkeeper's solicitous expressions of respect toward this individual.

At the baths there are no secrets; and so I soon found out that I was only a wall's thickness away from the former and famous Emir Abd-el-Kader, a native of Mascara in the district of Oran, the desert chieftain who for sixteen years fought with varied success against the conquerors of Algeria, spilling rivers of blood, his own and that of others, during the unhappy rule of Louis Philippe d'Orléans over that African colony, and who laid down the feared scimitar that he had wielded like none other in the service of his country only when, beaten and deceived in 1848, he was wrongfully taken prisoner and conveyed to France. He was set free on Napoleon III's ascension to the imperial throne and resided in Bursa in Anatolia until that unfortunate town was destroyed by an earthquake. When the Crimean War broke out he moved to Constantinople, and at its conclusion he had gone to Franzensbad to recover his health before heading for Damascus.

Friendships are struck at the baths with the same ease with which they are forgotten once one leaves the place; and so we soon went from greetings to visits, and from these to the most cordial and enjoyable relations.

The emir was of medium height and probably not more than forty-nine years old. His elegant pale white face displayed large wide-open eyes, dark blue in color. A line marked his forehead and part of his nose, a sign that he belonged to the powerful tribe of Haken. His nose was aquiline, his mouth well proportioned, and his beard rather sparse than heavy. Over his white Arab robe he wore a loose white burnoose, also of fine wool, whose hood, which always covered his head, was tied down on his forehead with a bright strip of rolled cashmere.

Abd-el-Kader, whom the Arabs considered a saint and a sage, was a handsome man, although his appearance was always more that of a hermit than that of a warrior. Anyone who saw him then, even knowing what he had been when, sowing death and terror wherever he appeared scimitar in hand, he had led the desert hordes in the annihilation of the invaders of his fatherland, could never guess that from his sweet and gently gazing eyes had gone forth those magnetic rays that had made even the lions of the desert quake, or that those small and delicate white hands had the strength to wield for so many years the cruel lance and the dreaded sword. He spoke slowly and solemnly, and his confidence in Allah and his resignation to the decrees of the Prophet were such that not even in the time of his unjust imprisonment in France did he betray the least sign of anger or impatience. The Koran said that a serene face heals the wounds of the heart, and that was enough for the devout emir.

But since it is not my aim to recount the political life or martial traits of this Moslem Templar, but to recall a conversation that I had with him about the special qualities of the Arabian horse, I shall leave the former task to the historians and limit myself to the latter, which, though modest, is not uninteresting.

As he was explaining to me the reverses suffered by the French army in its first Algerian campaigns, reverses that he attributed more to the poor quality of the European horses used in them than to the blunders of the generals charged with the conquest, he told me something that subsequently I also heard from the celebrated general and author Daumas: "Pity the man who enters on a campaign in the desert or the African mountains riding on the most famous animals that distinguish themselves in the races at Chantilly, the Champ-de-Mars, and Sartory. Those horses know nothing but to run, jump, and bolt. Horses without feelings, without a shred of intelligence, that do not adapt their character to that of their master, that do not seek or avoid danger in obedience to the rein or the leaning of the body, that do not dash like lightning from a dead rest, that cannot stop short at the very edge of a precipice, that cannot circle to the left or right with the speed of the whirlwind, like a compass in the hands of an architect, and that are merely the pampered spawn of luxury—such horses were not made for war in the Sahara. The Saharan horse, furthermore, can defy three things no other horse can defy: it can defy hunger, it can defy thirst, it can defy exhaustion."

"Hearing you speak of the Saharan horse, sir," I interrupted him, "has reminded me of the Chilean horse. Even if you knew it, you could not have given a more accurate description of its enviable qualities. But I think the Chilean horse has even more *defy's* in it than the Arabian; because it is generally larger, it can defy hunger, defy thirst, defy exhaustion, defy mistreatment, and defy going unshod! Your people consider a colt a member of the family from the moment of its birth; we wait two years to see whether or not it deserves our attentions. You keep it entire; we mutilate it. Affection, constant handling, and gentle treatment make the Arabian colt devoted to its master's service. In Chile harsh treatment, the spur, the whip, and the rider's strong arm force the wild colt to surrender. You shoe your horses with iron, while in Chile this practice is only now beginning to be common, since the hardness of our horses' hooves has for three centuries made it unnecessary to have recourse to artificial supplements. The Chilean horse can travel as much as thirty leagues; when it reaches the end of a rough and exhausting voyage, all that the noble brute requires to regain its vigor is a lively shake of the ears, a handful of dust on a sweat-soaked back, and the first corral that comes to hand.

"Affection attaches the Chilean horse to its master; and its instinct is such that it is even courteous and considerate with the fair sex, for we often see that a colt that is stubborn and unruly with a man will be gentle and submissive beneath a woman's weak hand. The Chilean horse obeys instantly, so much so that in the midst of the greatest excitement provoked by the character of its rider, a peremptory *Chit!* will root it in place, stamping on the ground but not moving until a new command frees it to resume its fiery movements."

I was not about to stop; but the emir, suddenly seizing me by the arm at this point and with his eyes filled with a fire that caused me to tremble, interrupted me, saying, "Those horses are Arabians; and whoever brought them to America must have been Arabian, too, because such a wealth of virtues can only be found in the horse of the Sahara!" Then, regaining his appearance of calm, he softly said, "Even that *Chit!* that you use to temper their ardor is Saharan. What wouldn't I do to take a Chilean horse with me to Damascus!"

Nothing is sweeter to the heart of man than the moment when he returns to his native soil from a distant land. What did I lack in Europe to be as happy as humanly possible? I enjoyed good health, I was twenty years younger than I am now, I had a steady income, not very abundant but sufficient easily to satisfy my needs and even allow for some luxuries. I had no chance to be bored, because my time was taken up with my light duties, pleasing studies, and interesting travel. I had visited all of Europe, gaining the favor of some crowned heads and being honored with the friendship of Humboldt, Pöppig, Wappaus, Korff, and other leading lights of human learning, whose affectionate letters, along with my appointments as honorary member of several scientific societies, I treasured with understandable pride. Still, there was an empty space within my heart. I lacked the bonds of tenderness, I lacked the sun of my beloved fatherland.

After five years of what many would consider an enviable life, I found myself at the baths of Marienbad, also in Upper Bohemia, when an unexpected stroke of fate brought into my hands a packet of communications from Chile, along with a letter from my worthy De Luines, secretary of the consulate in Hamburg, which began thus: "Sir: I have just received the most unhappy news for this your unfortunate protégé, although it is at the same time the most pleasing that you might hope for. The Chilean government calls you to continue in your own country some of the services that you have been rendering it in Germany!"

This letter produced in me a truly electrifying shock of joy; and considering it an unpardonable crime to waste a single day of those that I might need to reach Chile, I kissed the messages, wept with delight, and then devoted the whole night to writing. The next day, without even thinking of passing through Hamburg, where I resided, I headed directly for England; and then, full of bliss, I left on the *Nueva Granada* for the land that had seen my birth, where for the fifth time in my life I had a moment of complete happiness, that of my arrival!

What practical use might the detached reader find in this compilation of ancient histories, in which the censoring scissors have played a greater part than the narrating pen, and which I publish only in deference to the urging of my friends? I know not, unless it be found in the telling of events that prove the rightness of the precept "NEVER GIVE UP!" because misfortune is not eternal, and because just as an adverse fate can bring man down from the greatest heights to the humble rank of servant, so also, with the aid of steadfastness, honesty, and hard work, he can rise again until he occupies an envied seat at the banquet of kings.

THE END